Lambda-Calculus and Combinators, an Introduction

Combinatory logic and λ-calculus were originally devised in the 1920s for investigating the foundations of mathematics using the basic concept of 'operation' instead of 'set'. They have since evolved into important tools for the development and study of programming languages.

The authors' previous book *Introduction to Combinators and λ-Calculus* served as the main reference for introductory courses on λ-calculus for over twenty years: this long-awaited new version offers the same authoritative exposition and has been thoroughly revised to give a fully up-to-date account of the subject.

The grammar and basic properties of both combinatory logic and λ-calculus are discussed, followed by an introduction to type-theory. Typed and untyped versions of the systems, and their differences, are covered. λ-calculus models, which lie behind much of the semantics of programming languages, are also explained in depth.

The treatment is as non-technical as possible, with the main ideas emphasized and illustrated by examples. Many exercises are included, from routine to advanced, with solutions to most of them at the end of the book.

Review of *Introduction to Combinators and λ-Calculus:*

'This book is very interesting and well written, and is highly recommended to everyone who wants to approach combinatory logic and λ-calculus (logicians or computer scientists).' *Journal of Symbolic Logic*

'The best general book on λ-calculus (typed or untyped) and the theory of combinators.' Gérard Huet, *INRIA*

Lambda-Calculus and Combinators, an Introduction

J. ROGER HINDLEY

Department of Mathematics,
Swansea University, Wales, UK

JONATHAN P. SELDIN

Department of Mathematics and Computer Science,
University of Lethbridge, Alberta, Canada

CAMBRIDGE
UNIVERSITY PRESS

CAMBRIDGE UNIVERSITY PRESS
Cambridge, New York, Melbourne, Madrid, Cape Town,
Singapore, São Paulo, Delhi, Mexico City

Cambridge University Press
The Edinburgh Building, Cambridge CB2 8RU, UK

Published in the United States of America by Cambridge University Press, New York

www.cambridge.org
Information on this title: www.cambridge.org/9780521898850

First published 2008
Reprinted 2010

A catalogue record for this publication is available from the British Library

Library of Congress Cataloguing in Publication Data
Hindley, J. Roger.
Lambda-calculus and combinators : an introduction / J. Roger Hindley,
Jonathan P. Seldin.
p. cm.
Includes bibliographical references and index.
ISBN 978-0-521-89885-0 (hardback)
1. Lambda-calculus. 2. Combinatory logic. I. Seldin, J. P. II. Title.
QA9.5.H565 2008
511.3'5–dc22
2008006276

ISBN 978-0-521-89885-0 Hardback

To Carol, Goldie
and
Julie

Contents

Preface

The λ-calculus and combinatory logic are two systems of logic which can also serve as abstract programming languages. They both aim to describe some very general properties of programs that can modify other programs, in an abstract setting not cluttered by details. In some ways they are rivals, in others they support each other.

The λ-calculus was invented around 1930 by an American logician Alonzo Church, as part of a comprehensive logical system which included higher-order operators (operators which act on other operators). In fact the language of λ-calculus, or some other essentially equivalent notation, is a key part of most higher-order languages, whether for logic or for computer programming. Indeed, the first uncomputable problems to be discovered were originally described, not in terms of idealized computers such as Turing machines, but in λ-calculus.

Combinatory logic has the same aims as λ-calculus, and can express the same computational concepts, but its grammar is much simpler. Its basic idea is due to two people: Moses Schönfinkel, who first thought of it in 1920, and Haskell Curry, who independently re-discovered it seven years later and turned it into a workable technique.

The purpose of this book is to introduce the reader to the basic methods and results in both fields.

The reader is assumed to have no previous knowledge of these fields, but to know a little about propositional and predicate logic and recursive functions, and to have some experience with mathematical induction.

Exercises are included, and answers to most of them (those marked *) are given in an appendix at the end of the book. In the early chapters there are also some extra exercises without answers, to give more routine practice if needed.

References for further reading are included at the ends of appropriate chapters, for the reader who wishes to go deeper.

Some chapters on special topics are included after the initial basic chapters. However, no attempt has been made to cover all aspects of λ-calculus and combinatory logic; this book is only an introduction, not a complete survey.

This book is essentially an updated and re-written version of [HS86].[1] It assumes less background knowledge. Those parts of [HS86] which are still relevant have been retained here with only minor changes, but other parts have been re-written considerably. Many errors have been corrected. More exercises have been added, with more detailed answers, and the references have been brought up to date. Some technical details have been moved from the main text to a new appendix.

The three chapters on types in [HS86] have been extensively re-written here. Two of the more specialized chapters in [HS86], on higher-order logic and the consistency of arithmetic, have been dropped.

Acknowledgements The authors are very grateful to all those who have made comments on [HS86] which have been very useful in preparing the present book, especially Gérard Berry, Steven Blake, Naim Çağman, Thierry Coquand, Clemens Grabmayer, Yexuan Gui, Benedetto Intrigila, Kenichi Noguchi, Hiroakira Ono, Gabriele Ricci, Vincenzo Scianni, John Shepherdson, Lewis Stiller, John Stone, Masako Takahashi, Peter Trigg and Pawel Urzyczyn.

Their comments have led to many improvements and the correction of several errors. (Any errors that remain are entirely the authors' responsibility, however.)

On the production side, the authors wish to thank Larissa Kowbuz for her very accurate typing of an early draft, the designers of LaTeX and its associated software for the actual type-setting, and M. Tatsuta for the use of his macro 'proof.sty'. We are also very grateful to Chris Whyley for technical help, and to Cambridge University Press, especially David Tranah, for their expert input.

On the financial side we thank the National Sciences and Engineering Research Council of Canada for a grant which enabled a consultation visit by Hindley to Seldin in 2006, and the Department of Mathematics and Computer Science of the University of Lethbridge for helpful hospitality during that visit.

[1] Which itself was developed from [HLS72] which was written with Bruce Lercher.

Last but of course not least, the authors are very grateful to their wives, Carol Hindley and Goldie Morgentaler, for much encouragement and patient tolerance during this book's preparation.

Notes on the text This book uses a notation for functions and relations that is fairly standard in logic: *ordered pairs* are denoted by '$\langle\ ,\ \rangle$', a *binary relation* is regarded as a set of ordered pairs, and a *function* as a binary relation such that no two of its pairs have the same first member. If any further background material is needed, it can be found in textbooks on predicate logic; for example [Dal97], [Coh87], [End00], [Men97] or [Rau06].

The words '*function*', '*mapping*' and '*map*' are used interchangeably, as usual in mathematics. But the word '*operator*' is reserved for a slightly different concept of function. This is explained in Chapter 3, though in earlier chapters the reader should think of 'operator' and 'function' as meaning the same.

As usual in mathematics, the *domain* of a function ϕ is the set of all objects a such that $\phi(a)$ is defined, and the *range* of ϕ is the set of all objects b such that $(\exists a)(b = \phi(a))$. If A and B are sets, a *function from A to B* is a function whose domain is A and whose range is a subset of B.

Finally, a note about 'we' in this book: 'we' will almost always mean the reader and the authors together, not the authors alone.

1

The λ-calculus

1A Introduction

What is usually called λ-calculus is a collection of several formal systems, based on a notation invented by Alonzo Church in the 1930s. They are designed to describe the most basic ways that operators or functions can be combined to form other operators.

In practice, each λ-system has a slightly different grammatical structure, depending on its intended use. Some have extra constant-symbols, and most have built-in syntactic restrictions, for example type-restrictions. But to begin with, it is best to avoid these complications; hence the system presented in this chapter will be the 'pure' one, which is syntactically the simplest.

To motivate the λ-notation, consider the everyday mathematical expression '$x - y$'. This can be thought of as defining either a function f of x or a function g of y;

$$f(x) \;=\; x - y, \qquad\qquad g(y) \;=\; x - y,$$

or

$$f:\; x \mapsto x - y, \qquad\qquad g:\; y \mapsto x - y.$$

And there is a need for a notation that gives f and g different names in some systematic way. In practice, mathematicians usually avoid this need by various 'ad-hoc' special notations, but these can get very clumsy when higher-order functions are involved (functions which act on other functions).

Church's notation is a systematic way of constructing, for each expression involving 'x', a notation for the corresponding function of x (and similarly for 'y', etc.). Church introduced 'λ' as an auxiliary symbol and wrote

$$f = \lambda x \,.\, x - y \qquad\qquad g = \lambda y \,.\, x - y.$$

For example, consider the equations

$$f(0) = 0 - y, \qquad\qquad f(1) = 1 - y.$$

In the λ-notation these become

$$(\lambda x \,.\, x - y)(0) = 0 - y, \qquad\qquad (\lambda x \,.\, x - y)(1) = 1 - y.$$

These equations are clumsier than the originals, but do not be put off by this; the λ-notation is principally intended for denoting higher-order functions, not just functions of numbers, and for this it turns out to be no worse than others.[1] The main point is that this notation is systematic, and therefore more suitable for incorporation into a programming language.

The λ-notation can be extended to functions of more than one variable. For example, the expression '$x - y$' determines two functions h and k of two variables, defined by

$$h(x, y) = x - y, \qquad\qquad k(y, x) = x - y.$$

These can be denoted by

$$h = \lambda xy \,.\, x - y, \qquad\qquad k = \lambda yx \,.\, x - y.$$

However, we can avoid the need for a special notation for functions of several variables by using functions whose values are not numbers but other functions. For example, instead of the two-place function h above, consider the one-place function $h^\star$ defined by

$$h^\star = \lambda x \,.\, (\lambda y \,.\, x - y).$$

For each number a, we have

$$h^\star(a) = \lambda y \,.\, a - y;$$

hence for each pair of numbers a, b,

$$\begin{aligned} (h^\star(a))(b) &= (\lambda y \,.\, a - y)(b) \\ &= a - b \\ &= h(a, b). \end{aligned}$$

[1] For example, one fairly common notation in mathematics is $f = x \mapsto x - y$, which is essentially just the λ-notation in disguise, with '$x \mapsto$' instead of 'λx'.

Thus $h^\star$ can be viewed as 'representing' h. For this reason, we shall largely ignore functions of more than one variable in this book.

From now on, '*function*' will mean '*function of one variable*' unless explicitly stated otherwise. (The use of $h^\star$ instead of h is usually called *currying*.[2])

Having looked at λ-notation in an informal context, let us now construct a formal system of λ-calculus.

Definition 1.1 (λ-terms) Assume that there is given an infinite sequence of expressions $\mathbf{v}_0$, $\mathbf{v}_{00}$, $\mathbf{v}_{000}$, ... called *variables*, and a finite, infinite or empty sequence of expressions called *atomic constants*, different from the variables. (When the sequence of atomic constants is empty, the system will be called *pure*, otherwise *applied*.) The set of expressions called λ-*terms* is defined inductively as follows:

(a) all variables and atomic constants are λ-terms (called *atoms*);
(b) if M and N are any λ-terms, then (MN) is a λ-term (called an *application*);
(c) if M is any λ-term and x is any variable, then $(\lambda x.M)$ is a λ-term (called an *abstraction*).

Example 1.2 (Some λ-terms)

(a) $(\lambda \mathbf{v}_0.(\mathbf{v}_0\mathbf{v}_{00}))$ is a λ-term.

If x, y, z are any distinct variables, the following are λ-terms:

(b) $(\lambda x.(xy))$, (d) $(x(\lambda x.(\lambda x.x)))$,

(c) $((\lambda y.y)(\lambda x.(xy)))$, (e) $(\lambda x.(yz))$.

In (d), there are two occurrences of λx in one term; this is allowed by Definition 1.1, though not encouraged in practice. Part (e) shows a term of form $(\lambda x.M)$ such that x does not occur in M; this is called a *vacuous abstraction*, and such terms denote constant functions (functions whose output is the same for all inputs).

By the way, the expression 'λ' by itself is not a term, though it may occur in terms; similarly the expression 'λx' is not a term.

[2] Named after Haskell Curry, one of the inventors of combinatory logic. Curry always insisted that he got the idea of using $h^\star$ from M. Schönfinkel's [Sch24] (see [CF58, pp. 8, 10]), but most workers seem to prefer to pronounce 'currying' rather than 'schönfinkeling'. The idea also appeared in 1893 in [Fre93, Vol. 1, Section 4].

Notation 1.3 *Capital letters* will denote arbitrary λ-terms in this chapter. Letters 'x', 'y', 'z', 'u', 'v', 'w' will denote variables throughout the book, and distinct letters will denote distinct variables unless stated otherwise.

Parentheses will be omitted in such a way that, for example, '$MNPQ$' will denote the term $(((MN)P)Q)$. (This convention is called *association to the left.*) Other abbreviations will be

$$\lambda x.PQ \quad \text{for} \quad (\lambda x.(PQ)),$$
$$\lambda x_1 x_2 \ldots x_n.M \quad \text{for} \quad (\lambda x_1.(\lambda x_2.(\ldots(\lambda x_n.M)\ldots))).$$

Syntactic identity of terms will be denoted by '≡'; in other words

$$M \equiv N$$

will mean that M is exactly the same term as N. (The symbol '=' will be used in formal theories of equality, and for identity of objects that are not terms, such as numbers.) It will be assumed of course that if $MN \equiv PQ$ then $M \equiv P$ and $N \equiv Q$, and if $\lambda x.M \equiv \lambda y.P$ then $x \equiv y$ and $M \equiv P$. It will also be assumed that variables are distinct from constants, and applications are distinct from abstractions, etc. Such assumptions are always made when languages are defined, and will be left unstated in future.

The cases $k = 0$, $n = 0$ in statements like '$P \equiv MN_1 \ldots N_k$ $(k \geq 0)$' or 'T has form $\lambda x_1 \ldots x_n.PQ$ $(n \geq 0)$' will mean '$P \equiv M$' or 'T has form PQ'.

'λ' will often be used carelessly to mean 'λ-calculus in general'.

'*Iff*' will be used for 'if and only if'.

Exercise 1.4 * Insert the full number of parentheses and λ's into the following abbreviated λ-terms:

(a) $xyz(yx)$, (d) $(\lambda u.vuu)zy$,
(b) $\lambda x.uxy$, (e) $ux(yz)(\lambda v.vy)$,
(c) $\lambda u.u(\lambda x.y)$, (f) $(\lambda xyz.xz(yz))uvw$.

Informal interpretation 1.5 Not all systems based on λ-calculus use all the terms allowed by Definition 1.1, and in most systems, some terms are left uninterpreted, as we shall see later. But the interpretations of those λ-terms which are interpreted may be given as follows, roughly speaking.

In general, if M has been interpreted as a function or operator, then (MN) is interpreted as the result of applying M to argument N, provided this result exists.[3]

A term $(\lambda x.M)$ represents the operator or function whose value at an argument N is calculated by substituting N for x in M.

For example, $\lambda x.x(xy)$ represents the operation of applying a function twice to an object denoted by y; and the equation

$$(\lambda x.x(xy))N \;=\; N(Ny)$$

holds for all terms N, in the sense that both sides have the same interpretation.

For a second example, $\lambda x.y$ represents the constant function that takes the value y for all arguments, and the equation

$$(\lambda x.y)N \;=\; y$$

holds in the same sense as before.

This is enough on interpretation for the moment; but more will be said in Chapter 3, Discussion 3.27.

1B Term-structure and substitution

The main topic of the chapter will be a formal procedure for calculating with terms, that will closely follow their informal meaning. But before defining it, we shall need to know how to substitute terms for variables, and this is not entirely straightforward. The present section covers the technicalities involved. The details are rather boring, and the reader who is just interested in main themes should read only up to Definition 1.12 and then go to the next section.

By the way, in Chapter 2 a simpler system called combinatory logic will be described, which will avoid most of the boring technicalities; but for this gain there will be a price to pay.

Definition 1.6 The *length* of a term M (called *lgh*(M)) is the total number of occurrences of atoms in M. In more detail, define

[3] The more usual notation for function-application is $M(N)$, but historically (MN) has become standard in λ-calculus. This book uses the (MN) notation for formal terms (following Definition 1.1(b)), but reverts to the common notation, e.g. $f(a)$, in informal discussions of functions of numbers, etc.

(a) $lgh(a) \quad = \quad 1$ for atoms a;
(b) $lgh(MN) \quad = \quad lgh(M) + lgh(N)$;
(c) $lgh(\lambda x.M) \quad = \quad 1 + lgh(M)$.

The phrase '*induction on M*' will mean 'induction on $lgh(M)$'.

For example, if $M \equiv x(\lambda y.yux)$ then $lgh(M) = 5$.

Definition 1.7 For λ-terms P and Q, the relation P *occurs in* Q (or P *is a subterm of* Q, or Q *contains* P) is defined by induction on Q, thus:

(a) P occurs in P;
(b) if P occurs in M or in N, then P occurs in (MN);
(c) if P occurs in M or $P \equiv x$, then P occurs in $(\lambda x.M)$.

The meaning of '*an occurrence of P in Q*' is assumed to be intuitively clear. For example, in the term $((xy)(\lambda x.(xy)))$ there are two occurrences of (xy) and three occurrences of x.[4]

Exercise 1.8 * (Hint: in each part below, first write the given terms in full, showing all parentheses and λ's.)

(a) Mark all the occurrences of xy in the term $\lambda xy.xy$.
(b) Mark all the occurrences of uv in $x(uv)(\lambda u.v(uv))uv$.
(c) Does $\lambda u.u$ occur in $\lambda u.uv$?

Definition 1.9 (Scope) For a particular occurrence of $\lambda x.M$ in a term P, the occurrence of M is called the *scope* of the occurrence of λx on the left.

Example 1.10 Let

$$P \equiv (\lambda y.yx(\lambda x.y(\lambda y.z)x))vw.$$

The scope of the leftmost λy in P is $yx(\lambda x.y(\lambda y.z)x)$, the scope of λx is $y(\lambda y.z)x$, and that of the rightmost λy is z.

Definition 1.11 (Free and bound variables) An occurrence of a variable x in a term P is called

- *bound* if it is in the scope of a λx in P,

[4] The reader who wants more precision can define an occurrence of P in Q to be a pair $\langle P, p\rangle$ where p is some indicator of the position at which P occurs in Q. There are several definitions of suitable position indicators in the literature, for example in [Ros73, p. 167] or [Hin97, pp. 140–141]. But it is best to avoid such details for as long as possible.

- *bound and binding*, iff it is the x in λx,
- *free* otherwise.

If x has at least one binding occurrence in P, we call x a *bound variable of* P. If x has at least one free occurrence in P, we call x a *free variable of* P. The set of all free variables of P is called

$$\mathrm{FV}(P).$$

A *closed term* is a term without any free variables.

Examples Consider the term $xv(\lambda yz.yv)w$: this is really

$$\Big(((xv)(\lambda y.(\lambda z.(yv))))\,w\Big),$$

and in it the x on the left is free, the leftmost v is free, the leftmost y is both bound and binding, the only z is the same, the rightmost y is bound but not binding, the rightmost v is free, and the only w is free.

In the term P in Example 1.10, all four y's are bound, the leftmost and rightmost y's are also binding, the left-hand x is free, the central x is bound and binding, the right-hand x is bound but not binding, and z, v, w are free; hence

$$\mathrm{FV}(P) = \{x, z, v, w\}.$$

Note that x is both a free and a bound variable of P; this is not normally advisable in practice, but is allowed in order to keep the definition of 'λ-term' simple.

Definition 1.12 (Substitution) For any M, N, x, define $[N/x]M$ to be the result of substituting N for every free occurrence of x in M, and changing bound variables to avoid clashes. The precise definition is by induction on M, as follows (after [CF58, p. 94]).

(a) $[N/x]\,x \equiv N$;

(b) $[N/x]\,a \equiv a$ for all atoms $a \not\equiv x$;

(c) $[N/x](PQ) \equiv ([N/x]P\;[N/x]Q)$;

(d) $[N/x](\lambda x.P) \equiv \lambda x.P$;

(e) $[N/x](\lambda y.P) \equiv \lambda y.P$ if $x \notin \mathrm{FV}(P)$;

(f) $[N/x](\lambda y.P) \equiv \lambda y.[N/x]P$ if $x \in \mathrm{FV}(P)$ and $y \notin \mathrm{FV}(N)$;

(g) $[N/x](\lambda y.P) \equiv \lambda z.[N/x][z/y]P$ if $x \in \mathrm{FV}(P)$ and $y \in \mathrm{FV}(N)$.

(In 1.12(e)–(g), $y \not\equiv x$; and in (g), z is chosen to be the first variable $\notin \mathrm{FV}(NP)$.)

Remark 1.13 The purpose of clause 1.12(g) is to prevent the intuitive meaning of $[N/x](\lambda y.P)$ from depending on the bound variable y. For example, take three distinct variables w, x, y and look at

$$[w/x](\lambda y.x).$$

The term $\lambda y.x$ represents the constant function whose value is always x, so we should intuitively expect $[w/x](\lambda y.x)$ to represent the constant function whose value is always w. And this is what we get; by 1.12(f) and (a) we have

$$[w/x](\lambda y.x) \equiv \lambda y.w.$$

Now consider $[w/x](\lambda w.x)$. The term $\lambda w.x$ represents the constant function whose value is x, just as $\lambda y.x$ did. So we should hope that $[w/x](\lambda w.x)$ would represent the constant function whose value is always w.

But if $[w/x](\lambda w.x)$ was evaluated by (f), our hope would fail; we would have

$$[w/x](\lambda w.x) \equiv \lambda w.w,$$

which represents the identity function, not a constant function. Clause (g) rescues our hope. By (g) with $N \equiv y \equiv w$, we have

$$\begin{aligned} [w/x](\lambda w.x) &\equiv \lambda z.[w/x][z/w]x \\ &\equiv \lambda z.[w/x]x && \text{by 1.12 (b)} \\ &\equiv \lambda z.w, \end{aligned}$$

which represents the desired constant function.

Exercise 1.14* Evaluate the following substitutions:

(a) $[(uv)/x]\ (\lambda y.x(\lambda w.vwx))$,

(b) $[(\lambda y.xy)/x]\ (\lambda y.x(\lambda x.x))$,

(c) $[(\lambda y.vy)/x]\ (y\,(\lambda v.xv))$,

(d) $[(uv)/x]\ (\lambda x.zy)$.

Lemma 1.15 *For all terms M, N and variables x:*

(a) $[x/x]M \equiv M$;

(b) $x \notin \mathrm{FV}(M) \implies [N/x]M \equiv M$;

(c) $x \in \mathrm{FV}(M) \implies \mathrm{FV}([N/x]M) = \mathrm{FV}(N) \cup (\mathrm{FV}(M) - \{x\})$;

(d) $\mathit{lgh}([y/x]M) = \mathit{lgh}(M)$.

Proof Easy, by checking the clauses of Definition 1.12. □

Lemma 1.16 *Let x, y, v be distinct (the usual notation convention), and let no variable bound in M be free in vPQ. Then*

(a) $[P/v][v/x]M \equiv [P/x]M$ *if* $v \notin \mathrm{FV}(M)$;

(b) $[x/v][v/x]M \equiv M$ *if* $v \notin \mathrm{FV}(M)$;

(c) $[P/x][Q/y]M \equiv [([P/x]Q)/y][P/x]M$ *if* $y \notin \mathrm{FV}(P)$;

(d) $[P/x][Q/y]M \equiv [Q/y][P/x]M$ *if* $y \notin \mathrm{FV}(P)$, $x \notin \mathrm{FV}(Q)$;

(e) $[P/x][Q/x]M \equiv [([P/x]Q)/x]M$.

Proof The restriction on variables bound in M ensures that 1.12(g) is never used in the substitutions. Parts (a), (c), (e) are proved by straightforward but boring inductions on M. Part (b) follows from (a) and 1.15(a), and (d) follows from (c) and 1.15(b). □

Definition 1.17 (Change of bound variables, congruence) Let a term P contain an occurrence of $\lambda x.M$, and let $y \notin \mathrm{FV}(M)$. The act of replacing this $\lambda x.M$ by

$$\lambda y.[y/x]M$$

is called a *change of bound variable* or an *α-conversion* in P. Iff P can be changed to Q by a finite (perhaps empty) series of changes of bound variables, we shall say *P is congruent to Q*, or *P α-converts to Q*, or

$$P \equiv_\alpha Q.$$

Example 1.18

$$\begin{aligned} \lambda xy.x(xy) &\equiv \lambda x.(\lambda y.x(xy)) \\ &\equiv_\alpha \lambda x.(\lambda v.x(xv)) \\ &\equiv_\alpha \lambda u.(\lambda v.u(uv)) \\ &\equiv \lambda uv.u(uv). \end{aligned}$$

Definition 1.17 comes from [CF58, p. 91]. The name 'α-converts' comes from the same book, as do other Greek-letter names that will be used later; some will look rather arbitrary but they have become standard notation.

Lemma 1.19

(a) *If* $P \equiv_\alpha Q$ *then* $\mathrm{FV}(P) = \mathrm{FV}(Q)$;

(b) *The relation $\equiv_\alpha$ is reflexive, transitive and symmetric. That is, for all P, Q, R, we have:*

$$\begin{array}{ll} \textit{(reflexivity)} & P \equiv_\alpha P, \\ \textit{(transitivity)} & P \equiv_\alpha Q,\ Q \equiv_\alpha R \implies P \equiv_\alpha R, \\ \textit{(symmetry)} & P \equiv_\alpha Q \implies Q \equiv_\alpha P. \end{array}$$

Proof For (a), see A1.5(f) in Appendix A1. For (b): reflexivity and transitivity are obvious; for symmetry, if P goes to Q by a change of bound variable, further changes can be found that bring Q back to P; details are in Appendix A1, A1.5(e). □

Lemma 1.20 *If we remove from Lemma 1.16 the condition on variables bound in M, and replace '$\equiv$' by '$\equiv_\alpha$', that lemma stays true.*

Proof By [CF58, p. 95, Section 3E Theorem 2(c)]. □

Lemma 1.21 $M \equiv_\alpha M'$, $N \equiv_\alpha N' \implies [N/x]M \equiv_\alpha [N'/x]M'$.

Proof By Appendix A1's Lemma A1.10. □

Note 1.22 Lemma 1.21 can be viewed as saying that the operation of substitution is well-behaved with respect to α-conversion: if we α-convert the inputs of a substitution, then the output will not change by anything more complicated than $\equiv_\alpha$. All the operations to be introduced later will also be well-behaved in a similar sense. (More details are in Appendix A1.) Thus, when a bound variable in a term P threatens to cause some trouble, for example by making a particular substitution complicated, we can simply change it to a new harmless variable and use the resulting new term instead of P.

Further, two α-convertible terms play identical roles in nearly all applications of λ-calculus, and are always given identical interpretations; so it makes sense to think of them as identical. In fact most writers use '$P \equiv Q$' to mean '$P \equiv_\alpha Q$'; the present book will do the same from Chapter 3 onward.

Remark 1.23 (Simultaneous substitution) It is possible to modify the definition of $[N/x]M$ in 1.12 to define *simultaneous substitution*

$$[N_1/x_1, \ldots, N_n/x_n]M$$

for $n \geq 2$. We shall not need the details here, as only very simple special cases of simultaneous substitution will be used in this book. A full definition is in [Sto88, Section 2]; the key is to first change any bound variables in M that might cause problems.

By the way, $[N_1/x_1, \ldots, N_n/x_n]M$ should not be confused with the result of n successive substitutions

$$[N_1/x_1](\ldots([N_n/x_n]M)\ldots).$$

For example, take $n = 2$, $N_1 \equiv u$, $N_2 \equiv x_1$, $M \equiv x_1 x_2$; then

$$\begin{aligned} [u/x_1]([x_1/x_2]M) &\equiv [u/x_1](x_1 x_1) \\ &\equiv uu, \\ [u/x_1, x_1/x_2]M &\equiv ux_1. \end{aligned}$$

1C β-reduction

The topic of this section is the calculation procedure that lies at the heart of λ-calculus and gives it its power.

A term of form $(\lambda x.M)N$ represents an operator $\lambda x.M$ applied to an argument N. In the informal interpretation of $\lambda x.M$, its value when applied to N is calculated by substituting N for x in M, so $(\lambda x.M)N$ can be 'simplified' to $[N/x]M$. This simplification-process is captured in the following definition.

Definition 1.24 (β-contracting, β-reducing) Any term of form

$$(\lambda x.M)N$$

is called a *β-redex* and the corresponding term

$$[N/x]M$$

is called its *contractum.* Iff a term P contains an occurrence of $(\lambda x.M)N$ and we replace that occurrence by $[N/x]M$, and the result is P', we say we have *contracted* the redex-occurrence in P, and P *β-contracts* to P' or

$$P \rhd_{1\beta} P'.$$

Iff P can be changed to a term Q by a finite (perhaps empty) series of β-contractions and changes of bound variables, we say P *β-reduces to* Q, or

$$P \rhd_\beta Q.$$

Example 1.25

(a) $(\lambda x.x(xy))N \quad \rhd_{1\beta} \quad N(Ny)$.

(b) $(\lambda x.y)N \quad \rhd_{1\beta} \quad y$.

(c)
$$\begin{array}{llll} (\lambda x.(\lambda y.yx)z)v & \rhd_{1\beta} & [v/x]\,((\lambda y.yx)z) & \equiv (\lambda y.yv)z \\ & \rhd_{1\beta} & [z/y]\,(yv) & \equiv zv. \end{array}$$

(d)
$$\begin{array}{llll} (\lambda x.xx)(\lambda x.xx) & \rhd_{1\beta} & [(\lambda x.xx)/x]\,(xx) & \equiv (\lambda x.xx)(\lambda x.xx) \\ & \rhd_{1\beta} & [(\lambda x.xx)/x]\,(xx) & \equiv (\lambda x.xx)(\lambda x.xx) \\ & \ldots & \text{etc.} & \end{array}$$

(e)
$$\begin{array}{lll} (\lambda x.xxy)(\lambda x.xxy) & \rhd_{1\beta} & (\lambda x.xxy)(\lambda x.xxy)y \\ & \rhd_{1\beta} & (\lambda x.xxy)(\lambda x.xxy)yy \\ & \ldots & \text{etc.} \end{array}$$

Example 1.25(d) shows that the 'simplification' process need not always simplify. Even worse, (e) shows that it can actually complicate. These examples also show that the 'simplification' process need not terminate; in fact, it terminates iff it reaches a term containing no redexes.

Definition 1.26 A term Q which contains no β-redexes is called a *β-normal form* (or a *term in β-normal form* or just a *β-nf*). The class of all β-normal forms is called *β-nf* or *λβ-nf*. If a term P β-reduces to a term Q in β-nf, then Q is called a *β-normal form of* P.

The 'β' may be omitted when this causes no confusion.

Example 1.27

(a) In 1.25(c), zv is a β-normal form of $(\lambda x.(\lambda y.yx)z)v$.

(b) Let $L \equiv (\lambda x.xxy)(\lambda x.xxy)$. By 1.25(e) we have

$$L \rhd_{1\beta} Ly \rhd_{1\beta} Lyy \rhd_{1\beta} \ldots$$

This sequence is infinite and there is no other way that L can be β-reduced, so L has no β-normal form.

(c) Let $P \equiv (\lambda u.v)L$ for the above L. Then P can be reduced in two different ways (at least), thus:

$$
\begin{array}{llll}
\text{(i)} & P \equiv (\lambda u.v)L & \rhd_{1\beta} & [L/u]v \\
& & \equiv & v; \\
\text{(ii)} & P & \rhd_{1\beta} & (\lambda u.v)(Ly) \quad \text{by contracting } L \\
& & \rhd_{1\beta} & (\lambda u.v)(Lyy) \quad \text{by contracting } L \text{ again} \\
& & \ldots & \text{etc.}
\end{array}
$$

So P has a normal form v, but also has an infinite reduction.

(d) The term $(\lambda x.xx)(\lambda x.xx)$ in 1.25(d) is usually called Ω. It is not a normal form; indeed it does not reduce to one (because it reduces always to itself). But Ω is 'minimal' in the sense that it cannot be reduced to any different term. (In [Ler76] it is proved that no other redex is minimal in this sense.)

Exercise 1.28 * Reduce the following terms to β-normal forms:

(a) $(\lambda x.xy)(\lambda u.vuu)$,

(b) $(\lambda xy.yx)uv$,

(c) $(\lambda x\,.\,x(x(yz))x)(\lambda u.uv)$,

(d) $(\lambda x.xxy)(\lambda y.yz)$,

(e) $(\lambda xy.xyy)(\lambda u.uyx)$,

(f) $(\lambda xyz.xz(yz))((\lambda xy.yx)u)((\lambda xy.yx)v)\,w$.

Remark 1.29 Some terms can be reduced in more than one way. One such term, from Example 1.25(c), is $(\lambda x.(\lambda y.yx)z)v$. It has two reductions:

$$
\begin{array}{llll}
(\lambda x.(\lambda y.yx)z)v & \rhd_{1\beta} & (\lambda y.yv)z & \text{by contracting } (\lambda x.(\lambda y.yx)z)\,v \\
& \rhd_{1\beta} & zv & \text{by contracting } (\lambda y.yv)z;
\end{array}
$$

$$
\begin{array}{llll}
(\lambda x.(\lambda y.yx)z)v & \rhd_{1\beta} & (\lambda x.zx)v & \text{by contracting } (\lambda y.yx)z \\
& \rhd_{1\beta} & zv. &
\end{array}
$$

In this case both reductions reach the same normal form. Is this always true? Certainly, for any system claiming to represent computation the end-result should be independent of the path. So if this property failed for β-reduction, any claim by λ-calculus to be like a programming language would fail from the start.

The Church–Rosser theorem below will show that the normal form of a term is indeed unique, provided we ignore changes of bound variables. It will have many other applications too; in fact it is probably the most often quoted theorem on λ-calculus.

Before the theorem, here are two lemmas: the first says that nothing new can be introduced during a reduction, in a certain sense, and the second that the reducibility relation $\triangleright_\beta$ is preserved by substitution.

Lemma 1.30 $P \triangleright_\beta Q \implies \mathrm{FV}(P) \supseteq \mathrm{FV}(Q)$.

Proof First, $\mathrm{FV}((\lambda x.M)N) \supseteq \mathrm{FV}([N/x]M)$ by 1.15(b) and (c). Also α-conversions do not change $\mathrm{FV}(P)$, by 1.19(a). □

Lemma 1.31 (Substitution and $\triangleright_\beta$) *If $P \triangleright_\beta P'$ and $Q \triangleright_\beta Q'$, then*

$$[P/x]Q \triangleright_\beta [P'/x]Q'.$$

Proof By Appendix A1's A1.15. □

Theorem 1.32 (Church–Rosser theorem for $\triangleright_\beta$) *If $P \triangleright_\beta M$ and $P \triangleright_\beta N$ (see Figure 1:1), then there exists a term T such that*

$$M \triangleright_\beta T \quad \textit{and} \quad N \triangleright_\beta T.$$

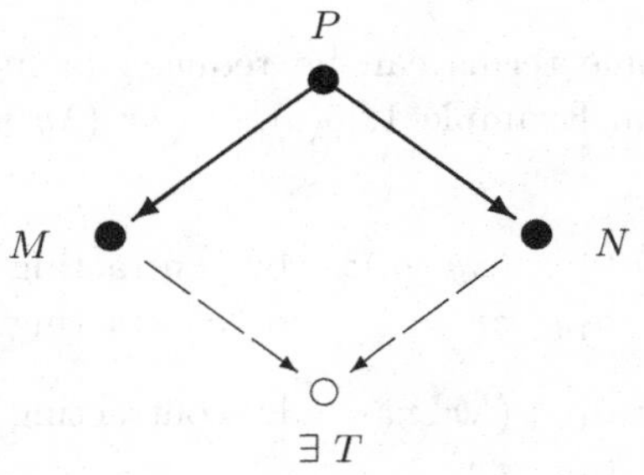

Fig. 1:1

Proof See Appendix A2's Theorem A2.11. □

Note The property described in the Church–Rosser theorem, that if a term can be reduced to two different terms then these two terms can be further reduced to one term, is called *confluence*. The theorem states that *β-reduction is confluent.*

As mentioned before, the most important application of this theorem is to show that a computation in λ-calculus cannot produce two essentially different results. This is done in the following corollary.

Corollary 1.32.1 *If P has a β-normal form, it is unique modulo $\equiv_\alpha$; that is, if P has β-normal forms M and N, then $M \equiv_\alpha N$.*

Proof Let $P \triangleright_\beta M$ and $P \triangleright_\beta N$. By 1.32, M and N reduce to a term T. But M and N contain no redexes, so $M \equiv_\alpha T$ and $N \equiv_\alpha T$. □

The following is an alternative characterization of β-normal forms which will be used in a later chapter.

Lemma 1.33 *The class β-nf is the smallest class such that*

(a) *all atoms are in β-nf;*

(b) $M_1, \ldots, M_n \in \beta\text{-nf} \implies aM_1 \ldots M_n \in \beta\text{-nf}$ *for all atoms a;*

(c) $M \in \beta\text{-nf} \implies \lambda x.M \in \beta\text{-nf}$.

Proof By induction on M, it is easy to prove that M is in the class defined by (a) – (c) iff M contains no redexes. □

Note 1.34 If $M \equiv aM_1 \ldots M_n$ where a is an atom, and $M \triangleright_\beta N$, then N must have form

$$N \equiv aN_1 \ldots N_n$$

where $M_i \triangleright_\beta N_i$ for $i = 1, \ldots, n$. To see this, note that M is really

$$((\ldots((aM_1)M_2)\ldots)M_n)$$

when its parentheses are fully shown; hence each β-redex in M must be in an M_i. Also the same holds for each subterm $\lambda x.P$ whose bound variable might be changed in the reduction of M.

Exercise 1.35 * Do not confuse *being* a β-nf with *having* a β-nf: first prove that

(a) $[N/x]M$ *is a β-nf* $\implies$ M *is a β-nf*;

then, in contrast (harder), find terms M and N such that $[N/x]M$ has a β-nf but M does not; this will prove that

(b) $[N/x]M$ *has a β-nf* $\not\Longrightarrow$ M *has a β-nf.*

Exercise 1.36* (Harder) Find terms P, Q such that neither of P, Q has a β-nf, but PQ has a β-nf.

1D β-equality

Reduction is non-symmetric, but it generates the following symmetric relation.

Definition 1.37 We say P is *β-equal* or *β-convertible* to Q (notation $P =_\beta Q$) iff Q can be obtained from P by a finite (perhaps empty) series of β-contractions and reversed β-contractions and changes of bound variables. That is, $P =_\beta Q$ iff there exist $P_0, \ldots, P_n$ $(n \geq 0)$ such that

$$(\forall i \leq n-1)\ \big(P_i \rhd_{1\beta} P_{i+1} \ \text{ or } \ P_{i+1} \rhd_{1\beta} P_i \ \text{ or } \ P_i \equiv_\alpha P_{i+1}\big),$$

$$P_0 \equiv P, \qquad P_n \equiv Q.$$

Exercise 1.38* Prove that $(\lambda xyz.xzy)(\lambda xy.x) =_\beta (\lambda xy.x)(\lambda x.x)$.

Lemma 1.39 *If $P =_\beta Q$ and $P \equiv_\alpha P'$ and $Q \equiv_\alpha Q'$, then $P' =_\beta Q'$.*

Lemma 1.40 (Substitution lemma for β-equality)

$$M =_\beta M',\ N =_\beta N' \implies [N/x]M =_\beta [N'/x]M'.$$

Theorem 1.41 (Church–Rosser theorem for $=_\beta$) *If $P =_\beta Q$, then there exists a term T such that*

$$M \rhd_\beta T \quad \text{and} \quad N \rhd_\beta T.$$

Proof By induction on the number n in 1.37. The basis, $n = 0$, is trivial. For the induction step, n to $n+1$, we assume:

$$P =_\beta P_n, \qquad P_n \rhd_{1\beta} P_{n+1} \ \text{ or } \ P_{n+1} \rhd_{1\beta} P_n$$

(see Figure 1:2); and the induction hypothesis gives a term T_n such that

$$P \rhd_\beta T_n, \qquad P_n \rhd_\beta T_n.$$

We want a T such that $P \rhd_\beta T$ and $P_{n+1} \rhd_\beta T$. If $P_{n+1} \rhd_{1\beta} P_n$, choose $T \equiv T_n$. If $P_n \rhd_{1\beta} P_{n+1}$, apply 1.32 to P_n, T_n, P_{n+1} as shown in Figure 1:2. □

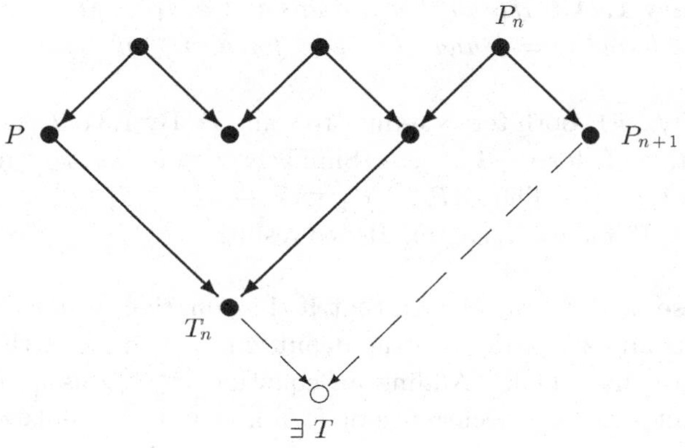

Fig. 1:2

The Church–Rosser theorem shows that two β-convertible terms both intuitively represent the same operator, since they can both be reduced to the same term. (This is why β-convertibility is called '='.)

Corollary 1.41.1 *If $P =_\beta Q$ and Q is a β-normal form, then $P \triangleright_\beta Q$.*

Proof By the Church–Rosser theorem, P and Q both reduce to some T. But Q contains no redexes, so $Q \equiv_\alpha T$. Hence $P \triangleright_\beta Q$. □

Corollary 1.41.2 *If $P =_\beta Q$, then either P and Q both have the same β-normal form or both P and Q have no β-normal form.*

Corollary 1.41.3 *If $P, Q \in \beta$-nf and $P =_\beta Q$, then $P \equiv_\alpha Q$.*

By Corollary 1.41.3 the relation $=_\beta$ is non-trivial, in the sense that not all terms are β-convertible to each other. For example, $\lambda xy.xy$ and $\lambda xy.yx$ are both in β-nf and $\lambda xy.xy \not\equiv_\alpha \lambda xy.yx$, so the corollary implies that $\lambda xy.xy \neq_\beta \lambda xy.yx$.

Corollary 1.41.4 (Uniqueness of nf) *A term is β-equal to at most one β-normal form, modulo changes of bound variables.*

The following more technical corollary will be needed later. Without using the Church–Rosser theorem it would be very hard to prove.

Corollary 1.41.5 *If a and b are atoms and $aM_1 \dots M_m =_\beta bN_1 \dots N_n$, then $a \equiv b$ and $m = n$ and $M_i =_\beta N_i$ for all $i \leq m$.*

Proof By 1.41, both terms reduce to some T. By 1.34, $T \equiv aT_1 \dots T_m$, where $M_i \triangleright_\beta T_i$ for $i = 1, \dots, m$. Similarly, $T \equiv bT'_1 \dots T'_n$ where $N_j \triangleright_\beta T'_j$ for $j = 1, \dots, n$. Thus $aT_1 \dots T_m \equiv T \equiv bT'_1 \dots T'_n$, so $a \equiv b$, $m = n$, and $T_i \equiv T'_i$ for $i = 1, \dots, m$. Hence result. □

Exercise 1.42 * (a) Prove that if the equation $\lambda xy.x = \lambda xy.y$ was added as an extra axiom to the definition of β-equality, then all terms would become equal. (Adding an equation $P = Q$ as an extra axiom means allowing any occurrence of P in a term to be replaced by Q and vice versa.)

(b) Do the same for the equation $\lambda x.x = \lambda xy.yx$.

Remark 1.43 (λI-terms) Terms without normal forms are like expressions which can be computed for ever without reaching a result. It is natural to think of such terms as meaningless, or at least as carrying less meaning than terms with normal forms. But it is possible for a term T to have a normal form, while one of its subterms has none. (An example is $T \equiv (\lambda u.v)\Omega$, where $\Omega \equiv (\lambda x.xx)(\lambda x.xx)$ from 1.25(d).) Thus a meaningful term can have a part which might be thought meaningless. To some logicians (including Church at certain stages of his work), this has seemed undesirable. From this viewpoint, it is better to work with a restricted set of terms called λI-*terms*, whose definition is the same as 1.1 except that $\lambda x.M$ is only allowed to be a λI-term when x occurs free in M. This restriction is enough to exclude the above term T, and by [CF58, Section 4E, Corollary 2.1], if a λI-term has a normal form then so do all its subterms.

There is an account of the λI-system in [Bar84, Chapter 9]. All the results stated so far are valid for the λI-system as well as for the full λ-system, but this will not always hold true for all future results.

Sometimes, to emphasise the contrast with the λI-system, the full system is called the λK-*system* and its terms are called λK-*terms*.

Exercise 1.44 (Extra practice)

(a) Insert all missing parentheses and λ's into the following abbreviated λ-terms:

(i) $xx(xxx)x$, (ii) $vw(\lambda xy.vx)$,
(iii) $(\lambda xy.x)uv$, (iv) $w(\lambda xyz.xz(yz))uv$.

(b) Mark all the occurrences of xy in the following terms:

(i) $(\lambda xy.xy)xy$, (ii) $(\lambda xy.xy)(xy)$, (iii) $\lambda xy.xy(xy)$.

(c) Do any of the terms in (a) or (b) contain any of the following terms as subterms? If so, which contains which?

(i) $\lambda y.xy$, (ii) $y(xy)$, (iii) $\lambda xy.x$.

(d) Evaluate the following substitutions:

(i) $[vw/x]\,(x(\lambda y.yx))$, (ii) $[vw/x]\,(x(\lambda x.yx))$,
(iii) $[ux/x]\,(x(\lambda y.yx))$, (iv) $[uy/x]\,(x(\lambda y.yx))$.

(e) Reduce the following terms to β-normal forms:

(i) $(\lambda xy.xyy)uv$, (ii) $(\lambda xy.yx)(uv)zw$,
(iii) $(\lambda xy.x)(\lambda u.u)$, (iv) $(\lambda xyz.xz(yz))(\lambda uv.u)$.

We shall leave λ-calculus now, and return again in Chapter 3. In fact Chapter 3 and most later chapters will apply equally well to both λ-calculus and combinatory logic.

Further reading

Before we move on, here are a few suggestions for supplementary reading. All of them are general works on λ-calculus; books on special subtopics will be mentioned in later chapters.

First, the Internet is a useful source: typing 'lambda calculus' into a search engine will show plenty of online introductions and summaries, as well as links to more specialized subtopics.

Also, most introductions to functional programming contain at least a quick introduction to λ-calculus. For example, [Mic88] and [Pie02] are well-written books of this kind.

[Chu41] is the first-ever textbook on λ, by the man who originated the subject. Its notation and methods are outdated now, but the early pages are still worth reading for motivation and some basic ideas.

[CF58] treats combinators and λ in parallel, and includes details such as substitution lemmas which many later accounts omit, as well as historical notes. But most of the book has long been superceded.

[Bar84] is an encyclopaedic and well-organized account of λ-calculus as known before 1984. It presents the deeper ideas underlying much of the theory, and even after over 20 years it is still essential for the intending specialist. (It does not cover type theory.)

[Kri93] is a sophisticated and smooth introduction (originally published in French). It covers less than the present book but treats several topics that will only be mentioned in passing here, such as intersection-types and Böhm's theorem. It also treats Girard's type-system F.

[Han04] is a short computer-science-oriented introduction. Its core topics overlap the present book. They are covered in less detail, but some useful extra topics are also included.

[Rév88] is a computer-science-oriented introduction demanding slightly less mathematical experience from the reader than the present book and covering less material. There are some exercises (but no answers). In Section 2.5 there is an interesting variant of β-reduction which generates the same equality as the usual one, and is confluent, but does not depend on a preliminary definition of substitution.

[Tak91] is a short introduction for Japanese readers on about the same level as the present book. It also contains an introduction to recursive functions, but does not treat types or combinatory logic.

[Wol04] is a Russian-language textbook of which a large part is an introduction to λ-calculus and combinators, covering the first five chapters of the present book as well as some more special topics such as types.

[Rez82] is a bibliography of all the literature up to 1982 on λ-calculus and combinators, valuable for the reader interested in history. It has very few omissions, and includes many unpublished manuscripts.

[Bet99] is a bibliography of works published from 1980 to 1999, based largely on items reviewed in the journal *Mathematical Reviews.* It is an electronic '.ps' file, for on-screen reading. (Printing-out is not recommended; it has over 500 pages!)

2
Combinatory logic

2A Introduction to CL

Systems of combinators are designed to do the same work as systems of λ-calculus, but without using bound variables. In fact, the annoying technical complications involved in substitution and α-conversion will be avoided completely in the present chapter. However, for this technical advantage we shall have to sacrifice the intuitive clarity of the λ-notation.

To motivate combinators, consider the commutative law of addition in arithmetic, which says

$$(\forall x, y) \;\; x + y \; = \; y + x.$$

The above expression contains bound variables 'x' and 'y'. But these can be removed, as follows. We first define an addition operator A by

$$A(x, y) \; = \; x + y \qquad \text{(for all } x, y\text{)},$$

and then introduce an operator C defined by

$$(\mathsf{C}(f))(x, y) \; = \; f(y, x) \qquad \text{(for all } f, x, y\text{)}.$$

Then the commutative law becomes simply

$$A \; = \; \mathsf{C}(A).$$

The operator C may be called a *combinator*; other examples of such operators are the following:

B,	which composes two functions:	$(\mathsf{B}(f, g))(x) \; = \; f(g(x))$;
B',	a reversed composition operator:	$(\mathsf{B}'(f, g))(x) \; = \; g(f(x))$;
I,	the identity operator:	$\mathsf{I}(f) \; = \; f$;
K,	which forms constant functions:	$(\mathsf{K}(a))(x) \; = \; a$;

S, a stronger composition operator: $(\mathsf{S}(f,g))(x) \;=\; f(x,g(x))$;
W, for doubling or 'diagonalizing': $(\mathsf{W}(f))(x) \;=\; f(x,x)$.

Instead of trying to define 'combinator' rigorously in this informal context, we shall build up a formal system of terms in which the above 'combinators' can be represented. Just as in the previous chapter, the system to be studied here will be the simplest possible one, with no syntactical complications or restrictions, but with the warning that systems used in practice are more complicated. The ideas introduced in the present chapter will be common to all systems, however.

Definition 2.1 (Combinatory logic terms, or CL-terms) Assume that there is given an infinite sequence of expressions $\mathbf{v}_0$, $\mathbf{v}_{00}$, $\mathbf{v}_{000}$, ... called *variables*, and a finite or infinite sequence of expressions called *atomic constants*, including three called *basic combinators*: I, K, S. (If I, K and S are the only atomic constants, the system will be called *pure*, otherwise *applied.*) The set of expressions called *CL-terms* is defined inductively as follows:

(a) all variables and atomic constants, including I, K, S, are CL-terms;
(b) if X and Y are CL-terms, then so is (XY).

An *atom* is a variable or atomic constant. A *non-redex constant* is an atomic constant other than I, K, S. A *non-redex atom* is a variable or a non-redex constant. A *closed term* is a term containing no variables. A *combinator* is a term whose only atoms are basic combinators. (In the pure system this is the same as a closed term.)

Examples of CL-terms (the one on the left is a combinator):

$$((\mathsf{S}(\mathsf{KS}))\mathsf{K}), \qquad\qquad ((\mathsf{S}(\mathsf{K}\mathbf{v}_0))((\mathsf{SK})\mathsf{K})).$$

Notation 2.2 Capital Roman letters will denote CL-terms in this chapter, and 'term' will mean 'CL-term'.

'CL' will mean 'combinatory logic', i.e. the study of systems of CL-terms. (In later chapters, particular systems will be called 'CLw', 'CLξ', etc., but never just 'CL'.)

The rest of the notation will be the same as in Chapter 1. In particular 'x', 'y', 'z', 'u', 'v', 'w' will stand for variables (distinct unless otherwise stated), and '$\equiv$' for syntactic identity of terms. Also parentheses will be omitted following the convention of association to the left, so that $(((UV)W)X)$ will be abbreviated to $UVWX$.

Definition 2.3 The *length of* X (or $lgh(X)$) is the number of occurrences of atoms in X:

(a) $lgh(a) = 1$ for atoms a;

(b) $lgh(UV) = lgh(U) + lgh(V)$.

For example, if $X \equiv x\mathsf{K}(\mathsf{SS}xy)$, then $lgh(X) \equiv 6$.

Definition 2.4 The relation X *occurs in* Y, or X *is a subterm of* Y, is defined thus:

(a) X occurs in X;

(b) if X occurs in U or in V, then X occurs in (UV).

The set of all variables occurring in Y is called $\mathrm{FV}(Y)$. (In CL-terms all occurrences of variables are free, because there is no λ to bind them.)

Example 2.5 Let $Y \equiv \mathsf{K}(x\mathsf{S})((x\mathsf{S}yz)(\mathsf{I}x))$. Then $x\mathsf{S}$ and x occur in Y (and $x\mathsf{S}$ has two occurrences and x has three). Also

$$\mathrm{FV}(Y) \equiv \{x, y, z\}.$$

Definition 2.6 (Substitution) $[U/x]Y$ is defined to be the result of substituting U for every occurrence of x in Y: that is,

(a) $[U/x]x \equiv U$,

(b) $[U/x]a \equiv a$ for atoms $a \not\equiv x$,

(c) $[U/x](VW) \equiv ([U/x]V\ [U/x]W)$.

For all $U_1, \ldots, U_n$ and mutually distinct $x_1, \ldots, x_n$, the result of simultaneously substituting U_1 for x_1, U_2 for x_2, ..., U_n for x_n in Y is called

$$[U_1/x_1, \ldots, U_n/x_n]Y.$$

Example 2.7

(a) $[(\mathsf{SK})/x](yxx) \equiv y(\mathsf{SK})(\mathsf{SK})$,

(b) $[(\mathsf{SK})/x, (\mathsf{KI})/y](yxx) \equiv \mathsf{KI}(\mathsf{SK})(\mathsf{SK})$.

Exercise 2.8* (a) Give a definition of $[U_1/x_1, \ldots, U_n/x_n]Y$ by induction on Y.

(b) An example in Remark 1.23 shows that the identity

$$[U_1/x_1, \ldots, U_n/x_n]Y \equiv [U_1/x_1]\big([U_2/x_2](\ldots [U_n/x_n]Y) \ldots\big)$$

can fail. State a non-trivial condition sufficient to make this identity true.

2B Weak reduction

In the next section, we shall see how I, K and S can be made to play a rôle that is essentially equivalent to 'λ'. We shall need the following reducibility relation.

Definition 2.9 (Weak reduction) Any term $\mathsf{I}X$, $\mathsf{K}XY$ or $\mathsf{S}XYZ$ is called a *(weak) redex*. *Contracting* an occurrence of a weak redex in a term U means replacing one occurrence of

$$\begin{array}{lll} \mathsf{I}X & \text{by} & X, \qquad \text{or} \\ \mathsf{K}XY & \text{by} & X, \qquad \text{or} \\ \mathsf{S}XYZ & \text{by} & XZ(YZ). \end{array}$$

Iff this changes U to U', we say that U *(weakly) contracts to* U', or

$$U \rhd_{1w} U'.$$

Iff V is obtained from U by a finite (perhaps empty) series of weak contractions, we say that U *(weakly) reduces to* V, or

$$U \rhd_{w} V.$$

Definition 2.10 A *weak normal form* (or *weak nf* or *term in weak normal form*) is a term that contains no weak redexes. Iff a term U weakly reduces to a weak normal form X, we call X a *weak normal form of* U.

(Actually the Church–Rosser theorem later will imply that a term cannot have more than one weak normal form.)

Example 2.11 Define $\mathsf{B} \equiv \mathsf{S}(\mathsf{KS})\mathsf{K}$. Then $\mathsf{B}XYZ \rhd_w X(YZ)$ for all terms X, Y and Z, since

$$\begin{array}{lll} \mathsf{B}XYZ \equiv & \mathsf{S}(\mathsf{KS})\mathsf{K}XYZ & \\ \rhd_{1w} & \mathsf{KS}X(\mathsf{K}X)YZ & \text{by contracting } \mathsf{S}(\mathsf{KS})\mathsf{K}X \text{ to } \mathsf{KS}X(\mathsf{K}X) \\ \rhd_{1w} & \mathsf{S}(\mathsf{K}X)YZ & \text{by contracting } \mathsf{KS}X \text{ to } \mathsf{S} \\ \rhd_{1w} & \mathsf{K}XZ(YZ) & \text{by contracting } \mathsf{S}(\mathsf{K}X)YZ \\ \rhd_{1w} & X(YZ) & \text{by contracting } \mathsf{K}XZ. \end{array}$$

Example 2.12 Define $\mathsf{C} \equiv \mathsf{S}(\mathsf{BBS})(\mathsf{KK})$. Then $\mathsf{C}XYZ \rhd_w XZY$, since

$$\begin{array}{lll} \mathsf{C}XYZ & \equiv & \mathsf{S}(\mathsf{BBS})(\mathsf{KK})XYZ \\ & \rhd_{1w} & \mathsf{BBS}X(\mathsf{KK}X)YZ \quad \text{by contracting } \mathsf{S}(\mathsf{BBS})(\mathsf{KK})X \\ & \rhd_{1w} & \mathsf{BBS}X\mathsf{K}YZ \quad \text{by contracting } \mathsf{KK}X \\ & \rhd_{w} & \mathsf{B}(\mathsf{S}X)\mathsf{K}YZ \quad \text{by 2.11} \\ & \rhd_{w} & \mathsf{S}X(\mathsf{K}Y)Z \quad \text{by 2.11} \\ & \rhd_{1w} & XZ(\mathsf{K}YZ) \quad \text{by contracting } \mathsf{S}X(\mathsf{K}Y)Z \\ & \rhd_{1w} & XZY \quad \text{by contracting } \mathsf{K}YZ. \end{array}$$

Incidentally, in line 4 of this reduction, a redex $\mathsf{K}YZ$ seems to occur; but this is not really so, since, when all its parentheses are inserted, $\mathsf{B}(\mathsf{S}X)\mathsf{K}YZ$ is really $((((\mathsf{B}(\mathsf{S}X))\mathsf{K})Y)Z)$.

Exercise 2.13* Reduce the following CL-terms to normal forms:

(i) $\mathsf{SIK}x$, (ii) $\mathsf{SSK}xy$, (iii) $\mathsf{S}(\mathsf{SK})xy$,
(iv) $\mathsf{S}(\mathsf{KS})\mathsf{S}xyz$, (v) $\mathsf{SBBI}xy$.

Lemma 2.14 (Substitution lemma for $\rhd_w$)

(a) $X \rhd_w Y \implies \mathrm{FV}(X) \supseteq \mathrm{FV}(Y)$;

(b) $X \rhd_w Y \implies [X/v]Z \rhd_w [Y/v]Z$;

(c) $X \rhd_w Y \implies [U_1/x_1, \ldots, U_n/x_n]X \rhd_w [U_1/x_1, \ldots, U_n/x_n]Y$.

Proof For (a): for all terms U, V, W, we have: $\mathrm{FV}(\mathsf{I}U) \supseteq \mathrm{FV}(U)$, $\mathrm{FV}(\mathsf{K}UV) \supseteq \mathrm{FV}(U)$, and $\mathrm{FV}(\mathsf{S}UVW) \supseteq \mathrm{FV}(UW(VW))$.

For (b): any contractions made in X can also be made in the substituted X's in $[X/v]Z$.

For (c): if R is a redex and contracts to T, then $[U_1/x_1, \ldots, U_n/x_n]R$ is also a redex and contracts to $[U_1/x_1, \ldots, U_n/x_n]T$. □

Theorem 2.15 (Church–Rosser theorem for $\rhd_w$) *If $U \rhd_w X$ and $U \rhd_w Y$, then there exists a CL-term T such that*

$$X \rhd_w T \quad \text{and} \quad Y \rhd_w T.$$

Proof Appendix A2, Theorem A2.13. □

Corollary 2.15.1 (Uniqueness of nf) *A CL-term can have at most one weak normal form.*

Exercise 2.16 Prove that $\mathsf{SKK}X \rhd_w X$ for all terms X. (Hence, by letting $I \equiv \mathsf{SKK}$, we obtain a term composed only of S and K which behaves like the combinator I. Thus CL could have been based on just two atoms, K and S. However, if we did this, a very simple correspondence between normal forms in CL and λ would fail; see Remark 8.23 and Exercise 9.19 later.)

Exercise 2.17* (Tricky) Construct combinators B' and W such that

$$\begin{array}{llll} \mathsf{B}'XYZ & \rhd_w & Y(XZ) & \text{(for all } X, Y, Z\text{)}, \\ \mathsf{W}XY & \rhd_w & XYY & \text{(for all } X, Y\text{)}. \end{array}$$

2C Abstraction in CL

In this section, we shall define a CL-term called '$[x].M$' for every x and M, with the property that

$$([x].M)N \rhd_w [N/x]M. \tag{1}$$

Thus the term $[x].M$ will play a role like $\lambda x.M$. It will be a combination of I's, K's, S's and parts of M, built up as follows.

Definition 2.18 (Abstraction) For every CL-term M and every variable x, a CL-term called $[x].M$ is defined by induction on M, thus:

$$\begin{array}{lllll} \text{(a)} & [x].M & \equiv \mathsf{K}M & & \text{if } x \notin \mathrm{FV}(M); \\ \text{(b)} & [x].x & \equiv \mathsf{I}; & & \\ \text{(c)} & [x].Ux & \equiv U & & \text{if } x \notin \mathrm{FV}(U); \\ \text{(f)} & [x].UV & \equiv \mathsf{S}([x].U)([x].V) & & \text{if neither (a) nor (c) applies.}^1 \end{array}$$

Example 2.19

$$\begin{array}{rcll} [x].xy & \equiv & \mathsf{S}([x].x)([x].y) & \text{by 2.18(f)} \\ & \equiv & \mathsf{SI}(\mathsf{K}y) & \text{by 2.18 (b) and (a).} \end{array}$$

[1] These clauses are from [CF58, Section 6A, clauses(a)–(f)], deleting (d)–(e), which are irrelevant here. The notation '$[x]$' is from [CF58, Section 6A]. In [Ros55], [Bar84] and [HS86] the notation '$\lambda^{\star}x$' was used instead, to stress similarities between CL and λ-calculus. But the two systems have important differences, and '$\lambda^{\star}x$' has since acquired some other meanings in the literature, so the '$[x]$' notation is used here.

Warning 2.20 In λ-calculus an expression λx can be part of a λ-term, for example the term $\lambda x.xy$. But in CL, the corresponding expression $[x]$ is not part of the formal language of CL-terms at all. In the above example, the expression $[x].xy$ is not itself a CL-term, but is merely a short-hand to denote the CL-term $\mathsf{SI}(\mathsf{K}y)$.

Theorem 2.21 *The clauses in Definition 2.18 allow us to construct* $[x].M$ *for all* x *and* M. *Further,* $[x].M$ *does not contain* x, *and, for all* N,

$$([x].M)N \ \triangleright_w \ [N/x]M.$$

Proof By induction on M we shall prove that $[x].M$ is always defined, does not contain x, and that

$$([x].M)\,x \ \triangleright_w \ M.$$

The theorem will follow by substituting N for x and using 2.14(c).

Case 1: $M \equiv x$. Then Definition 2.18(b) applies, and

$$([x].x)\,x \ \equiv \ \mathsf{I}x \ \triangleright_w \ x.$$

Case 2: M is an atom and $M \not\equiv x$. Then 2.18(a) applies, and

$$([x].M)\,x \ \equiv \ \mathsf{K}Mx \ \triangleright_w \ M.$$

Case 3: $M \equiv UV$. By the induction hypothesis, we may assume

$$([x].U)\,x \ \triangleright_w \ U, \qquad ([x].V)\,x \ \triangleright_w \ V.$$

Subcase 3(i): $x \notin \mathrm{FV}(M)$. Like Case 2.

Subcase 3(ii): $x \notin \mathrm{FV}(U)$ and $V \equiv x$. Then

$$\begin{aligned} ([x].M)\,x &\equiv ([x].Ux)\,x \\ &\equiv Ux && \text{by 2.18(c),} \\ &\equiv M. \end{aligned}$$

Subcase 3(iii): Neither of the above two subcases applies. Then

$$\begin{aligned} ([x].M)\,x &\equiv \mathsf{S}([x].U)([x].V)\,x && \text{by 2.18(f)} \\ &\triangleright_{1w} ([x].U)\,x\,(([x].V)\,x) \\ &\triangleright_w UV && \text{by induction hypothesis} \\ &\equiv M. \end{aligned}$$

(Note how the redexes and contractions for I, K, and S in 2.9 fit in with the cases in this proof; in fact this is their purpose.) □

Exercise 2.22* Evaluate

$$[x].u(vx), \qquad [x].x(\mathbf{S}y), \qquad [x].uxxv.$$

Remark 2.23 There are several other possible definitions of abstraction besides the one in Definition 2.18. For example, [Bar84, Definition 7.1.5] omits 2.18(c). But this omission enormously increases the lengths of terms $[x_1].(\ldots([x_n].M)\ldots)$ for most $x_1, \ldots, x_n, M$. Some alternative definitions of abstraction will be compared in Chapter 9.

Definition 2.24 For all variables $x_1, \ldots, x_n$ (not necessarily distinct),

$$[x_1, \ldots, x_n].M \equiv [x_1].([x_2].(\ldots([x_n].M)\ldots)).$$

Example 2.25

(a)
$$\begin{aligned} [x,y].x &\equiv [x].([y].x) \\ &\equiv [x].(\mathbf{K}x) && \text{by 2.18(a) for } [y] \\ &\equiv \mathbf{K} && \text{by 2.18(c).} \end{aligned}$$

(b)
$$\begin{aligned} [x,y,z].xz(yz) &\equiv [x].\big([y].\big([z].xz(yz)\big)\big) \\ &\equiv [x].\big([y].\big(\mathbf{S}([z].xz)([z].yz)\big)\big) && \text{by 2.18(f) for } [z] \\ &\equiv [x].\big([y].\mathbf{S}xy\big) && \text{by 2.18(c) for } [z] \\ &\equiv [x].\mathbf{S}x && \text{by 2.18(c) for } [y] \\ &\equiv \mathbf{S} && \text{by 2.18(c).} \end{aligned}$$

Exercise 2.26* Evaluate

$$[x,y,z].xzy, \qquad [x,y,z].y(xz), \qquad [x,y].xyy.$$

Compare $[x,y,z].xzy$ with the combinator $\mathbf{C}$ in Example 2.12. Note that $[x,y,z].y(xz)$ and $[x,y].xyy$ give answers to Exercise 2.17, combinators $\mathbf{B}'$ and $\mathbf{W}$. There are other possible answers to that exercise, but the the abstraction algorithm in Definition 2.18 has changed the formerly tricky task of finding an answer into a routine matter.

Theorem 2.27 *For all variables $x_1, \ldots, x_n$ (mutually distinct),*

$$([x_1, \ldots, x_n].M)\, U_1 \ldots U_n \;\triangleright_w\; [U_1/x_1, \ldots, U_n/x_n]M.$$

Proof By 2.14(c) it is enough to prove $([x_1, \ldots, x_n].M)x_1 \ldots x_n \;\triangleright_w\; M$. And this comes from 2.21 by an easy induction on n. □

Lemma 2.28 (Substitution and abstraction)

(a) $\mathrm{FV}([x].M) \ = \ \mathrm{FV}(M) - \{x\}$ *if* $x \in \mathrm{FV}(M)$;

(b) $[y].[y/x]M \ \equiv \ [x].M$ *if* $y \notin \mathrm{FV}(M)$;

(c) $[N/x]([y].M) \ \equiv \ [y].[N/x]M$ *if* $y \notin \mathrm{FV}(xN)$.

Proof Straightforward induction on M. □

Comment Part (b) of Lemma 2.28 shows that the analogue in CL of the λ-calculus relation $\equiv_\alpha$ is simply identity. Part (c) is an approximate analogue of Definition 1.12(f).

The last few results have shown that $[x]$ has similar properties to λx. But it must be emphasized again that, in contrast to λx, $[x]$ is not part of the formal system of terms; $[x].M$ is defined in the meta-theory by induction on M, and is constructed from **I**, **K**, **S**, and parts of M.

2D Weak equality

Definition 2.29 (Weak equality or weak convertibility) We shall say X is *weakly equal* or *weakly convertible* to Y, or $X =_w Y$, iff Y can be obtained from X by a finite (perhaps empty) series of weak contractions and reversed weak contractions. That is, $X =_w Y$ iff there exist $X_0, \ldots,$ X_n $(n \geq 0)$ such that

$$(\forall i \leq n-1)\ (\ X_i \rhd_{1w} X_{i+1} \ \text{ or } \ X_{i+1} \rhd_{1w} X_i\ ),$$

$$X_0 \equiv X, \qquad X_n \equiv Y.$$

Exercise 2.30* Prove that, if **B**, **W** are the terms in Example 2.11 and Exercise 2.17, then

$$\mathsf{BWBI}x \ =_w \ \mathsf{SII}x.$$

Lemma 2.31

(a) $X =_w Y \implies [X/v]Z =_w [Y/v]Z$;

(b) $X =_w Y \implies [U_1/x_1, \ldots, U_n/x_n]X =_w [U_1/x_1, \ldots, U_n/x_n]Y$.

Theorem 2.32 (Church–Rosser theorem for $=_w$) *If $X =_w Y$, then there exists a term T such that*

$$X \triangleright_w T \quad \text{and} \quad Y \triangleright_w T.$$

Proof From 2.15, like the proof of 1.41 from 1.32. □

Corollary 2.32.1 *If $X =_w Y$ and Y is a weak normal form, then we have $X \triangleright_w Y$.*

Corollary 2.32.2 *If $X =_w Y$, then either X and Y have no weak normal form, or they both have the same weak normal form.*

Corollary 2.32.3 *If X and Y are distinct weak normal forms, then $X \neq_w Y$; in particular $\mathsf{S} \neq_w \mathsf{K}$. Hence $=_w$ is non-trivial in the sense that not all terms are weakly equal.*

Corollary 2.32.4 (Uniqueness of nf) *A term can be weakly equal to at most one weak normal form.*

Corollary 2.32.5 *If a and b are atoms other than I, K and S, and $aX_1 \dots X_m =_w bY_1 \dots Y_n$, then $a \equiv b$ and $m = n$ and $X_i =_w Y_i$ for all $i \leq m$.*

Warning 2.33 Although the above results show that $=_w$ in CL behaves very like $=_\beta$ in λ, the two relations do not correspond exactly. The main difference is that $=_\beta$ has the property which [CF58] calls (ξ), namely

$$(\xi) \qquad X =_\beta Y \implies \lambda x.X =_\beta \lambda x.Y.$$

(This holds in λ because any contraction or change of bound variable made in X can also be made in $\lambda x.X$.) When translated into CL, (ξ) becomes

$$X =_w Y \implies [x].X =_w [x].Y.$$

But for CL-terms, $[x]$ is not part of the syntax, and (ξ) fails. For example, take

$$X \equiv \mathsf{S}xyz, \qquad Y \equiv xz(yz);$$

then $X =_w Y$, but

$$\begin{aligned}[x].X &\equiv \mathsf{S}(\mathsf{SS}(\mathsf{K}y))(\mathsf{K}z),\\ [x].Y &\equiv \mathsf{S}(\mathsf{SI}(\mathsf{K}z))(\mathsf{K}(yz)).\end{aligned}$$

These are normal forms and distinct, so by 2.32.3 they are not weakly equal.

For many purposes the lack of (ξ) is no problem and the simplicity of weak equality gives it an advantage over λ-calculus. This is especially true if all we want to do is define a set of functions in a formal theory, for example the recursive functions in Chapter 5. But for some other purposes (ξ) turns out to be indispensable, and weak equality is too weak. We then either have to abandon combinators and use λ, or add new axioms to weak equality to make it stronger. Possible extra axioms will be discussed in Chapter 9.

Exercise 2.34 *

(a) Construct a *pairing-combinator* D and two *projections* D_1, D_2 such that

$$\mathsf{D}_1(\mathsf{D}xy) \rhd_w x, \qquad \mathsf{D}_2(\mathsf{D}xy) \rhd_w y.$$

(b) Show that there is no combinator that distinguishes between atoms and composite terms; i.e. show that there is no A such that

$$\begin{aligned} AX &=_w \mathsf{S} && \text{if } X \text{ is an atom,} \\ AX &=_w \mathsf{K} && \text{if } X \equiv UV \text{ for some } U,\, V. \end{aligned}$$

(Operations involving decisions that depend on the syntactic structure of terms can hardly ever be done by combinators.)

(c) Prove that a term X is in weak normal form iff X is minimal with respect to weak reduction, i.e. iff

$$X \rhd_w Y \implies Y \equiv X.$$

(Contrast λ-calculus, 1.27(d).) Show that this would be false if there were an atom W with an axiom-scheme

$$\mathsf{W}XY \rhd_w XYY.$$

Extra practice 2.35

(a) Reduce the following CL-terms to weak normal forms. (For some of them, use the reductions for B, C and W shown in Examples 2.11 and 2.12 and Exercise 2.17.)

(i) $\mathsf{KS}uxyz$, (ii) $\mathsf{S}(\mathsf{K}x)(\mathsf{KI}y)z$,

(iii) $\mathsf{CSI}xy$, (iv) $\mathsf{S}(\mathsf{CI})xy$,

(v) $\mathsf{B}(\mathsf{BS})\mathsf{B}xyzu$, (vi) $\mathsf{BB}(\mathsf{BB})uvwxy$,

(vii) $\mathsf{B}(\mathsf{BW}(\mathsf{BC}))(\mathsf{BB}(\mathsf{BB}))xyzu$.

(b) Evaluate the following:

$$[x].xu(xv), \qquad [y].ux(uy), \qquad [x,y].ux(uy).$$

(c) Prove that $\mathsf{SK}xy =_w \mathsf{KI}xy$. (Cf. Example 8.16(a).)

Further reading

There are many informative websites: just type 'combinatory' into a search engine. Also several introductions to λ include CL as well. The following are some references that focus mainly on CL.

[Ste72], [Bun02] and [Wol03] are introductions to CL aimed at about the same level as the present book. If the reader is dissatisfied with this book, he or she might find one of these more useful!

[Bar84] contains only one chapter on CL explicitly (Chapter 7). But most of the ideas in that book apply to CL as well as λ.

[Smu85] contains a humorous and clever account of combinators and self-application, and is especially good for examples and exercises on the interdefinability of various combinators.

[Sch24] is the first-ever exposition of combinators, by the man who invented them, and is a very readable non-technical short sketch.

[CF58] was the only book on CL for many years, and is still valuable for a few things, for example its discussion of particular combinators and interdefinability questions (Chapter 5), alternative definitions of $[x]$ (Section 6A), strong equality and reduction (Sections 6B–6F), and historical comments at the ends of chapters.

[CHS72] is a continuation and updating of [CF58], and contains proofs of the main properties of weak reduction (Section 11B). Definitions of $[x]$ are discussed in Section 11C. References for other topics will be given as they crop up later in the present book.

[Bac78] has historical interest; it is a strong plea for a functional style of programming, using combinators as an analogy, and led to an upsurge of interest in combinators, and to several combinator-based programming languages. (But Backus was not the first to advocate this; some precursors were [Fit58], [McC60], [Lan65], [Lan66], [BG66] and [Tur76].)

3
The power of λ and combinators

3A Introduction

The purpose of this chapter and the next two is to show some of the expressive power of both λ and CL.

The present chapter describes three interesting theorems which hold for both λ and combinators, and are used frequently in the published literature: the *fixed-point theorem*, *Böhm's theorem*, and a theorem which helps in proving that a term has no normal form.

After these results, Section 3E will outline the history of λ and CL, and will discuss the question of whether they have any meaning, or are just uninterpretable formal systems.

Then Chapter 4 will show that all recursive functions are definable in both systems, and Chapter 5 will deduce from this a general undecidability theorem.

Notation 3.1 This chapter is written in a neutral notation, which may be interpreted in either λ or CL, as follows.

Notation	*Meaning for* λ	*Meaning for CL*
term	λ-term	CL-term
$X \equiv Y$	$X \equiv_\alpha Y$	X is identical to Y
$X \triangleright_{\beta,w} Y$	$X \triangleright_\beta Y$	$X \triangleright_w Y$
$X =_{\beta,w} Y$	$X =_\beta Y$	$X =_w Y$
λx	λx	$[x]$

Definition 3.2 A *combinator* is (in λ) a closed pure term, i.e. a term containing neither free variables nor atomic constants, and (in CL) a

term whose only atoms are the basic combinators **I**, **K**, **S**. In λ, the following combinators are given special names:

$$\mathbf{B} \equiv \lambda xyz.x(yz), \quad \mathbf{B}' \equiv \lambda xyz.y(xz), \quad \mathbf{C} \equiv \lambda xyz.xzy,$$
$$\mathbf{I} \equiv \lambda x.x, \quad \mathbf{K} \equiv \lambda xy.x, \quad \mathbf{S} \equiv \lambda xyz.xz(yz),$$
$$\mathbf{W} \equiv \lambda xy.xyy.$$

3B The fixed-point theorem

A *fixed point* of an operator or function is an object which does not change when the operator is applied to it. For example, the operation of squaring numbers has two fixed points 0 and 1, since $0^2 = 0$ and $1^2 = 1$; and the successor-function has none, since $n + 1 \neq n$ for all n.

The next theorem shows that every operator in λ and CL has a fixed point. More precisely, for every term X there is a term P (depending on X) such that

$$XP =_{\beta,w} P.$$

Furthermore, there is a combinator **Y** which finds these fixed points, i.e. such that, for every term X, the term $\mathbf{Y}X$ is a fixed point of X.

Theorem 3.3 (Fixed-point theorem) *In both λ and CL, there is a combinator* **Y** *such that*

(a) $\mathbf{Y}x =_{\beta,w} x(\mathbf{Y}x)$.

In fact, there is a **Y** *with the stronger property*

(b) $\mathbf{Y}x \rhd_{\beta,w} x(\mathbf{Y}x)$.

Proof A suitable **Y** was invented by Alan Turing in 1937. It is

$$\mathbf{Y} \equiv UU, \quad \text{where } U \equiv \lambda ux.x(uux).$$

It satisfies (b) (and therefore also (a)), because

$\mathbf{Y}x \equiv$	$(\lambda u.(\lambda x.x(uux)))Ux$	by the definition of U
$\rhd_{\beta,w}$	$[U/u](\lambda x.x(uux))\,x$	by Definition 1.24 or Theorem 2.21
$\equiv$	$(\lambda x.x(UUx))x$	by Definition 1.12 or Lemma 2.28(c) (noting that FV(U) is empty)
$\rhd_{\beta,w}$	$x(UUx)$	by Definition 1.24 or Theorem 2.21

$$\equiv \quad x(\mathbf{Y}x).$$

Note that the above reduction is correct for both λ and CL. For λ, each of the two steps above is a single contraction; for CL, each is a reduction given by Theorem 2.21. □

Corollary 3.3.1 *In λ and CL: for every Z and $n \geq 0$, the equation*

$$xy_1 \dots y_n \; = \; Z$$

can be solved for x. That is, there is a term X such that

$$Xy_1 \dots y_n \; =_{\beta,w} \; [X/x]Z.$$

Proof Choose $X \equiv \mathbf{Y}(\lambda xy_1 \dots y_n . Z)$. □

Comments The fixed-point theorem is most often used via this corollary. In the corollary, Z may contain any or none of $x, y_1, \dots, y_n$, although the most interesting cases occur when Z contains x.

The corollary can be used in representing the recursive functions by terms in λ or CL (Chapter 4, Note 4.15). In logical systems based on λ or CL, if the system's designer is not extremely careful the corollary may cause paradoxes (see [CF58, Section 8A]).

On a more trivial level, it provides the world of λ and CL with a garbage-disposer X_1 which swallows all arguments presented to it,

$$X_1 y \; =_{\beta,w} \; X_1,$$

and a bureaucrat X_2 which eternally permutes its arguments with no other effect,

$$X_2 yz \; =_{\beta,w} \; X_2 zy.$$

Corollary 3.3.2 (Double fixed-point theorem) *In λ and CL: for every pair of terms X, Y there exist P, Q such that*

$$XPQ \; =_{\beta,w} \; P, \qquad YPQ \; =_{\beta,w} \; Q.$$

Proof (From [Bar84, Section 6.5].) By Exercise 3.5(b) below, with $n = k = 2$, there exist terms X_1, X_2 such that (for $i = 1, 2$)

$$X_i \, y_1 y_2 \; =_{\beta,w} \; y_i \, (X_1 y_1 y_2)(X_2 y_1 y_2).$$

Choose $P \equiv X_1 XY$ and $Q \equiv X_2 XY$. □

Remark Turing's combinator Y in the proof of the fixed-point theorem is not the only possible one. The following definition gives another, first published by Paul Rosenbloom in [Ros50, pp. 130–131, Exs. 3e, 5f], but hinted at in 1929 by Curry in a letter. It is simpler than Turing's, but does not have the extra property 3.3(b). Some others are given in [CHS72, Section 11F7] and [Bar84, Section 6.5].

Definition 3.4 A *fixed-point combinator* is any combinator Y such that $\mathsf{Y}X =_{\beta,w} X(\mathsf{Y}X)$ for all terms X. Define

$$\mathsf{Y}_{\text{Turing}} \equiv UU, \qquad \text{where } U \equiv \lambda ux.x(uux),$$
$$\mathsf{Y}_{\text{Curry-Ros}} \equiv \lambda x.VV, \qquad \text{where } V \equiv \lambda y.x(yy).$$

Exercise 3.5* (a) Prove that $\mathsf{Y}_{\text{Curry-Ros}}$ is a fixed-point combinator.

(b) (Complicated) Extend Corollary 3.3.1 to prove that, in both λ and CL, every finite set of simultaneous equations of form

$$\left\{\begin{array}{rcl} x_1y_1\ldots y_n & = & Z_1 \\ \ldots & & \ldots \\ x_ky_1\ldots y_n & = & Z_k \end{array}\right\} \quad (n \geq 0, k \geq 1)$$

is solvable for $x_1, \ldots, x_k$. The terms $Z_1, \ldots, Z_n$ may contain any or none of $x_1, \ldots, x_k, y_1, \ldots, y_n$.

Extra practice 3.6 (a) Prove that the following terms are fixed-point combinators (in both λ and CL):

$$\mathsf{Y}_0 \equiv \mathsf{WS}(\mathsf{BWB}), \qquad \mathsf{Y}_1 \equiv \mathsf{WI}(\mathsf{B}(\mathsf{SI})(\mathsf{WI})).$$

(b) Prove that if a term Y is a fixed-point combinator, then

(i) $\mathsf{SI}Y =_{\beta,w} Y$ (and so $\mathsf{SI}Y$ is a fixed-point combinator),

(ii) $Y(\mathsf{SI})$ is a fixed-point combinator.

More on fixed points can be found in [Bar84, Sections 6.1, 6.5, 19.3].

3C Böhm's theorem

The next theorem shows that the members of a significant class of normal forms can be distinguished from each other in a very powerful way. It is due to Corrado Böhm [Böh68], and has applications in both the syntax and semantics of λ and CL.

To prepare for the theorem, the relevant class of normal forms will now be defined, first in λ and then in CL. These two classes will gain further significance in later chapters, but for the moment they are simply aids to stating Böhm's theorem.

Definition 3.7 ($\beta\eta$-normal forms) In λ-calculus, a term of form $\lambda x.Mx$ with $x \notin \mathrm{FV}(M)$ is called an *η-redex* and is said to *η-contract* to M. (Such redexes will be studied in Chapter 7.) A λ-term X which contains no β-redexes and no η-redexes is called a *$\beta\eta$-normal form*. The class of all such λ-terms is called *$\beta\eta$-nf* or *$\lambda\beta\eta$-nf*.

Example The λ-term $\lambda ux.ux$ is in β-nf but not in $\beta\eta$-nf. (It is really $\lambda u.(\lambda x.ux)$, which η-contracts to $\lambda u.u$.)

Definition 3.8 (Strong normal forms) In CL, the class *strong nf* is defined inductively as follows. Its members are called *strong normal forms*.

(a) All atoms other than I, K and S are in strong nf;

(b) if $X_1, \ldots, X_n$ are in strong nf, and a is any atom $\not\equiv \mathsf{I}, \mathsf{K}, \mathsf{S}$, then $aX_1 \ldots X_n$ is in strong nf;

(c) if X is in strong nf, then so is $[x].X$.

Exercise 3.9 (a) Notice that Definition 3.8 is like Lemma 1.33.

(b) Prove that the class strong nf contains I, K, S and all terms whose only atoms are variables.

Lemma 3.10 *In CL, every strong normal form is also a weak normal form.*

Proof Induction on Definition 3.8. □

Theorem 3.11 (Böhm's theorem) *In λ and CL: let M and N be combinators, either in $\beta\eta$-normal form (in λ) or in strong normal form (in CL). If $M \not\equiv N$, then there exist $n \geq 0$ and combinators $L_1, \ldots, L_n$ such that*

$$\begin{aligned} ML_1 \ldots L_n xy &\rhd_{\beta,w} x, \\ NL_1 \ldots L_n xy &\rhd_{\beta,w} y. \end{aligned}$$

Roughly speaking, Böhm's theorem says that M and N can be distinguished, not just by their structure, but by their behaviour. By feeding them a suitable diet, the same for both, they can be forced to behave in recognisably different ways, i.e. to act as different selectors.

Proof For λ, the original proof is in [Böh68]. More accessible proofs are in [Kri93, Chapter 9], [Bar84, Theorem 10.4.2], [CHS72, Section 11F8], and (in Japanese) [Tak91, Theorem 3.4.26, p. 148]. There are thorough analyses of the theorem and the principles behind it in [Bar84, Chapter 10] and [Hue93]. The above version of the theorem is the special case $P \equiv \lambda xy.x$, $Q \equiv \lambda xy.y$, of Theorem 10.4.2(ii) in [Bar84].

For CL, the theorem can be deduced from the λ-theorem as in [Hin79]. Alternatively, a careful check of the λ-proofs in [Böh68] or [CHS72] shows that all the reductions in these proofs become correct weak reductions when translated from λ into CL. □

(The theorem can be extended to three or more normal forms, see [BDPR79].)

Corollary 3.11.1 *In λ or CL: let M and N be distinct combinators in $\beta\eta$-nf (in λ) or strong nf (in CL). If we add the equation $M = N$ as a new axiom to the definition of $=_\beta$ or $=_w$, then all terms become equal.*

Proof The phrase 'add the equation $M = N$ as a new axiom' means allowing any occurrence of M in a term to be replaced by N, and vice versa. Then, for all X, Y:

$$
\begin{array}{llll}
X & =_{\beta,w} & ML_1 \dots L_n XY & \text{by Böhm's theorem for } M,\ N, \\
 & =_{\beta,w} & NL_1 \dots L_n XY & \text{by the new axiom } M = N, \\
 & =_{\beta,w} & Y & \text{by Böhm's theorem for } M,\ N.
\end{array}
$$

□

The above corollary is, in a sense, an extension of the Church–Rosser theorem. In λ, that theorem implied, via Corollary 1.32.1, that if two distinct combinators M and N are β-nfs the equation $M = N$ cannot be proved for $=_\beta$, and the present corollary says that, furthermore, if M and N are $\beta\eta$-nfs the equation cannot even be added as an extra axiom (without the system collapsing to triviality). Similarly for CL and $=_w$.

Corollary 3.11.2 *In λ or CL: if M is a combinator in $\beta\eta$-nf (in λ) or strong nf (in CL), and P is any other combinator whatever, then there* *exist $m \geq 0$ and combinators H_1, ..., H_m such that*

$$MH_1 \dots H_m \;\; \triangleright_{\beta,w} \;\; P.$$

Proof By Theorem 3.11 with N any normal form distinct from M, there exist $n \geq 0$ and $L_1, \dots, L_n$ such that $ML_1 \dots L_n xy \triangleright_{\beta,w} x$. Choose $m = n+2$ and H_1, ..., H_m to be L_1, ..., L_n, P, **I**. □

Exercise 3.12 *

(a) In λ, prove the following two special cases of Böhm's theorem directly, without using the general theorem:

$$\text{(i)} \quad M \equiv \lambda xyz.xz(yz), \quad N \equiv \lambda xyz.x(yz);$$
$$\text{(ii)} \quad M \equiv \lambda xy.x(yy), \quad N \equiv \lambda xy.x(yx).$$

(Hint for (ii): choose a value of $n \geq 3$. The main difficulty in the proof of Böhm's theorem is to deal with repeated variables such as the x in (ii).)

(b) In CL, prove that no combinator Y in strong normal form can satisfy the fixed-point equation

$$Yx =_w x(Yx).$$

Hence, to say that a CL-combinator is in strong nf is some restriction on the kind of operator it can represent.

(c) In contrast to (b), weak normal forms have no similar restriction. Show that the CL-version of $\mathbf{Y}_{\text{Curry-Ros}}$, which satisfies the fixed-point equation, is a weak nf. Show further that all combinators can be imitated in CL by weak nfs; that is, prove that, if

$$Xy_1 \dots y_n =_w Z,$$

where $n \geq 1$ and Z is a given combination of $y_1, \dots, y_n$ and constants, then there is a weak nf X' such that

$$X'y_1 \dots y_n =_w Z.$$

(Hint: why are terms such as $\mathbf{Y}_{\text{Curry-Ros}}$ and $[x, y, z].y(xz)$ in weak nf?)

3D The quasi-leftmost-reduction theorem

The topic of this section is the problem of proving that a given term X has no normal form. On the surface, this seems very hard: one must reduce X in all possible ways and show that all the reductions can be continued for ever. Fortunately there is a theorem which simplifies this task. It says that if just one of a certain restricted class of reductions called *quasi-leftmost reductions* is infinite, then all reductions of X can be continued for ever. This reduces the problem of testing all reductions to testing very few.

In this section we shall define quasi-leftmost reductions and state the above theorem precisely. The results will apply to $\triangleright_\beta$ and β-normal forms in λ, and $\triangleright_w$ and weak normal forms in CL.

But first we need to say precisely what a contraction or a reduction is, as follows.

Definition 3.13 (Contractions) Given a λ- or CL-term X, a *contraction in* X is an ordered triple $\langle X, R, Y\rangle$, where R is an occurrence of a redex in X, and Y is the result of contracting R in X. (For 'occurrence', see the end of Definition 1.7; for 'contracting', see 1.24 and 2.9.) Instead of '$\langle X, R, Y\rangle$', we may write

$$X \triangleright_R Y.$$

Example 3.14 In Remark 1.29, two contractions were shown in the λ-term $(\lambda x.(\lambda y.yx)z)v$; they are

$$(\lambda x.(\lambda y.yx)z)v \ \triangleright_{(\lambda x.(\lambda y.yx)z)v} \ (\lambda y.yv)z,$$

$$(\lambda x.(\lambda y.yx)z)v \ \triangleright_{(\lambda y.yx)z} \ (\lambda x.zx)v.$$

Definition 3.15 (Reductions) In CL, a *reduction* ρ is a finite or infinite series of contractions, thus:

$$X_1 \triangleright_{R_1} X_2 \triangleright_{R_2} X_3 \triangleright_{R_3} \ldots$$

In λ, a *reduction* ρ is a finite or infinite series of contractions separated by α-conversions (perhaps empty), thus:

$$X_1 \triangleright_{R_1} Y_1 \equiv_\alpha X_2 \triangleright_{R_2} Y_2 \equiv_\alpha X_3 \triangleright_{R_3} \ldots$$

In λ or CL, the *start* of ρ is X_1, and the *length* of ρ is the number of its contractions (finite or ∞), not counting α-steps. If the length of ρ is finite, say n, then X_{n+1} is called the reduction's *end* or *terminus*.

Definition 3.16 A reduction ρ *has maximal length* iff either ρ is infinite or its terminus contains no redexes (i.e. iff ρ continues as long as there are redexes to be contracted).

Example 3.17 (a) In CL, the length of the following weak reduction is 2. It is not maximal because the reduction can be continued one step further. (The redex-occurrence contracted at each step is underlined.)

$$\mathsf{S}(\mathsf{I}(\mathsf{K}xy))(\underline{\mathsf{I}z}) \;\triangleright_{1w}\; \mathsf{S}(\underline{\mathsf{I}(\mathsf{K}xy)})\,z \;\triangleright_{1w}\; \mathsf{S}(\mathsf{K}xy)\,z.$$

(b) In λ, let $X_1 \equiv (\lambda x.xx)(\lambda x.xx)$. Then the only redex in X_1 is $R_1 \equiv X_1$, and contracting R_1 does not change X_1. The following is counted as an infinite reduction with $X_i \equiv R_i \equiv X_1$ for all $i \geq 1$:

$$X_1 \;\triangleright_{1w}\; X_1 \;\triangleright_{1w}\; X_1 \;\triangleright_{1w}\; \ldots\;.$$

Definition 3.18 An occurrence of a redex in a term X_1 is called *maximal* iff it is not contained in any other redex-occurrence in X_1. It is *leftmost maximal* iff it is the leftmost of the maximal redex-occurrences in X_1. A reduction ρ such that, for each i, the contracted redex-occurrence R_i is leftmost maximal in X_i, and which has maximal length, is called the *leftmost reduction* of X_1, or the *normal reduction* of X_1. (It is uniquely determined, given X_1.)

Example 3.19 In CL, let $X_1 \equiv \mathsf{S}(\mathsf{I}(\mathsf{K}xy))(\mathsf{I}z)$. Then X_1 contains three redex-occurrences,

$$\mathsf{I}(\mathsf{K}xy), \quad \mathsf{K}xy, \quad \mathsf{I}z,$$

and $\mathsf{I}(\mathsf{K}xy)$, $\mathsf{I}z$ are maximal, and of these, $\mathsf{I}(\mathsf{K}xy)$ is leftmost. The leftmost reduction of X_1 is

$$\mathsf{S}(\underline{\mathsf{I}(\mathsf{K}xy)})(\mathsf{I}z) \;\triangleright_{1w}\; \mathsf{S}(\underline{\mathsf{K}xy})(\mathsf{I}z) \;\triangleright_{1w}\; \mathsf{S}x(\underline{\mathsf{I}z}) \;\triangleright_{1w}\; \mathsf{S}xz.$$

In 1958 Curry proved that if the leftmost reduction of a λ-term X_1 is infinite, then all reductions starting at X_1 can be continued for ever, i.e. X_1 has no normal form. (See [Bar84, Theorem 13.2.2].) Thus leftmost reductions neatly solve the problem of proving that a term has no normal form. But in practice, when writing out a leftmost reduction, it is often convenient to make a few non-leftmost steps between the leftmost steps, as in the following example.

Example 3.20 In CL, let $X_1 \equiv \mathsf{SII}(\mathsf{SII})$. Then the leftmost reduction of X_1 is infinite and proceeds as follows:

$$X_1 \equiv \underline{\mathsf{SII}(\mathsf{SII})} \ \triangleright_{1w} \ \underline{\mathsf{I}(\mathsf{SII})}(\mathsf{I}(\mathsf{SII})) \ \triangleright_{1w} \ \underline{\mathsf{SII}(\mathsf{I}(\mathsf{SII}))}$$

$$\triangleright_{1w} \ \underline{\mathsf{I}(\mathsf{I}(\mathsf{SII}))}(\mathsf{I}(\mathsf{I}(\mathsf{SII}))) \ \triangleright_{1w} \ \text{etc.}$$

But by inserting some non-leftmost steps between the leftmost ones, we can make a repetitive pattern obvious, thus:

$$X_1 \equiv \underline{\mathsf{SII}(\mathsf{SII})} \ \triangleright_{1w} \ \underline{\mathsf{I}(\mathsf{SII})}(\mathsf{I}(\mathsf{SII})) \ \triangleright_{1w} \ \mathsf{SII}(\underline{\mathsf{I}(\mathsf{SII})})$$

$$\triangleright_{1w} \ \underline{\mathsf{SII}(\mathsf{SII})} \ \triangleright_{1w} \ \text{etc.}$$

Examples like this led Henk Barendregt in [Bar84, Definition 8.4.8] to define the following class of reductions.

Definition 3.21 A *quasi-leftmost reduction* of a term X_1 is a reduction ρ with maximal length, such that, for each i, if X_i is not the terminus then there exists $j \geq i$ such that R_j is leftmost maximal.

Informally speaking, an infinite reduction is quasi-leftmost iff an infinity of its contractions are leftmost maximal, and is leftmost iff they all are. In the preceding example, the first reduction is leftmost and the second one is only quasi-leftmost.

Theorem 3.22 (Quasi-leftmost-reduction theorem) *For λ-terms and $\triangleright_\beta$, or CL-terms and $\triangleright_w$: if a term X has a normal form X^*, then every quasi-leftmost reduction of X is finite and ends at X^*.*

Corollary 3.22.1 *A term X has no normal form iff some quasi-leftmost reduction of X is infinite.*

Proof See the proof of [Bar84, Theorem 13.2.6]. That proof is written for λ but is also valid for CL. □

Exercise 3.23 In λ, prove that the **Y**-combinators in Definition 3.4 have no β-normal form, by finding infinite quasi-leftmost reductions for them. (By the way, these infinite reductions in λ have no analogues for $\triangleright_w$ in CL, and in fact the CL-versions of $\mathbf{Y}_{\text{Turing}}$ and $\mathbf{Y}_{\text{Curry-Ros}}$ both have weak normal forms; furthermore, $\mathbf{Y}_{\text{Curry-Ros}}$ is actually *in* weak normal form, see Exercise 3.12(c).)

Remark 3.24 The proof of Theorem 3.22 depends on a fact about reductions, called the *Standardization theorem*, which is proved for λ in [Bar84, Section 11.4, Theorem 11.4.7] and for CL in [CHS72, Section 11B3]. The study of reductions was begun as far back as 1936 by

Church and Rosser with their proof of the confluence of $\triangleright_\beta$, and was greatly deepened in the 1970s by Jan-Willem Klop and Jean-Jacques Lévy. Some of their results are reported in [Bar84, Chapters 3, 11–14]. (That account is written for λ, but most of its theorems hold also for CL and $\triangleright_w$.)

Remark 3.25 The study of reductions in λ and CL led Klop and his colleagues in the 1980s to look at reductions generated by different kinds of redexes in systems other than λ and CL. The outcome of this work was a very general theory of reductions and confluence on which a lot of work has been done. Good overall surveys are in [Klo92] (on systems like CL) and [KvOvR93] (on systems more like λ), and an introductory textbook is [BN98].

3E History and interpretation

Historical comment 3.26 Although CL has been introduced after λ in this book, it actually originated several years before λ. Combinators were invented in 1920 by a Ukrainian, Moses Schönfinkel, who described his idea in a talk which was published in [Sch24]. But Schönfinkel suffered from bouts of mental illness and did not develop his ideas; indeed [Sch24] was actually written for him by a helpful colleague who had attended his talk. He himself did little more mathematical work and died in poverty in a Moscow hospital in 1942.

Combinators were re-invented in 1927 by an American, Haskell Curry, who had not seen Schönfinkel's paper. Curry was the first to define CL as a precise system, and became responsible for the main line of work on it until about 1970.

The λ-calculus was invented by another American, Alonzo Church, in the early 1930s, and developed with the aid of his students Barkley Rosser and Stephen Kleene. In 1936 it was used as the key to the first-ever proof that first-order predicate logic is undecidable (see Remark 5.7).

Both λ and CL were originally introduced as parts of strong systems of higher-order logic designed to provide a type-free foundation for all of mathematics. But the systems of Church and Curry in the 1930s turned out to be inconsistent. This led Church to turn to type theory; and he published a neat system of typed λ in 1940, [Chu40]. On the other hand, Curry was still attracted by the generality of type-free logic, and turned to analysing its foundations with great care, through a series of very general but very weak systems.

Until about 1960, λ and CL were only studied by a few small groups. But around that time, logicians working on computability began to expand their interest from functions of numbers to functions of functions, and to ask what it meant for such a higher-order function to be computable. Formal systems were devised to try to express the properties of higher-order computable functions precisely, and most of these were based on some form of applied λ or CL. The same question also interested some of the leaders in the then-young subject of computer science, including John McCarthy in the late 1950s, who was one of the first advocates for the functional style of programming. McCarthy designed a higher-order programming language LISP which used a form of λ-notation.

From then on, interest in λ and CL began to grow.

In 1969, the American logician Dana Scott, while designing a formal theory of higher-order computation, realized, to his own surprise, that he could build a model for pure untyped λ and CL using only standard set-theoretical concepts. Until then, untyped λ and CL had been seen as incompatible with generally-accepted set-theories such as the well-known system ZF. Scott's model changed this view, and many logicians and computer-scientists began to study his model, and other models which were invented soon after. (See Chapter 16 below, or [Bar84, Chapters 18–20].)

Scott's model also stimulated an increased interest in the syntax of pure λ and CL. The leader in syntactical studies in the 1970s was Henk Barendregt in the Netherlands, and he and his students and colleagues made many new discoveries, particularly about the relationships between different reductions from the same term, see Remarks 3.24 and 3.25.

Today, λ and CL have become important topics in logic and computer science. Functional programming languages, and formal systems of higher-order logic, all need a version of λ or CL or something equivalent, as part of their syntax.

Conversely, the main value of λ and CL comes from their service as parts of other systems, so recent studies have focussed mainly on applied versions of λ and CL.

CL and λ are rather like the chassis of a bus, which gives the bus essential support but is definitely not the whole bus. Just as the chassis gains its purpose from the purpose to which the whole bus is put, so λ and CL gain their main purpose as parts of other systems of higher-order logic and programming.

Discussion 3.27 (Interpreting pure λ and CL) Up to now, this book has presented λ and CL as uninterpreted formal systems.

However, these systems were originally developed to formalize primitive properties of functions or operators. In particular, I represents the identity operator, K an operator which forms constant-functions, and S a substitution-and-composition operator.

But just what kind of operators are these? Most mathematicians think of functions as being sets of ordered pairs in some 'classical' set theory, for example Zermelo–Fraenkel set theory (ZF). To such a mathematician, I, K and S simply do not exist. In ZF, each set $\mathcal{S}$ has an identity-function $\mathsf{I}_{\mathcal{S}}$ with domain $\mathcal{S}$, but there is no 'universal' identity which can be applied to everything. (Similarly for K and S.)

In many practical applications of CL or λ this question does not arise: as we shall see in Chapter 10 the rules for building the systems' terms may be limited by type-restrictions, and then instead of one 'universal' identity-term I there would be a different term I_τ for each type-expression τ. Type-expressions would denote sets, and I_τ would denote the identity-function on the set denoted by τ.

But type-free systems also have their uses, and for these systems the question must still be faced: what kind of functions do the terms represent?

One possible answer was explained very clearly by Church in the introduction to his book [Chu41]. In the 1920s when λ and CL began, logicians did not automatically think of functions as sets of ordered pairs, with domain and range given, as mathematicians are trained to do today. Throughout mathematical history, right through to computer science, there has run another concept of function, less precise at first but strongly influential always; that of a function as an operation-process (in some sense) which may be applied to certain objects to produce other objects. Such a process can be defined by giving a set of rules describing how it acts on an arbitrary input-object. (The rules need not produce an output for every input.) A simple example is the permutation-operation ϕ defined by

$$\phi(\langle x, y, z\rangle) \;=\; \langle y, z, x\rangle.$$

Nowadays one would think of a computer program, though the 'operation-process' concept was not originally intended to have the finiteness and effectiveness limitations that are involved with computation.

From now on, let us reserve the word *'operator'* to denote this imprecise function-as-operation-process concept, and *'function'* and *'map'* for the set-of-ordered-pairs concept.

Perhaps the most important difference between operators and functions is that an operator may be defined by describing its action without defining the set of inputs for which this action produces results, i. e. without defining its domain. In a sense, operators are 'partial functions'.

A second important difference is that some operators have no restriction on their domain; they accept any inputs, including themselves. The simplest example is **I**, which is defined by the operation of doing nothing at all. If this is accepted as a well-defined concept, then surely the operation of doing nothing can be applied to it. We simply get

$$\mathbf{II} \;=\; \mathbf{I}.$$

Other examples of self-applicable operators are **K** and **S**; in formal CL we have

$$\mathbf{KK}xyz \;=_w\; y, \qquad\qquad \mathbf{SS}xyz \;=_w\; yz\,(xyz),$$

which suggest natural meanings for **KK** and **SS**. Of course, it is not claimed that every operator is self-applicable; this would lead to contradictions. But the self-applicability of at least such simple operators as **I**, **K** and **S** seems very reasonable.

The operator concept lies behind programming languages such as ML, in which a single piece of code may be applied to many different types of inputs. Such languages are called *polymorphic.*

It can be formalized in set theory if we weaken the axiom of foundation which prevents functions from being applied to themselves; see (1) in Remark 16.68.

The operator concept can be modelled in standard ZF set theory if, roughly speaking, we interpret operators as infinite sequences of functions (satisfying certain conditions), instead of as single functions. This was discovered by Dana Scott in 1969; see Chapter 16.

However, it must be emphasized that no experience with the operator concept, or sympathy with it, will be needed in the rest of this book.

4
Representing the computable functions

4A Introduction

In this chapter, a sequence of pure terms will be chosen to represent the natural numbers. It is then reasonable to expect that some of the other terms will represent functions of natural numbers, in some sense. This sense will be defined precisely below. The functions so representable will turn out to be exactly those computable by Turing machines.

In the 1930s, three concepts of computability arose independently: 'Turing-computable function', 'recursive function' and 'λ-definable function'. The inventors of these three concepts soon discovered that all three gave the same set of functions. Most logicians took this as strong evidence that the informal notion of 'computable function' had been captured exactly by these three formally-defined concepts.

Here we shall look at the recursive functions, and prove that all these functions can be represented in λ and CL. (We shall not work with the Turing-computable functions because their representability-proof is longer.)

An outline definition of the recursive functions will be given here; more details and background can be found in many textbooks on computability or textbooks on logic which include computability, for example [Coh87], [Men97] or the old but thorough [Kle52].

Notation 4.1 This chapter is written in the same neutral notation as the last one, and its results will hold for both λ and CL unless explicitly stated otherwise.

Recall that a *combinator* in λ or CL is any closed pure term.

The phrase '*X has a normal form*' will mean (in λ) that X β-reduces to a β-normal form, and (in CL) that X weakly reduces to a weak normal form.

Natural numbers will be denoted by 'i', 'j', 'k', 'm', 'n', 'p', 'q', and the set of all natural numbers by '$\mathbb{N}$'. (We shall assume $0 \in \mathbb{N}$.)

An *n-argument function* will be a function from a subset of $\mathbb{N}^n$ into $\mathbb{N}$. It will be convenient to include the case $n = 0$; a *0-argument function* will be simply a natural number.

In computability theory it is standard to use the name '*partial function*' for any function ϕ from a subset of $\mathbb{N}^n$ into $\mathbb{N}$, and to call ϕ '*total*' iff $\phi(m_1, \ldots, m_n)$ exists for all $m_1, \ldots, m_n \in \mathbb{N}$, and '*properly partial*' otherwise.

For λ- or CL-terms X and Y, we shall use the abbreviations

$$\left.\begin{array}{lcl} X^n Y & \equiv & \underbrace{X(X(\ldots\ldots(XY)\ldots))}_{n\ \text{`}X\text{'s}} \quad \text{if } n \geq 1, \\ X^0 Y & \equiv & Y. \end{array}\right\} \tag{1}$$

(*Warning:* the expression 'X^n' by itself will have no meaning in this book; the notation '$X^n Y$' will never be split, and will *not* mean the application of a term X^n to a term Y.)

Definition 4.2 (The Church numerals) For every $n \in \mathbb{N}$, the *Church numeral* for n is a term we shall call $\overline{n}$ or sometimes $\overline{n}_{\mathrm{Ch}}$,[1] defined (in λ) by

(a) $$\overline{n} \equiv \lambda xy.x^n y,$$

and (in CL) by

(b) $$\overline{n} \equiv (\mathbf{SB})^n(\mathbf{KI}) \qquad (\mathbf{B} \equiv \mathbf{S}(\mathbf{KS})\mathbf{K}).$$

Note 4.3 In both λ and CL, the Church numerals have the useful property that, for all terms F, X,

$$\overline{n}FX \ \triangleright_{\beta,w} \ F^n X. \tag{2}$$

Note 4.4 In CL, why are the Church numerals not chosen to be $\overline{n} \equiv [x,y].x^n y$, the exact analogue of those in λ? Well, in fact $[x,y].x^n y \equiv (\mathbf{SB})^n(\mathbf{KI})$ for all $n \neq 1$, by Definition 2.4. But for $n = 1$ this fails; we get $[x,y].xy \equiv \mathbf{I} \not=_w \mathbf{SB}(\mathbf{KI})$. Thus, if we defined $\overline{n} \equiv [x,y].x^n y$ in CL,

[1] In some books $\overline{n}$ is called $\ulcorner n \urcorner$ or $\mathbf{n}$, in Curry's work it was called $\mathbf{Z}_n$.

SB would not represent the successor function so neatly. (See Example 4.6.)

The λ-version of the Church numerals comes from [Chu41, p. 28]. Other representations of the natural numbers have also been proposed in the literature; for examples, see [CHS72, Section 13A1] and [Bar84, Definition 6.2.9, §6.4]. Each has its own technical advantages and disadvantages.

Definition 4.5 (Representability) Let ϕ be an n-argument partial function, i.e. a function from a subset of $\mathbb{N}^n$ into $\mathbb{N}$ ($n \geq 0$). A term X in λ or CL is said to *represent* ϕ iff, for all $m_1, \ldots, m_n \in \mathbb{N}$,

(a) $\phi(m_1, \ldots, m_n) = p \implies X\,\overline{m_1} \ldots \overline{m_n} =_{\beta,w} \overline{p}$,

and

(b) $\phi(m_1, \ldots, m_n)$ does not exist $\implies X\,\overline{m_1} \ldots \overline{m_n}$ has no nf.

Example 4.6 The *successor function* σ is defined by $\sigma(n) = n + 1$ for all $n \in \mathbb{N}$. It can be represented in λ by a term which we shall call $\overline{\sigma}$:

$$\overline{\sigma} \equiv \lambda uxy.x(uxy).$$

In fact it is easy to check that, for all $n \in \mathbb{N}$,

$$\overline{\sigma}\,\overline{n} \;\triangleright_\beta\; \overline{n+1}.$$

In CL, define $\overline{\sigma} \equiv [u, x, y].x(uxy)$. Then $\overline{\sigma} \equiv \mathbf{SB}$, so $\overline{\sigma}$ represents σ, because

$$\overline{\sigma}\,\overline{n} \equiv \overline{n+1}.$$

Remark 4.7 The main theorem of this chapter will be that every partial recursive function can be represented in both λ and CL.

The converse is also true, that every function representable in λ or CL is partial recursive. But its proof is too boring to include in this book. It comes from the fact that the definitions of $=_\beta$ and $=_w$ can be re-written as recursively axiomatized formal theories (see Chapter 6), and such theories can be coded into number-theory in such a way that their syntax can be described using recursive functions. This was first done for λ in [Kle36].

So, for both λ and CL, the representable partial functions are exactly the partial recursive functions.

After proving the main representability theorem, we shall extend it to say that every representable function can be represented by a normal form. This will turn out to be easy in CL, but not in λ.

The first step towards proving the representability of all partial recursive functions will be to prove the representability of the more restricted set of functions in the next definition.

4B Primitive recursive functions

Definition 4.8 (Primitive recursive functions) The set of all primitive recursive functions of natural numbers is defined by induction as follows, compare [Coh87, Section 3.1], [Kle52, Section 44, Remark 1, Basis B], [Men97, Chapter 3, Section 3], [Rau06, Section 6.1].

(I) The *successor function* σ is primitive recursive.

(II) The *number* 0 is a 0-argument primitive recursive function.

(III) For each $n \geq 1$ and $k \leq n$, the following *projection function* Π_k^n is primitive recursive:

$$\Pi_k^n(m_1, \ldots, m_n) \;=\; m_k \qquad \text{(for all } m_1, \ldots, m_n \in \mathbb{N}\text{)}.$$

(IV) If $n, p \geq 1$, and ψ, $\chi_1, \ldots, \chi_p$ are primitive recursive, then so is the function ϕ defined by *composition* as follows:

$$\phi(m_1, \ldots, m_n) \;=\; \psi(\chi_1(m_1, \ldots, m_n), \ldots, \chi_p(m_1, \ldots, m_n)).$$

(V) If $n \geq 0$ and ψ and χ are primitive recursive, then so is the function ϕ defined by *recursion* as follows:

$$\begin{aligned} \phi(0, m_1, \ldots, m_n) \;&=\; \psi(m_1, \ldots, m_n), \\ \phi(k+1, m_1, \ldots, m_n) \;&=\; \chi(k, \phi(k, m_1, \ldots, m_n), m_1, \ldots, m_n). \end{aligned}$$

(By checking the clauses of the above definition it can be seen that all primitive recursive functions are total.)

Example 4.9 The *predecessor function* π is defined thus:

$$\pi(0) = 0, \qquad \pi(k+1) = k. \tag{3}$$

It is primitive recursive. To prove this in detail, we first make its definition fit the pattern of (V) exactly, thus:

$$\pi(0) = 0, \qquad \pi(k+1) = \Pi_1^2(k, \pi(k)), \tag{4}$$

where $\Pi_1^2(m_1, m_2) = m_1$ for all $m_1, m_2 \in \mathbb{N}$. By (III), Π_1^2 is primitive recursive. By (II), 0 is primitive recursive. Hence π is primitive recursive, by (V) with

$$n = 0, \qquad \psi = 0, \qquad \chi = \Pi_1^2.$$

Exercise 4.10 * The *cut-off subtraction function* $\dot{-}$ is often used instead of subtraction in work with natural numbers, because subtraction is not a total function. (In the world of natural numbers, $2-5$ does not exist, for example.) Its definition is

$$\begin{aligned} m \dot{-} n &= m - n \quad \text{if } m \geq n, \\ m \dot{-} n &= 0 \qquad\quad \text{otherwise.} \end{aligned}$$

Prove, using Definition 4.8(I)–(V), that $\dot{-}$ is primitive recursive. (Hint: use the predecessor function.)

Theorem 4.11 (Representation of primitive recursion) *In λ with $=_\beta$ or CL with $=_w$: every primitive recursive function ϕ can be represented by a combinator $\overline{\phi}$.*

Proof The term $\overline{\phi}$ is chosen by induction, corresponding to the clauses in Definition 4.8.

(I) Choose $\overline{\sigma} \equiv \lambda uxy.x(uxy)$, as in Example 4.6.

(II) Choose $\overline{0} \equiv \lambda xy.y$, the Church numeral for 0.

(III) Choose $\overline{\Pi_k^n} \equiv \lambda x_1 \dots x_n . x_k$.

(IV) Given $\overline{\psi}, \overline{\chi_1}, \dots, \overline{\chi_p}$ representing $\psi, \chi_1, \dots, \chi_p$ respectively, choose

$$\overline{\phi} \equiv \lambda x_1 \dots x_n . \big(\overline{\psi} (\overline{\chi_1} x_1 \dots x_n) \dots (\overline{\chi_p} x_1 \dots x_n) \big).$$

(V) Given $\overline{\psi}$ and $\overline{\chi}$ representing ψ and χ respectively, choose

$$\overline{\phi} \equiv \lambda u x_1 \dots x_n . \big(\mathbf{R} (\overline{\psi} x_1 \dots x_n)(\lambda uv.\overline{\chi} uvx_1 \dots x_n) u \big), \qquad (5)$$

where $\mathbf{R}$ is a term to be constructed below, called a *recursion combinator.* This $\mathbf{R}$ will have the property that, for all X, Y, k,

$$\left.\begin{aligned} \mathbf{R}XY\overline{0} &=_{\beta,w} X, \\ \mathbf{R}XY(\overline{k+1}) &=_{\beta,w} Y\overline{k}(\mathbf{R}XY\overline{k}). \end{aligned}\right\} \qquad (6)$$

If an $\mathbf{R}$ exists satisfying (6), then the term $\overline{\phi}$ in (5) will represent the function ϕ in Case (V) of Definition 4.8; because

$$\begin{aligned} \overline{\phi}\,\overline{0}\,x_1 \dots x_n &=_{\beta,w} \mathbf{R} (\overline{\psi} x_1 \dots x_n)(\lambda uv.\overline{\chi} uvx_1 \dots x_n)\overline{0} \\ &=_{\beta,w} \overline{\psi} x_1 \dots x_n \qquad \text{by (6),} \end{aligned}$$

and

$$
\begin{aligned}
&\overline{\phi}\,(\overline{k+1})x_1 \dots x_n \\
&\quad =_{\beta,w}\ \mathbf{R}\,(\overline{\psi}x_1 \dots x_n)(\lambda uv.\overline{\chi}uvx_1 \dots x_n)\,(\overline{k+1}) \\
&\quad =_{\beta,w}\ (\lambda uv.\overline{\chi}uvx_1 \dots x_n)\,\overline{k}\,(\mathbf{R}\,(\overline{\psi}x_1 \dots x_n)(\lambda uv.\overline{\chi}uvx_1 \dots x_n)\,\overline{k}\,) \quad \text{by (6)} \\
&\quad =_{\beta,w}\ (\lambda uv.\overline{\chi}uvx_1 \dots x_n)\,\overline{k}\,(\overline{\phi}\,\overline{k}\,x_1 \dots x_n) \quad \text{by definition of } \overline{\phi} \\
&\quad =_{\beta,w}\ \overline{\chi}\,\overline{k}\,(\overline{\phi}\,\overline{k}\,x_1 \dots x_n)\,x_1 \dots x_n\,.
\end{aligned}
$$

We shall now construct an **R** to satisfy (6). There are many ways of doing this, see [CHS72, Section 13A3]; the one chosen here is from [Chu41, p. 39] and is due to Paul Bernays. It is one of the easiest to motivate, and gives an **R** which is shorter than most others, has a normal form, and is also typable in the sense of Chapters 11 and 12.

To motivate Bernays' **R**, consider for example a primitive recursive function ϕ defined by

$$\phi(0) \;=\; m, \qquad \phi(k+1) \;=\; \chi(k, \phi(k)). \tag{7}$$

One way of calculating $\phi(k)$ is to first write down the ordered pair $\langle 0, m\rangle$ and then iterate k times the function *Next* such that

$$\mathit{Next}(\langle n, x\rangle) \;=\; \langle\, n+1,\ \chi(n, x)\,\rangle, \tag{8}$$

and finally take the second member of the last pair produced. **R** will imitate this calculation-procedure.

The first step in constructing Bernays' **R** is to define a *pairing* combinator (compare Exercise 2.34):

$$\mathbf{D} \;\equiv\; \lambda xyz.z(\mathbf{K}y)x. \tag{9}$$

It is easy to check that, for all terms X and Y,

$$\left.\begin{aligned} \mathbf{D}XY\overline{0} \quad &\triangleright_{\beta,w}\ X, \\ \mathbf{D}XY\overline{k+1} \quad &\triangleright_{\beta,w}\ Y. \end{aligned}\right\} \tag{10}$$

We can think of $\mathbf{D}\overline{p}\,\overline{q}$ as an analogue of an ordered pair $\langle p, q\rangle$, since (10) gives a method of picking out the first or second member.

Using **D**, we now make a λ-analogue of the function *Next* in (8). Define

$$Q \;\equiv\; \lambda yv.\, \mathbf{D}(\overline{\sigma}\,(v\overline{0}\,))\,(y\,(v\overline{0}\,)(v\overline{1}\,)), \tag{11}$$

where $\overline{\sigma}$ was defined in Example 4.6. Then, for all X, Y, n,

$$\left.\begin{aligned} QY(\mathbf{D}\overline{n}X) \quad &\triangleright_{\beta,w}\ \mathbf{D}\,(\overline{\sigma}\,(\mathbf{D}\overline{n}X\overline{0}\,))\,(Y(\mathbf{D}\overline{n}X\overline{0}\,)\,(\mathbf{D}\overline{n}X\overline{1}\,)) \\ &\triangleright_{\beta,w}\ \mathbf{D}\,(\overline{\sigma}\,\overline{n})\,(Y\overline{n}X) \qquad \text{by (10)} \\ &\triangleright_{\beta,w}\ \mathbf{D}(\overline{n+1})(Y\overline{n}X) \qquad \text{by 4.6.} \end{aligned}\right\} \tag{12}$$

Thus QY would imitate the function *Next*, if Y represented the function χ in (7) and (8). Also, by using (12) repeatedly, we get, for all X, Y and all $k \geq 0$,

$$(QY)^k(\mathbf{D}\overline{0}X) \rhd_{\beta,w} \mathbf{D}\overline{k}X_k \tag{13}$$

for some term X_k, whose details will not matter.

Now define

$$\mathbf{R}_{\text{Bernays}} \equiv \lambda xyu.\, u(Qy)(\mathbf{D}\overline{0}x)\overline{1}. \tag{14}$$

Then, if $\mathbf{R}$ is $\mathbf{R}_{\text{Bernays}}$, we have, for all X, Y:

$$\left.\begin{array}{llll} \mathbf{R}XY\overline{k} & \rhd_{\beta,w} & \overline{k}\,(QY)(\mathbf{D}\overline{0}X)\overline{1} & \\ & \rhd_{\beta,w} & (QY)^k(\mathbf{D}\overline{0}X)\overline{1} & \text{by (2)} \\ & \rhd_{\beta,w} & \mathbf{D}\,\overline{k}\,X_k\,\overline{1} & \text{by (13)} \\ & \rhd_{\beta,w} & X_k & \text{by (10).} \end{array}\right\} \tag{15}$$

From this, the two parts of (6) follow, thus:

$$\begin{array}{llll} \mathbf{R}XY\overline{0} & \rhd_{\beta,w} & (QY)^0(\mathbf{D}\overline{0}X)\overline{1} & \text{by (14) and (2)} \\ & \rhd_{\beta,w} & \mathbf{D}\,\overline{0}\,X\,\overline{1} & \text{by (1), def. of ( )}^0\text{( )} \\ & \rhd_{\beta,w} & X & \text{by (10);} \end{array}$$

$$\begin{array}{llll} \mathbf{R}XY\overline{k+1} & \rhd_{\beta,w} & (QY)^{k+1}(\mathbf{D}\overline{0}X)\,\overline{1} & \text{by (14) and (2)} \\ & \rhd_{\beta,w} & (QY)\left((QY)^k(\mathbf{D}\overline{0}X)\right)\overline{1} & \text{by (1)} \\ & \rhd_{\beta,w} & QY(\mathbf{D}\overline{k}X_k)\overline{1} & \text{by (13)} \\ & \rhd_{\beta,w} & \mathbf{D}(\overline{k+1})(Y\overline{k}X_k)\overline{1} & \text{by (12)} \\ & \rhd_{\beta,w} & Y\overline{k}X_k & \text{by (10)} \\ & =_{\beta,w} & Y\,\overline{k}\,(\mathbf{R}XY\overline{k}) & \text{by (15).} \end{array}$$

□

Note 4.12 All the reductions in the preceding proof hold for $\rhd_w$ in CL as well as for $\rhd_\beta$ in λ. This is rather tedious to check in detail, but after Chapter 6 it will become clear that only one fact need be checked: never is a redex-occurrence contracted when it is in the scope of a λ. In fact, with one exception, all contractions in the proof of Theorem 4.11 have form

$$P_1 \ldots P_r\left((\lambda x.M)NQ_1 \ldots Q_s\right) \;\rhd\; P_1 \ldots P_r\left(([N/x]M)Q_1 \ldots Q_s\right)$$

$(r, s \geq 0)$, and such contractions translate into CL as correct weak reductions. The same will hold for other combined proofs for λ and CL later.

The one exception is $\overline{\sigma}\,\overline{n} \triangleright_\beta \overline{n+1}$; but that reduction translates into CL as an identity, as mentioned in Example 4.6.

Example 4.13 The *predecessor function* π is defined thus: $\pi(0) = 0$, $\pi(k+1) = k$. It is primitive recursive, as we saw in Example 4.9. We can build a term $\overline{\pi}$ to represent π by applying the proof of Theorem 4.11 to the equations

$$\pi(0) = 0, \qquad \pi(k+1) = k.$$

The result is

$$\overline{\pi}_{\text{Bernays}} \equiv \mathbf{R}_{\text{Bernays}}\overline{0}\,\mathbf{K}.$$

It is easy to check that this term represents π; it is enough to prove, using (6), that, if $\overline{\pi}$ is $\overline{\pi}_{\text{Bernays}}$, then

$$\overline{\pi}\,\overline{0} =_{\beta,w} \overline{0}, \qquad \overline{\pi}\,(\overline{\sigma}\,\overline{k}) =_{\beta,w} \overline{k}. \tag{16}$$

By the way, $\overline{\pi}_{\text{Bernays}}$ is not the shortest known representative of π; in fact it becomes rather long when $\mathbf{R}_{\text{Bernays}}$ is written out fully. The following term, due independently to Martin Bunder and F. Urbanek, is shorter and can easily be checked to represent π in both λ and CL:

$$\overline{\pi}_{\text{Bund-Urb}} \equiv \lambda x.\,\big(x\,(\lambda uv.v(u\overline{\sigma}))(\mathbf{K}\overline{0})\,\mathbf{I}\big).$$

Note 4.14 For the *pairing combinator* $\mathbf{D} \equiv \lambda xyz.z(\mathbf{K}y)x$ defined in (9), we can define two *projection combinators* $\mathbf{D}_1$, $\mathbf{D}_2$, thus:

$$\mathbf{D}_1 \equiv \lambda x.x\overline{0}, \qquad \mathbf{D}_2 \equiv \lambda x.x\overline{1}.$$

Then, by (10),

$$\mathbf{D}_1(\mathbf{D}X_1X_2) \triangleright_{\beta,w} X_1, \qquad \mathbf{D}_2(\mathbf{D}X_1X_2) \triangleright_{\beta,w} X_2.$$

Sometimes $\mathbf{D}$ is called a *conditional* operator, and $\mathbf{D}XY\overline{n}$ is called

$$\textit{If } n = 0 \textit{ then } X, \textit{ else } Y.$$

Note 4.15 (Recursion using fixed points) An alternative to Bernays' $\mathbf{R}$ can be made using any fixed-point combinator $\mathbf{Y}$. Let $\overline{\pi}$ be any representative of π, and consider the equation

$$\mathbf{R}xyz = \big(\textit{If } z = 0 \textit{ then } x, \textit{ else } y(\overline{\pi}z)(\mathbf{R}xy(\overline{\pi}z))\big),$$

or equivalently, the equation

$$\mathbf{R}xyz = \mathbf{D}\,x\,(y(\overline{\pi}z)(\mathbf{R}xy(\overline{\pi}z)))\,z.$$

By Corollary 3.3.1, this has a solution, which we shall call '$\mathbf{R}_{\mathrm{Fix}}$':

$$\mathbf{R}_{\mathrm{Fix}} \equiv \mathbf{Y}\,\big(\lambda uxyz.\,\mathbf{D}\,x\,(y(\overline{\pi}z)(uxy(\overline{\pi}z)))\,z\big).$$

This definition has an attractive simplicity of structure; and if a simple enough $\overline{\pi}$ could be found, $\mathbf{R}_{\mathrm{Fix}}$ would be shorter than $\mathbf{R}_{\mathrm{Bernays}}$.[2] However, $\mathbf{R}_{\mathrm{Fix}}$ has no normal form in λ-calculus, and this is sometimes a disadvantage.

Exercise 4.16 *

(a) Let $\phi(m) = 3m + 2$ for all $m \geq 0$; this ϕ is primitive recursive, and we have $\phi(0) = 2$ and $\phi(k+1) = 3 + \phi(k)$; use $\mathbf{R}$ in the proof of Theorem 4.11 to build a combinator that represents ϕ.

(b) Do the same for the functions *Add*, *Mult* and *Exp*, where

$$\begin{aligned} Add(m,n) &= m + n, \\ Mult(m,n) &= m \times n, \\ Exp(m,n) &= m^n. \end{aligned}$$

(c) Do the same for the cut-off subtraction function $\dot{-}$ defined in Exercise 4.10.

(d) (Harder) Although the proof of Theorem 4.11 gives a systematic way of representing every primitive recursive function, it does not claim to give the shortest possible representative. For the three functions in (b), find representatives without using $\mathbf{R}$ that are much shorter than those built with $\mathbf{R}$.

Extra practice 4.17 The following functions are primitive recursive; use $\mathbf{R}$ in the proof of Theorem 4.11 to build combinators that represent them:

(a) the function ϕ defined by $\phi(m) = m^2 + 2m + 3$,

(b) the factorial function $Fac(m) = m!$, where $0! = 1$ and

$$(k+1)! \;=\; (k+1) \times k \times \ldots \times 2 \times 1.$$

[2] In [Bar84] the numerals were chosen specially to make $\overline{\pi}$ simple, see [Bar84, Lemma 6.2.10]; but most other writers prefer the Church numerals.

4C Recursive functions

Definition 4.18 (Recursive total functions) A total function ϕ from $\mathbb{N}^n$ into $\mathbb{N}$ ($n \geq 0$) is called *recursive* iff there exist primitive recursive functions ψ and χ such that, for all $m_1, \ldots, m_n \in \mathbb{N}$,

$$\phi(m_1, \ldots, m_n) \;=\; \psi(\,\mu k[\,\chi(m_1, \ldots, m_n, k) = 0]\,),$$

where

(i) there exists a k such that $\chi(m_1, \ldots, m_n, k) = 0$,
(ii) $\mu k[\chi(m_1, \ldots, m_n, k) = 0]$ is the least such k.[3]

Note 4.19 Condition (i) ensures that $\phi(m_1, \ldots, m_n)$ exists for all m_1, …, $m_n \in \mathbb{N}$.

The above definition of 'recursive' has been chosen to make the next theorem's proof as easy as possible. The standard definition can be found in books on recursion theory, for example [Men97, Chapter 3 Section 3, Chapter 5 Section 3], and the above one is equivalent to it by Kleene's Normal Form theorem, [Kle52, Section 58] or [Men97, Corollary 5.11].

Theorem 4.20 (Representation of total recursion) *In λ with $=_\beta$ or CL with $=_w$: every recursive total function ϕ can be represented by a combinator $\overline{\phi}$.*

Proof Let ψ, χ be primitive recursive, and, for all $m_1, \ldots, m_n \in \mathbb{N}$, let

$$\phi(m_1, \ldots, m_n) = \psi(\,\mu k[\,\chi(m_1, \ldots, m_n, k) = 0]\,).$$

By Theorem 4.11, ψ and χ are representable by terms $\overline{\psi}$ and $\overline{\chi}$.

One way of computing $\mu k[\chi(m_1, \ldots, m_n, k) = 0]$ is to try to program a function θ such that $\theta(k)$ outputs k if $\chi(m_1, \ldots, m_n, k) = 0$, and moves on to $\theta(k+1)$ otherwise; when this program is started with $k = 0$, it will output the first k such that $\chi(m_1, \ldots, m_n, k) = 0$. The λ-analogue or CL-analogue of such a program would be a term H satisfying the following equation:

$$Hx_1...x_n y = (\textit{If } \overline{\chi}x_1...x_n y = 0 \textit{ then } y, \textit{ else } Hx_1...x_n(\overline{\sigma}y)\,). \qquad (17)$$

Given such an H, the following term could represent ϕ:

$$\overline{\phi} \equiv \lambda x_1 \ldots x_n \,.\, \overline{\psi}(Hx_1 \ldots x_n \overline{0}\,). \qquad (18)$$

[3] Recursive functions may also be called *total recursive* or *general recursive*.

A suitable H can be found by applying Corollary 3.3.1 to solve Equation (17), using any fixed-point combinator $\mathbf{Y}$, thus:

$$H \equiv \mathbf{Y}\big(\lambda u x_1 \dots x_n y.\, \mathbf{D}\, y\, (u x_1 \dots x_n (\overline{\sigma} y))(\overline{\chi}\, x_1 \dots x_n y)\,\big). \qquad (19)$$

However, the λ-version of the above H has no normal form. The following H is more complicated, but will be used in a later proof on representability by normal forms. First define

$$\left.\begin{array}{lcl} T & \equiv & \lambda x.\, \mathbf{D}\,\overline{0}\,(\lambda uv.\, u\,(x(\overline{\sigma} v))u(\overline{\sigma} v)\,), \\ P & \equiv & \lambda xy.\, Tx(xy)(Tx)y. \end{array}\right\} \qquad (20)$$

Then, for all terms X and Y, we have

$$\left.\begin{array}{lll} PXY =_{\beta,w} & Y & \text{if } XY =_{\beta,w} \overline{0}, \\ PXY =_{\beta,w} & PX(\overline{\sigma} Y) & \text{if } XY =_{\beta,w} \overline{m+1} \text{ for some } m. \end{array}\right\} \qquad (21)$$

To prove (21), note first that

$$\begin{array}{rl} PXY & =_{\beta,w} TX(XY)(TX)Y \\ & =_{\beta,w} \mathbf{D}\,\overline{0}\,(\lambda uv.\, u(X(\overline{\sigma} v))u(\overline{\sigma} v))\,(XY)\,(TX)\,Y \end{array}$$

where $u, v \notin \mathrm{FV}(XY)$. If $XY =_{\beta,w} \overline{0}$, then, by (10),

$$\begin{array}{rll} PXY & =_{\beta,w} \overline{0}\,(TX)Y & \\ & =_{\beta,w} Y & \text{because } \overline{0} \equiv \lambda xy.y. \end{array}$$

If $XY =_{\beta,w} \overline{m+1}$, then, by (10),

$$\begin{array}{rl} PXY & =_{\beta,w} (\lambda uv.\, u(X(\overline{\sigma} v))u(\overline{\sigma} v))\,(TX)\,Y \\ & =_{\beta,w} TX(X(\overline{\sigma} Y))(TX)(\overline{\sigma} Y) \\ & =_{\beta,w} PX(\overline{\sigma} Y). \end{array}$$

This proves (21). Now define

$$H \equiv \lambda x_1 \dots x_n y.\, P(\overline{\chi} x_1 \dots x_n)y. \qquad (22)$$

Then, for all $X_1, \dots, X_n, Y$, we have by (21),

$$\begin{array}{rl} HX_1 \dots X_n Y & =_{\beta,w} P(\overline{\chi} X_1 \dots X_n)Y \\ & =_{\beta,w} \left\{\begin{array}{ll} Y & \text{if } \overline{\chi} X_1 \dots X_n Y =_{\beta,w} \overline{0}, \\ HX_1 \dots X_n(\overline{\sigma} Y) & \text{if } \overline{\chi} X_1 \dots X_n Y =_{\beta,w} \overline{m+1}. \end{array}\right. \end{array}$$

Finally, using H, define $\overline{\phi}$ by (18). Thus all recursive total functions can be represented in λ and CL. □

Definition 4.21 (Partial recursive functions) A function ϕ from a subset of $\mathbb{N}^n$ into $\mathbb{N}$ ($n \geq 0$) is called *partial recursive*[4] iff there exist primitive recursive ψ and χ such that, for all $m_1, \ldots, m_n \in \mathbb{N}$,

$$\phi(m_1, \ldots, m_n) = \psi(\, \mu k[\, \chi(m_1, \ldots, m_n, k) = 0]\,),$$

where $\mu k[\chi(m_1, \ldots, m_n, k) = 0]$ is the least k such that $\chi(m_1, \ldots, m_n, k) = 0$, if such a k exists, and is undefined if no such k exists.

Example 4.22 The *subtraction* function is partial recursive. Because

$$m_1 - m_2 = \mu k[((m_2 + k) \dot{-} m_1) = 0],$$

where $\dot{-}$ is the cut-off subtraction introduced in Example 4.10. Note that when $m_1 < m_2$, we have $(m_2 + k) \dot{-} m_1 > 0$ for all $k \geq 0$, so $\mu k[((m_2 + k) \dot{-} m_1) = 0]$ does not exist. This agrees with $m_1 - m_2$ not existing when $m_1 < m_2$.

Theorem 4.23 (Representation of partial recursion) *In λ with $=_\beta$ or CL with $=_w$: every partial recursive function ϕ can be represented by a combinator $\overline{\phi}$.*

Proof Let ψ, χ be primitive recursive, and, for all $m_1, \ldots, m_n \in \mathbb{N}$, let

$$\phi(m_1, \ldots, m_n) = \psi(\, \mu k[\, \chi(m_1, \ldots, m_n, k) = 0]\,).$$

We shall modify the proof of Theorem 4.20, to construct a $\overline{\phi}$ such that $\overline{\phi}\,\overline{m_1} \ldots \overline{m_n}$ has no normal form when there is no k such that $\chi(m_1, \ldots, m_n, k) = 0$. We shall use a device due to Bruce Lercher, [Ler63].

First take the $\overline{\phi}$ from the proof of Theorem 4.20 and call it 'F':

$$F \equiv \lambda x_1 \ldots x_n \,.\, \overline{\psi}\,(Hx_1 \ldots x_n \overline{0}\,),$$

where H is defined by (19) or (22). For all $m_1, \ldots, m_n \in \mathbb{N}$, we have

$$F\,\overline{m_1} \ldots \overline{m_n} =_{\beta,w} \overline{\phi(m_1, \ldots, m_n)}. \tag{23}$$

Next, take the term P from (20) and define

$$\overline{\phi} \equiv \lambda x_1 \ldots x_n \,.\, P(\overline{\chi} x_1 \ldots x_n)\overline{0}\,\mathsf{I}\,(Fx_1 \ldots x_n). \tag{24}$$

To justify this choice of $\overline{\phi}$, suppose first that $m_1, \ldots, m_n$ are such that $\chi(m_1, \ldots, m_n, k) = 0$ for some k, and let j be the least such k. Then

[4] '*Recursive partial*' would be more systematic but 'partial recursive' is standard.

$$
\begin{aligned}
\overline{\phi}\,\overline{m_1}\ldots\overline{m_n} &=_{\beta,w} \overline{j}\,\mathbf{I}\,(F\,\overline{m_1}\ldots\overline{m_n}) && \text{by the proof of 4.20}\\
&=_{\beta,w} \mathbf{I}^j\,(F\,\overline{m_1}\ldots\overline{m_n}) && \text{by (2)}\\
&=_{\beta,w} F\,\overline{m_1}\ldots\overline{m_n} && \text{by the definition of } \mathbf{I}\\
&=_{\beta,w} \overline{\phi(m_1,\ldots,m_n)} && \text{by (23).}
\end{aligned}
$$

On the other hand, suppose $m_1, \ldots, m_n$ are such that there is no k such that $\chi(m_1, \ldots, m_n, k) = 0$. We must prove that $\overline{\phi}\,\overline{m_1}\ldots\overline{m_n}$ has no normal form.

First, since χ is total (being primitive recursive), for every k there is a $p_k \geq 0$ such that

$$\chi(m_1, \ldots, m_n, k) = p_k + 1.$$

Let $X \equiv \overline{\chi}\,\overline{m_1}\ldots\overline{m_n}$. Then $X\,\overline{k} =_{\beta,w} \overline{p_k + 1}$. Furthermore,

$$X\,\overline{k} \;\triangleright_{\beta,w}\; \overline{p_k + 1}, \tag{25}$$

by the Church–Rosser theorem, because the Church numerals are in normal form in both λ and CL.

To prove that $\overline{\phi}\,\overline{m_1}\ldots\overline{m_n}$ has no nf, it is enough to find an infinite quasi-leftmost reduction of this term, by Corollary 3.22.1 (which holds for both $\triangleright_\beta$ and $\triangleright_w$). Consider the following reduction (not every contraction is shown, and $F\,\overline{m_1}\ldots\overline{m_n}$ is written as 'G' for short):

$$
\begin{aligned}
\overline{\phi}\,\overline{m_1}\ldots\overline{m_n} &\triangleright_{\beta,w} PX\overline{0}\,\mathbf{I}G && \text{by (24)}\\
&\triangleright_{\beta,w} TX(X\overline{0})(TX)\overline{0}\,\mathbf{I}G && \text{by (20)}\\
&\triangleright_{\beta,w} TX(\overline{p_0+1})(TX)\overline{0}\,\mathbf{I}G && \text{by (25) } (k=0)\\
&\triangleright_{\beta,w} (\lambda uv.u(X(\overline{\sigma}v))u(\overline{\sigma}v))(TX)\overline{0}\,\mathbf{I}G && \text{by defs. of } T, \mathbf{D}\\
&\triangleright_{\beta,w} TX(X(\overline{\sigma}\,\overline{0}))(TX)(\overline{\sigma}\,\overline{0})\,\mathbf{I}G && \\
&\triangleright_{\beta,w} TX(X\overline{1})(TX)\overline{1}\,\mathbf{I}G && \text{by def. of } \overline{\sigma}\\
&\triangleright_{\beta,w} \;\ldots && \\
&\triangleright_{\beta,w} TX(X\overline{2})(TX)\overline{2}\,\mathbf{I}G && \text{similarly}\\
&\triangleright_{\beta,w} \;\ldots \text{ etc.} &&
\end{aligned}
$$

Clearly this reduction is infinite, and there is at least one leftmost maximal contraction in each part with form

$$TX(X\overline{i})(TX)\overline{i}\,\mathbf{I}G \;\triangleright_{\beta,w}\; TX(X\,(\overline{i+1}))(TX)\,(\overline{i+1})\,\mathbf{I}G.$$

□

The preceding theorem can be strengthened as follows.

Theorem 4.24 (Representation by normal forms) *In λ with $=_\beta$ or CL with $=_w$: every partial recursive function ϕ can be represented by a combinator $\overline{\phi}$ in normal form.*[5]

Proof In CL, the job is easy. Take the $\overline{\phi}$ from (24) in the proof of Theorem 4.23, and apply to it the procedure in the answer to Exercise 3.12(c). (Note that the notation '$\lambda x_1 \dots x_n$' in (24) means '$[x_1 \dots x_n]$' in CL.) The result is a weak normal form which represents ϕ.

In λ, the normal forms are a more restricted class, and the job of finding one to represent ϕ is less trivial. The following is based on a proof by Lercher, [Ler63]; details are omitted here.

Step 1: Prove the following general lemma about β-normal forms, for all variables y, z, by induction on $lgh(M)$ using Lemma 1.33:

$$M, N \text{ in nf} \quad \Longrightarrow \quad [(zN)/y]M \text{ in nf and } Mz \text{ has nf.} \tag{26}$$

Step 2: To prove the theorem for primitive recursive functions ϕ, consider the five cases in the proof of Theorem 4.11. In Cases (I)–(III), the terms $\overline{\phi}$ shown in the proof of 4.11 are clearly nfs.

In Case (IV), $\overline{\phi}$ was

$$\lambda x_1 \dots x_n . \big(\overline{\psi}\,(\overline{\chi_1}\, x_1 \dots x_n) \dots (\overline{\chi_p}\, x_1 \dots x_n)\big).$$

Assume that $\overline{\psi}, \overline{\chi_1}, \dots, \overline{\chi_p}$ are nfs. By (26), we can reduce $(\overline{\chi_1}\, x_1 \dots x_n)$, $\dots$, $(\overline{\chi_p}\, x_1 \dots x_n)$ to nfs, call them $N_1, \dots N_p$. Choose

$$\overline{\phi} \equiv \lambda x_1 \dots x_n \,.\, (x_1\, \mathbf{I}\, \overline{\psi}\, N_1 \dots N_p). \tag{27}$$

(Note that $n \geq 1$ in Case (IV) of Definition 4.8.) This is a nf. And it represents ϕ, because, for all $m_1 \geq 0$, we have

$$\overline{m_1}\, \mathbf{I}\, \overline{\psi} \quad \triangleright_\beta \quad \mathbf{I}^{m_1}\, \overline{\psi} \quad \triangleright_\beta \quad \overline{\psi}.$$

In Case (V), the $\overline{\phi}$ in (5) in the proof of 4.11 contains the terms $\mathbf{D}$, Q and $\mathbf{R}_{\text{Bernays}}$ defined in (9), (11) and (14). All these, including $\overline{\phi}$, can be proved to have nfs, using (26).

Step 3: For recursive total functions, look at the proof of 4.20. The terms T and P in (20) can be shown to have nfs, using (26). Instead of the H in (22), the following term has the same effect and has a nf:

$$H \;\equiv\; \lambda x_1 \dots x_n y \,.\, x_1\, \mathbf{I}\, P\, (\overline{\chi} x_1 \dots x_n)\, y.$$

[5] In [HS86] the proof of representation by nfs was incomplete. The authors are grateful to John Shepherdson for pointing this out.

Instead of the $\overline{\phi}$ in (18), use the normal form of the following:

$$\lambda x_1 \ldots x_n \, . \, x_1 \, \mathsf{I} \, \overline{\psi}\,(Hx_1 \ldots x_n \overline{0}\,). \tag{28}$$

Step 4: For partial recursive functions, modify the proof of 4.23 by changing the $\overline{\phi}$ in (24) to the normal form of

$$\lambda x_1 \ldots x_n \, . \, x_1 \, \mathsf{I} \, P(\overline{\chi} x_1 \ldots x_n)\overline{0}\, \mathsf{I}\,(Fx_1 \ldots x_n), \tag{29}$$

where F is the $\overline{\phi}$ obtained in Step 3. □

4D Abstract numerals and Z

Discussion 4.25 Instead of using pure terms to represent the numbers in λ or CL, it is possible to add two new atomic constants $\widehat{0}$ and $\widehat{\sigma}$ to the definition of 'term', and to represent each number n by

$$\widehat{n} \;\equiv\; \widehat{\sigma}^{\,n}\,\widehat{0}. \tag{30}$$

These are called the *abstract numerals.*

For these numerals, there is no way of constructing an **R** with the property (6), nor even of representing the predecessor function (see Exercise 4.27 below).

However, suppose we add a third new atom **Z**, and add to the definition of $\triangleright_\beta$ or $\triangleright_w$ the following new contractions (one for each $n \geq 0$):

$$\mathbf{Z}\widehat{n} \;\; \triangleright_1 \;\; \overline{n}_{\mathrm{Ch}}, \tag{31}$$

where $\overline{n}_{\mathrm{Ch}}$ is the Church numeral for n. (**Z** is called an *iteration operator.*) Let $\triangleright_{\beta,w\,\mathbf{Z}}$ be the resulting new reducibility relation. For both λ and CL, this relation is confluent (Appendix A2, Theorem A2.15). It can also be shown to satisfy a standardization theorem (using a modified definition of 'standard reduction'), and a theorem rather like the quasi-leftmost reduction theorem [Hin78, Theorems 1, 8].

Further, from **Z** we can build a recursion operator **R**. The following construction is from [CHS72, Section 13A3 p. 224, term **R**(Be)] and is very like that of $\mathbf{R}_{\mathrm{Bernays}}$ in (11) and (14):

$$\left.\begin{aligned} Q &\equiv \lambda yv.\, \mathbf{D}\,(\widehat{\sigma}(v\overline{0}_{\mathrm{Ch}}))\,(y(v\overline{0}_{\mathrm{Ch}})(v\overline{1}_{\mathrm{Ch}})),\\ \mathbf{R} &\equiv \lambda xyu.\, \mathbf{Z}\,u\,(Qy)(\mathbf{D}\widehat{0}x)\,\overline{1}_{\mathrm{Ch}}, \end{aligned}\right\} \tag{32}$$

where $\mathbf{D} \equiv \lambda xyz.z(\mathbf{K}y)x$ as in Note 4.14. By following the proof of (6), this $\mathbf{R}$ can be shown to satisfy

$$\left.\begin{array}{lll} \mathbf{R}XY\widehat{0} & \triangleright_{\beta,w\,\mathbf{Z}} & X, \\ \mathbf{R}XY(\widehat{k+1}) & =_{\beta,w\,\mathbf{Z}} & Y\widehat{k}\,(\mathbf{R}XY\widehat{k}\,). \end{array}\right\} \quad (33)$$

Also a term P like that in (20) can be constructed:

$$\left.\begin{array}{lll} T & \equiv & \lambda x.\,\mathbf{D}\,\overline{0}_{\mathrm{Ch}}\big(\lambda uv.\,u\,(x(\widehat{\sigma}v))u(\widehat{\sigma}v)\,\big), \\ P & \equiv & \lambda xy.\,Tx(\mathbf{Z}(xy))(Tx)y. \end{array}\right\} \quad (34)$$

It is straightforward to check that, for all terms X and Y,

$$\left.\begin{array}{llll} PXY & =_{\beta,w\,\mathbf{Z}}\; Y & \text{if } XY =_{\beta,w\,\mathbf{Z}} \widehat{0}, \\ PXY & =_{\beta,w\,\mathbf{Z}}\; PX(\widehat{\sigma}Y) & \text{if } XY =_{\beta,w\,\mathbf{Z}} \widehat{m+1}. \end{array}\right\} \quad (35)$$

Thus, if the numerals are abstract, all recursive total functions can be represented in terms of $\mathbf{Z}$.

For partial functions a representation theorem like Theorem 4.23 can probably be proved by a method like 4.23, but we have not seen a proof.

Definition 4.26 (Arithmetical extension) For λ or CL, the *arithmetical extension* $\lambda\beta\mathbf{Z}$ or CL$w\mathbf{Z}$, is obtained by adding to the set of terms three new atoms $\widehat{0}$, $\widehat{\sigma}$ and $\mathbf{Z}$, as suggested above, and adding to the definition of $\triangleright_\beta$ or $\triangleright_w$ the following new contractions:

$$\mathbf{Z}\widehat{n} \;\triangleright_1\; \overline{n}_{\mathrm{Ch}} \qquad (n = 0,\,1,\,2,\,\ldots),$$

where $\overline{n}_{\mathrm{Ch}}$ is the Church numeral $\lambda xy.x^n y$ or $(\mathbf{SB})^n(\mathbf{KI})$. The new reduction is called $\triangleright_{\beta\mathbf{Z}}$ (in λ) or $\triangleright_{w\mathbf{Z}}$ (in CL).

Exercise 4.27 * In λ or CL with abstract numerals, prove that if $\mathbf{Z}$ is absent then the predecessor-function π (such that $\pi(0) = 0$ and $\pi(k+1) = k$) cannot be represented by a term.

5
The undecidability theorem

The aim of this chapter is to prove a general undecidability theorem which will show in particular that the relation $=_\beta$ is recursively undecidable, and that there is no recursive way of deciding whether a λ-term has a normal form or not. These two were the first ever undecidability results to be discovered, and it was from them that Church deduced the undecidability of pure first-order predicate logic in 1936, answering a question posed by the leading mathematician David Hilbert over thirty years before (Hilbert's *Entscheidungsproblem*).

But the more general theorem we shall describe was first proved by Dana Scott in 1963 (in unpublished notes, but see [Bar84, Section 6.6]), and rediscovered independently by Curry [CHS72, Section 13B2]. It applies to CL as well as to λ.

Notation 5.1 This chapter will use the neutral notation of the preceding two chapters, which can be read in both λ and CL. All functions of natural numbers will here be total, i.e. will give outputs for all $n \in \mathbb{N}$. Numerals will be those of Church:

$$\overline{n} \equiv \lambda xy.x^n y \text{ in } \lambda\text{-calculus}, \qquad \overline{n} \equiv (\mathsf{SB})^n(\mathsf{KI}) \text{ in CL}.$$

Assumption 5.2 We assume that every term X has been given a number n by some coding algorithm. There are many possible such algorithms; indeed there is one in every word-processing software package, to translate expressions on the computer screen into the numbers with which the computer actually works. A simple coding algorithm is described in [Men97, Chapter 3, Section 4], though it is not intended to be practical or efficient. However, coding details will not matter here. The number assigned to X will be called the *Gödel number of X*, or

$gd(X)$, in honour of the man who first made use of such a coding. We shall assume that

(a) *there is a recursive total function* τ *of natural numbers, such that, for all terms* X, Y,

$$\tau(gd(X), gd(Y)) \; = \; gd((XY));$$

(b) *there is a recursive total function* ν *such that, for all* $n \in \mathbb{N}$,

$$\nu(n) \; = \; gd(\overline{n}).$$

For example, suitable functions τ and ν can be proved to exist for the coding algorithm in [Men97, Chapter 3, Section 4]; the underlying reason is that the operation of building a term (XY) from terms X and Y is effectively computable, and so is the operation of building $\overline{n}$ from n.

Definition 5.3 For all terms X, the Church numeral corresponding to $gd(X)$ will be called '$\ulcorner X \urcorner$':

$$\ulcorner X \urcorner \; \equiv \; \overline{gd(X)}.$$

Note If X is a term, then $gd(X)$ is a number and $\ulcorner X \urcorner$ is a term. For example, if the coding-algorithm assigns the number 5 to the term uv, then

$$gd(uv) \; = \; 5, \qquad \ulcorner uv \urcorner \; \equiv \; \lambda xy.x(x(x(x(xy)))).$$

Definition 5.4 A pair of sets $\mathcal{A}$, $\mathcal{B}$ of natural numbers is called *recursively separable* iff there is a recursive total function ϕ whose only output-values are 0 and 1, such that

$$n \in \mathcal{A} \implies \phi(n) = 0,$$
$$n \in \mathcal{B} \implies \phi(n) = 1.$$

A pair of *sets of terms* is called *recursively separable* iff the corresponding sets of Gödel numbers are recursively separable. A set $\mathcal{A}$ (of numbers or terms) is called *recursive* or *decidable* iff $\mathcal{A}$ and its complement are recursively separable.

Informally speaking, a pair $\mathcal{A}$, $\mathcal{B}$ is recursively separable iff $\mathcal{A} \cap \mathcal{B}$ is empty and there is an algorithm which decides whether a number or term is in $\mathcal{A}$ or in $\mathcal{B}$.

Definition 5.5 In λ with $=_\beta$ or CL with $=_w$, a set $\mathcal{A}$ of terms is said to be *closed under conversion* (or *equality*) iff, for all terms X, Y,

$$X \in \mathcal{A} \text{ and } Y =_{\beta,w} X \implies Y \in \mathcal{A}.$$

Theorem 5.6 (Scott–Curry undecidability theorem) *For sets of terms in λ with $=_\beta$ or CL with $=_w$: no pair of non-empty sets which are closed under conversion is recursively separable.*

Proof Let $\mathcal{A}$, $\mathcal{B}$ be sets of terms, non-empty and closed under conversion. Suppose there is a recursive total function ϕ whose only output-values are 0 and 1, which separates $\mathcal{A}$ from $\mathcal{B}$; i.e. such that

$$X \in \mathcal{A} \implies \phi(gd(X)) = 0, \tag{1}$$

$$X \in \mathcal{B} \implies \phi(gd(X)) = 1. \tag{2}$$

By Theorem 4.20, there is a combinator F which represents ϕ. Then

$$X \in \mathcal{A} \implies F\ulcorner X\urcorner =_{\beta,w} \overline{0}, \tag{3}$$

$$X \in \mathcal{B} \implies F\ulcorner X\urcorner =_{\beta,w} \overline{1}. \tag{4}$$

Also the functions τ and ν in Assumption 5.2(a) and (b) are recursive, so they can be represented by combinators, call them T and N respectively. So, for all X, Y, n,

$$T\ulcorner X\urcorner\ulcorner Y\urcorner =_{\beta,w} \ulcorner (XY)\urcorner, \tag{5}$$

$$N\overline{n} =_{\beta,w} \ulcorner \overline{n}\urcorner. \tag{6}$$

Choose any terms $A \in \mathcal{A}$ and $B \in \mathcal{B}$. We shall build a term J (which will depend on A and B), such that

$$F\ulcorner J\urcorner =_{\beta,w} \overline{0} \implies J =_{\beta,w} B, \tag{7}$$

$$F\ulcorner J\urcorner =_{\beta,w} \overline{1} \implies J =_{\beta,w} A. \tag{8}$$

This will cause a contradiction. To see this, let $j = gd(J)$; then $\phi(j) = 0$ or $\phi(j) = 1$, and (since ϕ is a function) not both at once. But

$$\begin{array}{rlll} \phi(j) = 0 & \implies & F\ulcorner J\urcorner =_{\beta,w} \overline{0} & \text{since } \ulcorner J\urcorner \equiv \overline{j} \text{ and } F \text{ represents } \phi, \\ & \implies & J =_{\beta,w} B & \text{by (7)}, \\ & \implies & J \in \mathcal{B} & \text{since } \mathcal{B} \text{ is closed under } =_{\beta,w}, \\ & \implies & \phi(j) = 1 & \text{by (2)}; \end{array}$$

$$\begin{array}{llll} \phi(j) = 1 & \Longrightarrow & F\lceil J\rceil =_{\beta,w} \overline{1} & \text{since } \lceil J\rceil \equiv \overline{j} \text{ and } F \text{ represents } \phi, \\ & \Longrightarrow & J =_{\beta,w} A & \text{by (8)}, \\ & \Longrightarrow & J \in \mathcal{A} & \text{since } \mathcal{A} \text{ is closed under } =_{\beta,w}, \\ & \Longrightarrow & \phi(j) = 0 & \text{by (1)}. \end{array}$$

Now (7) and (8) would hold if we could obtain

$$J =_{\beta,w} \mathbf{D}BA(F\lceil J\rceil), \tag{9}$$

where $\mathbf{D}$ is the pairing combinator from (9), $\mathbf{D} \equiv \lambda xyz.z(\mathbf{K}y)x$. Because, by (10) in Chapter 4,

$$\mathbf{D}BA\overline{0} =_{\beta,w} B, \qquad \mathbf{D}BA\overline{1} =_{\beta,w} A.$$

To build a J satisfying (9), choose $y \notin \mathrm{FV}(AB)$ and define

$$\left.\begin{array}{lll} H & \equiv & \lambda y.\mathbf{D}BA(F(Ty(Ny))), \\ J & \equiv & H\lceil H\rceil. \end{array}\right\} \tag{10}$$

This J satisfies (9), because

$$\begin{array}{lll} J =_{\beta,w} & \mathbf{D}BA(F(T\lceil H\rceil(N\lceil H\rceil))) & \text{by the definitions of } J, H, \\ =_{\beta,w} & \mathbf{D}BA(F(T\lceil H\rceil\lceil\lceil H\rceil\rceil)) & \text{by (6)}, \\ =_{\beta,w} & \mathbf{D}BA(F\lceil(H\lceil H\rceil)\rceil) & \text{by (5)}, \\ \equiv & \mathbf{D}BA(F\lceil J\rceil) & \text{since } J \equiv H\lceil H\rceil. \end{array}$$

□

Corollary 5.6.1 *In* λ *with* $=_\beta$ *or CL with* $=_w$*: if a set* $\mathcal{A}$ *of terms is closed under conversion and both* $\mathcal{A}$ *and its complement are non-empty, then* $\mathcal{A}$ *is not decidable.*

Proof In Theorem 5.6 let $\mathcal{B}$ be the complement of $\mathcal{A}$, i.e. the set of all terms not in $\mathcal{A}$. □

Corollary 5.6.2 *In* λ *with* $=_\beta$ *or CL with* $=_w$*: the set of all terms which have normal forms is not decidable.*

Roughly speaking, there is no algorithm which will decide, in finite time, whether a term X has a normal form or not.

Corollary 5.6.3 *The relations* $=_\beta$ *and* $=_w$ *are not decidable. That is, there is no recursive total function* ψ *such that*

$$\begin{array}{rcl} X =_{\beta,w} Y & \Longrightarrow & \psi(gd(X), gd(Y)) = 0, \\ X \neq_{\beta,w} Y & \Longrightarrow & \psi(gd(X), gd(Y)) = 1. \end{array}$$

Proof In 5.6.1, let $\mathcal{A}$ be the set of all terms convertible to one particular term (**I**, for example). □

Remark 5.7 (Entscheidungsproblem) As mentioned earlier, Church proved in 1936 that pure classical first-order predicate logic is undecidable. His proof can be summarized as follows. When λ-terms are given Gödel numbers, then $=_\beta$ corresponds to a relation between natural numbers. Natural numbers can be coded by terms in a pure predicate language which has function symbols, by choosing a variable z and a function-symbol f and letting

$$\begin{array}{lll} z & \text{represent} & 0, \\ f(z) & \text{represent} & 1, \\ f(f(z)) & \text{represent} & 2, \quad \text{etc.} \end{array}$$

Let $\overline{\overline{n}}$ be the representative of n in this coding. The definition of $=_\beta$ can be re-written as a formal theory with eight axiom-schemes and rules of inference, as we shall see in the next chapter (the theory $\lambda\beta$). These axiom-schemes and rules can be translated, via Gödel-numbering, into eight predicate-calculus formulas $F_1, \ldots, F_8$ containing a predicate-symbol E, such that the formula

$$(F_1 \wedge \ldots \wedge F_8) \to E(\overline{\overline{m}}, \overline{\overline{n}})$$

is provable in pure predicate logic iff m, n are Gödel numbers of interconvertible terms.

Hence, if we could decide all questions of provability in pure predicate logic, then we could decide whether arbitrary λ-terms are interconvertible, contrary to Corollary 5.6.3.

(The details of Church's proof are in [Chu36b] and [Chu36a]; in the former he proved the undecidability of $=_\beta$, and in the latter he deduced that of predicate logic.)

Exercise 5.8* Church's proof of the undecidability of $=_\beta$ in [Chu36b] was more direct than our proof via the Scott–Curry theorem. And the version of λ he used was the λI-calculus, described in Remark 1.43.

Prove that the general Scott–Curry theorem is not in fact true for this calculus. (Hint: to do this, you must find two non-empty sets of λI-terms which are closed under conversion yet are recursively separable; one approach is to use the fact that if $X =_\beta Y$ in the λI-calculus, then $\mathrm{FV}(X) = \mathrm{FV}(Y)$.)

Exercise 5.9 * (a) In λ or CL, the *range* of a combinator F may be defined to be the set of all combinators Y such that $Y =_{\beta,w} FX$ for some combinator X. Prove that the range of F is either infinite or a singleton, modulo $=_{\beta,w}$. (This was conjectured by Böhm and proved by Barendregt, [Bar84, Theorem 20.2.5]. Its proof is a neat application of Theorem 5.6 for a reader who knows some recursion theory.)

(b) The *second fixed-point theorem*, [Bar84, Theorem 6.5.9], states that for every λ- or CL-term F there exists a term X_F such that

$$F\ulcorner X_F \urcorner =_{\beta,w} X_F .$$

Prove this theorem. (Hint: modify J in the proof of Theorem 5.6.)

6

The formal theories $\lambda\beta$ and CLw

6A The definitions of the theories

The relations of reducibility and convertibility were defined in Chapters 1 and 2 via contractions of redexes. The present chapter gives alternative definitions, via formal theories with axioms and rules of inference.

These theories will be used later in describing the correspondence between λ and CL precisely, and will help to make the distinction between syntax and semantics clearer in the chapters on models to come. They will also give a more direct meaning to such phrases as 'add the equation $M = N$ as a new axiom to the definition of $=_\beta$ ...' (Corollary 3.11.1).

In books on logic, formal theories come in two kinds (at least): Hilbert-style and Gentzen-style. The theories in this chapter will be the former.

Notation 6.1 (Hilbert-style formal theories) A (Hilbert-style) *formal theory* $\mathcal{T}$ consists of three sets: *formulas*, *axioms* and *rules* (of inference). Each rule has one or more *premises* and one *conclusion*, and we shall write its premises above a horizontal line and its conclusion under this line; for examples, see the rules in Definition 6.2 below.

If Γ is a set of formulas, a *deduction* of a formula B from Γ is a tree of formulas, with those at the tops of branches being axioms or members of Γ, the others being deduced from those immediately above them by a rule, and the bottom one being B. Non-axioms at the tops of branches are called *assumptions*. Iff such a deduction exists, we say

$$\mathcal{T}, \Gamma \vdash B, \qquad \text{or} \qquad \Gamma \vdash_{\mathcal{T}} B.$$

Iff Γ is empty, we call the deduction a *proof*, call B a *provable formula* or *theorem* of $\mathcal{T}$, and say

$$\mathcal{T} \vdash B, \qquad \text{or} \qquad \vdash_{\mathcal{T}} B.$$

Finally, in this book an *axiom-scheme* will be any set of axioms which all conform to some given pattern.

(This sense of 'formal theory' comes from [Men97, Chapter 1, Section 4], except that deductions were viewed there as linear sequences, not trees.)

Definition 6.2 ($\lambda\beta$, formal theory of β-equality) The *formulas* of $\lambda\beta$ are just equations $M = N$, for all λ-terms M and N. The *axioms* are the particular cases of (α), (β) and (ρ) below, for all λ-terms M, N, and all variables x, y. The *rules* are (μ), (ν), (ξ), (τ) and (σ) below. (Their names are from [CF58].)

Axiom-schemes:

$$(\alpha) \quad \lambda x.M = \lambda y.[y/x]M \qquad \text{if } y \notin FV(M);$$

$$(\beta) \quad (\lambda x.M)N = [N/x]M;$$

$$(\rho) \quad M = M.$$

Rules of inference:

$$(\mu) \quad \frac{M = M'}{NM = NM'}; \qquad (\tau) \quad \frac{M = N \quad N = P}{M = P};$$

$$(\nu) \quad \frac{M = M'}{MN = M'N}; \qquad (\sigma) \quad \frac{M = N}{N = M};$$

$$(\xi) \quad \frac{M = M'}{\lambda x.M = \lambda x.M'}.$$

Iff an equation $M = N$ is provable in $\lambda\beta$, we say

$$\lambda\beta \vdash M = N.$$

Definition 6.3 ($\lambda\beta$, formal theory of β-reduction) This theory is called $\lambda\beta$ like the previous one. (The context will always make clear which theory the name '$\lambda\beta$' means.) Its *formulas* are expressions $M \triangleright N$, for all λ-terms M and N. Its *axiom-schemes* and *rules* are the same as in Definition 6.2, but with '=' changed to '$\triangleright$' and rule (σ) omitted. Iff an expression $M \triangleright N$ is provable in $\lambda\beta$, we say

$$\lambda\beta \vdash M \triangleright N.$$

Lemma 6.4

$$(a) \qquad M \rhd_\beta N \iff \lambda\beta \vdash M \rhd N;$$

$$(b) \qquad M =_\beta N \iff \lambda\beta \vdash M = N.$$

Proof Straightforward and boring. □

Definition 6.5 (CLw, formal theory of weak equality) The *formulas* of CLw are equations $X = Y$, for all CL-terms X and Y. The *axioms* are the particular cases of the four axiom-schemes below, for all CL-terms X, Y and Z. The *rules* are (μ), (ν), (τ) and (σ) below.

Axiom-schemes:

$$(\mathsf{I}) \quad \mathsf{I}X = X;$$

$$(\mathsf{K}) \quad \mathsf{K}XY = X;$$

$$(\mathsf{S}) \quad \mathsf{S}XYZ = XZ(YZ);$$

$$(\rho) \quad X = X.$$

Rules of inference:

$$(\mu) \quad \frac{X = X'}{ZX = ZX'}; \qquad (\tau) \quad \frac{X = Y \quad Y = Z}{X = Z};$$

$$(\nu) \quad \frac{X = X'}{XZ = X'Z}; \qquad (\sigma) \quad \frac{X = Y}{Y = X}.$$

Iff an equation $X = Y$ is provable in CLw, we say

$$\text{CL}w \ \vdash \ X = Y.$$

Definition 6.6 (CLw, formal theory of weak reduction) The *formulas* of CLw are expressions $X \rhd Y$, for all CL-terms X and Y. The *axiom-schemes* and *rules* are the same as in Definition 6.5, but with '=' changed to '$\rhd$' and (σ) omitted. Iff $X \rhd Y$ is provable in CLw, we say

$$\text{CL}w \ \vdash \ X \rhd Y.$$

Lemma 6.7

$$(a) \qquad X \rhd_w Y \iff CLw \vdash X \rhd Y;$$

$$(b) \qquad X =_w Y \iff CLw \vdash X = Y.$$

Remark 6.8 By the Church–Rosser theorems and Lemmas 6.4 and 6.7, the theories $\lambda\beta$ and CLw are consistent in the sense that not all their formulas are provable. (It is standard in logic to call a theory without negation 'inconsistent' when all formulas in its language are provable.)

6B First-order theories

This section and the next one contain some general background material from logic and proof-theory that will be used later.

Notation 6.9 (First-order theories) Most textbooks on predicate logic, for example [Dal97, Chapter 2], [Men97, Chapter 2] or [End00, Chapter 2], are concerned with *first-order languages*. With minor variations, such a language has three kinds of expressions: *terms*, built up from atomic constants and variables by some given operations, *atomic formulas* in which terms are related by some given predicates (for example '='), and *composite formulas* built up from atomic ones using connectives such as '$\wedge$', '$\vee$', '$\rightarrow$', '$\leftrightarrow$', '$\neg$', and the quantifiers '$\forall$', '$\exists$'.

Following [Men97, Chapter 2, Sections 3 and 8], a *first-order theory* $\mathcal{T}$ is a special kind of Hilbert-style formal theory. Its *formulas* are the formulas of a given first-order language. Its *axioms* are divided into two classes: *proper axioms*, which are peculiar to $\mathcal{T}$, and *logical axioms*, which are the usual axioms of classical predicate logic (including axioms for '='). The *rules* of $\mathcal{T}$ are the usual rules of predicate logic.

Remark 6.10 Neither of the equality-theories $\lambda\beta$ and CLw is a first-order theory, because they contain no connectives or quantifiers. However, could they be made into first-order theories by simply adding connectives and quantifiers to their languages and adding appropriate rules?

For $\lambda\beta$, the answer is 'no', because each 'λ' in a λ-term binds a variable, and operators that bind variables are not allowed in first-order terms.

But in CL-terms there are no variable-binding operators, and CLw can easily be extended to a first-order theory CLw^+, as follows.

Definition 6.11 (The first-order theory CLw^+) The *terms* of CLw^+ are CL-terms. The *atomic formulas* are equations $X = Y$, and *composite formulas* are built from them using connectives and quantifiers in the normal way. The *rules of inference* and *logical axioms* are the usual ones for classical first-order logic with equality (e.g. those in [Men97, Chapter 2, Sections 3 and 8] or [End00, Section 2.4]). The *proper axioms* are the following three:

(a) $(\forall x, y)\,(\mathbf{K}xy = x)$,

(b) $(\forall x, y, z)\,(\mathbf{S}xyz = xz(yz))$,

(c) $\neg(\mathbf{S} = \mathbf{K})$.

Lemma 6.12 $\mathrm{CL}w^{+}$ *has the same set of provable equations as* $\mathrm{CL}w$.

Proof By [Bar73, Theorem 2.12]. (Axiom (c) can be included in $\mathrm{CL}w^{+}$ because, by the Church–Rosser theorem, $\mathbf{S} = \mathbf{K}$ is not provable in $\mathrm{CL}w$.) □

Note The difference between $\mathrm{CL}w^{+}$ and $\mathrm{CL}w$ lies in their languages. In $\mathrm{CL}w$ we can prove two separate equations such as $\mathbf{II} = \mathbf{I}$ and $\mathbf{IK} = \mathbf{K}$; but we cannot prove their conjunction $(\mathbf{II} = \mathbf{I}\ \wedge\ \mathbf{IK} = \mathbf{K})$; in fact we cannot even express it, because '$\wedge$' is not in the language of $\mathrm{CL}w$. In $\mathrm{CL}w^{+}$ we can prove logical combinations of equations, but, by the above lemma, we cannot prove any more single equations than in $\mathrm{CL}w$. $\mathrm{CL}w^{+}$ is said to be a 'conservative extension' of $\mathrm{CL}w$.

6C Equivalence of theories

Suppose we have a Hilbert-style formal theory $\mathcal{T}$, and we consider extending $\mathcal{T}$ by adding a new rule $\mathcal{R}$. It is natural to ask first whether $\mathcal{R}$ is already derivable in $\mathcal{T}$. But what exactly does '$\mathcal{R}$ is derivable' mean? Mainstream proof-theory gives several answers to this question (e.g. in [TS00, Definition 3.4.4]), and those that have turned out useful in comparing λ with CL will be described here.

But first, what does 'a new rule $\mathcal{R}$' mean? Let $\mathcal{F}$ be the set of all formulas of the language of $\mathcal{T}$, and let $n \geq 1$. Then every function ϕ from a subset of $\mathcal{F}^n$ to $\mathcal{F}$ determines a rule $\mathcal{R}(\phi)$ thus: each n-tuple of formulas $\langle A_1, \ldots, A_n \rangle$ in the domain of ϕ may be called a sequence of *premises*, and if $\phi(A_1, \ldots, A_n) = B$, then B is called the corresponding *conclusion*, and the expression

$$\frac{A_1, \ldots, A_n}{B}$$

is called an *instance* of the rule $\mathcal{R}(\phi)$.

Definition 6.13 (Derivable and admissible rules) Let $\mathcal{R}$ be a rule determined by a function ϕ from a subset of $\mathcal{F}^n$ to $\mathcal{F}$, as above. $\mathcal{R}$ is said to be *derivable* in $\mathcal{T}$ iff, for each instance of $\mathcal{R}$, its conclusion is deducible in $\mathcal{T}$ from its premises: i.e.

$$\mathcal{T},\ A_1,\ \ldots\ A_n\ \ \vdash\ \ B.$$

$\mathcal{R}$ is said to be *admissible* in $\mathcal{T}$ iff adding $\mathcal{R}$ to $\mathcal{T}$ as a new rule will not increase the set of theorems of $\mathcal{T}$.

$\mathcal{R}$ is said to be *correct* in $\mathcal{T}$ iff, for each instance of $\mathcal{R}$, if all the premises are provable in $\mathcal{T}$ then so is the conclusion; i.e. iff

$$(\mathcal{T} \vdash A_1),\ \ldots,\ (\mathcal{T} \vdash A_n)\ \ \Longrightarrow\ \ (\mathcal{T} \vdash B).$$

Finally, a single formula C, for example a proposed new axiom, is said to be both *derivable* and *admissible* in $\mathcal{T}$ iff

$$\mathcal{T}\ \vdash\ C.$$

Lemma 6.14 *In a Hilbert-style formal theory $\mathcal{T}$, let $\mathcal{R}$ be a rule determined by a function ϕ as above.*

(a) $\mathcal{R}$ is admissible in $\mathcal{T}$ iff $\mathcal{R}$ is correct in $\mathcal{T}$.

(b) If $\mathcal{R}$ is derivable in $\mathcal{T}$, it is also admissible in $\mathcal{T}$.

(c) If $\mathcal{R}$ is derivable in $\mathcal{T}$, then $\mathcal{R}$ is derivable in every extension of $\mathcal{T}$ obtained by adding new axioms or rules.

Proof Straightforward. □

Lemma 6.14(b) says, in effect, that derivability is a stronger property than admissibility. In fact it is strictly stronger, i.e. for some theories there exist rules which are admissible but not derivable. An example will occur in Remark 15.2, in the language of CL.

Definition 6.15 (Equivalence of theories) Let $\mathcal{T}$ and $\mathcal{T}'$ be Hilbert-style formal theories with the same set of formulas. We shall call $\mathcal{T}$ and $\mathcal{T}'$ *theorem-equivalent* iff every rule and axiom of $\mathcal{T}$ is admissible in

$\mathcal{T}'$ and vice versa, and *rule-equivalent* iff every rule and axiom of $\mathcal{T}$ is derivable in $\mathcal{T}'$ and vice versa.

Clearly, theorem-equivalence is weaker than rule-equivalence. The following easy lemma shows why it is called 'theorem-equivalence'.

Lemma 6.16 *Let $\mathcal{T}$ and $\mathcal{T}'$ be Hilbert-style formal theories with the same set of formulas. Then $\mathcal{T}$ and $\mathcal{T}'$ are theorem-equivalent iff they have the same set of theorems.*

Definition 6.17 Let $\mathcal{T}$ be a Hilbert-style formal theory whose set of formulas includes some equations $X = Y$, where X and Y are terms according to some definition. The *equality relation determined by $\mathcal{T}$* is called $=_{\mathcal{T}}$ and is defined by

$$X =_{\mathcal{T}} Y \iff \mathcal{T} \vdash X = Y.$$

Lemma 6.18 *Let $\mathcal{T}$ and $\mathcal{T}'$ be Hilbert-style formal theories with the same set of formulas, and let this set include some equations. If $\mathcal{T}$ and $\mathcal{T}'$ are theorem-equivalent, then they both determine the same equality-relation.*

A more detailed treatment of derivability, admissability and correctness of rules can be found in the thesis [Gra05, Section 4.2.4].

7
Extensionality in λ-calculus

7A Extensional equality

The concept of function-equality used in most of mathematics is what is called '*extensional*'; that is, it includes the assumption that for functions ϕ and ψ with the same domain,

$$(\forall x)\big(\,\phi(x) = \psi(x)\,\big) \quad\Longrightarrow\quad \phi = \psi.$$

In contrast, in computing, the main subjects are programs, whose equality is '*intensional*'; i.e. if two programs compute the same mathematical function, we do not say they are the same program. (One of them may be more efficient than the other.)

The theory $\lambda\beta$ is also intensional: there exist two terms F and G such that

$$\lambda\beta \;\vdash\; FX = GX \qquad \text{(for all terms } X\text{)},$$

but not $\lambda\beta \vdash F = G$. For example, take any variable y and choose

$$F \;\equiv\; y, \qquad G \;\equiv\; \lambda x.yx.$$

This chapter is about adding an extensionality rule to the theory $\lambda\beta$. In the next chapter we shall do the same for CL.

The discussion of extensionality will help to clarify the relationship between λ and CL, and this relationship will be examined in Chapter 9.

Notation 7.1 In this chapter, 'term' means 'λ-term'. Recall that a *closed term* is one without free variables. Recall also the formal theory $\lambda\beta$ of β-equality, Definition 6.2.

The following two rules and one axiom-scheme have been proposed at various times to express the concept of extensionality in λ-calculus.

$$(\zeta) \qquad \frac{Mx = Nx}{M = N} \qquad \text{if } x \notin \mathrm{FV}(MN);$$

$$(ext) \qquad \frac{MP = NP \ \text{ for all terms } P}{M = N};$$

$$(\eta) \qquad \lambda x.Mx = M \qquad \text{if } x \notin \mathrm{FV}(M).$$

Rule (ζ) says, roughly speaking, that if M and N have the same effect on an unspecified object x, then $M = N$.

Rule (ext) has an infinite number of premises, namely a premise $MP = NP$ for each term P, so deductions involving this rule are infinite trees. Such deductions are beyond the scope of this book, but it can be shown that the theory obtained by adding (ext) to $\lambda\beta$ is theorem-equivalent to that obtained by adding (ζ). So nothing would be gained by studying (ext) instead of (ζ), and we shall ignore (ext) from now on.

Axiom-scheme (η) is of course simpler than any rule, and the idea of expressing extensionality by a single axiom-scheme is very attractive. In fact, Theorem 7.4 will show that (η) is just as strong as (ζ) and (ext). (By the way, in (η) the notation '$\lambda x.Mx$' means, as always, '$\lambda x.(Mx)$' not '$(\lambda x.M)x$'.)

Definition 7.2 Let $\lambda\beta$ be the theory of equality in Definition 6.2; we define two new formal theories of equality:

$$\lambda\beta\zeta: \quad \text{add rule } (\zeta) \text{ to } \lambda\beta;$$
$$\lambda\beta\eta: \quad \text{add axiom-scheme } (\eta) \text{ to } \lambda\beta.$$

(Adding (η) means adding all equations $\lambda x.Mx = M$ as new axioms, for all terms M and all $x \notin \mathrm{FV}(M)$.)

Remark 7.3 (Rule (ω)) In 1950, Paul Rosenbloom suggested the following variant of rule (ext) [Ros50, Chapter 3, rule E5]:

$$(\omega) \qquad \frac{MQ = NQ \ \text{ for all closed terms } Q}{M = N.}$$

Rule (ω) is stronger than rules (ext) and (ζ), in the sense that (ext) and (ζ) are easily derivable from (ω) but (ω) is not derivable, nor even admissible, in the theory $\lambda\beta\zeta$. (The non-admissibility of (ω) was proved by Gordon Plotkin in [Plo74]; he constructed terms M and N such that

$MQ = NQ$ was provable in $\lambda\beta\zeta$ (even in $\lambda\beta$) for all closed Q, yet $\lambda\beta\zeta \nvdash M = N$.)

Rule (ω) has been discussed in detail in [Bar84, Sections 17.3, 17.4], and a little in [HL80, Sections 5ff.]; it will not be studied further here.

Theorem 7.4 *The theories $\lambda\beta\zeta$ and $\lambda\beta\eta$ are rule-equivalent in the sense of Definition 6.15, and hence also theorem-equivalent. Thus both theories determine the same equality-relation.*

Proof First, rule (ζ) is derivable in the theory $\lambda\beta\eta$. Because, from a premise $Mx = Nx$ with $x \notin \mathrm{FV}(MN)$, we can deduce $\lambda x.Mx = \lambda x.Nx$ by rule (ξ) in 6.2, and hence, by (η) twice,

$$M \;=\; \lambda x.Mx \;=\; \lambda x.Nx \;=\; N.$$

Conversely, every (η)-axiom $\lambda x.Mx = M$ (with $x \notin \mathrm{FV}(M)$) is provable in $\lambda\beta\zeta$; because the equation

$$(\lambda x.Mx)x \;=\; Mx$$

is provable by (β) in 6.2, and $\lambda x.Mx = M$ follows by (ζ). □

Definition 7.5 (Extensional ($\beta\eta$) equality in λ) The equality determined by the theories $\lambda\beta\zeta$ and $\lambda\beta\eta$ will be called $=_{ext}$ or $=_{\beta\eta}$ (or $=_{\lambda ext}$ or $=_{\lambda\beta\eta}$ if confusion with CL needs to be avoided); i.e. we define

$$M =_{ext} N \iff \lambda\beta\zeta \vdash M = N,$$
$$M =_{\beta\eta} N \iff \lambda\beta\eta \vdash M = N.$$

By Theorem 7.4, $M =_{ext} N \iff M =_{\beta\eta} N$, so '$=_{ext}$' and '$=_{\beta\eta}$' both denote the same relation, and we can use whichever notation we like for it. The main tool for proving results about this relation is the reduction to be described in the next section.

Exercise 7.6 * The theory $\lambda\beta\zeta$ includes all the rules of $\lambda\beta$ in Definition 6.2, in particular rule (ξ). Let $\lambda\beta_{-\xi+\zeta}$ be the theory of equality obtained by deleting (ξ) from $\lambda\beta$ and adding (ζ) instead. Prove that $\lambda\beta_{-\xi+\zeta}$ is rule-equivalent to $\lambda\beta\zeta$. Thus, roughly speaking, (ζ) renders (ξ) redundant.

7B $\beta\eta$-reduction in λ-calculus

Definition 7.7 (η-reduction) An *η-redex* is any λ-term

$$\lambda x.Mx$$

with $x \notin \mathrm{FV}(M)$. Its *contractum* is

$$M.$$

The phrases '*P η-contracts to Q*' and '*P η-reduces to Q*' are defined by replacing η-redexes by their contracta, like '*β-contracts*' and '*β-reduces*' in Definition 1.24, with notation

$$P \rhd_{1\eta} Q, \qquad P \rhd_{\eta} Q.$$

Definition 7.8 ($\beta\eta$-reduction) A *$\beta\eta$-redex* is a β-redex or an η-redex. The phrases '*P $\beta\eta$-contracts to Q*' and '*P $\beta\eta$-reduces to Q*' are defined like '*β-contracts*' and '*β-reduces*' in Definition 1.24, with notation

$$P \rhd_{1\beta\eta} Q, \qquad P \rhd_{\beta\eta} Q.$$

Definition 7.9 ($\beta\eta$-normal forms) (Same as Definition 3.7) A λ-term Q containing no $\beta\eta$-redexes is said to be *in $\beta\eta$-normal form* (or *$\beta\eta$-nf*), and we say such a term *Q is a $\beta\eta$-normal form of P* iff $P \rhd_{\beta\eta} Q$.

Definition 7.10 (The formal theory $\lambda\beta\eta$ of $\beta\eta$-reduction) This is defined by adding to the theory of β-reduction in Definition 6.3 the axiom-scheme

$$(\eta) \qquad \lambda x.Mx \rhd M \qquad (\text{if } x \notin \mathrm{FV}(M)).$$

Lemma 7.11 *For all P, Q: $P \rhd_{\beta\eta} Q \iff \lambda\beta\eta \vdash P \rhd Q$.*

Lemma 7.12

(a) $\quad P \rhd_{\beta\eta} Q \implies \mathrm{FV}(P) \supseteq \mathrm{FV}(Q)$;

(b) $\quad P \rhd_{\beta\eta} Q \implies [P/x]M \rhd_{\beta\eta} [Q/x]M$;

(c) $\quad P \rhd_{\beta\eta} Q \implies [N/x]P \rhd_{\beta\eta} [N/x]Q$.

Proof For β-steps, use 1.30 and 1.31. For an η-step $\lambda y.Hy \rhd_{1\eta} H$ with $y \notin \mathrm{FV}(H)$, we have $\mathrm{FV}(\lambda y.Hy) = \mathrm{FV}(H)$, giving (a). Also, if $\lambda y.Hy$ is an η-redex, so is $[N/x](\lambda y.Hy)$, giving (c). Part (b) is easy. □

Theorem 7.13 (Church–Rosser theorem for $\triangleright_{\beta\eta}$) *If $P \triangleright_{\beta\eta} M$ and $P \triangleright_{\beta\eta} N$, then there exists a λ-term T such that*

$$M \triangleright_{\beta\eta} T \quad \text{and} \quad N \triangleright_{\beta\eta} T.$$

Proof See Appendix A2, Theorem A2.12. □

Corollary 7.13.1 *If P has a $\beta\eta$-normal form, it is unique modulo $\equiv_\alpha$.*

Proof Like Corollary 1.32.1. □

Theorem 7.14 *A λ-term has a $\beta\eta$-normal form iff it has a β-normal form.*

Proof First, if $P \triangleright_\beta N$ and N is a β-nf, we can change N to a $\beta\eta$-nf by simply η-reducing N. (By checking cases, it can be proved that an η-contraction cannot create new β-redexes in a term. Also an η-reduction cannot continue for ever, because η-contractions make terms shorter.)

The converse part of the theorem looks easy, but actually is not; for a proof of it, see [CHS72, Section 11E, Lemma 13.1], [Bar84, Section 15.1] or [Tak95, end of Section 3]. □

Theorem 7.15 (η-postponement) *In a $\beta\eta$-reduction, all the η-contractions can be postponed to the end; i.e. if $M \triangleright_{\beta\eta} N$ then there exists a P such that*

$$M \triangleright_\beta P \triangleright_\eta N.$$

Proof [Bar84, Corollary 15.1.6] or [Tak95, Theorem 3.5]. □

The following theorem connects $\triangleright_{\beta\eta}$ with extensional equality.

Theorem 7.16 *For all λ-terms P and Q: $P =_{ext} Q$ iff Q can be obtained from P by a finite (perhaps empty) series of $\beta\eta$-contractions and reversed $\beta\eta$-contractions and changes of bound variables.*

Proof Straightforward, using 7.4. □

Corollary 7.16.1 (Church–Rosser theorem for $=_{ext}$) *If $P =_{\beta\eta} Q$, then there exists a λ-term T such that*

$$M \triangleright_{\beta\eta} T \quad \text{and} \quad N \triangleright_{\beta\eta} T.$$

Proof By 7.13 and 7.16, like the proof of 1.41. □

Corollary 7.16.2 (Consistency of $=_{\beta\eta}$) *There exist λ-terms M and N such that* $M \neq_{\beta\eta} N$.

Corollary 7.16.3 (Uniqueness of nf) *A λ-term is extensionally equal to at most one βη-nf, modulo changes of bound variables.*

Remark 7.17 The above results show that $\triangleright_{\beta\eta}$ is very well behaved, almost as easy to use as $\triangleright_{\beta}$. In fact, it is a bit surprising that we have managed to add extensionality to λ with so little effort. However, in the deeper theory of reductions, $\triangleright_{\beta\eta}$ gets significantly more difficult; for example, although there is an analogue of the quasi-leftmost-reduction theorem for $\triangleright_{\beta\eta}$, its proof is much harder than for $\triangleright_{\beta}$ [Klo80, Chapter IV, Corollary 5.13].

Also, it is not certain that (ζ), (*ext*), (η), (ω) or any other rule in pure λ can describe the concept of extensionality exactly. (We have highlighted (ζ) and (η) here because they are fairly easy to work with and the reader might meet them in the literature.) Another approach to extensionality will be made in Chapter 14 and the two approaches will be compared in Remark 14.25.

8

Extensionality in combinatory logic

8A Extensional equality

In this chapter we shall look at axioms and rules to add to weak equality in CL to make it extensional.

Notation 8.1 'Term' means 'CL-term' in this chapter. We shall study here the following two rules and one axiom-scheme:

$$(\zeta) \qquad \frac{Xx = Yx}{X = Y} \qquad \text{if } x \notin \mathrm{FV}(XY);$$

$$(\xi) \qquad \frac{X = Y}{[x].X = [x].Y};$$

$$(\eta) \qquad [x].Ux = U \qquad \text{if } x \notin \mathrm{FV}(U).$$

The first rule, (ζ), is the same as in the λ-calculus. But the other two, (ξ) and (η), will turn out to have a different status in CL from that in λ.

Definition 8.2 Let CLw be the theory of weak equality, Definition 6.5; we define two new formal theories of equality:

$$\begin{aligned} \mathrm{CL}\zeta: &\quad \text{add rule } (\zeta) \text{ to } \mathrm{CL}w; \\ \mathrm{CL}\xi: &\quad \text{add rule } (\xi) \text{ to } \mathrm{CL}w. \end{aligned}$$

Exercise 8.3* Prove that neither (ζ) nor (ξ) is admissible in the theory CLw. Hence both the theories CLζ and CLξ contain provable equations that are not provable for weak equality.

Remark 8.4 The following rule could also be studied:

$$(ext) \qquad \frac{XZ = YZ \text{ for all terms } Z}{X = Y};$$

but it gives the same set of provable equations as (ζ), although the proof of that fact is beyond the scope of this book.[1]

We shall give the name 'extensional equality' to the equality determined by rule (ζ), just as we did in λ-calculus.

Definition 8.5 (Extensional equality in CL) The relation $=_{ext}$ (or $=_{C\,ext}$ when confusion with λ needs to be avoided)[2] is defined thus:

$$X =_{ext} Y \quad \Longleftrightarrow \quad \mathrm{CL}\zeta \;\vdash\; X = Y.$$

Example 8.6

(a) $\mathbf{SK} \; =_{ext} \; \mathbf{KI}$.

This is proved by applying rule (ζ) twice to the weak equation $\mathbf{SK}xy \; =_w \; \mathbf{KI}xy$, which is proved thus:

$$\begin{aligned} \mathbf{SK}xy \;&=_w\; \mathbf{K}y(xy) && \text{by axiom-scheme } (\mathbf{S}) \text{ in 6.5,}\\ &=_w\; y && \text{by } (\mathbf{K}) \text{ in 6.5,}\\ &=_w\; \mathbf{I}y && \text{by } (\mathbf{I}) \text{ and rule } (\sigma),\\ &=_w\; \mathbf{KI}xy && \text{by } (\mathbf{K}) \text{ and rules } (\sigma), (\mu). \end{aligned}$$

(b) $\mathbf{S}(\mathbf{K}X)(\mathbf{K}Y) \; =_{ext} \; \mathbf{K}(XY)$ for all terms X, Y.

To prove this, choose $v \notin \mathrm{FV}(XY)$ and apply (ζ) to the weak equation $\mathbf{S}(\mathbf{K}X)(\mathbf{K}Y)v =_w \mathbf{K}(XY)v$, which comes thus:

$$\begin{aligned} \mathbf{S}(\mathbf{K}X)(\mathbf{K}Y)v \;&=_w\; \mathbf{K}Xv(\mathbf{K}Yv) && \text{by } (\mathbf{S}) \text{ in 6.5,}\\ &=_w\; XY && \text{by } (\mathbf{K}) \text{ twice and } (\mu), (\nu),\\ &=_w\; \mathbf{K}(XY)v && \text{by } (\mathbf{K}) \text{ and } (\sigma). \end{aligned}$$

[1] It was set as an exercise in [HS86, p. 79], but to prove (ζ) admissible in CLw+(ext), one must first prove that deductions in CLw+(ext) remain correct deductions after simultaneous substitutions, and this is not trivial (since such deductions may be infinite). In λ this complication is avoided by using rule (ξ), which is not available in CLw+(ext).

[2] This relation is often called $=_{\beta\eta}$ in the literature, by supposed analogy with λ-calculus, but that notation is misleading; we shall see below that the meaning of (η) in CL differs from that in λ.

(c) $\mathsf{S}(\mathsf{K}X)\mathsf{I} \ =_{ext} \ X$ for all terms X.

This is proved by applying (ζ) to the following, for $v \notin \mathrm{FV}(X)$:

$$\begin{array}{rcll} \mathsf{S}(\mathsf{K}X)\mathsf{I}v & =_w & \mathsf{K}Xv(\mathsf{I}v) & \text{by } (\mathsf{S}) \text{ in 6.5,} \\ & =_w & Xv & \text{by } (\mathsf{K}), (\mathsf{I}), (\mu), (\nu). \end{array}$$

Remark 8.7 (The rôles of (ξ) and (η)) In CL, (η) says $[x].Ux = U$ if $x \notin \mathrm{FV}(U)$.

In λ, we saw that (η) acted as an extensionality-principle equivalent to (ζ). But in the proof of that fact (Theorem 7.4), the step from (η) to (ζ) used rule (ξ) as well as (η). This passed without comment in λ-calculus, where (ξ) is a permanent underlying assumption for equality.

But in CL, the definition of $=_w$ does not include (ξ), and (η) by itself is not an extensionality principle at all. Indeed, (η) holds in CL as an identity:

$$[x].Ux \ \equiv \ U \quad \text{if } x \notin \mathrm{FV}(U)$$

(by Definition 2.18(c)), but despite this, $=_w$ is not extensional, as we saw in Exercise 8.3. All we can get from (η) in CL is that every term is equal to an abstraction: $U = [x].Ux$.

However, if we extended the theory CLw by adding rule (ξ), the strengthened theory CLξ would be extensional by the argument in the proof of Theorem 7.4.

In CL, (ξ) can be regarded as a weak form of extensionality principle that asserts

$$Xx = Yx \quad \vdash \quad X = Y$$

whenever X and Y are abstractions. (Because, if $X \equiv [x].V$ and $Y \equiv [x].W$, then $Xx =_w V$ and $Yx =_w W$, so from $Xx = Yx$ we could deduce $V = W$ in CLw, and then (ξ) would imply $X = Y$.)

Roughly speaking, (ξ) says that extensionality holds for abstractions, while (η) says that all terms are equal to abstractions, so the two together give extensionality for all terms.

Theorem 8.8 *The theory* CLξ *determines the same equality-relation* $=_{ext}$ *as* CLζ *does.*

Proof It is enough to prove CLξ theorem-equivalent to CLζ. We shall actually prove rule-equivalence.

First we derive (ζ) in the theory $CL\xi$ (see 8.7 and 7.4). Given an equation $Xx = Yx$ with $x \notin FV(XY)$, apply (ξ) to give

$$[x].Xx \;=\; [x].Yx,$$

and this is $X = Y$ by the definition of $[x]$-abstraction, 2.18(c).

Next we derive (ξ) in $CL\zeta$. Given $X = Y$, deduce

$$\begin{array}{rcll} ([x].X)x & = & X & \text{by 2.21} \\ & = & Y & \text{given} \\ & = & ([x].Y)x & \text{by 2.21;} \end{array}$$

then $[x].X = [x].Y$ follows by (ζ). □

Remark 8.9 In some accounts of CL, abstraction is defined by clauses (a), (b) and (f) of Definition 2.18 without clause (c); see for example [Bar84, Definition 7.1.5]. For this definition of abstraction, the above proof would fail and the corresponding theory $CL\xi$ would determine an equality weaker than $=_{ext}$, as shown in [BHS89]. (To get $=_{ext}$ we would have to add (η) as well as (ξ), just as in λ-calculus.)

8B Axioms for extensionality in CL

We now have two ways of 'strengthening' weak equality to make extensional equality: via $CL\zeta$ or via $CL\xi$. But unfortunately neither of these theories is very easy to work with.

However, as far back as the 1920s, Curry discovered a simpler theory. He found that the same effect as rule (ζ) could be obtained by adding just a finite set of axioms to the theory of weak equality, [Cur30, p. 832 Satz 4]. Each axiom was an equation $A = B$ where A and B were closed terms. These terms were rather long, but it is still interesting that a rule such as (ζ) can be replaced by just a small set of equations.

(By the way, in the last chapter we seemed to do better than that, replacing (ζ) by just one equation (η); but in fact (η) was an axiom-scheme not an axiom, and represented an infinite number of axioms, one for each choice of M, x. In the present section the total number of axioms, not just of axiom-schemes, will be finite.)

The axioms to be given here will be taken from [CF58, p. 203, the set ω_η] with some modifications. There is a different set in [Bar84,

Corollary 7.3.15, the set $A_{\beta\eta}$], and several axiomatizations are compared in [CHS72, Section 11D].

Definition 8.10 (Extensionality axioms) The theory CLext_{ax} is defined by adding to CLw (Definition 6.5) the following five axioms:

$$\textit{E-ax 1:}\quad \mathsf{S}\,(\mathsf{S}\,(\mathsf{KS})\,(\mathsf{S}(\mathsf{KK})(\mathsf{S}(\mathsf{KS})\mathsf{K})))\,(\mathsf{KK}) \;=\; \mathsf{S}(\mathsf{KK});$$

$$\textit{E-ax 2:}\quad \mathsf{S}\,(\mathsf{S}(\mathsf{KS})\mathsf{K})\,(\mathsf{KI}) \;=\; \mathsf{I};$$

$$\textit{E-ax 3:}\quad \mathsf{S}(\mathsf{KI}) \;=\; \mathsf{I};$$

$$\textit{E-ax 4:}\quad \mathsf{S}(\mathsf{KS})(\mathsf{S}(\mathsf{KK})) \;=\; \mathsf{K};$$

$$\textit{E-ax 5:}\quad \mathsf{S}\,(\mathsf{K}(\mathsf{S}(\mathsf{KS})))\,(\mathsf{S}(\mathsf{KS})(\mathsf{S}(\mathsf{KS}))) \;=\; \mathsf{S}\,(\mathsf{S}\,(\mathsf{KS})\,(\mathsf{S}(\mathsf{KK})(\mathsf{S}(\mathsf{KS})(\mathsf{S}(\mathsf{K}(\mathsf{S}(\mathsf{KS})))\mathsf{S}))))\,(\mathsf{KS}).$$

Note 8.11 These mysterious axioms can be made very slightly less mysterious by expressing them thus:

$$\textit{E-ax 1:}\quad [x,y,v].(\mathsf{K}xv)(\mathsf{K}yv) \;=\; [x,y,v].xy,$$
$$\text{or}\quad [x,y].\mathsf{S}(\mathsf{K}x)(\mathsf{K}y) \;=\; [x,y].\mathsf{K}(xy);$$

$$\textit{E-ax 2:}\quad [x,v].(\mathsf{K}xv)(\mathsf{I}v) \;=\; [x,v].xv,$$
$$\text{or}\quad [x].\mathsf{S}(\mathsf{K}x)\mathsf{I} \;=\; [x].x;$$

$$\textit{E-ax 3:}\quad [x,v].\mathsf{I}(xv) \;=\; [x,v].xv,$$
$$\text{or}\quad [x].\mathsf{S}(\mathsf{KI})x \;=\; [x].x;$$

$$\textit{E-ax 4:}\quad [x,y,v].\mathsf{K}(xv)(yv) \;=\; [x,y,v].xv,$$
$$\text{or}\quad [x,y].\mathsf{S}(\mathsf{S}(\mathsf{KK})x)y \;=\; [x,y].x;$$

$$\textit{E-ax 5:}\quad [x,y,z,v].\mathsf{S}(xv)(yv)(zv) \;=\; [x,y,z,v].xv(zv)(yv(zv)),$$
$$\text{or}\quad [x,y,z].\mathsf{S}(\mathsf{S}(\mathsf{S}(\mathsf{KS})x)y)z \;=\; [x,y,z].\mathsf{S}(\mathsf{S}xz)(\mathsf{S}yz).$$

Discussion 8.12 But how on earth can the above axioms be connected with extensionality?

Well, to add extensionality to CLw, it is enough to find axioms which make CLext_{ax} theorem-equivalent to CLζ or CLξ. We choose CLξ. So we must find axioms which will make rule (ξ) admissible in CLext_{ax}; that is, which will give

$$\mathrm{CL}ext_{ax} \vdash X = Y \quad\Longrightarrow\quad \mathrm{CL}ext_{ax} \vdash [v].X = [v].Y \qquad (1)$$

for all variables v.

In particular, for the special case that the equation $X = Y$ is an axiom from ($\mathbf{I}$), ($\mathbf{K}$) or ($\mathbf{S}$) in Definition 6.5, the new axioms must be strong enough to give, for all U, V, W, v,

$$\mathrm{CL}ext_{ax} \vdash \quad [v].\mathbf{I}U \ = \ [v].U,$$

$$\mathrm{CL}ext_{ax} \vdash \quad [v].\mathbf{K}UV \ = \ [v].U,$$

$$\mathrm{CL}ext_{ax} \vdash \quad [v].\mathbf{S}UVW \ = \ [v].UW(VW).$$

The proof of the next theorem will show that E-axs 3–5 do this job. Before that theorem, a lemma will show the use of E-axs 1–2.

Lemma 8.13 *For all X, Y, v:*

$$\mathrm{CL}ext_{ax} \quad \vdash \quad [v].XY \ = \ \mathbf{S}([v].X)([v].Y).$$

Proof By the definition of $[v]$ in 2.18, the desired equation is already an identity, unless either (a) $v \notin \mathrm{FV}(XY)$, or (c) $v \notin \mathrm{FV}(X)$ and $Y \equiv v$. The purpose of E-axs 1–2 is to deal with these two exceptional cases, as follows.

$$\begin{array}{llll} \text{Case (a):} \ [v].XY & \equiv & \mathbf{K}(XY) & \text{by 2.18(a)} \\ & =_w & ([x,y].\mathbf{K}(xy))XY & \text{by 2.27} \\ & = & ([x,y].\mathbf{S}(\mathbf{K}x)(\mathbf{K}y))XY & \text{by } E\text{-}ax \text{ 1 as in 8.11} \\ & =_w & \mathbf{S}(\mathbf{K}X)(\mathbf{K}Y) & \text{by 2.27} \\ & \equiv & \mathbf{S}([v].X)([v].Y) & \text{by 2.18(a).} \end{array}$$

$$\begin{array}{llll} \text{Case (c):} \ [v].XY & \equiv & X & \text{by 2.18(c)} \ \ (\,Y \equiv v \notin \mathrm{FV}(X)\,) \\ & = & \mathbf{S}(\mathbf{K}X)\mathbf{I} & \text{by 2.27 and } E\text{-}ax \text{ 2 as in 8.11} \\ & \equiv & \mathbf{S}([v].X)([v].v) & \text{by 2.18(a), (b).} \end{array}$$

□

Theorem 8.14 *The theory* $\mathrm{CL}ext_{ax}$ *is theorem-equivalent to the theories* $\mathrm{CL}\zeta$ *and* $\mathrm{CL}\xi$, *and hence determines the same equality-relation as they do, namely* $=_{ext}$.

Proof It is enough to prove $\mathrm{CL}ext_{ax}$ theorem-equivalent to $\mathrm{CL}\xi$, i.e. every equation provable in one is provable in the other.

First, every equation provable in $\mathrm{CL}ext_{ax}$ is provable in $\mathrm{CL}\xi$. In fact each of E-axs 1 – 5 can easily be proved in $\mathrm{CL}\xi$, using 8.11, and the other axioms and rules of CLext_{ax} are just those of CLw, which are also in CLξ.

For the converse, we must prove rule (ξ) admissible in CLext_{ax}; that is, we must show that if an equation $X = Y$ is provable in CLext_{ax} by a proof with, say, n steps, then $[v].X = [v].Y$ is also provable in CLext_{ax} for every v. This we shall do by induction on n. Recall the axioms and rules of CLext_{ax} (given in 8.10), which include those of CLw (in 6.5).

If $n = 1$, the equation $X = Y$ is an axiom of CLext_{ax}. If it is one of E-axs 1–5, then no variables occur in XY, so in CLext_{ax} we have

$$\begin{aligned} [v].X &\equiv \mathsf{K}X && \text{by 2.18(a)},\\ &= \mathsf{K}Y && \text{by rule } (\mu) \text{ in CL}w \text{ (see 6.5)},\\ &\equiv [v].Y && \text{by 2.18(a)}. \end{aligned}$$

The other axioms of CLext_{ax} are instances of axiom-schemes (I), (K), (S), (ρ) in 6.5. Suppose $X = Y$ is an instance of (K). Then $X \equiv \mathsf{K}UV$ and $Y \equiv U$ for some U and V, and we must prove $[v].\mathsf{K}UV = [v].U$ in CLext_{ax}. This is done as follows.

$$\begin{aligned} [v].\mathsf{K}UV &= \mathsf{S}\,(\mathsf{S}(\mathsf{KK})([v].U))\,([v].V) && \text{using 8.13}\\ &= ([x,y].\mathsf{S}(\mathsf{S}(\mathsf{KK})x)y)\,([v].U)\,([v].V) && \text{by 2.27}\\ &= ([x,y].x)([v].U)([v].V) && \text{by } E\text{-}ax \text{ 4 in 8.11}\\ &= [v].U && \text{by 2.27}. \end{aligned}$$

The cases of (I) and (S) are similar. The case of (ρ) is trivial.

For the induction step, suppose $n \geq 2$ and the equation $X = Y$ is the conclusion of rule (μ), (ν), (τ) or (σ) in 6.5. If the rule is (μ), then $X \equiv ZU$ and $Y \equiv ZV$ for some Z, U, V, and there is an $n-1$-step proof that

$$\text{CL}ext_{ax} \quad \vdash \quad U = V.$$

The induction-hypothesis is that

$$\text{CL}ext_{ax} \quad \vdash \quad [v].U = [v].V.$$

From this, in CLext_{ax} we can prove

$$\begin{aligned} [v].X &= \mathsf{S}([v].Z)([v].U) && \text{by 8.13}\\ &= \mathsf{S}([v].Z)([v].V) && \text{by induc. hyp. and rule } (\mu)\\ &= [v].Y && \text{by 8.13}. \end{aligned}$$

Rule (ν) is handled like (μ). Rules (τ) and (σ) are easy. □

Warning The above proof has shown only that rule (ξ) is admissible in the theory CLext_{ax}, not that it is derivable (see Definition 6.13). That is, we have proved

$$\mathrm{CL}ext_{ax} \vdash X = Y \quad \Longrightarrow \quad \mathrm{CL}ext_{ax} \vdash [v].X = [v].Y,$$

but *not* that the equation $[v].X = [v].Y$ can be deduced from $X = Y$ in CLext_{ax} for all X, Y and v. Such a strong statement is not needed in proving the above theorem.

8C Strong reduction

Corresponding to $=_{\mathrm{ext}}$ in λ-calculus in the last chapter there was a reduction $\triangleright_{\beta\eta}$ with useful properties, such as confluence and an easily-decidable set of normal forms, so it is natural to try to define a reduction here for $=_{ext}$ in CL.

Definition 8.15 (Strong reduction, $\succ$) The formal theory of *strong reduction* has as formulas all expressions $X \succ Y$, for all CL-terms X and Y. Its *axiom-schemes* and *rules* are the same as those for CLw in Definition 6.5, but with '=' changed to ' $\succ$ ', rule (σ) omitted, and the following new rule added:

$$(\xi) \qquad \frac{X \succ Y}{[x].X \succ [x].Y}.$$

Iff $X \succ Y$ is provable in this theory, we say X *strongly reduces to* Y, or just

$$X \succ Y.$$

Example 8.16

(a) $\mathsf{SK} \succ \mathsf{KI}$.

To prove this, first note that $\mathsf{SK}xy \triangleright_w \mathsf{K}y(xy) \triangleright_w y$. Since the axiom-schemes and rules for $\succ$ include those for $\triangleright_w$, this gives

$$\mathsf{SK}xy \succ y.$$

Hence, by rule (ξ) twice,

$$[x,y].\mathsf{SK}xy \succ [x,y].y.$$

But $[x,y].\mathsf{SK}xy \equiv \mathsf{SK}$ and $[x,y].y \equiv \mathsf{KI}$.

(b) $\mathsf{S}(\mathsf{K}X)(\mathsf{K}Y) \;\succ\!\!-\; \mathsf{K}(XY)$.
To prove this for all terms X, Y, choose $v \notin \mathrm{FV}(XY)$; then

$$\mathsf{S}(\mathsf{K}X)(\mathsf{K}Y) \equiv [v].(\mathsf{K}Xv)(\mathsf{K}Yv), \quad \mathsf{K}(XY) \equiv [v].XY.$$

Also $(\mathsf{K}Xv)(\mathsf{K}Yv) \;\triangleright_w\; XY$, so by (ξ),

$$[v].(\mathsf{K}Xv)(\mathsf{K}Yv) \succ\!\!- [v].XY.$$

(c) $\mathsf{S}(\mathsf{K}X)\mathsf{I} \;\succ\!\!-\; X$.
To prove this for all terms X, choose $v \notin \mathrm{FV}(X)$; then

$$\mathsf{S}(\mathsf{K}X)\mathsf{I} \equiv [v].(\mathsf{K}Xv)(\mathsf{I}v), \quad X \equiv [v].Xv.$$

Also $(\mathsf{K}Xv)(\mathsf{I}v) \;\triangleright_w\; Xv$, so by (ξ),

$$[v].(\mathsf{K}Xv)(\mathsf{I}v) \succ\!\!- [v].Xv.$$

(d) For each of *E-ax*s 1–5 in Definition 8.10, the left side strongly reduces to the right side. In fact, each of these axioms was obtained by applying (ξ) to a weak reduction, as shown in 8.11.

Lemma 8.17 *The relation* $\succ\!\!-$ *is transitive and reflexive. Also*

(a) $X \succ\!\!- Y \implies \mathrm{FV}(X) \supseteq \mathrm{FV}(Y)$;
(b) $X \succ\!\!- Y \implies [X/v]Z \succ\!\!- [Y/v]Z$;
(c) $X \succ\!\!- Y \implies [U_1/x_1,\dots,U_n/x_n]X \succ\!\!- [U_1/x_1,\dots,U_n/x_n]Y$;
(d) *the equivalence relation generated by* $\succ\!\!-$ *is the same as* $=_{ext}$*; that is,* $X =_{ext} Y$ *iff* X *goes to* Y *by a finite series of strong reductions and reversed strong reductions.*

Proof Straightforward. □

Theorem 8.18 (Church–Rosser theorem for $\succ\!\!-$) *The relation* $\succ\!\!-$ *is confluent; i.e. if* $U \succ\!\!- X$ *and* $U \succ\!\!- Y$*, there exists* Z *such that*

$$X \succ\!\!- Z \quad \text{and} \quad Y \succ\!\!- Z.$$

Proof See Exercise 9.19(a). (That exercise deduces the confluence of $\succ\!\!-$ from that of $\triangleright_\beta$ via a translation between CL and λ. The authors do not know of a proof that is independent of λ.) □

Definition 8.19 X is called *strongly irreducible* iff, for all Y,

$$X \succ\!\!- Y \implies Y \equiv X.$$

Theorem 8.20 *The strongly irreducible CL-terms are exactly the terms in the class* strong nf *defined thus (from 3.8 and like 1.33):*

(a) *all atoms other than* **I**, **K** *and* **S** *are in strong nf;*

(b) *if* $X_1, \ldots, X_n$ *are in strong nf, and a is any atom* $\not\equiv$ **I**, **K**, **S**, *then* $aX_1 \ldots X_n$ *is in strong nf;*

(c) *if* X *is in strong nf, then so is* $[x].X$.

Proof [Ler67b]. □

Definition 8.21 X has a strong nf $X^\star$ iff $X^\star$ is a strong nf and $X \succ\!\!- X^\star$.

Lemma 8.22 *(a) A CL-term cannot have more than one strong nf.*

(b) *If* $X^\star$ *is a strong nf and* $U =_{ext} X^\star$, *then* $U \succ\!\!- X^\star$.

(c) $X^\star$ *is the strong nf of* X *iff* $X^\star$ *is a strong nf and* $X =_{ext} X^\star$.

Proof By 8.18 and 8.20. □

A few more facts about strong nfs will be given in Exercise 9.19.

Remark 8.23 By the way, why do we not simplify the basis of CL by defining **I** $\equiv$ **SKK**? (See Exercise 2.16.) One reason is that, if this was done, Theorem 8.20 would fail. **I** would still be in strong nf since **I** $\equiv [x].x$, but **I** would become (infinitely) reducible, since

$$\begin{array}{lll} \mathbf{I} \equiv \mathbf{SKK} & \succ\!\!- \ \mathbf{KIK} & \text{since } \mathbf{SK} \succ\!\!- \mathbf{KI} \text{ by 8.16(a)} \\ & \succ\!\!- \ \mathbf{K(KIK)K} & \text{etc.} \end{array}$$

Remark 8.24 So far, strong reduction is behaving reasonably well. However, the proof that the irreducibles are exactly the normal forms is by no means easy, and it is a bit worrying that no λ-independent proof of confluence is known. In fact, further properties of $\succ\!\!-$ turn out to be just as messy to prove as those of $\triangleright_{\beta\eta}$ in λ, perhaps more so, and, as a result, $\succ\!\!-$ has attracted very little interest.

However, some significant properties were proved in the 1960s. A clear short account was given in [HLS72, Chapter 7], and a more detailed one in [CHS72, Section 11E]. The latter contains a standardization theorem. Also rule (ξ) for $\succ\!\!-$ can be replaced by axioms (an infinite but recursively decidable set), and this can be used to simplify the characterization proof for the irreducibles [Hin67, Ler67a, HL70].

9

Correspondence between λ and CL

9A Introduction

Everything done so far has emphasized the close correspondence between λ and CL, in both motivation and results, but only now do we have the tools to describe this correspondence precisely. This is the aim of the present chapter.

The correspondence between the 'extensional' equalities will be described first, in Section 9B.

The non-extensional equalities are less straightforward. We have $=_\beta$ in λ-calculus and $=_w$ in combinatory logic, and despite their many parallel properties, these differ crucially in that rule (ξ) is admissible in the theory $\lambda\beta$ but not in CLw. To get a close correspondence, we must define a new relation in CL to be like β-equality, and a new relation in λ to be like weak equality. The former will be done in Section 9D below. (An account of the latter can be found in [ÇH98].)

Notation 9.1 This chapter is about both λ- and CL-terms, so 'term' will never be used without 'λ-' or 'CL-'.

For λ-terms we shall ignore changes of bound variables, and '$M \equiv_\alpha N$' will be written as '$M \equiv N$'. (So, in effect, the word 'λ-term' will mean 'α-convertibility class of λ-terms', i.e. the class of all λ-terms α-convertible to a given one.)

Define

$$\begin{aligned} \Lambda &= \text{the class of all (α-convertibility classes of) λ-terms},\\ \mathcal{C} &= \text{the class of all CL-terms.} \end{aligned}$$

We shall assume that the variables in $\mathcal{C}$ are the same as those in Λ.

For CL-terms, in this chapter the $[x].M$ of Definition 2.18 will be called '$[x]^\eta . M$', to distinguish it from a modified definition of abstraction to be described later in the chapter.

The letters 'I', 'K' and 'S' will denote only the atomic combinators of CL, not anything in λ.

Recall the four main equality relations defined earlier; two in λ:

$=_\beta$ (determined by the theory $\lambda\beta$ in 6.2),
$=_{\lambda ext}$ or $=_{\lambda\beta\eta}$ (determined by $\lambda\beta\zeta$ or $\lambda\beta\eta$ in 7.2),

and two in CL:

$=_w$ (determined by the theory CLw in 6.5),
$=_{Cext}$ (determined by any of CLζ, CLξ, CLext_{ax} in 8.2, 8.10).

The following very natural mapping is the basis of the correspondence between λ and CL.

Definition 9.2 (The λ-mapping) With each CL-term X we associate a λ-term X_λ called its λ-*transform*, by induction on X, thus:

(a) $x_\lambda \equiv x,$
(b) $\mathsf{I}_\lambda \equiv \lambda x.x, \quad \mathsf{K}_\lambda \equiv \lambda xy.x, \quad \mathsf{S}_\lambda \equiv \lambda xyz.xz(yz),$
(c) $(XY)_\lambda \equiv X_\lambda Y_\lambda.$

Note 9.3 Clearly X_λ is uniquely defined (modulo changes of bound variables). Also $X \not\equiv Y$ implies $X_\lambda \not\equiv Y_\lambda$, so the λ-mapping is one-to-one. It maps $\mathcal{C}$ onto a subclass of Λ, which will be called $\mathcal{C}_\lambda$:

$$\mathcal{C}_\lambda = \left\{ X_\lambda : X \in \mathcal{C} \right\}.$$

The class $\mathcal{C}_\lambda$ is not the whole of Λ; for example, it is easy to see that the λ-term $\lambda x.y$ is not the λ-transform of any CL-term.

Lemma 9.4 *For all CL-terms X, Z and variables v:*

(a) $\mathrm{FV}(X_\lambda) = \mathrm{FV}(X);$
(b) $([Z/v]X)_\lambda \equiv [Z_\lambda/v](X_\lambda).$

Proof Part (a) is easy, and (b) is proved by induction on X. □

Lemma 9.5 *For all CL-terms X and Y:*

(a) $X \triangleright_w Y \implies X_\lambda \triangleright_\beta Y_\lambda;$

(b) $X =_w Y \implies X_\lambda =_\beta Y_\lambda$;

(c) $X =_{Cext} Y \implies X_\lambda =_{\lambda ext} Y_\lambda$;

Proof Part (a) is proved by induction on the axioms and rules of the theory CLw in 6.5, 6.6. Cases (ρ), (μ), (ν), (τ) are trivial, because these rules are also valid for $\triangleright_\beta$. The other cases are (**S**), (**K**), (**I**), as follows.

$$\begin{aligned} \text{Case } (\mathbf{S})\text{:} \quad (\mathbf{S}XYZ)_\lambda &\equiv (\lambda xyz.xz(yz))\,X_\lambda Y_\lambda Z_\lambda \\ &\triangleright_\beta X_\lambda Z_\lambda (Y_\lambda Z_\lambda) \\ &\equiv (XZ(YZ))_\lambda. \end{aligned}$$

$$\text{Case } (\mathbf{K})\text{:} \quad (\mathbf{K}XY)_\lambda \equiv (\lambda xy.x)\,X_\lambda Y_\lambda \quad \triangleright_\beta \quad X_\lambda.$$

$$\text{Case } (\mathbf{I})\text{:} \quad (\mathbf{I}X)_\lambda \equiv (\lambda x.x)\,X_\lambda \quad \triangleright_\beta \quad X_\lambda.$$

For (b), the proof is similar. Finally, (c) comes by induction on the rules of the theory CLζ defined in 8.2. □

The following terms in CL play a rôle rather like abstractions $\lambda x.M$.

Definition 9.6 (Functional CL-terms) A CL-term with one of the six forms $\mathbf{S}XY$ (for some X, Y), $\mathbf{S}X$, $\mathbf{K}X$, **S**, **K**, **I**, is called *functional* or *fnl.*

Lemma 9.7 *For all functional CL-terms U:*

(a) $U_\lambda \triangleright_\beta \lambda x.M$ *for some λ-term M;*

(b) $U \triangleright_w V \implies V$ *is functional.*

Lemma 9.8 *A CL-term X is weakly equal to a functional term iff X_λ is β-equal to an abstraction-term (i.e. a λ-term of form $\lambda x.M$).*

Proof First, let $X =_w U$ and U be fnl. Then, by 2.32, $X \triangleright_w V$ and $U \triangleright_w V$ for some V. By 9.7(b), V is fnl. Hence, by 9.7(a), $V_\lambda \triangleright_\beta \lambda x.M$ for some M. But $X_\lambda \triangleright_\beta V_\lambda$ by 9.5(a), so $X_\lambda \triangleright_\beta \lambda x.M$.

For the converse, see Exercise 9.28. □

9B The extensional equalities

Remark 9.9 Via the λ-mapping, the extensional equality relation $=_{\lambda\,ext}$ in λ-calculus induces the following relation between CL-terms:

$$X \;=_{ext\text{-}induced}\; Y \quad\Longleftrightarrow\quad X_\lambda \;=_{\lambda ext}\; Y_\lambda .$$

The main aim of the present section is to prove that this induced relation is the same as the relation $=_{C\,ext}$ defined in 8.5, i.e. to prove

$$X \;=_{C\,ext}\; Y \quad\Longleftrightarrow\quad X_\lambda \;=_{\lambda\,ext}\; Y_\lambda .$$

Our principal tool is the following mapping from Λ to $\mathcal{C}$.

Definition 9.10 (The H_η-mapping) With each λ-term M we associate a CL-term called M_{H_η} (or just M_H when no confusion is likely), thus:

(a) $x_{H_\eta} \equiv x$,

(b) $(MN)_{H_\eta} \equiv M_{H_\eta} N_{H_\eta}$,

(c) $(\lambda x.M)_{H_\eta} \equiv [x]^\eta.(M_{H_\eta})$. ('$[x]^\eta$' is the '$[x]$' defined in 2.18.)

Lemma 9.11 *For all CL-terms X:*

$$(X_\lambda)_{H_\eta} \;\equiv\; X.$$

Proof Induction on X. The cases $X \equiv x$, $X \equiv YZ$ are trivial. The other cases are $X \equiv \mathbf{S}, \mathbf{K}$ or $\mathbf{I}$, and for these we have:

$$\begin{aligned}
\mathbf{S}_{\lambda\,H} &\equiv (\lambda xyz.xz(yz))_H \\
&\equiv [x,y,z]^\eta.xz(yz) \quad \equiv \mathbf{S} \quad \text{by 2.25(b)};\\
\mathbf{K}_{\lambda\,H} &\equiv (\lambda xy.x)_H \\
&\equiv [x,y]^\eta.x \quad \equiv \mathbf{K} \quad \text{by 2.25(a)};\\
\mathbf{I}_{\lambda\,H} &\equiv (\lambda x.x)_H \\
&\equiv [x]^\eta.x \quad \equiv \mathbf{I} \quad \text{by 2.18(b)}.
\end{aligned}$$

□

Remark 9.12 Lemma 9.11 says the H_η-mapping reverses the effect of the λ-mapping; it is called a *left inverse* of the λ-mapping.

If we also had $(M_{H_\eta})_\lambda \equiv M$ for all λ-terms M, then H_η would be the

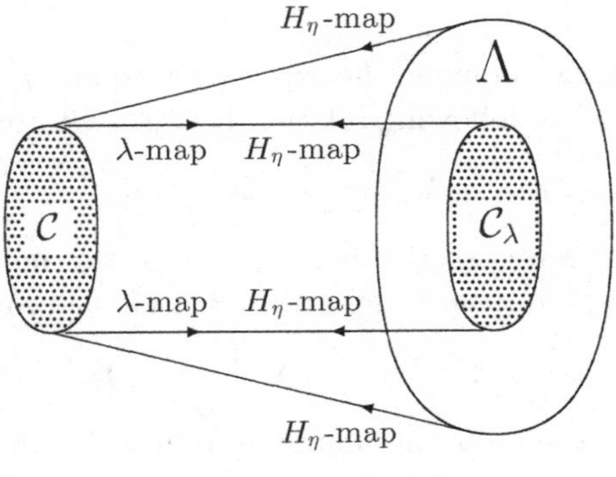

Fig. 9:1

(two-sided) inverse of the λ-mapping. But we do not have this, since, for example,

$$\big((\lambda u.vu)_{H_\eta}\big)_\lambda \;\equiv\; \big([u].vu\big)_\lambda \;\equiv\; v_\lambda \;\equiv\; v,$$

and $v \not\equiv \lambda u.vu$.

The λ-mapping takes $\mathcal{C}$ to $\mathcal{C}_\lambda \subset \Lambda$; see Figure 9:1. In Note 9.3 we saw that this mapping is one-to-one but its range is not the whole of Λ. On the other hand, by Lemma 9.11 the range of the H_η-mapping is the whole of $\mathcal{C}$.

It is easy to see that the H_η-mapping is not one-to-one. But when the domain of this mapping is restricted to $\mathcal{C}_\lambda$, it becomes one-to-one, and this restricted H_η-mapping becomes the two-sided inverse of the λ-mapping. (Because, for every $M \in \mathcal{C}_\lambda$ we have $M \equiv X_\lambda$ for an $X \in \mathcal{C}$, and hence

$$\begin{aligned}\big(M_{H_\eta}\big)_\lambda \;\equiv\; \big((X_\lambda)_{H_\eta}\big)_\lambda \;&\equiv\; X_\lambda \quad \text{by Lemma 9.11}\\ &\equiv\; M.)\end{aligned}$$

The next two lemmas will be needed in proving that $=_{C\,ext}$ corresponds to $=_{\lambda ext}$. In Lemma 9.13, part (b) is a special case of (d), but (b) must be proved before (d) can be proved.

Lemma 9.13 *For all λ-terms M and N:*

(a) $\mathrm{FV}(M_{H_\eta}) \;=\; \mathrm{FV}(M)$;

(b) $\big([y/x]M\big)_{H_\eta} \;\equiv\; [y/x]\big(M_{H_\eta}\big)$ *if y does not occur in M;*

(c) $M \equiv_\alpha N \implies M_{H_\eta} \equiv N_{H_\eta}$;

(d) $\big([N/x]M\big)_{H_\eta} \equiv [N_{H_\eta}/x]\big(M_{H_\eta}\big)$.

Proof Parts (a) and (b) come by straightforward inductions on M.

For (c): it is enough to prove that $(\lambda x.M)_{H_\eta} \equiv (\lambda y.[y/x]M)_{H_\eta}$ if $y \notin \mathrm{FV}(M)$. This is done as follows.

$$\begin{array}{rcccl} (\lambda x.M)_H & \equiv & [x]^\eta.(M_H) & \equiv & [y]^\eta.([y/x](M_H)) \quad \text{by 2.28(b)} \\ & & & \equiv & [y]^\eta.(([y/x]M)_H) \quad \text{by (b) above} \\ & & & \equiv & (\lambda y.[y/x]M)_H. \end{array}$$

For (d): by (b) and (c), it is enough to prove (d) when no variable bound in M is free in xN. This is done by induction on M. The cases that M is an atom or an application are routine. The remaining case is that $M \equiv \lambda y.P$ and $y \notin \mathrm{FV}(xN)$; then

$$\begin{array}{rcll} ([N/x](\lambda y.P))_H & \equiv & (\lambda y.[N/x]P)_H & \text{by 1.12(f)} \\ & \equiv & [y]^\eta.(([N/x]P)_H) & \text{by 9.10(c)} \\ & \equiv & [y]^\eta.([N_H/x](P_H)) & \text{by induc. hypoth.} \\ & \equiv & [N_H/x]([y]^\eta.(P_H)) & \text{by 2.28(c)} \\ & \equiv & [N_H/x]((\lambda y.P)_H) & \text{by 9.10(c).} \end{array}$$

□

Lemma 9.14 *For all λ-terms M and N:*

$$\lambda\beta\zeta \vdash M = N \quad\implies\quad \mathrm{CL}\zeta \vdash M_{H_\eta} = N_{H_\eta}.$$

Proof By 7.4 we can use $\lambda\beta\eta$ instead of $\lambda\beta\zeta$. We use induction on the definition of $\lambda\beta\eta$ in 6.2 and 7.2. Cases (ρ), (μ), (ν), (τ), (σ) are trivial because these rules of $\lambda\beta\eta$ are also rules of $\mathrm{CL}\zeta$. For case (α), use 9.13(c). For case (ξ): this rule is admissible in $\mathrm{CL}\zeta$ by 8.8.

Case (β): Let $M \equiv (\lambda x.P)Q$ and $N \equiv [Q/x]P$. Then

$$\begin{array}{rcccll} M_H & \equiv & ([x]^\eta.P_H)Q_H & =_w & [Q_H/x](P_H) & \text{by 2.21} \\ & & & \equiv & N_H & \text{by 9.13(d).} \end{array}$$

Case (η): Let $M \equiv \lambda x.Nx$ and $x \notin \mathrm{FV}(N)$. Then

$$M_H \equiv [x]^\eta.(N_H x) \equiv N_H \quad \text{by 2.18(c).}$$

□

Theorem 9.15 (Equivalence of extensional equalities) *For all CL-terms X and Y,*

$$X =_{C\,ext} Y \iff X_\lambda =_{\lambda\,ext} Y_\lambda.$$

Proof Part '⇒' is 9.5(c), and '⇐' comes from 9.11 and 9.14. □

By the way, $[\,]^\eta$ and the H_η-mapping have not been mentioned at all in the preceding theorem; they have simply been tools in its proof.

On the other hand, the next theorem will summarize all the main points of the correspondence between extensional λ and CL, including points involving H_η. Its proof will need the following lemma.

Lemma 9.16 *For all CL-terms Y:*

$$\big([x]^\eta.Y\big)_\lambda =_{\lambda\,ext} \lambda x.(Y_\lambda).$$

Proof

$$\begin{array}{lll} \big([x]^\eta.Y\big)_\lambda & =_\eta & \lambda x.\,\big(\big([x]^\eta.Y\big)_\lambda x\big) \quad \text{by } (\eta), \\ & \equiv & \lambda x.\,\big(([x]^\eta.Y)x\big)_\lambda \quad \text{by 9.2(c), (a)} \\ & =_\beta & \lambda x.(Y_\lambda) \quad \text{by 9.5(b) since } ([x]^\eta.Y)x =_w Y. \end{array}$$

□

Theorem 9.17 (Linking extensional λ and CL) *For all CL-terms X, Y and all λ-terms M, N:*

(a) $(X_\lambda)_{H_\eta} \equiv X;$

(b) $(M_{H_\eta})_\lambda =_{\lambda\,ext} M;$

(c) $X =_{C\,ext} Y \iff X_\lambda =_{\lambda\,ext} Y_\lambda;$

(d) $M =_{\lambda\,ext} N \iff M_{H_\eta} =_{C\,ext} N_{H_\eta}.$

Proof Part (a) is 9.11 and (c) is 9.15. For (d), '⇒' is 9.14, and '⇐' comes from (b) and (c). Part (b) is proved by induction on M. For example, if $M \equiv \lambda x.P$, then

$$\begin{array}{lll} (M_H)_\lambda & \equiv & \big([x]^\eta.(P_H)\big)_\lambda \\ & =_{\lambda\,ext} & \lambda x.\big((P_H)_\lambda\big) \quad \text{by 9.16} \\ & =_{\lambda\,ext} & \lambda x.P \quad \text{by induc. hypoth. and } (\xi). \end{array}$$

□

Discussion 9.18 (Reduction) The correspondence between λ and CL is nowhere near as neat for reduction as for equality. In λ, the 'extensional' reduction is $\triangleright_{\beta\eta}$ (Definition 7.8), and in CL it is $\succ\!\!-$ (Definition 8.15). It is easy to prove a one-way connection

$$M \triangleright_{\beta\eta} N \quad \Longrightarrow \quad M_{H_\eta} \succ\!\!- N_{H_\eta} \tag{1}$$

by a proof like that of Lemma 9.14. But if we ask for the converse of (1), we shall be disappointed, because $X \succ\!\!- Y$ does not imply $X_\lambda \triangleright_{\beta\eta} Y_\lambda$, but only $X_\lambda =_{\lambda ext} Y_\lambda$ (Exercise 9.19(b) below). Some of the problems involved were discussed in [Hin77, Section 3].

The lack of a two-way correspondence between the two reductions is no great drawback, however. Equality is the main thing, and all we should ask of a reduction-concept is that it helps in the study of equality (and, perhaps, that it behaves in some sense like the informal process of calculating the value of a function). Reduction's main use is to help us get results of the form '$X = Y$ is not provable in the theory of equality'.

Exercise 9.19 (Strong reduction and strong nfs)

(a) * Prove that the relation $\succ\!\!-$ is confluent (Theorem 8.18). (Hint: use 9.18(1) and the confluence of $\triangleright_{\beta\eta}$, 7.13.)

(b) * Find CL-terms X, Y such that $X \succ\!\!- Y$ but $X_\lambda \not\triangleright_{\beta\eta} Y_\lambda$.

(c) * Prove that, for all CL-terms X,

$$\begin{aligned} X \text{ is in strong nf} \quad &\Longleftrightarrow \quad X \equiv M_{H_\eta} \text{ for some } M \text{ in } \beta\eta\text{-nf} \\ &\Longleftrightarrow \quad X \equiv M_{H_\eta} \text{ for some } M \text{ in } \beta\text{-nf}. \end{aligned}$$

(d) Using (c) and 8.22(c) and 9.17, prove that, for all CL-terms X and λ-terms M,

(i) X has a strong nf iff X_λ has a $\beta\eta$-nf;

(ii) M has a $\beta\eta$-nf iff M_{H_η} has a strong nf.

(e) Using (d)(i) and 3.23, prove that, in CL, the **Y**-combinators in Definition 3.4 have no strong nf. (Though, as remarked in 3.23, they have weak nfs, and one is actually *in* weak nf.)

(f) In CL just as in λ, do not confuse *having* a nf with *being in* nf. Although every CL-term *in* strong nf is also in weak nf, it is possible for a CL-term X to *have* a strong nf without having a weak nf. Prove that **SK**(**SII**(**SII**)) is one such X.

9C New abstraction algorithms in CL

Having successfully connected the extensional equalities in λ and CL, it is natural to look next at β-equality.

However, for this we shall need a new definition of [ ]-abstraction in CL. The one used so far, Definition 2.18, contains the clause

$$\text{(c)} \qquad [x].Ux \;\equiv\; U \quad \text{if } x \notin \mathrm{FV}(U)$$

which is like axiom-scheme (η), and the latter is not admissible in the theory λβ. So, if we wish to find a correspondence between λβ and CL, we are unlikely to be helped much by $[\ ]^{\eta}$ and H_{η}: we must restrict or omit clause (c).

The following [ ]-definition is from [CF58, Section 6A algorithm (abf)] and [Bar84, Definition 7.1.5]; it simply omits (c).

Definition 9.20 (Weak abstraction) For all CL-terms Y, $[x]^{w}.Y$ is defined thus:

$$\begin{array}{lll} \text{(a)} & [x]^{w}.Y \;\equiv\; \mathsf{K}Y & \text{if } x \notin \mathrm{FV}(Y); \\ \text{(b)} & [x]^{w}.x \;\equiv\; \mathsf{I}; & \\ \text{(f)} & [x]^{w}.UV \equiv \mathsf{S}([x]^{w}.U)([x]^{w}.V) & \text{if } x \in \mathrm{FV}(UV). \end{array}$$

Remark 9.21 Weak abstraction was not used in Chapter 2 because the terms $[x]^{w}.Y$ it produces are in many cases much longer than $[x]^{\eta}.Y$. For example, calculate and compare

$$[x,y,z]^{w}.xz(yz), \qquad [x,y,z]^{\eta}.xz(yz).$$

Lemma 9.22 *For all CL-terms Y and Z:*

(a) $[x]^{w}.Y$ *is defined for all x and Y, and does not contain x;*

(b) $([x]^{w}.Y)Z \;\triangleright_{w}\; [Z/x]Y;$

(c) $[z]^{w}.[z/x]Y \;\equiv\; [x]^{w}.Y \quad$ *if* $z \notin \mathrm{FV}(Y)$*;*

(d) $[Z/v]([x]^{w}.Y) \;\equiv\; [x]^{w}.([Z/v]Y) \quad$ *if* $x \notin \mathrm{FV}(vZ)$*;*

(e) $\left([x]^{w}.Y\right)_{\lambda} \;=_{\beta}\; \lambda x.(Y_{\lambda}).$

Proof Parts (a) and (b) are proved together just like 2.21. Parts (c) and (d) are proved by a straightforward induction on Y, like 2.28(c). Part (e) also comes by induction on Y. □

Lemma 9.23 *For all CL-terms Y, $[x]^w.Y$ is functional in the sense of Definition 9.6.*

Proof Obvious from the definition of $[\ ]^w$. (This lemma does not hold for $[\ ]^\eta$, as the example $[x]^\eta.ux \equiv u$ shows.) □

Definition 9.24 (The H_w-mapping) For all λ-terms M, define M_{H_w} as in Definition 9.10, but using $[\ ]^w$ instead of $[\ ]^\eta$; in particular, define

$$(\lambda x.M)_{H_w} \equiv [x]^w.(M_{H_w}).$$

Lemma 9.25 *For all λ-terms M and N:*

(a) $\mathrm{FV}(M_{H_w}) = \mathrm{FV}(M)$;

(b) $M \equiv_\alpha N \implies M_{H_w} \equiv N_{H_w}$;

(c) $([N/x]M)_{H_w} \equiv [N_{H_w}/x](M_{H_w})$.

Proof Like the proof of 9.13. (The proof of (c) uses 9.22(d).) □

The above lemma shows that H_w has the same basic properties as H_η. We shall use these properties in the next section. But before doing that, it might be of interest to look at two other possible definitions of $[\ ]$-abstraction.

Remark 9.26 (Abstraction $[\ ]^{fab}$) The definition of $[\ ]^w$ could be made neater by restricting clause 9.20(a) to the case that Y is an atom, as in [CF58, Section 6A algorithm (fab)]. But this would make Lemma 9.22(d) fail. For example, calculate and compare

$$[uz/v]([x]^{fab}.v), \qquad [x]^{fab}.[uz/v]v\ .$$

And 9.22(d) is useful for comparing λ with CL, as it says substitution and $[x]^w$ behave very like substitution and λx in λ.

Remark 9.27 (Abstraction $[\ ]^\beta$) The H_w-mapping is not a left inverse of the λ-mapping, since by the example in Remark 9.21, $(\mathbf{S}_\lambda)_{H_w} \not\equiv \mathbf{S}$. In [CHS72, p. 71], Curry defined an abstraction, today called '$[\ ]^\beta$', which does not admit clause (c) in all cases but in just enough cases to give the property

$$(X_\lambda)_{H_\beta} \equiv X$$

to its associated mapping H_β. His definition consists of clauses 9.20(a) and (b), plus the following:

$$(\mathrm{c}_\beta) \quad [x]^\beta.Ux \equiv U \qquad \text{if } U \text{ is fnl and } x \notin \mathrm{FV}(U);$$

$$(\mathrm{f}_\beta) \quad [x]^\beta.UV \equiv \mathbf{S}([x]^\eta.U)([x]^\eta.V) \quad \text{if neither (a) nor } (\mathrm{c}_\beta) \text{ applies.}$$

Note the two 'η's in (f_β); their effect is to say that clause (c) can be used unrestrictedly in computing $[x]^\beta.Y$ if it is not the first clause used in the computation. (To see this, compute $[x,y,z]^\beta.xz(yz)$ and show that $(\mathbf{S}_\lambda)_{H_\beta} \equiv \mathbf{S}$.)

This definition is more complicated than $[\,]^\eta$ and $[\,]^w$ but has some of the virtues of both: like $[\,]^w$, $[x]^\beta.Y$ is functional for all Y, and like H_η, H_β is a left inverse of the λ-mapping.

But a cost of getting these virtues is that the useful Lemma 9.22(d) has to be weakened to

$$(\forall \text{ non-fnl } Z)\ \Big([Z/v]([x]^\beta.Y) \equiv [x]^\beta.([Z/v]Y) \ \text{ if } x \notin \mathrm{FV}(vZ) \Big).$$

By the way, both the H_β- and H_η-mappings are left inverses of the λ-mapping, but this does *not* imply that the two H-mappings are the same, because a mapping can have many left inverses (although it cannot have more than one two-sided inverse).

Exercise 9.28* For the reader who knows the standardization theorem, [Bar84, Theorem 11.4.7]: prove, using this theorem, that, for all CL-terms X, if $X_\lambda =_\beta \lambda x.M$ for some M, then X is weakly equal to a fnl term. (Hint: $[\,]^\beta$ and its associated H_β-mapping may be useful.)

9D Combinatory β-equality

The relation of β-equality in λ-calculus induces the following equality between CL-terms.

Definition 9.29 (Combinatory β-equality) For all CL-terms X and Y, define

$$X =_{C\beta} Y \iff X_\lambda =_\beta Y_\lambda.$$

The aim of this section is to find a new definition of $=_{C\beta}$ which is entirely within CL and does not mention λ.

Exercise 9.30 * It is easy to prove that $=_{C\beta}$ is intermediate between $=_w$ and $=_{C\,ext}$; i.e. to prove that

(a) $X =_w Y \implies X =_{C\beta} Y \implies X =_{C\,ext} Y.$

Show that these implications cannot be reversed, by proving

(b) $\mathsf{SK} =_{C\beta} \mathsf{KI}, \qquad \mathsf{SK} \neq_w \mathsf{KI};$

(c) $\mathsf{S(KI)} =_{C\,ext} \mathsf{I}, \qquad \mathsf{S(KI)} \neq_{C\beta} \mathsf{I}.$

Exercise 9.31 For all CL-terms X, prove that $\mathsf{K}(\mathsf{K}X)$ is a fixed point of S with respect to $=_{C\beta}$. That is, prove $\mathsf{S}(\mathsf{K}(\mathsf{K}X)) =_{C\beta} \mathsf{K}(\mathsf{K}X)$.

To re-define $=_{C\beta}$ without mentioning λ, we shall use the following formal theory. It is a modification of the theory CLζ in the previous chapter.

Definition 9.32 (The formal theory CLζ_β) CLζ_β is obtained by adding the following rule to the theory CLw of weak equality in Definition 6.5:

$$(\zeta_\beta) \qquad \frac{Ux = Vx}{U = V} \quad \text{if } x \notin \mathrm{FV}(UV) \text{ and } U,\ V \text{ are fnl.}$$

Example 9.33 CLζ_β $\vdash$ $\mathsf{SK} = \mathsf{KI}$.
To see this, first note that the following can be proved in CLw:

$$\mathsf{SK}yz \;=\; \mathsf{K}z(yz) \;=\; z \;=\; \mathsf{I}z.$$

Then rule (ζ_β) can be applied, since $\mathsf{SK}y$ and I are fnl, to give

$$\mathsf{SK}y \;=\; \mathsf{I}.$$

But CLw $\vdash$ $\mathsf{I} = \mathsf{KI}y$, so CL$\zeta_\beta$ $\vdash$ $\mathsf{SK}y = \mathsf{KI}y$. Since SK and KI are fnl, rule (ζ_β) can be applied to give

$$\mathsf{SK} \;=\; \mathsf{KI}.$$

Lemma 9.34 *For all CL-terms X, Y and λ-terms M, N:*

(a) $\mathrm{CL}\zeta_\beta \vdash X = Y \implies \lambda\beta \vdash X_\lambda = Y_\lambda;$

(b) $\lambda\beta \vdash M = N \implies \mathrm{CL}\zeta_\beta \vdash M_{H_w} = N_{H_w}.$

Proof (a) We use induction on the axiom-schemes and rules defining CLζ_β in 9.32 and 6.5. For those in CLw, see the proof of 9.5.

For rule (ζ_β): let $x \notin \mathrm{FV}(UV)$ and U, V be fnl CL-terms, and suppose, as induction hypothesis, that $(Ux)_\lambda =_\beta (Vx)_\lambda$. We must deduce that $U_\lambda =_\beta V_\lambda$. By 9.7(a), there exist λ-terms M, N such that

$$U_\lambda \rhd_\beta \lambda x.M, \qquad V_\lambda \rhd_\beta \lambda x.N.$$

Hence

$$\begin{array}{llll} U_\lambda =_\beta \lambda x.M & =_\beta & \lambda x.((\lambda x.M)x) & \text{since } (\lambda x.M)x \rhd_\beta M, \\ & =_\beta & \lambda x.(U_\lambda x) & \text{since } U_\lambda \rhd_\beta \lambda x.M, \\ & =_\beta & \lambda x.(V_\lambda x) & \text{by induc. hypoth.,} \\ & =_\beta & V_\lambda & \text{similarly.} \end{array}$$

(b) We use induction on the definition of $\lambda\beta$ in 6.2. For cases (α) and (β), use 9.25(b) and (c). Cases (ρ), (μ), (ν), (τ), (σ) are easy.

For case (ξ): suppose, as induction hypothesis, that

$$\mathrm{CL}\zeta_\beta \ \vdash \ M_{H_w} = N_{H_w}.$$

We must deduce $(\lambda x.M)_{H_w} = (\lambda x.N)_{H_w}$, that is $[x]^w.M_{H_w} = [x]^w.N_{H_w}$. Now, by 2.21,

$$([x]^w.M_{H_w})x =_w M_{H_w},$$

and similarly for N; so

$$\mathrm{CL}\zeta_\beta \ \vdash \ ([x]^w.M_{H_w})x = ([x]^w.N_{H_w})x.$$

But $[x]^w.M_{H_w}$ and $[x]^w.N_{H_w}$ are fnl by 9.23, so rule (ζ_β) applies, giving

$$\mathrm{CL}\zeta_\beta \ \vdash \ [x]^w.M_{H_w} = [x]^w.N_{H_w}.$$

□

Lemma 9.35 *For all CL-terms X:*

$$\mathrm{CL}\zeta_\beta \ \vdash \ (X_\lambda)_{H_w} = X.$$

Proof We use induction on X. The cases $X \equiv YZ$, $X \equiv x$ and $X \equiv \mathbf{I}$ are easy, and the case $X \equiv \mathbf{K}$ is like $X \equiv \mathbf{S}$. For $X \equiv \mathbf{S}$, we have

$$\begin{array}{lll} (\mathbf{S}_\lambda)_{H_w} uvw \ \equiv \ ([x,y,z]^w.xz(yz))uvw & =_w & uw(vw) \\ & =_w & \mathbf{S}uvw. \end{array}$$

Also $\mathbf{S}uv$, $\mathbf{S}u$, $\mathbf{S}$ and $(\mathbf{S}_\lambda)_{H_w}$ are fnl, and $(\mathbf{S}_\lambda)_{H_w}uv$ and $(\mathbf{S}_\lambda)_{H_w}u$ can easily be weakly reduced to fnl terms, so rule (ζ_β) can be applied three times to give

$$\mathrm{CL}\zeta_\beta \ \vdash \ (\mathbf{S}_\lambda)_{H_w} = \mathbf{S}.$$

□

Theorem 9.36 (Equivalence of β-equalities) *The equality $=_{C\beta}$, induced on CL-terms by $=_\beta$ in λ-calculus, is the same as the equality determined by the formal theory* $\mathrm{CL}\zeta_\beta$*; i.e. for all CL-terms X and Y,*

$$\begin{aligned} X =_{C\beta} Y \quad &\Longleftrightarrow \quad X_\lambda =_\beta Y_\lambda \\ &\Longleftrightarrow \quad \mathrm{CL}\zeta_\beta \ \vdash \ X = Y. \end{aligned}$$

Proof The first '$\Longleftrightarrow$' is Definition 9.29. For the second: '$\Leftarrow$' is 9.34(a), and '$\Rightarrow$' comes from 9.34(b) and 9.35. □

Theorem 9.37 (Summary) *For all CL-terms X and Y, and λ-terms M and N:*

(a) $(X_\lambda)_{H_w} \ =_{C\beta} \ X;$

(b) $(M_{H_w})_\lambda \ =_\beta \ M;$

(c) $X =_{C\beta} Y \quad \Longleftrightarrow \quad X_\lambda =_\beta Y_\lambda \quad \Longleftrightarrow \quad \mathrm{CL}\zeta_\beta \ \vdash \ X = Y;$

(d) $M =_\beta N \quad \Longleftrightarrow \quad M_{H_w} \ =_{C\beta} \ N_{H_w}.$

Proof Part (a) is 9.35 with 9.36, and (c) is just 9.36. Part (b) is proved by induction on M like 9.17(b), using 9.22(e).

For (d): '$\Leftarrow$' comes from (b) and (c), and '$\Rightarrow$' is 9.34(b). □

Remark 9.38 (Axioms for β-equality) It is possible to find axioms for $=_{C\beta}$, just as was done for extensional equality in Section 8B. A suitable set of five axioms is in [CF58, Section 6C4, p. 203]. Another set (for the version of CL in which **I** is not an atom) is the set A_β in [Bar84, Definition 7.3.6]. (Two members of that set are redundant, namely (A.1′) and (A.2′), as stated in the proof of [Bar84, Corollary 7.3.15].)

We shall never need the details of these axioms in the present book, but the formal theory obtained by adding them to CLw will be mentioned several times; it will be called

$$\mathrm{CL}\beta_{ax}.$$

Remark 9.39 (Rule (ξ) again) A CL-version of rule (ξ) was introduced in the last chapter (Notation 8.1); in the present chapter's notation, it says

$$(\xi) \qquad \frac{X = Y}{[x]^\eta.X = [x]^\eta.Y.}$$

The corresponding theory CLξ was proved equivalent to CLζ. It is natural to ask whether there is a modified version of (ξ) that would produce a theory equivalent to CLζ_β.

An obvious first attempt is to change $[\ ]^\eta$ to $[\ ]^w$. But this fails: the resulting theory CLξ turns out strictly weaker than CLζ_β, [BHS89, Section 6]. A second attempt is to change $[\ ]^\eta$ to the $[\ ]^\beta$ that was defined in Remark 9.27. This succeeds.

In more detail: let the formal theory CLξ_β be defined by adding to CLw (the theory of weak equality in Definition 6.5) the rule

$$(\xi_\beta) \qquad \frac{X = Y}{[x]^\beta.X = [x]^\beta.Y.}$$

Then the following theorem holds.

Theorem 9.40 *The equality determined by* CLξ_β *is the same as* $=_{C\beta}$*; i.e., for all CL-terms* X, Y,

$$\text{CL}\xi_\beta \ \vdash \ X = Y \qquad \Longleftrightarrow \qquad X =_{C\beta} Y.$$

Proof By 9.36, it is enough to prove that CL$\xi_\beta \ \vdash \ X = Y$ iff CL$\zeta_\beta \vdash X = Y$. This is done in [BHS89, Theorem 4]. □

Remark 9.41 (β-strong reduction) Several definitions of reduction have been proposed for $=_{C\beta}$, but unfortunately none is very easy to work with. If we simply modified the definition of strong reduction (Definition 8.15) by changing abstraction from $[\ ]^\eta$ to $[\ ]^w$, we would get a reduction that is not confluent (pointed out by Bruce Lercher in correspondence and discussed in [Hin77, Section 3]). If we changed abstraction to $[\ ]^\beta$, we would get confluence but not some other desirable properties.

Several other alternative β-strong reductions have been proposed. The one defined by Mohamed Mezghiche in [Mez89, Section 2] has the fewest snags; it depends on an ingenious modification to the definition of $[\ ]$.

10
Simple typing, Church-style

10A Simple types

In mathematics the definition of a particular function usually includes a statement of the kind of inputs it will accept, and the kind of outputs it will produce. For example, the squaring function accepts integers n as inputs and produces integers n^2 as outputs, and the zero-test function accepts integers and produces Boolean values ('true' or 'false' according as the input is zero or not).

Corresponding to this way of defining functions, λ and CL can be modified by attaching expressions called 'types' to terms, like labels to denote their intended input and output sets. In fact almost all programming languages that use λ and CL use versions with types.

This chapter and the next two will describe two different approaches to attaching types to terms: (i) called *Church-style* or sometimes *explicit* or *rigid*, and (ii) called *Curry-style* or sometimes *implicit*. Both are used extensively in programming.

The Church-style approach originated in [Chu40], and is described in the present chapter. In it, a term's type is a built-in part of the term itself, rather like a person's fingerprint or eye-colour is a built-in part of the person's body. (In Curry's approach a term's type will be assigned after the term has been built, like a passport or identity-card may be given to a person some time after birth.)

The first step is to define expressions called 'types' (or 'simple types' to distinguish them from other more complicated type-systems.)

Definition 10.1 (Simple types) Assume we have a finite or infinite sequence of symbols called *atomic types*; then we define *types* as follows.

(a) every atomic type is a type;

(b) if σ and τ are types, then the expression $(\sigma \to \tau)$ is a type, called a *function type*.

Comments 10.2 An atomic type is intended to denote a particular set; for example we may have the atomic type N for the set of natural numbers, and H for the set of Boolean values {'true', 'false'}. In general, the atomic types will depend on the intended use of the system we wish to build.[1]

A function type $(\sigma \to \tau)$ is intended to denote some given set of *functions from σ to τ*. That is, functions which accept as inputs the members of the set denoted by σ, and produce outputs in the set denoted by τ. In mathematical language, the *domain* of such a function is the set denoted by σ, and its *range* is a subset of the set denoted by τ.

The exact set of functions denoted by $(\sigma \to \tau)$ will depend on the intended use of whatever system of typed terms we build. For example, it might be the set of *all* functions from σ to τ, or just the *computable* functions from σ to τ. When this set of functions is specified, then every type comes to denote a set of individuals or functions. For example,

$(\mathsf{N} \to \mathsf{N})$:	functions from numbers to numbers;
$(\mathsf{N} \to \mathsf{H})$:	functions from numbers to Boolean values;
$(\mathsf{N} \to (\mathsf{N} \to \mathsf{N}))$:	functions from numbers to functions;
$((\mathsf{N} \to \mathsf{N}) \to \mathsf{N})$:	functions from functions to numbers;
$((\mathsf{N} \to \mathsf{N}) \to (\mathsf{N} \to \mathsf{N}))$:	functions from functions to functions;
etc.	

Notation Lower-case Greek letters will denote arbitrary types. We shall use the abbreviations

$$\begin{array}{lll} \sigma \to \tau & \text{for} & (\sigma \to \tau), \\ \rho \to \sigma \to \tau & \text{for} & (\rho \to (\sigma \to \tau)), \\ \sigma_1 \to \ldots \to \sigma_n \to \tau & \text{for} & (\sigma_1 \to (\ldots \to (\sigma_n \to \tau)\ldots)). \end{array}$$

(*Warning*: an expression such as '$\sigma \to \tau$' containing Greek letters is not itself a type; it is only a name in the meta-language for an unspecified type.)[2]

[1] In many works on type-theory an atomic type 0 is used for the set of all natural numbers. We use N here instead to avoid confusion with the number zero.

[2] By the way, although '$\sigma \to \tau$' is now the standard notation for function-types, older writers used different notations: for example '$\mathsf{F}\sigma\tau$' (used by Curry and, in early works, by the present authors), '$\tau\sigma$' (used by Church and his former students), also '$\sigma\tau$', 'τ^{σ}' and '${}^{\sigma}\tau$' (by various writers).

10B Typed λ-calculus

Definition 10.3 (Typed variables) Assume that there is given an infinite sequence of expressions $\mathbf{v}_0$, $\mathbf{v}_{00}$, $\mathbf{v}_{000}$, ... called *untyped variables* (compare Definition 1.1). We make *typed variables* x^τ by attaching type-superscripts to untyped variables, in such a way that

(a) (*consistency condition*) no untyped variable receives more than one type, i.e. we do not make x^τ, x^σ with $\tau \not\equiv \sigma$;

(b) every type τ is attached to an infinite sequence of variables.

Note 10.4 We call x^τ a *variable of type* τ; it is intended to denote an arbitrary member of whatever set is denoted by τ. Condition (a) ensures that, for example, if we make a typed variable x^{N}, to denote an arbitrary number, we cannot also make $x^{\mathsf{N}\to\mathsf{N}}$, which would denote a function.

Condition (b) ensures that, roughly speaking, for every τ, there are enough variables to discuss as many members of this set as we like.

There are many ways of attaching types to variables to satisfy (a) and (b). The details will not matter in this book, but here is one way of doing it. First, list all the untyped variables, without repetitions (call them v_1, v_2, v_3, ... for convenience, instead of $\mathbf{v}_0$, $\mathbf{v}_{00}$, $\mathbf{v}_{000}$, ...), and list all the types, without repetitions (call them τ_1, τ_2, τ_3, ...). Then, for each $i \geq 1$, attach τ_i to all of

$$v_{\psi(i,1)},\ v_{\psi(i,2)},\ v_{\psi(i,3)},\ \ldots,$$

where ψ is a function that maps $\mathbb{N}^{\mathrm{pos}} \times \mathbb{N}^{\mathrm{pos}}$ one-to-one onto $\mathbb{N}^{\mathrm{pos}}$, where $\mathbb{N}^{\mathrm{pos}} = \{1, 2, 3, \ldots\}$. Many such functions ψ are known; one is

$$\psi(i,j) \quad = \quad j + \frac{(i+j-2)(i+j-1)}{2}.$$

Definition 10.5 (Simply typed λ-terms) Assume that, besides the typed variables, we have a (perhaps empty) finite or infinite sequence of expressions called *typed atomic constants*, c^τ, each with an attached type. Then the set of all *typed λ-terms* is defined as follows:

(a) all typed variables x^τ and atomic constants c^τ are typed λ-terms of type τ;

(b) if $M^{\sigma\to\tau}$ and N^{σ} are typed λ-terms of types $\sigma\to\tau$ and σ respectively, then the following is a typed λ-term of type τ:

$$(M^{\sigma\to\tau}N^{\sigma})^{\tau};$$

(c) if x^{σ} is a variable of type σ and M^{τ} is a typed λ-term of type τ, then the following is a typed λ-term of type $\sigma\to\tau$:

$$(\lambda x^{\sigma}.M^{\tau})^{\sigma\to\tau}.$$

Note 10.6 A typed term M^{τ} is intended to denote a member of whatever set is denoted by τ. The clauses of the above definition have been chosen with this intention in mind; for example, in (b), if $M^{\sigma\to\tau}$ denotes a function ϕ from σ to τ, and N^{σ} denotes a member a of σ, then the term $(M^{\sigma\to\tau}N^{\sigma})^{\tau}$ denotes $\phi(a)$, which is in τ.

The atomic constants might include atoms $\overline{0}^{\mathsf{N}}$ and $\overline{\sigma}^{\mathsf{N}\to\mathsf{N}}$ to denote zero and the successor function.

When writing typed terms, type-superscripts will often be omitted when it is obvious from the context what they should be. Other notation-conventions for terms will be the same as in Chapter 1.

Example 10.7 For every type σ, the following is a typed term:

$$\mathsf{I}_{\sigma} \equiv (\lambda x^{\sigma}.x^{\sigma})^{\sigma\to\sigma}.$$

It may be written informally as $(\lambda x^{\sigma}.x)^{\sigma\to\sigma}$ or $(\lambda x.x)^{\sigma\to\sigma}$ or simply

$$\lambda x^{\sigma}.x.$$

Example 10.8 For every pair of types σ and τ, the following is a typed term:

$$\mathsf{K}_{\sigma,\tau} \equiv \left(\lambda x^{\sigma}.(\lambda y^{\tau}.x^{\sigma})^{\tau\to\sigma}\right)^{\sigma\to(\tau\to\sigma)}.$$

It may be written as $(\lambda x^{\sigma}y^{\tau}.x)^{\sigma\to(\tau\to\sigma)}$ or $(\lambda xy.x)^{\sigma\to(\tau\to\sigma)}$ or

$$\lambda x^{\sigma}y^{\tau}.x.$$

Example 10.9 For every triple of types ρ, σ and τ, the following is a typed term, called $\mathsf{S}_{\rho,\sigma,\tau}$:

$$\left(\lambda x^{\rho\to\sigma\to\tau}.\left(\lambda y^{\rho\to\sigma}.\left(\lambda z^{\rho}.\left((x^{\rho\to\sigma\to\tau}z^{\rho})^{\sigma\to\tau}(y^{\rho\to\sigma}z^{\rho})^{\sigma}\right)^{\tau}\right)^{\rho\to\tau}\right)^{\delta}\right)^{\theta},$$

where

$$\delta \equiv (\rho \to \sigma) \to (\rho \to \tau),$$
$$\theta \equiv (\rho \to \sigma \to \tau) \to (\rho \to \sigma) \to \rho \to \tau.$$

To check that this expression satisfies the definition of typed term, it is best to look at its construction step by step. First, $x^{\rho\to\sigma\to\tau}$, $y^{\rho\to\sigma}$ and z^{ρ} are typed terms by Definition 10.5(a). Then the expressions

$$(x^{\rho\to\sigma\to\tau} z^{\rho})^{\sigma\to\tau}, \qquad (y^{\rho\to\sigma} z^{\rho})^{\sigma}$$

are typed terms by 10.5(b). Hence the expression

$$\big(\,(x^{\rho\to\sigma\to\tau} z^{\rho})^{\sigma\to\tau}\;(y^{\rho\to\sigma} z^{\rho})^{\sigma}\big)^{\tau}$$

is a typed term, again by 10.5(b). Next, the expression

$$\big(\,\lambda z^{\rho}\,.\,\big(\,(x^{\rho\to\sigma\to\tau} z^{\rho})^{\sigma\to\tau}\;(y^{\rho\to\sigma} z^{\rho})^{\sigma}\big)^{\tau}\,\big)^{\rho\to\tau}$$

is a typed term by 10.5(c). Finally, by 10.5(c) used twice more, the whole expression $\mathbf{S}_{\rho,\sigma,\tau}$ is a typed term.

This procedure, for constructing $\mathbf{S}_{\rho,\sigma,\tau}$ and checking that types are correct at each step, can be displayed as a tree-diagram, see below. The same procedure will crop up again in a different context in the next chapter.

$$\dfrac{\dfrac{\dfrac{\dfrac{\dfrac{x^{\rho\to\sigma\to\tau} \qquad z^{\rho}}{(xz)^{\sigma\to\tau}} \qquad \dfrac{y^{\rho\to\sigma} \qquad z^{\rho}}{(yz)^{\sigma}}}{(xz(yz))^{\tau}}}{(\lambda z^{\rho}.(xz(yz))^{\tau})^{\rho\to\tau}}}{(\lambda y^{\rho\to\sigma}.(\lambda z.xz(yz))^{\rho\to\tau})^{\delta}}}{(\lambda x^{\rho\to\sigma\to\tau}.(\lambda yz.xz(yz))^{\delta})^{\theta}.}$$

Notation As mentioned before, type-superscripts are often omitted; for example, this was done in several places in the preceding tree-diagram to avoid obscuring the main structure. The term $\mathbf{S}_{\rho,\sigma,\tau}$ may be written as

$$(\lambda xyz.xz(yz))^{(\rho\to\sigma\to\tau)\to(\rho\to\sigma)\to\rho\to\tau}$$

or

$$\lambda x^{\rho\to\sigma\to\tau} y^{\rho\to\sigma} z^{\rho}.xz(yz).$$

Definition 10.10 (Substitution) $[N^\sigma/x^\sigma](M^\tau)$ is defined in the same way as the substitution of untyped terms in Definition 1.12.

It is routine to check that $[N^\sigma/x^\sigma](M^\tau)$ is a typed term of type τ. Note that we do not define $[N^\rho/x^\sigma](M^\tau)$ when $\rho \not\equiv \sigma$.

Lemma 10.11

(a) In a typed term M^τ, if we replace an occurrence of a typed term P^σ by another term of type σ, then the result is a typed term of type τ.

(b) (for α-conversion) If $(\lambda x^\sigma . M^\tau)^{\sigma\to\tau}$ is a typed term, then so is $(\lambda y^\sigma . [y^\sigma/x^\sigma]M^\tau)^{\sigma\to\tau}$, and both terms have the same type.

(c) (for β-conversion) If $\left((\lambda x^\sigma . M^\tau)^{\sigma\to\tau} N^\sigma\right)^\tau$ is a typed term, then so is $[N^\sigma/x^\sigma]M^\tau$, and both terms have the same type.

Proof Tedious but straightforward. □

All the lemmas on substitution and α-conversion in Chapter 1 and Appendix A1 hold for typed terms, with unchanged proofs.

Definition 10.12 (Simply typed β-equality and reduction) The formal theory of simply typed β-equality will be called $\lambda\beta^\to$.[3] It has equations $M^\sigma = N^\sigma$ as its formulas, and the following as its axiom-schemes and rules:

(α) $\lambda x^\sigma . M^\tau \;=\; \lambda y^\sigma . [y^\sigma/x^\sigma]M^\tau$ if $y^\sigma \notin \mathrm{FV}(M^\tau)$;

(β) $\left((\lambda x^\sigma . M^\tau)^{\sigma\to\tau} N^\sigma\right)^\tau \;=\; [N^\sigma/x^\sigma]M^\tau$;

(ρ) $M^\sigma \;=\; M^\sigma$;

(μ) $M^\sigma = N^\sigma \;\vdash\; P^{\sigma\to\tau}M^\sigma = P^{\sigma\to\tau}N^\sigma$;

(ν) $M^{\sigma\to\tau} = N^{\sigma\to\tau} \;\vdash\; M^{\sigma\to\tau}P^\sigma = N^{\sigma\to\tau}P^\sigma$;

(ξ) $M^\tau = N^\tau \;\vdash\; \lambda x^\sigma . M^\tau = \lambda x^\sigma . N^\tau$;

(τ) $M^\sigma = N^\sigma,\; N^\sigma = P^\sigma \;\vdash\; M^\sigma = P^\sigma$.

(σ) $M^\sigma = N^\sigma \;\vdash\; N^\sigma = M^\sigma$;

[3] It is very like the systems called '$\lambda\!\to$-Church' in [Bar92, Section 3.2] and '$\lambda^\to$' in [Mit96].

The formal theory of simply typed β-reduction will be called $\lambda\beta^{\rightarrow}$ like that of equality. Its axioms and rules are the same as above but with (σ) omitted and '=' replaced by '$\triangleright$'.

For provability in these theories we shall write

$$\lambda\beta^{\rightarrow} \vdash M^{\sigma} = N^{\sigma}, \qquad \lambda\beta^{\rightarrow} \vdash M^{\sigma} \triangleright N^{\sigma}.$$

Note 10.12.1 By induction on the above clauses it can be seen that if $M^{\sigma} = N^{\tau}$ or $M^{\sigma} \triangleright N^{\tau}$ is provable in $\lambda\beta^{\rightarrow}$, then $\sigma \equiv \tau$. Hence, if $\sigma \not\equiv \tau$ then no equation $M^{\sigma} = N^{\tau}$ can be proved in $\lambda\beta^{\rightarrow}$. In particular, if $\sigma \not\equiv \tau$ then

$$(\lambda x^{\sigma}.x^{\sigma})^{\sigma\rightarrow\sigma} \not\equiv_{\alpha} (\lambda y^{\tau}.y^{\tau})^{\tau\rightarrow\tau}.$$

Remark 10.13 *Redex, contraction, reduction* ($\triangleright_{\beta}$), and *β-normal form* are defined in typed λ exactly as in untyped λ, see 1.24 and 1.26. It is routine to prove that

(a) $\quad M^{\sigma} \triangleright_{\beta} N^{\tau} \quad\Longrightarrow\quad \sigma \equiv \tau,$

(b) $\quad M^{\sigma} \triangleright_{\beta} N^{\sigma} \quad\Longleftrightarrow\quad \lambda\beta^{\rightarrow} \vdash M^{\sigma} \triangleright N^{\sigma}.$

Also, *β-equality* ($=_{\beta}$) is defined as in 1.37, and it is routine to prove that

(c) $\quad M^{\sigma} =_{\beta} N^{\sigma} \quad\Longleftrightarrow\quad \lambda\beta^{\rightarrow} \vdash M^{\sigma} = N^{\sigma}.$

All the other properties of reduction and equality in Chapter 1 hold for typed terms, with the same proofs as before. Note in particular the *substitution lemmas* (1.31 and 1.40), the *Church–Rosser theorems* (1.32, 1.41 and A2.16), and the *uniqueness of normal forms* (1.41.4).

Besides these properties, typed λ has one extra property that untyped λ does not have, and which plays a key role in all its applications. It will be stated in the next theorem. First recall the definitions of *reductions* and *reductions with maximal length* in 3.15 and 3.16.

Definition 10.14 (Normalizability, WN, SN) In a typed or untyped λ-calculus, a term M is called *normalizable* or *weakly normalizable* or *WN* iff it has a normal form. It is called *strongly normalizable* or *SN* iff all reductions starting at M have finite length.

Clearly SN implies WN. To illustrate, consider the untyped terms

$$\Omega \equiv (\lambda x.xx)(\lambda x.xx), \qquad T_2 \equiv (\lambda x.y)\Omega, \qquad T_3 \equiv (\lambda x.y)(\lambda x.x).$$

The first has an infinite reduction $\Omega \triangleright_1 \Omega \triangleright_1$ etc., and has no normal form, so it is neither SN nor WN. The second has (at least) two reductions, one finite and the other infinite:

$$(\lambda x.y)\Omega \rhd_1 y, \qquad (\lambda x.y)\Omega \rhd_1 (\lambda x.y)\Omega \rhd_1 \ldots$$

Thus T_2 is WN but not SN. Finally, T_3 has no infinite reduction, so T_3 is both SN and WN.

One can think of an SN term as being 'safe' in the sense that it cannot lead to an endless computation. And in this view a WN term is a term T that can be reduced to a safe term (although, like T_2 above, T itself might not be safe).

Theorem 10.15 (SN for simply typed $\rhd_\beta$) *In the simply typed λ-calculus $\lambda\beta^{\rightarrow}$, all terms are SN, i.e. no infinite β-reductions are possible.*

Proof See Appendix A3, Theorem A3.3. □

Corollary 10.15.1 (WN for simply typed $\rhd_\beta$) *Every typed term M^τ in $\lambda\beta^{\rightarrow}$ has a β-normal form $M^{*\tau}$. Further, all β-reductions of M^τ which have maximal length end at $M^{*\tau}$.*

Proof By 10.15 and the Church–Rosser confluence theorem. □

Corollary 10.15.2 *In simply typed λ-calculus the relation $=_\beta$ is decidable.*

Proof (Decidability was defined at the end of 5.4.) To decide whether $M^\sigma =_\beta N^\tau$, reduce both terms to their normal forms, by 10.15.1, and decide whether these are identical. By 1.41.2, this is enough. □

The above theorem and its corollaries contrast strongly with untyped λ, in which reductions may be infinitely long and there is no decision-procedure for the relation $=_\beta$ (Corollary 5.6.3). They say that the world of typed terms is completely safe, in the sense that all computations terminate and their results are unique.

Having looked at typed β, we turn next to $\beta\eta$ (compare Chapter 7).

Definition 10.16 (Simply typed $\beta\eta$) The equality-theory $\lambda\beta\eta^{\rightarrow}$ is defined by adding to Definition 10.12 ($\lambda\beta^{\rightarrow}$) the following axiom-scheme:

$$(\eta) \qquad (\lambda x^\sigma.(M^{\sigma\rightarrow\tau}x^\sigma)^\tau)^{\sigma\rightarrow\tau} = M^{\sigma\rightarrow\tau} \qquad \text{if } x^\sigma \notin \mathrm{FV}(M^{\sigma\rightarrow\tau}).$$

The reduction-theory $\lambda\beta\eta^{\rightarrow}$ is defined similarly (using '$\triangleright$' instead of '$=$'). The notations *η-redex*, *η-contraction*, *η-reduction*, $\triangleright_\eta$, *βη-reduction*, $\triangleright_{\beta\eta}$ and *βη-normal form* are defined as in 7.7–7.9.

Remark 10.17 The main properties of the untyped $\beta\eta$-system were stated in 7.11–7.16; these hold for the typed system as well, and the proofs are the same. The SN theorem also holds for typed $\beta\eta$-reductions; see Theorem A3.13 in Appendix A3. Hence Corollaries 10.15.1 and 10.15.2 also extend to $\beta\eta$.

Remark 10.18 (Representability of functions) In Chapter 4 it was shown that all recursive functions can be represented in untyped λ, in the sense of Definition 4.5. It is natural to ask what subset of these functions can be represented by typed terms.

By Corollary 10.15.1, every function that is representable by a typed term must be total.

In [Sch76], Helmut Schwichtenberg showed that if we represent the natural numbers by typed analogues of the Church numerals in Definition 4.2, the functions representable by typed terms form a very limited class; namely the polynomials and the conditional function 'if $x = 0$ then y else z', and certain simple combinations of these. This class is often called the *extended polynomials*; see [TS00, p. 21] for its precise definition.

10C Typed CL

The types for typed CL-terms are the same as those for λ-terms, see Definition 10.1.

Definition 10.19 (Simply typed CL-terms) Assume we have *typed variables* as in Definition 10.3. Assume we have an infinite number of *typed atomic constants*, including the following ones, called *basic combinators*, with types as shown:

$$\mathsf{I}^{\sigma\to\sigma} \quad \text{(one constant for each type } \sigma\text{);}$$

$$\mathsf{K}^{\sigma\to\tau\to\sigma} \quad \text{(one for each pair } \sigma,\tau\text{);}$$

$$\mathsf{S}^{(\rho\to\sigma\to\tau)\to(\rho\to\sigma)\to\rho\to\tau} \quad \text{(one for each triple } \rho,\sigma,\tau\text{).}$$

Then we define *typed CL-terms* as follows:

(a) all the typed variables and typed atomic constants (including the basic combinators) are typed CL-terms;

(b) if $X^{\sigma\to\tau}$ and Y^{σ} are typed CL-terms, with types as shown, then the following is a typed CL-term of type τ:

$$(X^{\sigma\to\tau}Y^{\sigma})^{\tau}.$$

Notation 10.20 Type-superscripts will often be omitted. The notation conventions for CL-terms from Chapter 2 will be used.

The typed basic combinators will often be abbreviated to

$$\mathsf{I}_{\sigma}, \qquad \mathsf{K}_{\sigma,\tau}, \qquad \mathsf{S}_{\rho,\sigma,\tau}.$$

Their types are motivated by the types of their λ-counterparts in Examples 10.7–10.9.[4]

Definition 10.21 *Substitution* $[U^{\sigma}/x^{\sigma}](Y^{\tau})$ is defined just as for untyped terms in Definition 2.6. (We do not define $[U^{\rho}/x^{\sigma}](X^{\tau})$ when $\rho \not\equiv \sigma$.)

Just as for λ-terms, $[U^{\sigma}/x^{\sigma}](X^{\tau})$ can be shown to be a typed term with the same type as X^{τ}.

Definition 10.22 (Simply typed weak equality and reduction) The formal theory of simply typed weak equality will be called $\mathrm{CL}w^{\to}$. It has equations $X^{\sigma} = Y^{\sigma}$ as its formulas, and the following as its axiom-schemes and rules:

(I) $\mathsf{I}_{\sigma}X^{\sigma} = X^{\sigma}$;

(K) $\mathsf{K}_{\sigma,\tau}X^{\sigma}Y^{\tau} = X^{\sigma}$;

(S) $\mathsf{S}_{\rho,\sigma,\tau}X^{\rho\to\sigma\to\tau}Y^{\rho\to\sigma}Z^{\rho} = X^{\rho\to\sigma\to\tau}Z^{\rho}(Y^{\rho\to\sigma}Z^{\rho})$;

(ρ) $X^{\sigma} = X^{\sigma}$;

(μ) $X^{\sigma} = Y^{\sigma} \ \vdash\ Z^{\sigma\to\tau}X^{\sigma} = Z^{\sigma\to\tau}Y^{\sigma}$;

(ν) $X^{\sigma\to\tau} = Y^{\sigma\to\tau} \ \vdash\ X^{\sigma\to\tau}Z^{\sigma} = Y^{\sigma\to\tau}Z^{\sigma}$;

(τ) $X^{\sigma} = Y^{\sigma},\ Y^{\sigma} = Z^{\sigma} \ \vdash\ X^{\sigma} = Z^{\sigma}$;

(σ) $X^{\sigma} = Y^{\sigma} \ \vdash\ Y^{\sigma} = X^{\sigma}$.

[4] An alternative motivation independent of λ was given in [CF58, Section 8C].

The formal theory of simply typed weak reduction will be called $CLw^{\rightarrow}$ like that of equality. Its axioms and rules are the same as above but with (σ) omitted and '=' replaced by '$\triangleright$'.

For provability in these theories we shall write

$$CLw^{\rightarrow} \vdash X^{\sigma} = Y^{\sigma}, \qquad CLw^{\rightarrow} \vdash X^{\sigma} \triangleright Y^{\sigma}.$$

Remark 10.23 *Redex, contraction, reduction,* $\triangleright_w$ and *weak normal form* are defined in typed CL exactly as in untyped CL, see 2.9 and 2.10. It is routine to prove that

(a) $X^{\sigma} \triangleright_w Y^{\tau} \implies \sigma \equiv \tau$,

(b) $X^{\sigma} \triangleright_w Y^{\sigma} \iff CLw^{\rightarrow} \vdash X^{\sigma} \triangleright Y^{\sigma}$.

Also, *weak equality* ($=_w$) is defined as in 2.29, and it is routine to prove

(c) $X^{\sigma} =_w Y^{\sigma} \iff CLw^{\rightarrow} \vdash X^{\sigma} = Y^{\sigma}$.

All the other properties of reduction and equality in Chapter 2 hold for typed CL with the same proofs as in Chapter 2. Note in particular the *substitution lemmas* (2.14 and 2.31), the *Church–Rosser theorems* (2.15, 2.32 and A2.16), and the *uniqueness of normal forms* (2.32.4).

Definition 10.24 (Abstraction) For every typed term X^{τ} and variable x^{σ}, a term called $[x^{\sigma}].X^{\tau}$ is defined by induction on the length of X^{τ} as follows (compare Definition 2.18).

(a) $[x^{\sigma}].X^{\tau} \equiv \mathsf{K}_{\sigma,\tau}X^{\tau}$ if $x^{\sigma} \notin FV(X^{\tau})$;

(b) $[x^{\sigma}].x^{\sigma} \equiv \mathsf{I}_{\sigma}$;

(c) $[x^{\sigma}].(U^{\sigma\rightarrow\tau}x^{\sigma}) \equiv U^{\sigma\rightarrow\tau}$ if $x^{\sigma} \notin FV(U^{\sigma\rightarrow\tau})$;

(f) $[x^{\sigma}].(U^{\rho\rightarrow\tau}V^{\rho}) \equiv \mathsf{S}_{\sigma,\rho,\tau}([x^{\sigma}].U^{\rho\rightarrow\tau})([x^{\sigma}].V^{\rho})$
if neither (a) nor (c) applies.

Exercise 10.25 Write all the missing type-superscripts into the above definition, and verify that $[x^{\sigma}].X^{\tau}$ always has type $\sigma\rightarrow\tau$.

Abstraction of typed terms has the same properties as untyped abstraction in Chapter 2, with the same proofs as in that chapter. Note in particular Theorems 2.21 and 2.27 and Lemma 2.28.

Typed CL-terms also have the following 'safety' properties with respect to $\triangleright_w$. Just as for λ in Definition 10.14, a term is called *SN* iff all weak reductions starting at that term are finite, and *WN* iff it has a normal form.

Theorem 10.26 (SN for simply typed $\triangleright_w$) *In simply typed CL, all terms are SN, i.e. there are no infinite weak reductions.*

Proof Appendix A3, Theorem A3.14. □

Corollary 10.26.1 (WN for simply typed $\triangleright_w$) *Every simply typed CL-term has a weak normal form.*

Corollary 10.26.2 *In simply typed CL the relation $=_w$ is decidable.*

Remark 10.27 (Strong reduction) A typed version of $\succ\!-$ can be defined and a WN theorem proved for it; the proof is like Theorem 11.28. However, for SN, no theorem in known. The first step towards such a theorem would be to give a satisfactory definition of the concept of SN for strong reduction, and this is not as easy as it looks.

Further reading See the end of Chapter 12.

11 Simple typing, Curry-style in CL

11A Introduction

The typed terms in Chapter 10 correspond to functions as they are usually defined in set theory and mathematics. On the other hand, if one takes the 'functions as operators' approach of Discussion 3.27, Chapter 10 leaves one with the feeling that something essential to the interpretation of untyped λ-terms has been lost.

For example, for different pairs σ, τ of types, the terms $\mathsf{K}_{\sigma,\tau} \equiv \lambda x^{\sigma} y^{\tau} . x^{\sigma}$ are all distinct. But in a sense they all represent special cases of the same operation, that of forming constant-functions. An even simpler example is given by the terms $\mathsf{I}_{\sigma} \equiv \lambda x^{\sigma} . x^{\sigma}$, which are distinct for different types σ but which all represent special cases of the one operation of doing nothing. If we feel that these two operations are single intuitive concepts, then a theory that tries to formalize them by splitting them into an infinity of special cases seems to be heading in the wrong direction.

It seems better to aim for a formalism in which each operation is represented by a single term, and this term is given an infinite number of types. This is what will be done in the present chapter. We shall take the untyped terms as given, and state a set of axioms and rules that will assign certain types to certain terms. Most terms that receive types will receive infinitely many of them, corresponding to the idea that they represent operators with an infinite number of special cases. (But some terms, such as $\lambda x . xx$, will receive no types.)

A type-system in which a term may have many types is called *polymorphic*. A type-system in which a term's types are not part of its structure, but are assigned to it after the term is built, is called

Curry-style, or sometimes *implicit*, in contrast to Chapter 10's *Church-style* systems.

In a Curry-style system a type assigned to a term is like a label to tell the kinds of combinations that can 'safely' be made with the term. Although at first Curry's approach will seem very different from Church's, it will turn out that if we take the same types here as were used in Chapter 10 and adopt the simplest rules to assign them to terms, then a term X will receive a type τ in the present chapter if and only if there is a corresponding typed term X^τ in Chapter 10.

A Curry-style system will not be a mere notational variant of Church's style, however; it will have more expressive power and more flexibility. For example, a natural question to ask about an untyped term X is whether it has any typed analogues (just as K had the typed analogues $\mathsf{K}_{\sigma,\tau}$ in Chapter 10, for all σ and τ); but although this question is about Church's system, it turns out that the easiest way to answer it is to re-state it in Curry's language. Then we shall see that its answer can be given for each X by a fairly simple algorithm.

Furthermore, Curry-style systems can be generalized in ways that Church's style cannot; an example will be given in 11.43.[1]

The present chapter will treat only CL-terms. The rules for λ-terms are slightly more complicated and will be postponed to the next chapter.

We shall begin by extending the definition of simple types in 10.1 by adding type-variables. An expression containing type-variables may be used to describe an infinite set of types all at once.

Definition 11.1 (Parametric types) Assume that we have an infinite sequence of *type-variables* and a finite, infinite or empty sequence of *type-constants*. Then we define *parametric types* as follows:[2]

(a) all type-constants and type-variables are (atomic) parametric types;

(b) if σ and τ are types, then $(\sigma \to \tau)$ is a parametric (function-) type.

In the rest of this chapter we shall omit 'parametric' since no other types will be discussed. A *closed type* will be a type containing no type-variables. An *open type* will be a type containing *only* type-variables.

1 The name '*Curry-style*' arose because this kind of type-assignment originated with Curry in the 1930s, and he was its main advocate until Robin Milner used it in the programming language ML in the 1970s, [Mil78].

2 In [HS86], parametric types were called 'type-schemes'.

Notation 11.2 Lower-case Greek letters will denote types, and the same abbreviations will be used here as in Chapter 10. In discussing the types of the Church numerals we shall use the abbreviation

$$\mathsf{N}_\tau \ \equiv \ (\tau \to \tau) \to \tau \to \tau.$$

Type-variables will be denoted by letters 'a', 'b', 'c', 'd', 'e'. The variables in terms will be called here *term-variables.* (Type-variables and term-variables need not be different.)

The result of simultaneously substituting types $\sigma_1, \ldots, \sigma_n$ for type-variables $a_1, \ldots, a_n$ in a type τ will be called

$$[\sigma_1/a_1, \ldots, \sigma_n/a_n]\tau.$$

The type-constants may include the symbol **N** for the set of all natural numbers and **H** for truth-values. In this case, some examples of types would be

$$\begin{array}{lll} \mathsf{N} \to \mathsf{H}, & \mathsf{N} \to \mathsf{N}, & \mathsf{N} \to \mathsf{N} \to \mathsf{H}, \\ a \to b, & \mathsf{N} \to b, & (b \to a) \to a, \\ \text{etc.} & & \end{array}$$

Terms in this chapter will be CL-terms (i.e. the untyped terms from Chapter 2, not the typed terms from Chapter 10). As usual, a *non-redex atom* is an atom other than **S**, **K** and **I**. A *non-redex constant* is a constant other than **S**, **K** and **I**. A *pure term* is a term whose only atoms are **S**, **K**, **I** and variables. A *combinator* is a term whose only atoms are **S**, **K**, **I**.

Remark 11.3 In this chapter and the next, a function-type $\sigma \to \tau$ is intended to denote some set of operators ϕ such that

$$x \in \sigma \implies \phi(x) \text{ is defined and } \phi(x) \in \tau.$$

This contrasts with Chapter 10: there, a claim that ϕ was in $\sigma \to \tau$ implied that the domain of ϕ was exactly σ, but here it only implies that the domain $\supseteq \sigma$. This comes from our intention that one operator ϕ may have many types $\sigma \to \tau$; correspondingly, the domain of ϕ may include many different sets σ.

11B The system $TA_C^{\to}$

Definition 11.4 A *type-assignment formula* or $TA_C^{\to}$*-formula* is any expression

$$X : \tau ,$$

where X is a CL-term and τ is a type. We call X its *subject* and τ its *predicate*.

A formula $X{:}\tau$ can be read informally as 'we assign to X the type τ' or 'X receives type τ', or very informally as 'X is a member of τ'.[3]

Definition 11.5 (The type-assignment system $TA_C^{\to}$) $TA_C^{\to}$ is a formal theory in the sense of Notation 6.1. Its *axioms* are given by three *axiom-schemes*, motivated by the types of I_σ, $\mathsf{K}_{\sigma,\tau}$ and $\mathsf{S}_{\rho,\sigma,\tau}$ in Definition 10.19; they are:

$$(\to \mathsf{I}) \qquad \mathsf{I} : \sigma \to \sigma,$$

$$(\to \mathsf{K}) \qquad \mathsf{K} : \sigma \to \tau \to \sigma,$$

$$(\to \mathsf{S}) \qquad \mathsf{S} : (\rho \to \sigma \to \tau) \to (\rho \to \sigma) \to \rho \to \tau.$$

The only *rule* of $TA_C^{\to}$ is called the $\to$*-elimination* rule, or $(\to \mathrm{e})$; it is motivated by Definition 10.19(b), and says:

$$(\to \mathrm{e}) \qquad \frac{X : \sigma \to \tau \qquad Y : \sigma}{XY : \tau\,.}$$

Notation Let Γ be any finite, infinite or empty set of $TA_C^{\to}$-formulas. Iff there exists a deduction of a formula $X{:}\tau$ whose non-axiom assumptions are all in Γ, we write

$$\Gamma \vdash_{TA_C^{\to}} X{:}\tau ,$$

or just $\Gamma \vdash X{:}\tau$ when no confusion is likely. Iff Γ is empty, we call the deduction a ($TA_C^{\to}$ -) *proof* and write

$$\vdash_{TA_C^{\to}} X : \tau\,.$$

[3] [HS86] used the notation '$X \in \tau$' for type-assignment formulas, but '$X : \tau$' has now come into standard use. Some older works used 'τX' or '$\vdash \tau X$' (thinking of τ as a propositional function rather than a set).

Example 11.6 The term **SKK**, which behaves like **I** (since $\mathbf{SKK}X \triangleright X$), also has all the types that **I** has. That is, for all σ,

$$\vdash_{\mathrm{TA}_{\mathrm{C}}^{\rightarrow}} \quad \mathbf{SKK} : \sigma \rightarrow \sigma .$$

Proof Let σ be any type. In axiom-scheme ($\rightarrow$**S**), take ρ, σ, τ to be σ, $\sigma \rightarrow \sigma$, σ respectively; this gives us an axiom

$$\mathbf{S} : (\sigma \rightarrow (\sigma \rightarrow \sigma) \rightarrow \sigma) \rightarrow (\sigma \rightarrow \sigma \rightarrow \sigma) \rightarrow \sigma \rightarrow \sigma .$$

Also, from axiom-scheme ($\rightarrow$**K**) we can get the following two axioms:

$$\mathbf{K} : \sigma \rightarrow (\sigma \rightarrow \sigma) \rightarrow \sigma ,$$
$$\mathbf{K} : \sigma \rightarrow \sigma \rightarrow \sigma .$$

Using these three axioms and rule ($\rightarrow$e), we make the $\mathrm{TA}_{\mathrm{C}}^{\rightarrow}$-proof below:

$$\dfrac{\dfrac{\overset{(\rightarrow \mathbf{S})}{\mathbf{S} : (\sigma \rightarrow (\sigma \rightarrow \sigma) \rightarrow \sigma) \rightarrow (\sigma \rightarrow \sigma \rightarrow \sigma) \rightarrow \sigma \rightarrow \sigma} \quad \overset{(\rightarrow \mathbf{K})}{\mathbf{K} : \sigma \rightarrow (\sigma \rightarrow \sigma) \rightarrow \sigma}}{\mathbf{SK} : (\sigma \rightarrow \sigma \rightarrow \sigma) \rightarrow \sigma \rightarrow \sigma} \quad \overset{(\rightarrow \mathbf{K})}{\mathbf{K} : \sigma \rightarrow \sigma \rightarrow \sigma}}{\mathbf{SKK} : \sigma \rightarrow \sigma .}$$

Example 11.7 Recall that $\mathbf{B} \equiv \mathbf{S(KS)K}$. Then, for all ρ, σ, τ:

$$\vdash_{\mathrm{TA}_{\mathrm{C}}^{\rightarrow}} \quad \mathbf{B} : (\sigma \rightarrow \tau) \rightarrow (\rho \rightarrow \sigma) \rightarrow \rho \rightarrow \tau .$$

Proof The required proof is shown below. To make it fit into the width of the page, it uses the following abbreviations:

$$\begin{aligned}
\theta &\equiv (\rho \rightarrow \sigma \rightarrow \tau) \rightarrow (\rho \rightarrow \sigma) \rightarrow \rho \rightarrow \tau, \\
\mu &\equiv \sigma \rightarrow \tau, \\
\nu &\equiv \rho \rightarrow \sigma \rightarrow \tau, \\
\pi &\equiv (\rho \rightarrow \sigma) \rightarrow \rho \rightarrow \tau.
\end{aligned}$$

(We have $\nu \equiv \rho \rightarrow \mu$, so the formula $\mathbf{K} : \mu \rightarrow \nu$ is an axiom under axiom-scheme ($\rightarrow$**K**). Also $\nu \rightarrow \pi \equiv \theta$, so $\mu \rightarrow \nu \rightarrow \pi \equiv \mu \rightarrow \theta$.)

$$\dfrac{\dfrac{\overset{(\rightarrow \mathbf{S})}{\mathbf{S} : (\mu \rightarrow \nu \rightarrow \pi) \rightarrow (\mu \rightarrow \nu) \rightarrow \mu \rightarrow \pi} \quad \dfrac{\overset{(\rightarrow \mathbf{K})}{\mathbf{K} : \theta \rightarrow \mu \rightarrow \theta} \quad \overset{(\rightarrow \mathbf{S})}{\mathbf{S} : \theta}}{\mathbf{KS} : \mu \rightarrow \theta}}{\mathbf{S(KS)} : (\mu \rightarrow \nu) \rightarrow \mu \rightarrow \pi} \quad \overset{(\rightarrow \mathbf{K})}{\mathbf{K} : \mu \rightarrow \nu}}{\mathbf{S(KS)K} : \mu \rightarrow \pi .}$$

Exercise 11.8* For each of the terms on the left in the following table, give a $TA_C^{\rightarrow}$-proof to show it has all the types on the right (one type for each ρ, σ, τ).

	Term		*Type*
(a)	$\overline{0} \equiv \mathsf{KI}$	(see 4.2)	$\tau \to \sigma \to \sigma$
(b)	$\overline{\sigma} \equiv \mathsf{SB}$	(see 4.6)	$((\sigma \to \tau) \to \rho \to \sigma) \to (\sigma \to \tau) \to \rho \to \tau$
(c)	$\mathsf{W} \equiv \mathsf{SS}(\mathsf{KI})$	(see 2.17)	$(\sigma \to \sigma \to \tau) \to \sigma \to \tau$
(d)	KK		$\rho \to \sigma \to \tau \to \sigma$
(e)	$\overline{0} \equiv \mathsf{KI}$		$\mathsf{N}_\tau \quad (\mathsf{N}_\tau \equiv (\tau \to \tau) \to \tau \to \tau.)$
(f)	$\overline{\sigma} \equiv \mathsf{SB}$		$\mathsf{N}_\tau \to \mathsf{N}_\tau$
(g)	$\overline{n} \equiv (\mathsf{SB})^n(\mathsf{KI})$		$\mathsf{N}_\tau.$

Exercise 11.9* Give $TA_C^{\rightarrow}$-deductions to show that, for all ρ, σ, τ,

(a) $U : \rho \to \sigma \to \tau, \;\; V : \rho \to \sigma, \;\; W : \rho \;\; \vdash \;\; \mathsf{S}UVW : \tau,$

(b) $U : \rho \to \sigma \to \tau, \;\; V : \rho \to \sigma, \;\; W : \rho \;\; \vdash \;\; UW(VW) : \tau,$

(c) $U : \rho, \;\; V : \sigma \;\; \vdash \;\; \mathsf{K}UV : \rho,$

(d) $U : \rho \;\; \vdash \;\; \mathsf{I}U : \rho,$

(e) $x : \rho \to \sigma, \;\; x : \rho \;\; \vdash \;\; xx : \sigma.$

These examples and exercises raise some points which will be discussed below, before we move on to the main properties of $TA_C^{\rightarrow}$.

Note 11.10 (Axioms) The three axiom-schemes for $TA_C^{\rightarrow}$ in Definition 11.5 are not axioms, but just patterns to show what the axioms look like. The actual axioms are particular cases of these three schemes. For example, if the type-constants include N, the axioms for I are

$\mathsf{I} : a \to a,$	$\mathsf{I} : (c \to c) \to (c \to c),$
$\mathsf{I} : \mathsf{N} \to \mathsf{N},$	$\mathsf{I} : ((a \to b) \to c) \to ((a \to b) \to c),$
$\mathsf{I} : (a \to b) \to (a \to b),$	etc.

Thus there are an infinite number of axioms. Also, if we perform a substitution in an axiom, say by substituting $b \to c$ for a in the axiom $\mathsf{I} : (a \to b) \to (a \to b)$, we get

$$\mathsf{I} : ((b \to c) \to b) \to ((b \to c) \to b),$$

and this is another axiom: the set of axioms is *closed under substitution.*

The following lemma takes this remark further; it says in effect that the set of all deductions is closed under substitution.

Lemma 11.11 (Closure under type-substitutions) *Let* Γ *be any set of* $\mathrm{TA}_{\mathrm{C}}^{\rightarrow}$*-formulas, and let*

$$\Gamma \vdash_{\mathrm{TA}_{\mathrm{C}}^{\rightarrow}} X:\tau\,.$$

For any types $\sigma_1,\ldots,\sigma_k$ *and type-variables* $a_1,\ldots,a_k$ *(distinct as usual), let* $[\sigma_1/a_1,\ldots,\sigma_k/a_k]\Gamma$ *be the result of substituting* $\sigma_1,\ldots,\sigma_k$ *for* $a_1,\ldots,$ a_k *simultaneously in all the predicates in* Γ. *Then*

$$[\sigma_1/a_1,\ldots,\sigma_k/a_k]\Gamma \;\; \vdash_{\mathrm{TA}_{\mathrm{C}}^{\rightarrow}} \;\; X:[\sigma_1/a_1,\ldots,\sigma_k/a_k]\tau\,.$$

Proof Substitute $[\sigma_1/a_1,\ldots,\sigma_k/a_k]$ throughout the given deduction. The result is still a genuine deduction, because substitution creates from an axiom for **I**, **K** or **S** a new axiom of the same kind, and from an instance of rule ($\rightarrow$e) a new instance of this rule. □

Note 11.12 (Principal axioms) All the axioms for **I** are substitution-instances of the single axiom $\mathbf{I}: a \rightarrow a$; this axiom is called a *principal axiom* for **I**. Similarly, **K** and **S** have the following as principal axioms:

$$\mathbf{K}: a\rightarrow b\rightarrow a, \qquad \mathbf{S}: (a\rightarrow b\rightarrow c)\rightarrow(a\rightarrow b)\rightarrow a\rightarrow c\,.$$

(A principal axiom plays a similar role to an axiom-scheme, though on a different level: the axiom $\mathbf{I}: a \rightarrow a$ is an expression in the formal language of $\mathrm{TA}_{\mathrm{C}}^{\rightarrow}$, while the axiom-scheme '$\mathbf{I}:\sigma\rightarrow\sigma$' is an expression in the informal meta-language in which we are discussing $\mathrm{TA}_{\mathrm{C}}^{\rightarrow}$.)

Note 11.13 (Deductions from assumptions) Exercise 11.9 shows an interesting way in which the Curry-style approach to types is more expressive than Church's: in $\mathrm{TA}_{\mathrm{C}}^{\rightarrow}$ we can already answer questions of a kind that could not even have been asked in Chapter 10, namely "What type would X have if certain parts of X had certain types?". The possibility of making deductions from assumptions is an important advantage of the present approach. (See Section 11I.)

11C Subject-construction

Looking again at Examples 11.6 and 11.7 and your answers to Exercises 11.8 and 11.9, notice that the deduction of a formula $X:\tau$ closely follows the construction of X. Rule ($\rightarrow$e) says

$$\frac{X : \sigma \rightarrow \tau \qquad Y : \sigma}{XY : \tau\,,}$$

and in this rule the subject of the conclusion is built from the subjects of the premises. Hence, as we move down a deduction the subject grows in length and contains all earlier subjects.

In more detail: let $\mathcal{D}$ be a tree-form deduction of a formula $X:\tau$ from some assumptions

$$\text{(a)} \qquad U_1 : \pi_1, \; \ldots \; , U_n : \pi_n \qquad (n \geq 0),$$

such that each of these formulas actually occurs in $\mathcal{D}$.

Suppose, for the moment, that each U_i is a non-redex atom. Then $\{U_1, \ldots, U_n\}$ will be exactly the set of non-redex atoms occurring in X, and if we strip all types from $\mathcal{D}$, we shall get the construction-tree for X (i.e. the tree which shows how X is built up from U_1, ..., U_n and perhaps also some occurrences of **I**, **K** and **S**). To each occurrence of U_i in X there will correspond an assumption $U_i : \pi_i$ in $\mathcal{D}$, and to each occurrence of **I**, **K** or **S** in X there will correspond an axiom in $\mathcal{D}$. (Hence $n = 0$ iff X is a combinator.) In general, if Z is any subterm of X, then to each occurrence of Z in X there will correspond a formula in $\mathcal{D}$ with Z as subject.

For example, look at the deduction for Exercise 11.9(b):

$$\text{(b)} \qquad \cfrac{\cfrac{U : \rho\rightarrow\sigma\rightarrow\tau \qquad W : \rho}{UW : \sigma\rightarrow\tau}\,(\rightarrow\text{e}) \qquad \cfrac{V : \rho\rightarrow\sigma \qquad W : \rho}{VW : \sigma}\,(\rightarrow\text{e})}{UW(VW) : \tau\,.}\,(\rightarrow\text{e})$$

Here $X \equiv UW(VW)$, and there are three assumptions (so $n = 3$ in (a)):

$$U : \rho\rightarrow\sigma\rightarrow\tau, \qquad V : \rho\rightarrow\sigma, \qquad W : \rho.$$

Stripping the types away, we get the following tree, which is the construction-tree of X if U, V, W are atoms:

$$\text{(c)} \qquad \dfrac{\dfrac{U \quad W}{UW} \qquad \dfrac{V \quad W}{VW}}{UW(VW)\,.}$$

On the other hand, returning to (a), suppose some of $U_1, \ldots, U_n$ are not atoms. Then X will be an applicative combination of $U_1, \ldots, U_n$ and I, K, S, and the stripped tree will show how X is built up from these terms; it will not be the whole construction-tree of X, but only a lower part. Each term-occurrence Z in X will either

(i) be inside an occurrence of a U_i corresponding to an assumption $U_i : \pi_i$, or
(ii) be an applicative combination of $U_1, \ldots, U_n, \mathsf{I}, \mathsf{K}, \mathsf{S}$, and have a corresponding formula in $\mathcal{D}$ with Z as subject.

For example, in (b) above, if $U \equiv V(VW)$ and

$$X \equiv V(VW)\,W\,(VW), \qquad Z \equiv VW,$$

then there are two occurrences of Z in X: the first is in U and has no corresponding formula in (b), but the second corresponds to the formula $VW : \sigma$ in (b).

The correspondence between deductions and term-constructions is the key to the study of $\mathrm{TA}_{\mathrm{C}}^{\rightarrow}$, and will be used repeatedly throughout this chapter. (It has been described formally in the *Subject-construction theorem* of [CF58, Section 9B].)

One of its corollaries is that if $\Gamma \vdash_{\mathrm{TA}_{\mathrm{C}}^{\rightarrow}} X : \tau$ and all the subjects in Γ are atoms, then every non-redex atom q in X must occur as a subject of a formula in Γ, say $q : \pi$ for some type π.

11D Abstraction

The aim of this section is to show that the type of $[x].X$ is exactly what one would expect from the informal interpretation of $[x].X$ as a function. Its main theorem will show how to deduce the type of $[x].X$ from the types of x and X, and will help in assigning types quickly to complex terms.[4]

[4] It was called the Stratification Theorem in [CF58, Section 9D Corollary 1.1], and is an analogy of the deduction theorem for Hilbert-style versions of propositional logic.

Theorem 11.14 (Abstraction and types) *Let Γ be any set of $\mathrm{TA}_{\mathrm{C}}^{\rightarrow}$-formulas. If x does not occur in any subject in Γ, and*

$$\Gamma,\ x:\sigma \quad \vdash_{\mathrm{TA}_{\mathrm{C}}^{\rightarrow}} \quad X:\tau\,,$$

then

$$\Gamma \ \vdash_{\mathrm{TA}_{\mathrm{C}}^{\rightarrow}} \ [x].X : \sigma \rightarrow \tau\,,$$

where $[\,]$ is any of the three abstraction algorithms $[\,]^{\eta}$, $[\,]^{w}$, $[\,]^{\beta}$ defined in 9.1 (with 2.18), 9.20, 9.27 respectively.

Proof We use induction on X, with cases corresponding to Definition 2.18, which includes all the cases in 9.20 and 9.27. Let $\mathcal{D}$ be the given deduction of $X:\tau$ from $x:\sigma$ and members of Γ. The restriction that x not occur in Γ implies that whenever x occurs in $\mathcal{D}$, its type must be σ.

Case 1: $x \notin \mathrm{FV}(X)$ and $[x].X \equiv \mathbf{K}X$. Since $x \notin \mathrm{FV}(X)$, the assumption $x:\sigma$ is not used in $\mathcal{D}$, so $\mathcal{D}$ is a deduction of

$$\Gamma \ \vdash \ X:\tau\,.$$

Now by axiom-scheme $(\rightarrow\mathbf{K})$ we have an axiom $\mathbf{K}:\tau\rightarrow\sigma\rightarrow\tau$. Hence, by rule $(\rightarrow\mathrm{e})$,

$$\Gamma \ \vdash \ \mathbf{K}X : \sigma\rightarrow\tau\,.$$

Case 2: $X \equiv x$ and $[x].X \equiv \mathbf{I}$. By axiom-scheme $(\rightarrow\mathbf{I})$ we have an axiom $\mathbf{I}:\sigma\rightarrow\sigma$. But $X \equiv x$, so $\tau \equiv \sigma$, and the axiom says $\mathbf{I}:\sigma\rightarrow\tau$. Hence

$$\Gamma \ \vdash \ \mathbf{I}:\sigma\rightarrow\tau\,.$$

Case 3: $X \equiv Ux$ with $x \notin \mathrm{FV}(U)$, and $[x].X \equiv U$. Then, by the correspondence between deductions and constructions, $\mathcal{D}$ must have form

$$\dfrac{\begin{matrix}\mathcal{D}_1\\ U:\sigma\rightarrow\tau\end{matrix} \qquad x:\sigma}{Ux:\tau\,,}\ (\rightarrow\mathrm{e})$$

where $\mathcal{D}_1$ is a deduction in which x does not occur. (The above notation means that $\mathcal{D}_1$ is a deduction of the formula $U:\sigma\rightarrow\tau$, and $\mathcal{D}$ is the result of applying $(\rightarrow\mathrm{e})$ to $\mathcal{D}_1$ and an assumption $x:\sigma$.) But $[x].X \equiv U$. Hence $\mathcal{D}_1$ gives

$$\Gamma \ \vdash \ [x].X : \sigma\rightarrow\tau\,.$$

Case 4: $X \equiv X_1X_2$ and $[x].X \equiv \mathbf{S}([x]'.X_1)([x]'.X_2)$, where $[\,]'$ is the same as $[\,]$ if $[\,]$ is $[\,]^\eta$ or $[\,]^w$, but $[\,]'$ is $[\,]^\eta$ if $[\,]$ is $[\,]^\beta$.

In $\mathcal{D}$, the formula $X_1X_2 : \tau$ must be the conclusion of rule ($\rightarrow$e). (The only other possibility is that it be in Γ; but then, by assumption, X_1X_2 would not contain x and we would be in Case 1 not Case 4.) Therefore $\mathcal{D}$ must have form

$$\dfrac{\begin{matrix}\mathcal{D}_1 & & \mathcal{D}_2 \\ X_1 : \rho\rightarrow\tau & & X_2 : \rho\end{matrix}}{X_1X_2 : \tau\,,}\ (\rightarrow\mathrm{e})$$

for some ρ. We are proving the theorem for three forms of $[x]$ at once, so in the induction hypothesis we can assume

$$\Gamma \;\vdash\; ([x]'.X_1) : \sigma\rightarrow\rho\rightarrow\tau,$$

$$\Gamma \;\vdash\; ([x]'.X_2) : \sigma\rightarrow\rho.$$

Now by axiom-scheme ($\rightarrow\mathbf{S}$) we have an axiom

$$\mathbf{S} : (\sigma\rightarrow\rho\rightarrow\tau)\rightarrow(\sigma\rightarrow\rho)\rightarrow\sigma\rightarrow\tau.$$

Hence, by ($\rightarrow$e) twice we get

$$\Gamma \;\vdash\; \mathbf{S}\,([x]'.X_1)\,([x]'.X_2) : \sigma\rightarrow\tau.$$

This completes Case 4 and the proof. □

Note The axiom-schemes for **I**, **K** and **S** exactly fit the cases in the preceding proof. If they had not already been motivated by analogy with $\mathbf{I}_\sigma$, $\mathbf{K}_{\sigma,\tau}$ and $\mathbf{S}_{\rho,\sigma,\tau}$ in Chapter 10 (which were motivated by a λ-analogy), this proof would have been their principal motivation.

Corollary 11.14.1 *Let Γ be any set of $\mathrm{TA}_C^{\rightarrow}$-formulas. If no subject in Γ contains any of the (distinct) variables $x_1, \ldots, x_n$, and*

$$\Gamma,\ x_1:\sigma_1,\ \ldots,\ x_n:\sigma_n \;\;\vdash_{\mathrm{TA}_C^{\rightarrow}}\;\; X : \tau,$$

and $[\,]$ is any of $[\,]^\eta$, $[\,]^w$, $[\,]^\beta$, then

$$\Gamma \;\vdash_{\mathrm{TA}_C^{\rightarrow}}\; ([x_1,\ldots,x_n].X) : \sigma_1\rightarrow\ldots\rightarrow\sigma_n\rightarrow\tau.$$

Corollary 11.14.2 *If all subjects in Γ are atoms, the above theorem and corollary extend to the abstraction algorithm $[\,]^{fab}$ defined in 9.26.*

Proof The proof of 11.14 needs no change. (But if Γ contained a composite subject, the statement in Case 4 that $X_1X_2 : \tau$ must be the conclusion of rule ($\to$e) would fail for $[\ ]^{fab}$, and so would the theorem.) □

Exercise 11.15* Using Corollary 11.14.1, prove the following in $\mathrm{TA}_C^{\to}$.

(a) Let $C \equiv [x, y, z].xzy$; prove (for all types ρ, σ, τ):

$$C : (\rho \to \sigma \to \tau) \to \sigma \to \rho \to \tau.$$

(b) Let $\mathbf{D} \equiv [x, y, z].z(\mathbf{K}y)x$, as defined in (9) in Chapter 4, and let $\mathbf{N}_\tau \equiv (\tau \to \tau) \to \tau \to \tau$. Prove, for all types τ:

$$\mathbf{D} : \tau \to \tau \to \mathbf{N}_\tau \to \tau.$$

(c) Let $\mathbf{R}_{\mathrm{Bernays}}$ be as defined in Chapter 4 (11) and (14), i.e.

$$\mathbf{R}_{\mathrm{Bernays}} \equiv [x, y, u].\, u(Qy)(\mathbf{D}\overline{0}x)\overline{1},$$

where $\overline{0} \equiv \mathbf{KI}$, $\overline{\sigma} \equiv \mathbf{SB}$, $\overline{1} \equiv (\mathbf{SB})(\mathbf{KI})$, and

$$Q \equiv [y, v].\, \mathbf{D}\,(\overline{\sigma}\,(v\overline{0}))\,(y\,(v\overline{0})(v\overline{1})).$$

For every type τ let $\tau^\star \equiv \mathbf{N}_{\mathbf{N}_\tau} \to \mathbf{N}_\tau$. Prove, for all τ:

$$\mathbf{R}_{\mathrm{Bernays}} : \mathbf{N}_\tau \to (\mathbf{N}_\tau \to \mathbf{N}_\tau \to \mathbf{N}_\tau) \to \mathbf{N}_{\tau^\star} \to \mathbf{N}_\tau.$$

(Hint: since $\overline{0} \equiv \mathbf{KI}$, it can be given an infinite number of types in $\mathrm{TA}_C^{\to}$, and in your proof, two occurrences of $\overline{0}$ in $\mathbf{R}_{\mathrm{Bernays}}$ must be given two different types, $\mathbf{N}_\tau$ and $\mathbf{N}_{\mathbf{N}_\tau}$.)

Exercise 11.16 The advantage of using Corollary 11.14.1 can be seen by writing out the term C in Exercise 11.15(a) in terms of **S**, **K** and **I**, and proving (a) directly from Theorem 11.14 without using that corollary.

11E Subject-reduction

The second main theorem about $\mathrm{TA}_C^{\to}$ will show that type-assignments are preserved by both weak and strong reduction. (If one thinks of a type as a safety-label and reduction as a computation-process, it will say that a term will not lose any labels during a computation; i.e. it will not become less safe.)

The theorem's proof will need the following definition and lemma.

Definition 11.17 (Inert assumptions) A CL-term U will be called [*weakly* or *strongly*] *inert* iff it is a normal form [weak or strong, respectively] whose leftmost atom is a non-redex atom; i.e. iff it has form

$$U \equiv qV_1 \ldots V_k$$

where q is an atom $\not\equiv \mathsf{I}, \mathsf{K}, \mathsf{S}$, and $V_1, \ldots, V_k$ are normal forms. A set Γ of $\mathrm{TA}_{\mathrm{C}}^{\rightarrow}$-formulas $\{U_1 : \pi_1,\ U_2 : \pi_2,\ \ldots\}$ will be called *inert* iff all of U_1, U_2, etc. are inert.[5]

The following lemma says, roughly speaking, that if we replace a part V of a term X by a new term W with the same type as V, then the type of X will not change.

Lemma 11.18 (Replacement) *Let* Γ_1 *and* Γ_2 *be any sets of* $\mathrm{TA}_{\mathrm{C}}^{\rightarrow}$-*formulas, and let* $\mathcal{D}$ *be a deduction giving*

$$\Gamma_1 \vdash_{\mathrm{TA}_{\mathrm{C}}^{\rightarrow}} X : \tau.$$

Let V *be a term-occurrence in* X, *such that there is a formula* $V : \rho$ *in* $\mathcal{D}$ *in the same position as* V *has in the construction-tree of* X. *Let* $X^\star$ *be the result of replacing* V *by a term* W *such that*

$$\Gamma_2 \vdash_{\mathrm{TA}_{\mathrm{C}}^{\rightarrow}} W : \rho.$$

Then

$$\Gamma_1 \cup \Gamma_2 \vdash_{\mathrm{TA}_{\mathrm{C}}^{\rightarrow}} X^\star : \tau.$$

Proof First cut off from $\mathcal{D}$ the subtree above the formula $V : \rho$. The result is a deduction $\mathcal{D}_1$ with form

$$\begin{array}{c} V : \rho \\ \mathcal{D}_1 \\ X : \tau. \end{array}$$

(This notation means that $\mathcal{D}_1$ has conclusion $X : \tau$ and one of its assumptions is the formula $V : \rho$.) Then replace V by W in the assumption $V : \rho$ and make corresponding replacements in all formulas below it in $\mathcal{D}_1$. The result is a deduction ${\mathcal{D}_1}^\star$ with form

$$\begin{array}{c} W : \rho \\ {\mathcal{D}_1}^\star \\ X^\star : \tau. \end{array}$$

[5] In [HS86], 'normal-subjects' was used instead of 'inert'.

Then take the given deduction of $W : \rho$ (call this deduction $\mathcal{D}_2$), and place it over the assumption $W\!:\!\rho$ in $\mathcal{D}_1{}^\star$. The result is a deduction

$$\begin{array}{c} \mathcal{D}_2 \\ W : \rho \\ \mathcal{D}_1{}^\star \\ X^\star : \tau \end{array}$$

as desired. □

Theorem 11.19 (Subject-reduction) *Let* Γ *be a weakly* [*strongly*] *inert set of* $\mathrm{TA}_{\mathrm{C}}^{\rightarrow}$*-formulas. If*

$$\Gamma \ \vdash_{\mathrm{TA}_{\mathrm{C}}^{\rightarrow}} \ X\!:\!\tau$$

and $X \rhd_w X'$ [$X \succ\!\!- X'$], *then*

$$\Gamma \ \vdash_{\mathrm{TA}_{\mathrm{C}}^{\rightarrow}} \ X'\!:\!\tau.$$

Proof The proofs for $\rhd_w$ and $\succ\!\!-$ first appeared in [CF58, Sections 9C2, 9C6] and [CHS72, Section 14B2]. We shall keep to $\rhd_w$ here for simplicity.

By the replacement lemma, it is enough to take care of the case that X is a redex and X' is its contractum.

Case 1: $X \equiv \mathsf{I}X'$. Let $\mathcal{D}$ be a deduction of $\mathsf{I}X'\!:\!\tau$ from Γ. By the given condition on Γ, the formula $\mathsf{I}X'\!:\!\tau$ itself cannot be in Γ, nor can the leftmost I in $\mathsf{I}X'$ be a subject in Γ; hence this I must correspond to an instance of axiom-scheme $(\rightarrow \mathsf{I})$. Therefore, using the correspondence between deductions and term-constructions, $\mathcal{D}$ must have form

$$\dfrac{\begin{array}{c}(\rightarrow \mathsf{I}) \\ \mathsf{I} : \tau \rightarrow \tau\end{array} \qquad \begin{array}{c}\mathcal{D}_1 \\ X' : \tau\end{array}}{\mathsf{I}X' : \tau.}\ (\rightarrow \mathrm{e})$$

That is, $\mathcal{D}$ must contain a deduction $\mathcal{D}_1$ of $X'\!:\!\tau$. Thus $\Gamma \vdash X'\!:\!\tau$.

Case 2: $X \equiv \mathsf{K}X'Y$. Let $\mathcal{D}$ be a deduction of $\mathsf{K}X'Y\!:\!\tau$ from Γ. By the given condition on Γ, none of $\mathsf{K}X'Y$, $\mathsf{K}X'$, K can be a subject in Γ; hence the leftmost K in $\mathsf{K}X'Y$ must correspond to an instance of axiom-scheme $(\rightarrow \mathsf{K})$. Therefore, using the correspondence between deductions and term-constructions, $\mathcal{D}$ must have form (for some σ):

$$\dfrac{\dfrac{\begin{array}{c}(\rightarrow \mathsf{K}) \\ \mathsf{K} : \tau \rightarrow \sigma \rightarrow \tau\end{array} \qquad \begin{array}{c}\mathcal{D}_1 \\ X' : \tau\end{array}}{\mathsf{K}X' : \sigma \rightarrow \tau}\ (\rightarrow \mathrm{e}) \qquad \begin{array}{c}\mathcal{D}_2 \\ Y : \sigma\end{array}}{\mathsf{K}X'Y : \tau.}\ (\rightarrow \mathrm{e})$$

Therefore $\mathcal{D}$ must contain a deduction $\mathcal{D}_1$ of $X':\tau$. Thus $\Gamma \vdash X':\tau$.

Case 3: $X \equiv \mathbf{S}UVW$ and $X' \equiv UW(VW)$. Let $\mathcal{D}$ be a deduction of $\mathbf{S}UVW:\tau$ from Γ. None of $\mathbf{S}UVW$, $\mathbf{S}UV$, $\mathbf{S}U$, $\mathbf{S}$ can be a subject in Γ, so $\mathcal{D}$ must have the following form (for some ρ, σ):

$$\dfrac{\dfrac{\dfrac{\overset{(\to\mathbf{S})}{\mathbf{S} : (\rho\to\sigma\to\tau)\to(\rho\to\sigma)\to\rho\to\tau} \quad \overset{\mathcal{D}_1}{U : \rho\to\sigma\to\tau}}{\mathbf{S}U : (\rho\to\sigma)\to\rho\to\tau} \quad \overset{\mathcal{D}_2}{V : \rho\to\sigma}}{\mathbf{S}UV : \rho\to\tau} \quad \overset{\mathcal{D}_3}{W : \rho}}{\mathbf{S}UVW : \tau.}$$

From $\mathcal{D}_1$, $\mathcal{D}_2$, $\mathcal{D}_3$ we can construct a deduction of $UW(VW):\tau$ thus:

$$\dfrac{\dfrac{\overset{\mathcal{D}_1}{U : \rho\to\sigma\to\tau} \quad \overset{\mathcal{D}_3}{W : \rho}}{UW : \sigma\to\tau} \quad \dfrac{\overset{\mathcal{D}_2}{V : \rho\to\sigma} \quad \overset{\mathcal{D}_3}{W : \rho}}{VW : \sigma}}{UW(VW) : \tau.}$$

□

Remark 11.20 (Subject-expansion) It is natural to ask whether the subject-reduction theorem can be reversed; that is, if X reduces to X', whether

$$\Gamma \vdash X':\tau \quad \Longrightarrow \quad \Gamma \vdash X:\tau.$$

The answer is that reversal is possible only under certain very restrictive conditions, [CF58, Section 9C3].

For an example where reversal is not possible, take

(a) $$X \equiv \mathbf{SKSI}, \quad X' \equiv \mathbf{KI}(\mathbf{SI}).$$

Here $X \rhd_w X'$, and $\vdash_{\mathrm{TA}_C^{\to}} X' : \sigma \to \sigma$ for all types σ, but, by Exercise 11.38 later, it is only possible to prove $X:\sigma\to\sigma$ for composite σ.

A stronger example of non-reversal is

(b) $$X \equiv \mathbf{SIII}, \quad X' \equiv \mathbf{II}(\mathbf{II}).$$

In this case we can prove $X':\sigma\to\sigma$ for every σ, but X has no types at all (by Example 11.37 later).

The non-reversibility of Theorem 11.19 means that the set of types assigned to a term is not invariant under conversion. Thus the system $\mathrm{TA}_C^{\to}$ is not as tidy as we might like. One way to tidy it up would be to add an equality-invariance rule to $\mathrm{TA}_{\mathrm{C}}^{\to}$, and this will be done in Section 11K. Since convertibility is not a recursively decidable relation, the new rule will not be decidable, but we shall see that this apparently serious problem will have less effect than we might expect.

11F Typable CL-terms

In this section we study pure terms, i.e. terms whose only atoms are combinators and variables.

Some untyped terms have typed analogues in Chapter 10, for example **B**, **K** and $xz(yz)$; but others have not, for example xx. In this section and the next, the set of untyped pure terms that have typed analogues will be characterized precisely. This set will turn out to be decidable.

Definition 11.21 (Type-contexts) A *(type-)context* is a finite or infinite set of $\mathrm{TA}_{\mathrm{C}}^{\to}$-formulas $\Gamma = \{x_1 : \rho_1,\ x_2 : \rho_2,\ \ldots\}$ whose subjects are variables, and which is *consistent* in the sense that no variable receives more than one type in Γ, i.e.

$$x_i \equiv x_j \implies \rho_i \equiv \rho_j. \tag{1}$$

If X is a term, an $\mathrm{FV}(X)$*-context* is a context whose subjects are exactly the variables in $\mathrm{FV}(X)$.[6]

Note 11.22 (a) The consistency condition says that a context is essentially just a mapping from a set of term-variables, to types. For example, the assumptions used in assigning a type to xx in Exercise 11.9(e) were $x : \rho$, $x : \rho \to \sigma$; this pair does *not* form a context, because it is not consistent.

(b) Contexts are inert, in the sense of Definition 11.17 (both weakly and strongly). Hence the subject-reduction theorem applies to deductions from contexts.

Definition 11.23 (Typable pure terms) Let X be any pure CL-term, with $\mathrm{FV}(X) = \{x_1, \ldots, x_n\}$ $(n \geq 0)$. We say X is *typable*[7] iff

[6] The word 'context' has also another meaning in many books on λ and CL: a term with 'holes' in it, cf. [Bar84, Definition 2.1.18]. For this reason, type-contexts are often called 'type-environments'. But the word 'environment' has also other meanings, so 'context' is preferred in this book.

[7] In Curry's works and [HS86], typable terms were called 'stratified'.

there exist a context $\{x_1 : \rho_1, \ldots, x_n : \rho_n\}$ and a type τ such that

$$x_1 : \rho_1, \ldots, x_n : \rho_n \quad \vdash_{\mathrm{TA}_C^{\rightarrow}} \quad X : \tau.$$

In particular, if $n = 0$, X is typable iff there exists τ such that

$$\vdash_{\mathrm{TA}_C^{\rightarrow}} \quad X : \tau.$$

Example 11.24

(a) The following closed terms are typable (by 11.5–11.8 and 11.15):

$$\mathbf{I},\ \mathbf{K},\ \mathbf{S},\ \mathbf{B},\ \mathbf{W},\ \mathbf{KK},\ \mathbf{SB},\ \mathbf{KI},\ \overline{n},\ \mathbf{D},\ \mathbf{R}_{\mathrm{Bernays}}.$$

(b) The non-closed terms x and $xz(yz)$ are typable, since

$$x : a \ \vdash_{\mathrm{TA}_C^{\rightarrow}} \ x : a,$$

$$x : a \rightarrow b \rightarrow c,\ \ y : a \rightarrow b,\ \ z : a \quad \vdash_{\mathrm{TA}_C^{\rightarrow}} \quad xz(yz) : c.$$

(c) In contrast, xx is not typable. A $\mathrm{TA}_C^{\rightarrow}$-deduction which assigned a type to xx would have to have form

$$\frac{x : \sigma \rightarrow \tau \qquad x : \sigma}{xx : \tau\,,} \ (\rightarrow \mathrm{e})$$

compare Exercise 11.9(e). But, as noted earlier, the two assumptions $x : \sigma \rightarrow \tau,\ \ x : \sigma$ are not consistent.

In a sense, xx represents the most general possible self-application. Self-applications were not allowed at all in Chapter 10; they were regarded as too 'risky'. But in this chapter we allow ourselves to come closer to danger; some particular self-applications such as **KK** are typable, but not xx.

Lemma 11.25

(a) A pure CL-term X is typable iff every subterm of X is typable.

(b) A pure CL-term X is typable iff there exist closed *types $\rho_1, \ldots, \rho_n$, τ satisfying Definition 11.23.*

(c) The set of all typable pure CL-terms is closed under weak and strong reduction, but not expansion.

(d) The set of all typable pure CL-terms is closed under [ ]-abstraction, but not under application.

Proof (a) By the subject-construction property in Section 11C.

(b) By the type-substitution lemma, 11.11.

(c) By the subject-reduction theorem (11.19), and Remark 11.20.

(d) By 11.14 and 11.14.2, and the result in 11.24 that x is typable but xx is not. □

Theorem 11.26 (Decidability of typability) *The set of all typable pure CL-terms is decidable.*

Proof The *principal-type algorithm* in [Cur69] or [Hin69, Theorem 1] includes a decision-procedure to tell whether a term is typable; see Theorem 11.36 below. □

Theorem 11.27 (SN theorem for $\triangleright_w$) *Every typable pure CL-term is strongly normalizable with respect to $\triangleright_w$. Further, if Γ is weakly inert and $\Gamma \vdash_{\mathrm{TA}_C^{\rightarrow}} X : \tau$, then X is SN with respect to $\triangleright_w$.*

Proof See Corollary 11.56.1 later. □

Corollary 11.27.1 (WN theorem for $\triangleright_w$) *Every typable pure CL-term has a weak normal form.*

Theorem 11.28 (WN theorem for $\succ\!-$) *Every typable pure CL-term has a strong normal form.*[8]

Proof A proof is in [HLS72, Italian edition, Theorems 9.19–9.21].[9] □

Corollary 11.28.1 *In CL, the fixed-point combinators* $\mathbf{Y}_{\mathrm{Turing}}$ *and* $\mathbf{Y}_{\mathrm{Curry-Ros}}$ *in Definition 3.4 are untypable.*

Proof By 9.19(e), these combinators have no strong nf. □

[8] No SN theorem for strong reduction is known; see Remark 10.27.

[9] In Theorem 9.19, the second 'M' should be 'X'. The English edition has a less trivial error: the Y in the conclusion of Theorem 9.19 should be a $Y^\star$ such that $Y \succ\!- Y^\star$, and Theorem 9.20 needs a similar change; but Theorem 9.21 is correct.

11G Link with Church's approach

The definition of 'typable term' in 11.23 was obviously intended to imitate the definition of 'typed term' in Chapter 10. And indeed, for closed terms the connection is straightforward, as will be shown below. But for terms containing variables, there will be a slight complication.

We assume here that the type-constants in Definition 11.1 are the same as the atomic types in Chapter 10.

Definition 11.29 For every typed CL-term Y^τ, define $|Y^\tau|$ to be the untyped term obtained by deleting all type-superscripts from Y^τ. In particular, define

$$|\mathsf{S}^{(\rho\to\sigma\to\tau)\to(\rho\to\sigma)\to\rho\to\tau}| \equiv \mathsf{S}, \qquad |\mathsf{K}^{\sigma\to\tau\to\sigma}| \equiv \mathsf{K},$$
$$|\mathsf{I}^{\sigma\to\sigma}| \equiv \mathsf{I}, \qquad |x^\tau| \equiv x.$$

If X is untyped and $|Y^\tau| \equiv X$, we call Y^τ a *typed analogue* of X.

A single untyped term may have many typed analogues, for example

$$\mathsf{I} \equiv |\mathsf{I}^{\mathsf{N}\to\mathsf{N}}| \equiv |\mathsf{I}^{(\mathsf{N}\to\mathsf{N})\to(\mathsf{N}\to\mathsf{N})}| \equiv \text{etc.}$$

So the correspondence between terms in Chapters 10 and 11 is not one-to-one. However, if in Chapter 11 we pass from terms to $\mathrm{TA}_\mathrm{C}^{\to}$-proofs, the correspondence between the two chapters becomes one-to-one, at least for closed pure terms and closed types. (A closed type contains no type-variables, and hence is a genuine type in both Chapters 10 and 11.)

Let τ be closed. By following the clauses in Definition 10.5, we can see that every closed pure typed term Y^τ can be re-written as a $\mathrm{TA}_\mathrm{C}^{\to}$-proof. Conversely, every $\mathrm{TA}_\mathrm{C}^{\to}$-proof of a formula $X : \tau$ can be re-written as a typed term Y^τ with $|Y^\tau| \equiv X$. In fact, closed pure typed terms and $\mathrm{TA}_\mathrm{C}^{\to}$-proofs are just different notations for the same ideas.

This gives the following lemma.

Lemma 11.30 *A closed pure CL-term X is typable iff it has a typed analogue, i.e. a Y^τ such that $|Y^\tau| \equiv X$.*

Proof By 11.25(b) and by comparing Definitions 10.5, 11.23 and 11.29.[10] □

[10] In [HS86] the condition 'closed' was wrongly omitted from the lemma on p. 186 corresponding to 11.30.

Discussion 11.31 (Non-closed terms) Let Y^τ be a pure typed term containing variables, say $\mathrm{FV}(Y^\tau) = \{x_1^{\rho_1}, \ldots, x_n^{\rho_n}\}$ $(n \geq 1)$. Then Y^τ can easily be re-written as a $\mathrm{TA}_{\mathrm{C}}^{\rightarrow}$-deduction, giving

$$x_1 : \rho_1, \ \ldots, x_n : \rho_n \ \ \vdash_{\mathrm{TA}_{\mathrm{C}}^{\rightarrow}} \ \ X : \tau \qquad \text{(where } X \equiv |Y^\tau|\text{)}.$$

However, the converse procedure, re-writing $\mathrm{TA}_{\mathrm{C}}^{\rightarrow}$-deductions as typed terms, needs a little care, because not every $\mathrm{TA}_{\mathrm{C}}^{\rightarrow}$-deduction $\mathcal{D}$ corresponds to a typed term, even when all types in $\mathcal{D}$ are closed. To see this, let x^τ be any typed variable and let $\sigma \not\equiv \tau$. Then, by the consistency condition in Definition 10.3, x^σ is not a typed variable. Hence the one-step deduction which gives

$$x : \sigma \ \ \vdash \ \ x : \sigma$$

does not correspond to a typed term.

In fact, referring to Note 10.4, the only $\mathrm{TA}_{\mathrm{C}}^{\rightarrow}$-deductions that correspond to typed terms are those whose assumptions are in the infinite set

$$\{\, v_{\psi(i,j)} : \tau_i \ \ : \ 1 \leq i, \ 1 \leq j \,\}.$$

For such deductions, the correspondence with typed terms is one-to-one.

11H Principal types

The axioms and rule of $\mathrm{TA}_{\mathrm{C}}^{\rightarrow}$ allow more than one type to be assigned to a term; this raises the natural question of what the set of types assigned to a term looks like. The present section will show that if a pure term is typable, all its types turn out to be substitution-instances of one 'principal type'. Thus the situation described for **I**, **K** and **S** in Note 11.12 holds for composite terms as well as atoms.

Definition 11.32 (Principal type, p.t.) Let X be any pure CL-term, with $\mathrm{FV}(X) = \{x_1, \ldots, x_n\}$ $(n \geq 0)$.

(a) If $n = 0$: a *principal type* or *p.t.* of X is any type π such that

  (i) $\vdash_{\mathrm{TA}_{\mathrm{C}}^{\rightarrow}} X : \pi$, and

  (ii) if $\vdash_{\mathrm{TA}_{\mathrm{C}}^{\rightarrow}} X : \tau$ then τ is a substitution-instance of π.

(b) If $n \geq 0$: a pair $\langle \Gamma, \pi \rangle$ is a *principal pair* (*p.p.*) of X, and π is a *p.t.* of X, iff

(i) Γ is an FV(X)-context and $\Gamma \vdash_{\mathrm{TA}_C^{\rightarrow}} X : \pi$, and

(ii) if $\Gamma' \vdash_{\mathrm{TA}_C^{\rightarrow}} X : \tau$ for some FV(X)-context Γ' and type τ, then $\langle \Gamma', \tau \rangle$ is a substitution-instance of $\langle \Gamma, \pi \rangle$.

Notation In the above definition a *substitution-instance* of a pair $\langle \Gamma, \pi \rangle$ is a pair $\langle \Gamma', \pi' \rangle$ that is the result of a simultaneous substitution

$$[\rho_1/a_1, \ldots, \rho_k/a_k]$$

of types for type-variables in π and the predicates in Γ. The subjects in Γ are unchanged.

Example 11.33 The term **SKK** has a principal type $a \rightarrow a$.

Proof If there exists a $\mathrm{TA}_C^{\rightarrow}$-proof of $\mathbf{SKK} : \tau$ for some τ, that proof must follow the construction of **SKK**, so it must have form

$$\dfrac{\dfrac{\overset{(\rightarrow \mathbf{S})}{\mathbf{S} : \rho \rightarrow \sigma \rightarrow \tau} \qquad \overset{(\rightarrow \mathbf{K})}{\mathbf{K} : \rho}}{\mathbf{SK} : \sigma \rightarrow \tau}\,(\rightarrow \mathrm{e}) \qquad \overset{(\rightarrow \mathbf{K})}{\mathbf{K} : \sigma}}{\mathbf{SKK} : \tau\,.}\,(\rightarrow \mathrm{e}) \tag{2}$$

for some ρ, σ, τ. The formula $\mathbf{K} : \sigma$ must be an instance of axiom-scheme $(\rightarrow \mathbf{K})$. Hence σ must have form $\mu \rightarrow \nu \rightarrow \mu$ for some μ, ν. We record this 'equation':

$$\sigma \equiv \mu \rightarrow \nu \rightarrow \mu. \tag{3}$$

Next, the formula $\mathbf{S} : \rho \rightarrow \sigma \rightarrow \tau$ must be an $(\rightarrow \mathbf{S})$-axiom, and all such axioms have form

$$\mathbf{S} : (\xi \rightarrow \eta \rightarrow \zeta) \rightarrow (\xi \rightarrow \eta) \rightarrow \xi \rightarrow \zeta\,;$$

hence, for some ξ, η, ζ,

$$\rho \equiv \xi \rightarrow \eta \rightarrow \zeta, \qquad \sigma \equiv \xi \rightarrow \eta, \qquad \tau \equiv \xi \rightarrow \zeta\,. \tag{4}$$

Also the formula $\mathbf{K} : \rho$ must be a $(\rightarrow \mathbf{K})$-axiom, so

$$\rho \equiv \xi \rightarrow \eta \rightarrow \xi. \tag{5}$$

A type can be assigned to **SKK** iff the five equations in (3)–(5) can be solved simultaneously, and the p.t. of **SKK** will be given by the most general possible solution of these equations.

The two equations for ρ in (4) and (5), and those for σ in (3) and (4), imply that

$$\zeta \equiv \xi, \qquad \xi \equiv \mu, \qquad \eta \equiv \nu \rightarrow \mu. \tag{6}$$

These equations can be solved by taking any types μ, ν, and setting $\zeta \equiv \xi \equiv \mu$ and $\eta \equiv \nu \to \mu$. Then (4) can be satisfied by setting

$$\rho \;\equiv\; \mu \to (\nu \to \mu) \to \mu, \qquad \tau \;\equiv\; \mu \to \mu. \tag{7}$$

To get the most general solution we take μ, ν to be type-variables a, b. This gives the following $\mathrm{TA}_{\mathrm{C}}^{\to}$-proof:

$$\dfrac{\dfrac{\overset{(\to\mathbf{S})}{\mathbf{S} : (a \to (b \to a) \to a) \to (a \to b \to a) \to a \to a} \quad \overset{(\to\mathbf{K})}{\mathbf{K} : a \to (b \to a) \to a}}{\mathbf{SK} : (a \to b \to a) \to a \to a} \quad \overset{(\to\mathbf{K})}{\mathbf{K} : a \to b \to a}}{\mathbf{SKK} : a \to a\,.}$$

□

Example 11.34 The term $x\mathbf{I}$ has a principal type b and a principal pair

$$\Big\langle \{x : (a \to a) \to b\},\ b \Big\rangle .$$

Proof If there exists a deduction giving $\Gamma \vdash_{\mathrm{TA}_{\mathrm{C}}^{\to}} x\mathbf{I} : \tau$ for some τ and some $\mathrm{FV}(x\mathbf{I})$-context Γ, it must have form

$$\dfrac{x : \xi \to \tau \qquad \overset{(\to\mathbf{I})}{\mathbf{I} : \xi}}{x\mathbf{I} : \tau}\ (\to \mathrm{e})$$

for some ξ. But $\mathbf{I} : \xi$ must be an $(\to\mathbf{I})$-axiom, so $\xi \equiv \eta \to \eta$ for some η. Hence the deduction must have form

$$\dfrac{x : (\eta \to \eta) \to \tau \qquad \overset{(\to\mathbf{I})}{\mathbf{I} : \eta \to \eta}}{x\mathbf{I} : \tau\,.}\ (\to \mathrm{e}) \tag{8}$$

Conversely, for all types η, τ, the above is a genuine $\mathrm{TA}_{\mathrm{C}}^{\to}$-deduction. By taking the special case $\eta \equiv a$, $\tau \equiv b$, we get a deduction

$$\dfrac{x : (a \to a) \to b \qquad \overset{(\to\mathbf{I})}{\mathbf{I} : a \to a}}{x\mathbf{I} : b\,.}\ (\to \mathrm{e}) \tag{9}$$

Hence

$$x : (a \to a) \to b \ \ \vdash_{\mathrm{TA}_{\mathrm{C}}^{\to}} \ \ x\mathbf{I} : b. \tag{10}$$

Also, if $x:\rho \vdash_{\text{TA}_C^{\rightarrow}} x\mathbf{I}:\tau$ for some ρ and τ, then $\rho \equiv (\eta \rightarrow \eta) \rightarrow \tau$ by (8), so the pair $\langle \{x:\rho\}, \tau \rangle$ must be a substitution-instance of

$$\Big\langle \{x:(a \rightarrow a) \rightarrow b\},\ b \Big\rangle.$$

□

Remark 11.35 (Pseudo-uniqueness of p.t.) Example 11.33 showed that $a \rightarrow a$ is a p.t. of **SKK**. Clearly $c \rightarrow c$ and $d \rightarrow d$, etc. are also p.t.s. So the p.t. of a term is not unique. However, it is easy to see that the p.t.s of a term X differ only by the substitution of distinct variables for distinct variables, and it is normal to say 'the p.t. of X' as if it was unique.

Theorem 11.36 (Principal-types theorem) *Every typable pure CL-term has a principal type and a principal pair.*

Proof Full proofs are in [Cur69] and [Hin69, Theorem 1]; they also give Theorem 11.26, the decidability of typability.

We just outline the method here. The key is the subject-construction property in Section 11C, that the deduction-tree for a formula $X:\tau$ must follow the structure of the construction-tree of X. To decide whether a pure term X is typable, one writes down the construction-tree of X and tries to fill in a suitable type at each stage, conforming to the patterns demanded by the axiom-schemes and rule ($\rightarrow$e).

If there is no way to fill in the types that is consistent with these patterns, the attempt will lead to a contradiction, and one can conclude that X is not typable. But if suitable types can be filled in throughout the tree, the process of filling them in will indicate the most general possible type at each stage, and the type at the bottom of the tree will be a principal type for X.

The method can be seen in action in the examples before this theorem. In an example below it will be applied to prove that a particular term is untypable.

This procedure can be written out as a formal algorithm, known as the *principal-type* algorithm (or the *type-reconstruction* or *type-inference* algorithm). It is part of the type-inference algorithm used in the programming language ML, see [Mil78]. A comprehensive introduction to the algorithm is in [Pie02, Chapter 22]. A detailed account of a version for pure λ-terms is in [Hin97, Chapter 3], including a proof that the algorithm works. □

Example 11.37 The term **SII** is untypable.

Proof A $TA_C^{\rightarrow}$-proof of $\mathbf{SII}:\tau$ would have form

$$\dfrac{\dfrac{\dfrac{(\rightarrow\mathbf{S})}{\mathbf{S}:\rho\rightarrow\sigma\rightarrow\tau} \qquad \dfrac{(\rightarrow\mathbf{I})}{\mathbf{I}:\rho}}{\mathbf{SI}:\sigma\rightarrow\tau}\,(\rightarrow\mathrm{e}) \qquad \dfrac{(\rightarrow\mathbf{I})}{\mathbf{I}:\sigma}}{\mathbf{SII}:\tau\,.}\,(\rightarrow\mathrm{e}) \tag{11}$$

Reading upward: first, the formula $\mathbf{I}:\sigma$ would have to be an $(\rightarrow\mathbf{I})$-axiom, so, for some type ν,

$$\sigma \;\equiv\; \nu\rightarrow\nu. \tag{12}$$

The formula $\mathbf{I}:\rho$ would also have to be an $(\rightarrow\mathbf{I})$-axiom, so, for some μ,

$$\rho \equiv \mu\rightarrow\mu. \tag{13}$$

Finally, the $(\rightarrow\mathbf{S})$-axiom in the above proof would have to have form

$$\mathbf{S} : (\xi\rightarrow\eta\rightarrow\zeta)\rightarrow(\xi\rightarrow\eta)\rightarrow\xi\rightarrow\zeta$$

for some ξ, η, ζ; hence

$$\rho \;\equiv\; \xi\rightarrow\eta\rightarrow\zeta, \qquad \sigma \;\equiv\; \xi\rightarrow\eta, \qquad \tau \;\equiv\; \xi\rightarrow\zeta. \tag{14}$$

The two equations for ρ in (13) and (14), and the two for σ in (12) and (14), imply that

$$\mu \equiv \xi, \qquad \mu \;\equiv\; \eta\rightarrow\zeta, \qquad \nu \equiv \xi, \qquad \nu \;\equiv\; \eta. \tag{15}$$

Hence

$$\eta\rightarrow\zeta \;\;\equiv\;\; \mu \;\;\equiv\;\; \xi \;\equiv\; \nu \;\;\equiv\;\; \eta,$$

which is impossible because $\eta\rightarrow\zeta$ is a longer expression than η. □

Exercise 11.38 Prove that **SKSI** is typable and has a principal type $(a\rightarrow b)\rightarrow a\rightarrow b$.

Summary 11.39 The following is a table of some pure terms and their principal types. (The term $\mathbf{R}_{\mathrm{Bernays}}$ from Example 11.15(c) is not included; the type assigned to it in that example was *not* principal.)

Term	*Principal type*
I	$a\rightarrow a$
K	$a\rightarrow b\rightarrow a$

$\mathbf{S}$		$(a \to b \to c) \to (a \to b) \to a \to c$
$\mathbf{B}$	$(\equiv \mathbf{S(KS)K})$	$(b \to c) \to (a \to b) \to a \to c$
$\mathbf{C}$	$(\equiv \mathbf{S(BBS)(KK)})$	$(a \to b \to c) \to b \to a \to c$
$\mathbf{W}$	$(\equiv \mathbf{SS(KI)})$	$(a \to a \to b) \to a \to b$
$\mathbf{CI}$		$a \to (a \to b) \to b$
$\mathbf{CB}$		$(a \to b) \to (b \to c) \to a \to c$
$\mathbf{SKSI}$		$(a \to b) \to a \to b$
$\overline{\sigma}$	$(\equiv \mathbf{SB})$	$((b \to c) \to a \to b) \to (b \to c) \to a \to c$
$\overline{0}$	$(\equiv \mathbf{KI})$	$a \to b \to b$
$\overline{1}$	$(\equiv \mathbf{SB(KI)})$	$(a \to b) \to a \to b$
$\overline{n}$	$(n \geq 2)$	$(a \to a) \to a \to a \quad (\equiv \mathbf{N}_a)$
$\mathbf{D}$	$(\equiv [x,y,z].z(\mathbf{K}y)x)$	$a_1 \to a_2 \to ((b \to a_2) \to a_1 \to c) \to c.$

11I Adding new axioms

The system $\mathrm{TA}_{\mathrm{C}}^{\to}$ can be extended by adding extra axioms, either by adding new atomic terms with appropriate type-assignment axioms for each new atom, or by assigning new types to old terms to express some special role these terms may have.

We shall call a set of proposed new axioms a *basis.*

Example 11.40 (The arithmetical basis $\mathcal{B}_{\mathbf{Z}}$)

The *arithmetical extension* of CL was introduced in Discussion 4.25 and Definition 4.26. It was made by adding three new atoms $\widehat{0}$, $\widehat{\sigma}$, $\mathbf{Z}$ to the definition of term (for zero, successor and iterator) and adding the following contractions to the definition of weak reduction:

$$\mathbf{Z}\widehat{n} \;\; \triangleright_{w\mathbf{Z}} \;\; \overline{n} \qquad \big(\overline{n} \equiv (\mathbf{SB})^n(\mathbf{KI}),\ n = 0,1,2,\ldots\big). \tag{16}$$

Corresponding to this, let the *arithmetical basis* $\mathcal{B}_{\mathbf{Z}}$ be the following set of formulas:

$$\widehat{0} : \mathbf{N}, \qquad \widehat{\sigma} : \mathbf{N} \to \mathbf{N}, \qquad \mathbf{Z} : \mathbf{N} \to \mathbf{N}_\tau, \tag{17}$$

where $\mathbf{N}$ is a type-constant and $\mathbf{N}_\tau$ is $(\tau \to \tau) \to \tau \to \tau$ (cf. Exercise 11.8(g)). In the third part of (17) there is one formula for each type τ. Hence $\mathcal{B}_{\mathbf{Z}}$ is an infinite set. But all the formulas $\mathbf{Z} : \mathbf{N} \to \mathbf{N}_\tau$ are substitution-instances of $\mathbf{Z}:\mathbf{N}\to\mathbf{N}_a$, so these formulas could be summarized by one 'principal axiom'.

Exercise 11.41 Given $\widehat{0}$, $\widehat{\sigma}$, $\mathbf{Z}$ as above, let $\mathbf{R}$ be the recursion operator defined in Chapter 4 (32), namely

$$\left.\begin{array}{rcl} Q & \equiv & [y,v].\,\mathbf{D}\,(\widehat{\sigma}(v\overline{0}))\,(y(v\overline{0})(v\overline{1})), \\ \mathbf{R} & \equiv & [x,y,u].\,\mathbf{Z}\,u\,(Qy)(\mathbf{D}\widehat{0}x)\,\overline{1}, \end{array}\right\} \tag{18}$$

where $\overline{n} \equiv (\mathbf{SB})^n(\mathbf{KI})$ and $\mathbf{D} \equiv [x,y,z].z(\mathbf{K}y)x$. Prove that

$$\mathcal{B}_{\mathbf{Z}} \quad \vdash_{\mathrm{TA}_{\mathrm{C}}^{\to}} \quad \mathbf{R}:\ \mathbf{N}\to(\mathbf{N}\to\mathbf{N}\to\mathbf{N})\to\mathbf{N}\to\mathbf{N}. \tag{19}$$

Example 11.42 (Two bases for the Church numerals) Suppose we take pure terms, and a type-constant $\mathbf{N}$, and look at the Church numerals. It seems natural to wish to add axioms assigning the following new types to the combinators for zero and successor:

$$\mathbf{KI}:\mathbf{N}, \qquad \mathbf{SB}:\mathbf{N}\to\mathbf{N}. \tag{20}$$

Alternatively, the following could be added as an infinite set of new axioms:

$$(\mathbf{SB})^n(\mathbf{KI}):\mathbf{N} \qquad (n=0,1,2,\ldots). \tag{21}$$

Example 11.43 (Proper inclusions) A new axiom with the form

$$\mathbf{I}:\mu\to\nu \tag{22}$$

for some types μ, ν with $\mu \not\equiv \nu$, says intuitively that the identity operator maps μ into ν, i.e. that μ is a subset of ν. Such an axiom is called a *proper inclusion*. By rule ($\to$e),

$$X:\mu,\ \ \mathbf{I}:\mu\to\nu \quad \vdash \quad \mathbf{I}X:\nu.$$

To use proper inclusions effectively, one needs to be able to deduce $X:\nu$ from $\mathbf{I}X:\nu$. But we cannot do this by the subject-reduction theorem, since a proper inclusion is not inert in the sense of Definition 11.17. In fact there is no way to deduce $X:\nu$ in $\mathrm{TA}_{\mathrm{C}}^{\to}$ as it stands, so when proper inclusions are of interest a rule of equality-invariance of types has to be added to $\mathrm{TA}_{\mathrm{C}}^{\to}$; see Section 11K below.

Definition 11.44 (Monoschematic bases) A set of $\mathrm{TA}_{\mathrm{C}}^{\rightarrow}$-formulas

$$\mathcal{B} = \{U_1 : \pi_1, \quad U_2 : \pi_2, \quad U_3 : \pi_3, \ \ldots\}$$

is called a *monoschematic basis* iff each U_i is a non-redex constant and $\mathcal{B}$ contains a 'principal axiom' for each U_i like the principal axioms for **I**, **K** and **S** in Note 11.12. More precisely, $\mathcal{B}$ is monoschematic iff each U_i is a non-redex constant and, for each constant U occurring as a subject in $\mathcal{B}$ (say $U \equiv U_{i_1} \equiv U_{i_2} \equiv U_{i_3} \equiv \ldots$), there is one i_j such that $\{\pi_{i_1}, \pi_{i_2}, \pi_{i_3}, \ldots\}$ is exactly the set of all substitution-instances of π_{i_j}. (The formula $U_{i_j} : \pi_{i_j}$ is called the *principal axiom* for U in $\mathcal{B}$.)

Remark 11.45 An example of a monoschematic basis is $\mathcal{B}_{\mathbf{Z}}$ in Example 11.40. But the bases in Examples 11.42–11.43 are not monoschematic, because their subjects are not non-redex constants.

If a basis is monoschematic, it has many of the convenient properties of the axioms for **I**, **K** and **S**. For example, it is closed under substitution, so in Lemma 11.11, if Γ is a monoschematic basis we can replace '$[\sigma_1/a_1, \ldots, \sigma_k/a_k]\Gamma$' by just '$\Gamma$'.

Every monoschematic basis is inert (because its subjects are non-redex constants).

Definition 11.46 (Relative typability) Let $\mathcal{B}$ be any set of $\mathrm{TA}_{\mathrm{C}}^{\rightarrow}$-formulas. Let X be any CL-term, with $\mathrm{FV}(X) = \{x_1, \ldots, x_n\}$ $(n \geq 0)$.

(a) We call X *typable relative to* $\mathcal{B}$ iff there exist a context $\{x_1 : \rho_1, \ldots, x_n : \rho_n\}$ and a type τ such that

$$\mathcal{B},\ x_1 : \rho_1, \ldots, x_n : \rho_n \quad \vdash_{\mathrm{TA}_{\mathrm{C}}^{\rightarrow}} \quad X : \tau.$$

(b) We call a type π a *principal type of* X *relative to* $\mathcal{B}$, and a pair $\langle \Gamma, \pi \rangle$ a *p.p. of* X *relative to* $\mathcal{B}$, iff

(i) Γ is an $\mathrm{FV}(X)$-context and $\mathcal{B} \cup \Gamma \vdash_{\mathrm{TA}_{\mathrm{C}}^{\rightarrow}} X : \pi$, and

(ii) if $\mathcal{B} \cup \Gamma' \vdash_{\mathrm{TA}_{\mathrm{C}}^{\rightarrow}} X : \tau$ for some $\mathrm{FV}(X)$-context Γ' and type τ, then $\langle \Gamma', \tau \rangle$ is a substitution-instance of $\langle \Gamma, \pi \rangle$.

Remarks 11.47 (Extending previous theorems) Suppose $\mathrm{TA}_{\mathrm{C}}^{\rightarrow}$ is extended by adding a basis $\mathcal{B}$, and suppose $\mathcal{B}$ is monoschematic or inert.

Then the *abstraction-and-types theorem* (11.14) can easily be shown to still hold.

The *principal-types theorem* (11.36) holds for p.t. and p.p. relative to $\mathcal{B}$, if $\mathcal{B}$ is monoschematic.

The *decidability of typability* (11.26) does not extend to relative typability unless $\mathcal{B}$ satisfies some decidability conditions.

The *strong normalization theorem* (11.27) still holds for $\triangleright_w$ if $\mathcal{B}$ is weakly inert. That is, every term typable relative to a weakly inert $\mathcal{B}$ is SN with respect to $\triangleright_w$.

Further, for the particular basis $\mathcal{B}_{\mathbf{Z}}$ in 11.40, the SN theorem extends in another sense. Let $\triangleright_{w\mathbf{Z}}$ be the modified reduction suggested in 11.40(16); then the subject-reduction theorem and SN theorem both hold for $\triangleright_{w\mathbf{Z}}$. (The former is easy to prove; for the latter, see Theorem A3.22 in Appendix A3.)

Remark 11.48 (Extending subject-reduction) Let $\mathrm{TA}_{\mathrm{C}}^{\rightarrow}$ be extended by adding a basis $\mathcal{B}$.

(a) If $\mathcal{B}$ is weakly or strongly inert, then the subject-reduction theorem (11.19) still holds, for $\triangleright_w$ or $\succ\!\!-$ as appropriate, since the union of two inert assumption-sets is clearly inert.

Further, this theorem also holds for some non-inert bases. For example, its proof still works if the condition on the set Γ in 11.19 is relaxed slightly, to say that every subject in Γ is in nf, and if a subject in Γ begins with **S**, **K** or **I**, then every type that Γ gives to it is atomic. An example of such a set Γ is the basis

$$\{\,(\mathbf{SB})^n(\mathbf{KI}) : \mathbf{N} \;:\; n = 0, 1, 2, \ldots\,\}$$

in Example 11.42 (21), so the subject-reduction theorem holds for that basis, even though it is not inert.

(b) In contrast, an example of a basis for which the theorem's conclusion fails, yet might have some interest, is

$$\overline{0} : \mathbf{N}, \qquad \mathbf{BW}(\mathbf{BB}) : \mathbf{N} \to \mathbf{N},$$

where $\overline{0} \equiv \mathbf{KI}$ as usual. The interest is that $\mathbf{BW}(\mathbf{BB})$ behaves rather like $\overline{\sigma}$, since

$$\begin{array}{lcll}
\mathbf{BW}(\mathbf{BB})\overline{n}xy & \triangleright_w & \mathbf{W}(\mathbf{BB}\overline{n})xy & \text{where } \overline{n} \equiv (\mathbf{SB})^n(\mathbf{KI}), \\
& \triangleright_w & \mathbf{BB}\overline{n}xxy & \\
& \triangleright_w & \mathbf{B}(\overline{n}x)xy & \\
& \triangleright_w & \overline{n}x(xy) & \\
& \triangleright_w & x^n(xy) & \text{by 4.3} \\
& \equiv & x^{n+1}y. &
\end{array}$$

The theorem's conclusion fails for this basis because, although we can easily deduce $\mathsf{BW(BB)}\overline{0} : \mathsf{N}$ from this basis, and easily see that

$$\mathsf{BW(BB)}\overline{0} \triangleright_w \mathsf{W(BB}\overline{0}),$$

there is no way to deduce $\mathsf{W(BB}\overline{0}) : \mathsf{N}$ from this basis.

11J Propositions-as-types and normalization

Discussion 11.49 (Propositions as types) A type such as $a \to b \to a$, which is open, i.e. contains no type-constants, can be interpreted as a formula of propositional calculus by reading '$\to$' as implication.

Further, if $\mathcal{D}$ is a $\mathrm{TA}_{\mathrm{C}}^{\to}$-deduction whose types are all open, and we remove all subjects from $\mathcal{D}$, then the result will be a deduction in propositional calculus. This is because the above transformation changes rule $(\to \mathrm{e})$, which says

$$\frac{X : \sigma \to \tau \qquad Y : \sigma}{XY : \tau},$$

to the propositional rule of *modus ponens*, which says

$$\frac{\sigma \to \tau \qquad \sigma}{\tau},$$

and changes the axiom-schemes $(\to \mathsf{I})$, $(\to \mathsf{K})$ and $(\to \mathsf{S})$ to provable formula-schemes of propositional calculus, namely

$$\sigma \to \sigma, \qquad \sigma \to \tau \to \sigma, \qquad (\rho \to \sigma \to \tau) \to (\rho \to \sigma) \to \rho \to \tau .$$

For example, if this transformation is carried out on the deduction of $\mathsf{SKK} : \sigma \to \sigma$ in Example 11.6, the result is the following propositional deduction of $\sigma \to \sigma$:

$$\cfrac{\cfrac{(\sigma \to (\sigma \to \sigma) \to \sigma) \to (\sigma \to \sigma \to \sigma) \to \sigma \to \sigma \qquad \sigma \to (\sigma \to \sigma) \to \sigma}{(\sigma \to \sigma \to \sigma) \to \sigma \to \sigma} \qquad \sigma \to \sigma \to \sigma}{\sigma \to \sigma .}$$

Furthermore, the term SKK which has been deleted from the conclusion determines the tree-structure of the propositional deduction. Even better, the whole propositional deduction can be coded as a single typed term

$$\mathsf{S}_{\sigma, \sigma \to \sigma, \sigma} \mathsf{K}_{\sigma, \sigma \to \sigma} \mathsf{K}_{\sigma, \sigma}$$

in the system of Chapter 10, if we extend that system by allowing its types to contain variables.

Thus, roughly speaking, open types correspond to propositional formulas, and typed terms correspond to propositional deductions.

More precisely, the correspondence is not with the propositional calculus which arises from classical truth-table logic, but with that which arises from intuitionistic logic, which is weaker but plays a crucial role in studying the foundations of computing. Intuitionistic logic is described in several books and websites, for example, [TS00, Section 2.1.1, system Ni] and [SU06, Chapter 2]. In it, certain classical tautologies are not provable, for example the formula known as Peirce's law (after Charles Sanders Peirce),

$$((a \to b) \to a) \to a.$$

This logic has other connectives besides implication, but since simple types have only '$\to$', they correspond only to the implicational fragment of intuitionistic logic.

This correspondence is called the *propositions-as-types* or *Curry–Howard* correspondence. The propositions-to-types part was first hinted at in [Cur34, p. 588] and first described explicitly in [CF58, Section 9E]. The deductions-to-terms part was described in [How80] (written in 1969). A number of other people also noticed the correspondence in the 1960s and extended it to other connectives and quantifiers. Some sources are [Läu65], [Läu70] and [Sco70a], also [Bru70], in which it was used as the basis of the proof-system *Automath*.

Definition 11.50 A type σ is said to be *inhabited* if and only if there is a closed term M such that

$$\vdash M : \sigma.$$

Under the propositions-as-types correspondence, inhabited types correspond to provable propositional formulas, and the closed terms which inhabit them correspond to propositional proofs.

Non-closed terms, i.e. terms containing free variables, correspond, not to proofs, but to deductions from assumptions.

The correspondence between terms and deductions plays an important role in the study of deductions and their structure. Indeed, in the proof-theory book [TS00] it is introduced in the first chapter, and in at least three other books it has been made the main theme: [GLT89], [Sim00] and [SU06].

Discussion 11.51 (Reducing deductions) The deductions-to-terms correspondence suggests that we should be able to reduce or simplify deductions just like terms, and perhaps define a concept of irreducible or 'simplest' deduction of a formula, corresponding to terms in normal form, and even prove confluence and normalization theorems for deductions, corresponding to those theorems for typed terms. And indeed all this can be done, [TS00, Chapter 6].

In fact, the theory of proof-reductions was begun independently of the correspondence with terms, by Dag Prawitz in 1965 [Pra65], and it is now a standard tool in proof-theory. The correspondence with terms has helped illuminate parts of this theory, and it, in turn, has illuminated parts of the theory of typed terms, for example the strong normalization theorem, 10.26.

To get a little of its flavour, let us just sketch the basic definitions for a reduction-theory of deductions. Since the present book is not about propositional logic, we shall do it for $TA_C^{\rightarrow}$-deductions, not propositional deductions. (The latter are described, for example, in [Pra65] and [TS00, Chapter 6].)

Definition 11.52 (Deduction-reductions for $TA_C^{\rightarrow}$) A *reduction* of one deduction to another consists of a sequence of replacements by the following three reduction-rules.

I-*reductions for deductions:* A deduction of the form

$$\dfrac{\mathsf{I}:\tau\to\tau \qquad \begin{matrix}\mathcal{D}_1\\ X:\tau\end{matrix}}{\begin{matrix}\mathsf{I}X:\tau\\ \mathcal{D}_2\end{matrix}}\,(\to \mathrm{e})$$

may be reduced to

$$\begin{matrix}\mathcal{D}_1\\ X:\tau\\ \mathcal{D}_2{}',\end{matrix}$$

where $\mathcal{D}_2{}'$ is obtained from $\mathcal{D}_2$ by replacing appropriate occurrences of $\mathsf{I}X$ by X.

K-*reductions for deductions:* A deduction of the form

$$\dfrac{\dfrac{\mathsf{K}:\tau\to\sigma\to\tau \qquad \begin{matrix}\mathcal{D}_1\\ X:\tau\end{matrix}}{\mathsf{K}X:\sigma\to\tau}\,(\to e) \qquad \begin{matrix}\mathcal{D}_2\\ Y:\sigma\end{matrix}}{\mathsf{K}XY:\tau}\,(\to e)$$
$$\mathcal{D}_3$$

may be reduced to

$$\begin{matrix}\mathcal{D}_1\\ X:\tau\\ \mathcal{D}_3{}',\end{matrix}$$

where $\mathcal{D}_3{}'$ is obtained from $\mathcal{D}_3$ by replacing appropriate occurrences of $\mathsf{K}XY$ by X.

S-*reductions for deductions:* A deduction of the form

$$\dfrac{\dfrac{\dfrac{\mathsf{S}:(\rho\to\sigma\to\tau)\to(\rho\to\sigma)\to\rho\to\tau \qquad \begin{matrix}\mathcal{D}_1\\ X:\rho\to\sigma\to\tau\end{matrix}}{\mathsf{S}X:(\rho\to\sigma)\to\rho\to\tau} \qquad \begin{matrix}\mathcal{D}_2\\ Y:\rho\to\sigma\end{matrix}}{\mathsf{S}XY:\rho\to\tau} \qquad \begin{matrix}\mathcal{D}_3\\ Z:\rho\end{matrix}}{\mathsf{S}XYZ:\tau}$$
$$\mathcal{D}_4$$

may be reduced to

$$\dfrac{\dfrac{\begin{matrix}\mathcal{D}_1\\ X:\rho\to\sigma\to\tau\end{matrix} \qquad \begin{matrix}\mathcal{D}_3\\ Z:\rho\end{matrix}}{XZ:\sigma\to\tau} \qquad \dfrac{\begin{matrix}\mathcal{D}_2\\ Y:\rho\to\sigma\end{matrix} \qquad \begin{matrix}\mathcal{D}_3\\ Z:\rho\end{matrix}}{YZ:\sigma}}{XZ(YZ):\tau}$$
$$\mathcal{D}_4{}',$$

where $\mathcal{D}_4{}'$ is obtained from $\mathcal{D}_4$ by replacing appropriate occurrences of $\mathsf{S}XYZ$ by $XZ(YZ)$.

Remark 11.53 Let Γ be any set of $\mathrm{TA}_C^{\to}$-formulas, and let $\mathcal{D}$ be a deduction giving

$$\Gamma \vdash_{\mathrm{TA}_C^{\to}} X:\tau.$$

(a) From the above definition it is clear that if a reduction of $\mathcal{D}$ is possible, then X must contain a weak redex. Also, if $\mathcal{D}$ reduces to $\mathcal{D}'$, then X will be weakly reduced to a term X', and $\mathcal{D}'$ will give

$$\Gamma \quad \vdash_{\mathrm{TA}_C^{\rightarrow}} \quad X' : \tau \qquad\qquad (X \rhd_w X').$$

(b) Conversely, if X contains a weak redex, and Γ is weakly inert, then by the proof of the subject-reduction theorem (11.19) a reduction of $\mathcal{D}$ is possible. And if $X \rhd_w Y$, then $\mathcal{D}$ can be reduced to a deduction giving

$$\Gamma \quad \vdash_{\mathrm{TA}_C^{\rightarrow}} \quad Y : \tau\,.$$

(c) A deduction that cannot be reduced is called *normal.*

One of the most important properties of deduction-reductions is that they cannot go on for ever. This can be proved directly, but here it will be deduced from the corresponding property for typed terms (Theorem 10.26), via the following definition and lemma.

Definition 11.54 (Assignment of typed terms to deductions) To each deduction $\mathcal{D}$ in $\mathrm{TA}_C^{\rightarrow}$, assign a typed term $T(\mathcal{D})$ as follows. This $T(\mathcal{D})$ will encode just enough of the structure of $\mathcal{D}$ to serve in the proof of the SN theorem and no more.

First, choose any atomic type from the definition of types in 10.1 (call it c), and substitute c for all type-variables in $\mathcal{D}$. Call the result $\mathcal{D}'$. Then, for each type τ, choose one typed term-variable, call it v^τ.

Assign a typed term to each part of $\mathcal{D}'$, thus:

(a) to an assumption $x : \rho$, assign v^ρ;

(b) to an assumption $U : \rho$ where U is not a variable, assign v^ρ;

(c) to an axiom $\mathbf{I} : \sigma \rightarrow \sigma$, assign $\mathbf{I}_\sigma$;

(d) to an axiom $\mathbf{K} : \sigma \rightarrow \tau \rightarrow \sigma$, assign $\mathbf{K}_{\sigma,\tau}$;

(e) to an axiom $\mathbf{S} : (\rho \rightarrow \sigma \rightarrow \tau) \rightarrow (\rho \rightarrow \sigma) \rightarrow \rho \rightarrow \tau$, assign $\mathbf{S}_{\rho,\sigma,\tau}$;

(f) to the conclusion of an application of rule $(\rightarrow \mathrm{e})$, say

$$\frac{U : \sigma \rightarrow \tau \qquad V : \sigma}{UV : \tau\,,} \;(\rightarrow \mathrm{e})$$

assign $(X^{\sigma\rightarrow\tau} Y^\sigma)^\tau$, where $X^{\sigma\rightarrow\tau}$ has been assigned to the premise $U : \sigma \rightarrow \tau$, and Y^σ to the premise $V : \sigma$.

The typed term $T(\mathcal{D})$ contains only one variable of each type (though that variable may occur many times), and contains no non-redex constants. But it contains all the occurrences of **S**, **K** and **I** that have been introduced into $\mathcal{D}$ by axioms, and this is enough to give us the following key lemma.

Lemma 11.55 *Let $\mathcal{D}$, $\mathcal{E}$ be any $\mathrm{TA}_C^{\rightarrow}$-deductions, and let $\mathcal{D}$ reduce to $\mathcal{E}$ by one of the replacements in Definition 11.52. Then $T(\mathcal{D})$ reduces to $T(\mathcal{E})$ by one weak contraction.*

Proof Straightforward. □

Theorem 11.56 (SN for deductions) *Every reduction of a $\mathrm{TA}_C^{\rightarrow}$-deduction is finite.*

Proof Suppose we had an infinite reduction of deductions. Then, by Lemma 11.55, we would get an infinite weak reduction of typed terms. But this would contradict the SN theorem for these terms, Theorem 10.26. □

Corollary 11.56.1 (SN for CL-terms) *Let Γ be weakly inert, and let $\Gamma \vdash_{\mathrm{TA}_C^{\rightarrow}} X:\tau$. Then all weak reductions of X are finite.*

Proof By the theorem and Remark 11.53(b). □

Remark 11.57 If the inertness condition in the above corollary is omitted, the corollary might fail. In fact we could have a deduction $\mathcal{D}$ giving

$$\Gamma \vdash_{\mathrm{TA}_C^{\rightarrow}} X:\tau\,,$$

such that $\mathcal{D}$ was normal but X had an infinite reduction. For example, let $X \equiv \mathbf{YK}$ where $\mathbf{Y}$ is a fixed-point combinator, and let $\Gamma = \{\mathbf{YK}:\tau\}$ for some τ; then $\Gamma \vdash \mathbf{YK}:\tau$ by a one-step normal deduction; but **YK** has no weak normal form.

However, there are some non-inert assumption-sets for which the conclusion of the corollary is true or partly true. Two such sets have been used in the literature as bases of axioms for extensions of $\mathrm{TA}_C^{\rightarrow}$; they are discussed in the following two remarks.

Remark 11.58 (Bases with a universal type) Suppose there is a type-constant ω (standing for the universal set), and suppose a basis $\mathcal{B}$ contains a formula $X:\omega$ for every term X. Then $\mathcal{B}$ is clearly not inert. However, suppose the part of $\mathcal{B}$ left over after all the formulas $X:\omega$ are removed is weakly inert. Then, if $\mathcal{D}$ is a normal deduction giving, say,

$$\mathcal{B} \vdash_{\mathrm{TA}_{\mathrm{C}}^{\rightarrow}} Y:\tau\,,$$

all weak redexes in Y will be in components which receive type ω in $\mathcal{D}$. (See [Sel77, pp. 26–27], where, as in the work of Curry, ω is called E.)

With a basis $\mathcal{B}$ that assigns a type ω to every term, types no longer serve as 'safety labels'; instead, they become labels describing a term's behaviour in some more complex way. For example, the system called *intersection types* that originated in [Sal78] and [CDS79] contains such a basis; in that system, the rules allow other types to be assigned besides ω, and it can be proved that the positions of the ω's in a term's types indicate certain aspects of the term's reduction-behaviour, for example whether it has a normal form. (More references on this system are in the list of further reading at the end of Chapter 12.)

Remark 11.59 (Bases with proper inclusions) Suppose a basis $\mathcal{B}$ contains a proper inclusion $\mathsf{I}:\mu\to\nu$ (see Example 11.43). Then $\mathcal{B}$ is clearly not inert. Further, if an assumption $\mathsf{I}:\mu\to\nu$ is used in a normal deduction $\mathcal{D}$ of a formula $Y:\tau$, there can easily be a redex in Y.

For example, let a, b, c, d be type-variables, let G and H be non-redex atoms, and let

$$\mathcal{B} \;=\; \{\mathsf{I}:(a\to b)\to c\to d,\;\; G:b,\;\; H:c\}.$$

Then, using the axiom $\mathsf{K}:b\to a\to b$, we can easily deduce

$$\mathcal{B} \;\vdash_{\mathrm{TA}_{\mathrm{C}}^{\rightarrow}}\; \mathsf{I}(\mathsf{K}G)H:d$$

by a normal deduction. Yet $\mathsf{I}(\mathsf{K}G)$ is a redex; furthermore, if this redex is contracted to $\mathsf{K}G$, then the term becomes $\mathsf{K}GH$, which is also a redex. This shows that contracting all redexes of the form $\mathsf{I}U$ need not lead to a term in normal form.

However, if that part of $\mathcal{B}$ left over when the proper inclusions are removed is inert, then it can be proved that $\mathcal{B}\vdash Y:\tau$ implies that Y has a normal form, provided that each proper inclusion $\mathsf{I}:\mu\to\nu$ in $\mathcal{B}$ satisfies either of the following two conditions: (1) ν is a type-constant; or (2) for each term U such that $\mathcal{B}\vdash U:\mu$ and for each $n\geq 0$, each reduction of $Ux_1\dots x_n$ proceeds entirely inside U. (See [Sel77, Remark 2, p. 23].)

Proper inclusions satisfying (1) can occur in a system of transfinite type theory, where a type constant T is made into a transfinite type by postulating $\mathsf{I}:\mu\rightarrow T$ for every finite type μ. (See [And65].)

To see an application of condition (2), it is necessary to consider a type theory that is to include statements about types. In this case each type must be a term. This can be accomplished by making each type-constant a non-redex constant, each type-variable an ordinary term-variable, and taking another non-redex constant, say F (Curry's notation), so that $\sigma\rightarrow\tau$ will be regarded as an abbreviation for $\mathsf{F}\sigma\tau$. Then if H is the type-constant of propositions, we can turn each type into a propositional function by making a new type-constant L, postulating $\tau:\mathsf{L}$ for each type τ in which L does not occur, and postulating the proper inclusion

$$\mathsf{I}:\ \mathsf{L}\rightarrow\tau\rightarrow\mathsf{H}$$

for each type τ in which L does not occur. (See [CHS72, Chapter 17].)

Remark 11.60 ($\beta\eta$-reducing a deduction) It is possible to add to the definition of deduction-reduction (11.52) the following new rule, analogous to the definition of strong reduction of terms (Definition 8.15):

$\beta\eta$-strong reductions for deductions If

$$\begin{array}{c} x:\sigma \\ \mathcal{D}_1 \\ X:\tau \end{array} \quad \text{reduces to} \quad \begin{array}{c} x:\sigma \\ \mathcal{D}_2 \\ Y:\tau \end{array}$$

and the corresponding deductions obtained by Theorem 11.14 are

$$\begin{array}{c} \mathcal{D}_1{}' \\ [x]^\eta.X:\sigma\rightarrow\tau \end{array} \quad \text{and} \quad \begin{array}{c} \mathcal{D}_2{}' \\ [x]^\eta.Y:\sigma\rightarrow\tau, \end{array}$$

then

$$\begin{array}{c} \mathcal{D}_1{}' \\ [x]^\eta.X:\sigma\rightarrow\tau \\ \mathcal{D}_3 \end{array} \quad \text{reduces to} \quad \begin{array}{c} \mathcal{D}_2{}' \\ [x]^\eta.Y:\sigma\rightarrow\tau \\ \mathcal{D}_3{}', \end{array}$$

where $\mathcal{D}_3{}'$ is obtained from $\mathcal{D}_3$ by replacing appropriate occurrences of $[x].X$ by $[x].Y$.

It has been proved [Sel77, Remark 3, p. 24] that every deduction from a strongly inert basis has a normal form with respect to this 'strong' reduction.

11K The equality-rule Eq′

As we have seen in Remark 11.20, $\mathrm{TA}_{\mathrm{C}}^{\rightarrow}$ is not invariant under combinatory equality. For example, **SKSI** does not have all of the types that **KI**(**SI**) has; furthermore, although **II**(**II**) has p.t. $a \rightarrow a$, **SIII** is untypable. In a system using combinators this is a defect, because the usefulness of combinators comes from the transformations that can be carried out using their reduction properties. To remedy this defect we can add the following rule:

Rule Eq′
$$\frac{X : \tau \qquad X =_{\star} Y}{Y : \tau\,,}$$

where '$=_{\star}$' stands for $=_{w}$, $=_{\mathrm{C}\beta}$, or the extensional equality $=_{\mathrm{C}\,ext}$. Of course this is really three rules; when we need to distinguish them, they will be called, respectively,

$$\mathrm{Eq}'_{w}\,, \qquad \mathrm{Eq}'_{\beta}\,, \qquad \mathrm{Eq}'_{ext}\,.$$

Definition 11.61 (The systems $\mathbf{TA}_{\mathrm{C}=}^{\rightarrow}$) The systems $\mathrm{TA}_{\mathrm{C}=w}^{\rightarrow}$, $\mathrm{TA}_{\mathrm{C}=\beta}^{\rightarrow}$ and $\mathrm{TA}_{\mathrm{C}=ext}^{\rightarrow}$ are defined by adding the above rules Eq'_{w}, Eq'_{β} and Eq'_{ext}, respectively, to the definition of $\mathrm{TA}_{\mathrm{C}}^{\rightarrow}$ (Definition 11.5).

The name $\mathrm{TA}_{\mathrm{C}=}^{\rightarrow}$ will mean any or all of these systems, according to context.

Remark 11.62 (Undecidability) Note that the relation $\vdash X : \tau$ in $\mathrm{TA}_{\mathrm{C}=}^{\rightarrow}$ is undecidable, unlike that in $\mathrm{TA}_{\mathrm{C}}^{\rightarrow}$ which is decidable (see Theorem 11.26). The underlying reason for this is that in systems with rule Eq′, deductions need not follow the constructions of the terms as they do in $\mathrm{TA}_{\mathrm{C}}^{\rightarrow}$ (see Section 11C), because it is possible for a deduction in $\mathrm{TA}_{\mathrm{C}=}^{\rightarrow}$ to consist of a $\mathrm{TA}_{\mathrm{C}}^{\rightarrow}$-deduction followed by an inference by rule Eq′. Since combinatory equality is undecidable, so is $\mathrm{TA}_{\mathrm{C}=}^{\rightarrow}$.

Discussion 11.63 It might seem that, since rule Eq′ can occur anywhere in a deduction, $\mathrm{TA}_{\mathrm{C}=}^{\rightarrow}$ is a much richer system than $\mathrm{TA}_{\mathrm{C}}^{\rightarrow}$. But this is not the case. Every deduction in $\mathrm{TA}_{\mathrm{C}=}^{\rightarrow}$ can be replaced by one in which rule Eq′ occurs only at the end.

For, suppose an inference by Eq′ occurs before the end of a deduction. Then its conclusion is a premise for an inference by ($\rightarrow$ e), or else for another inference by Eq′. Since equality is transitive, successive inferences by Eq′ can always be combined into one; so we may assume that the next rule is $(\to e)$, and assume our deduction has one of the forms

$$\dfrac{\dfrac{\begin{matrix}\mathcal{D}_1\\ X:\sigma\to\tau\end{matrix}\qquad X=_\star Y}{Y:\sigma\to\tau}\,\mathrm{Eq}' \qquad \begin{matrix}\mathcal{D}_2\\ Z:\sigma\end{matrix}}{\begin{matrix}YZ:\tau\\ \mathcal{D}_3\end{matrix}}\,(\to\mathrm{e})$$

or

$$\dfrac{\begin{matrix}\mathcal{D}_2\\ Z:\sigma\to\tau\end{matrix} \qquad \dfrac{\begin{matrix}\mathcal{D}_1\\ X:\sigma\end{matrix}\qquad X=_\star Y}{Y:\sigma}\,\mathrm{Eq}'}{\begin{matrix}ZY:\tau\\ \mathcal{D}_3\,.\end{matrix}}\,(\to\mathrm{e})$$

These deductions can be replaced, respectively, by

$$\dfrac{\dfrac{\begin{matrix}\mathcal{D}_1\\ X:\sigma\to\tau\end{matrix}\qquad \begin{matrix}\mathcal{D}_2\\ Z:\sigma\end{matrix}}{XZ:\tau}\,(\to\mathrm{e}) \qquad \begin{matrix}(X=_\star Y)\\ XZ=_\star YZ\end{matrix}}{\begin{matrix}YZ:\tau\\ \mathcal{D}_3\end{matrix}}\,\mathrm{Eq}'$$

or

$$\dfrac{\dfrac{\begin{matrix}\mathcal{D}_2\\ Z:\sigma\to\tau\end{matrix}\qquad \begin{matrix}\mathcal{D}_1\\ X:\sigma\end{matrix}}{ZX:\tau}\,(\to\mathrm{e}) \qquad \begin{matrix}(X=_\star Y)\\ ZX=_\star ZY\end{matrix}}{\begin{matrix}ZY:\tau\\ \mathcal{D}_3\,.\end{matrix}}\,\mathrm{Eq}'$$

If these replacements are made systematically in a deduction, beginning at the top, and if consecutive inferences by rule Eq′ are combined whenever they occur in this process, we will eventually wind up with a new deduction of the same formula, in which there is at most one inference by Eq′, and that inference occurs at the end. This proves the following theorem.

Theorem 11.64 (Eq′-postponement) *If* $=_\star$ *is* $=_w$ *or* $=_{C\beta}$ *or* $=_{C\,ext}$*, and* Γ *ia any set of formulas, and*

$$\Gamma \ \vdash_{\mathrm{TA}_{C=}^{\to}} \ X:\tau\,,$$

then there is a term Y *such that* $Y =_\star X$ *and*

$$\Gamma \ \vdash_{\mathrm{TA}_{C}^{\to}} \ Y:\tau\,.$$

Corollary 11.64.1 (WN theorem for $\mathrm{TA}_{\mathrm{C=}}^{\rightarrow}$) *Let Γ be weakly [strongly] inert. If $\Gamma \vdash X : \tau$ in $\mathrm{TA}_{\mathrm{C}=w}^{\rightarrow}$ [$\mathrm{TA}_{\mathrm{C}=ext}^{\rightarrow}$], then X has a weak [strong] normal form.*

Proof By 11.27.1 and 11.28. □

Remarks 11.65

(a) An extension of Corollary 11.64.1 to $=_{\mathrm{C}\beta}$ would depend on the theory of β-strong reduction, see Remark 9.41.

(b) Corollary 11.64.1 cannot be strengthened to conclude that X is SN. To see this, take a term X which has a normal form but also has an infinite reduction, say $X \equiv \mathbf{Y}(\mathbf{KI})$. This X has a normal form, since

$$X \rhd_w \mathbf{KI}X \rhd_w \mathbf{I};$$

but it also has the infinite reduction

$$X \rhd_w \mathbf{KI}X \rhd_w \mathbf{KI}(\mathbf{KI}X) \rhd_w \mathbf{KI}(\mathbf{KI}(\mathbf{KI}X)) \rhd_w \text{etc.}$$

Now $\mathbf{I}:a\to a$ is provable in $\mathrm{TA}_{\mathrm{C}}^{\rightarrow}$, so by rule Eq′, $X:a\to a$ is provable in $\mathrm{TA}_{\mathrm{C}=w}^{\rightarrow}$. But X is not SN.

Definition 11.66 (Typability in $\mathrm{TA}_{\mathrm{C=}}^{\rightarrow}$) The definitions of *typable*, *p.t.* and *p.p.* for $\mathrm{TA}_{\mathrm{C=}}^{\rightarrow}$ are exactly the same as for $\mathrm{TA}_{\mathrm{C}}^{\rightarrow}$ (Definitions 11.23 and 11.32), but with $\vdash_{\mathrm{TA}_{\mathrm{C=}}^{\rightarrow}}$ instead of $\vdash_{\mathrm{TA}_{\mathrm{C}}^{\rightarrow}}$.

However, the class of typable terms in $\mathrm{TA}_{\mathrm{C=}}^{\rightarrow}$ differs from that in $\mathrm{TA}_{\mathrm{C}}^{\rightarrow}$. The following theorem gives the relation between the two classes.

Theorem 11.67 *Let $=_\star$ be $=_w$ or $=_{ext}$. Then a pure CL-term X is typable in $\mathrm{TA}_{\mathrm{C=}}^{\rightarrow}$ iff X has a normal form $X^\star$ which is typable in $\mathrm{TA}_{\mathrm{C}}^{\rightarrow}$. Further, the types that $\mathrm{TA}_{\mathrm{C=}}^{\rightarrow}$ assigns to X are exactly those that $\mathrm{TA}_{\mathrm{C}}^{\rightarrow}$ assigns to $X^\star$.*

Proof Exercise. (Hint: use the Eq′-postponement and WN theorems, with the p.t. theorem for $\mathrm{TA}_{\mathrm{C}}^{\rightarrow}$ (11.36).) □

Theorem 11.68 (Principal types in $\mathrm{TA}_{\mathrm{C=}}^{\rightarrow}$) *Let $=_\star$ be $=_w$ or $=_{\mathrm{C}\beta}$ or $=_{\mathrm{C}\,ext}$.*

(a) Every pure CL-term that is typable in $\mathrm{TA}_{\mathrm{C=}}^{\rightarrow}$ has a p.t. and a p.p. in $\mathrm{TA}_{\mathrm{C=}}^{\rightarrow}$.

(b) If $\mathcal{B}$ is a monoschematic basis of axioms, then every term typable relative to $\mathcal{B}$ has a p.t. and a p.p. relative to $\mathcal{B}$.

Proof From 11.67. (The proof is valid for both (a) and (b), see Discussion 11.47.) □

Warning 11.69 Although the above theorem may appear to be the same as the p.t. theorem for $\mathrm{TA}_C^{\rightarrow}$, it is not quite. This is because a term may be typable in both $\mathrm{TA}_C^{\rightarrow}$ and $\mathrm{TA}_{C=}^{\rightarrow}$, but have different principal types in both systems. For example, **SKSI** is typable in $\mathrm{TA}_C^{\rightarrow}$ and its p.t. is $(a \rightarrow b) \rightarrow a \rightarrow b$ (by Exercise 11.38); but **SKSI** $\triangleright_w$ **I**, so in $\mathrm{TA}_{C=}^{\rightarrow}$ its p.t. is $a \rightarrow a$.

However, despite this warning, the Eq′-postponement theorem has essentially reduced the study of $\mathrm{TA}_{C=}^{\rightarrow}$ to the study of $\mathrm{TA}_C^{\rightarrow}$. The latter is much easier, which is why so much of the present chapter has been devoted to it, despite the fact that $\mathrm{TA}_C^{\rightarrow}$ is incomplete with respect to equality.

Further reading See the end of the next chapter.

12
Simple typing, Curry-style in λ

12A The system $\mathbf{TA}_\lambda^{\rightarrow}$

This chapter will do for λ-terms what Chapter 11 did for CL-terms. There is not a major difference between the two chapters in either the basic ideas or the main results, but there is a major technical complication in the proofs for λ, caused by the fact that λ-terms have bound variables while CL-terms do not.

In this chapter the terms are λ-terms exactly as defined in Chapter 1 (not the typed terms of Chapter 10). Recall the abbreviations

$$\mathsf{I} \equiv \lambda x.x, \quad \mathsf{K} \equiv \lambda xy.x, \quad \mathsf{S} \equiv \lambda xyz.xz(yz).$$

Types are defined here exactly as in Definition 11.1 (parametric types). The basic conventions for these types are those of Notation 11.2, and the types are interpreted exactly as in Remark 11.3.

Type-assignment formulas are as defined in Definition 11.4, except that now their subjects are λ-terms, not CL-terms.

The $\rightarrow$*-elimination rule* from Definition 11.5 will be used also in the present chapter; for λ-terms M and N, it says

$$\frac{M : \sigma \rightarrow \tau \qquad N : \sigma}{MN : \tau\,.} \ (\rightarrow \mathrm{e})$$

Discussion 12.1 (The $\rightarrow$ introduction rule) A comparison of Definitions 11.5 and 10.19 shows that the axiom-schemes $(\rightarrow \mathsf{I})$, $(\rightarrow \mathsf{K})$ and $(\rightarrow \mathsf{S})$ of the former correspond to the constants I_σ, $\mathsf{K}_{\sigma,\tau}$ and $\mathsf{S}_{\rho,\sigma,\tau}$ of the latter, and that rule $(\rightarrow \mathrm{e})$ of the former corresponds to the construction of application-terms $(M^{\sigma\rightarrow\tau}N^{\sigma})^{\tau}$ in the latter.

To assign types to λ-terms, we shall not need $(\rightarrow \mathsf{I})$, $(\rightarrow \mathsf{K})$ and $(\rightarrow \mathsf{S})$, but instead we shall need a new rule corresponding to the construction of

$$(\lambda x^{\sigma} . M^{\tau})^{\sigma\to\tau}$$

in the definition of typed λ-terms (10.5). This new rule will not be a straightforward rule like (→e), but will be like the implication-introduction rule in Gerhard Gentzen's 'Natural Deduction' system of propositional logic.[1]

The new rule is called →-*introduction* or (→i), and says

$$(\to \mathrm{i}) \quad \begin{cases} \text{If } x \notin \mathrm{FV}(L_1 \dots L_n) \text{ and} \\ \qquad L_1 : \rho_1, \ \dots, L_n : \rho_n, \ x : \sigma \quad \vdash \quad M : \tau, \\ \text{then} \\ \qquad L_1 : \rho_1, \ \dots, \ L_n : \rho_n \quad \vdash \quad (\lambda x . M) : (\sigma \to \tau) . \end{cases}$$

It is usually written thus:

$$\frac{\begin{array}{c}[x : \sigma] \\ M : \tau\end{array}}{(\lambda x . M) : (\sigma \to \tau) .} \ (\to \mathrm{i})$$

This needs some explanation. Gentzen's Natural Deduction systems are very like formal theories as defined in Chapter 6, but they are not quite the same. A deduction is a tree of formulas just like deductions in Notation 6.1, but Gentzen allowed that some of the assumptions in branch-tops may be only temporary assumptions, to be employed at an early stage in the deduction and then 'discharged' (or 'cancelled') at a later stage. After an assumption has been discharged, it is marked in some way; we shall enclose it in brackets.

In such a system, rule (→i) is read as *'If $x \notin \mathrm{FV}(L_1 \dots L_n)$, and the formula $M : \tau$ is the conclusion of a deduction whose not-yet-discharged assumptions are $L_1 : \rho_1, \ \dots, L_n : \rho_n, \ x : \sigma$, then you may deduce*

$$(\lambda x . M) : (\sigma \to \tau),$$

and wherever the assumption $x : \sigma$ occurs undischarged at a branch-top above $M : \tau$, you must enclose it in brackets to show that it has now been discharged.'

When an assumption has been discharged, it ceases to count as an assumption. More formally, in a completed deduction-tree in a Natural

[1] Natural Deduction is described in several textbooks and websites, for example [Dal97, Section 1.4], [Coh87, Section 11.4], [RC90], [SU06, Section 2.2].

Deduction system, some formulas at branch-tops may be enclosed in brackets; and if Γ is any set of formulas, the notation

$$\Gamma \vdash M:\tau$$

is defined to mean that there is a deduction-tree whose bottom formula is $M:\tau$, and whose *unbracketed* top-formulas are members of Γ. As usual, when Γ is empty, we say

$$\vdash M:\tau.$$

Here are three examples.

Example 12.2 In this chapter, $\mathsf{S} \equiv \lambda xyz.xz(yz)$. In any system whose rules include $(\to\mathrm{e})$ and $(\to\mathrm{i})$, we have, for all types ρ, σ, τ,

$$\vdash \mathsf{S} : (\rho \to \sigma \to \tau) \to (\rho \to \sigma) \to \rho \to \tau.$$

Proof First, we can assume $x : \rho \to \sigma \to \tau$, $y : \rho \to \sigma$ and $z : \rho$, and make a deduction for $xz(yz)$ thus. (For ease of reference later, each assumption is numbered.)

$$\dfrac{\dfrac{\overset{1}{x : \rho \to \sigma \to \tau} \qquad \overset{2}{z : \rho}}{xz : \sigma \to \tau}\,(\to\mathrm{e}) \qquad \dfrac{\overset{3}{y : \rho \to \sigma} \qquad \overset{2}{z : \rho}}{yz : \sigma}\,(\to\mathrm{e})}{xz(yz) : \tau}\,(\to\mathrm{e})$$

Then we can apply rule $(\to\mathrm{i})$ three times. The result is the following deduction. In it, whenever rule $(\to\mathrm{i})$ is used, the number of the assumption it discharges is shown, e.g. '$(\to\mathrm{i} - 2)$'.

$$\dfrac{\dfrac{\dfrac{\dfrac{\dfrac{\overset{1}{[x : \rho \to \sigma \to \tau]} \quad \overset{2}{[z : \rho]}}{xz : \sigma \to \tau}\,(\to\mathrm{e}) \qquad \dfrac{\overset{3}{[y : \rho \to \sigma]} \quad \overset{2}{[z : \rho]}}{yz : \sigma}\,(\to\mathrm{e})}{xz(yz) : \tau}\,(\to\mathrm{e})}{\lambda z.xz(yz) : (\rho \to \tau)}\,(\to\mathrm{i}\ - 2)}{\lambda yz.xz(yz) : (\rho \to \sigma) \to \rho \to \tau}\,(\to\mathrm{i}\ - 3)}{\lambda xyz.xz(yz) : (\rho \to \sigma \to \tau) \to (\rho \to \sigma) \to \rho \to \tau.}\,(\to\mathrm{i}\ - 1)$$

□

Comments on Example 12.2 (a) Although all the branch-top formulas have brackets in the completed deduction above, each one starts its life without brackets, and only receives brackets when it is discharged after a use of $(\to\mathrm{i})$.

(b) Only formulas at branch-tops can be discharged, never those in the body of a deduction.

(c) If an assumption occurs several times at branch-tops, such as $z:\rho$ above, rule ($\rightarrow$i) discharges every branch-top occurrence that is above the place where ($\rightarrow$i) is applied.

(d) The rule-names and the numbers shown in the deduction are included for the reader's convenience, but are not really part of the deduction and are not actually necessary; if they were omitted, the form of each rule would still show which rule it was, and which assumptions (if any) it discharged.

Example 12.3 In this chapter, $\mathsf{K} \equiv \lambda xy.x$. In any system whose rules include ($\rightarrow$e) and ($\rightarrow$i), we have, for all σ, τ,

$$\vdash \ \mathsf{K} : \sigma \rightarrow \tau \rightarrow \sigma.$$

Proof Here is a deduction of the required formula. In it, the first application of ($\rightarrow$i) discharges all assumptions $y:\tau$ that occur. But none in fact occur, so nothing is discharged. This is perfectly legitimate; it is called a '*vacuous discharge*', and is shown by '($\rightarrow$i – v)'.

$$\dfrac{\dfrac{\overset{1}{[x:\sigma]}}{\lambda y.x : \tau \rightarrow \sigma}\ (\rightarrow\text{i} - \text{v})}{\lambda xy.x : \sigma \rightarrow \tau \rightarrow \sigma.}\ (\rightarrow\text{i} \ - 1)$$ □

Example 12.4 In this chapter, $\mathsf{I} \equiv \lambda x.x$. In any system with rule ($\rightarrow$i), we have, for all σ,

$$\vdash \ \mathsf{I} : \sigma \rightarrow \sigma.$$

Proof The following deduction begins with a one-step deduction $x:\sigma$, whose conclusion is the same as its only assumption. A deduction with only one step is a genuine deduction, and rule ($\rightarrow$i) can legitimately be applied to it.

$$\dfrac{\overset{1}{[x:\sigma]}}{\lambda x.x : \sigma \rightarrow \sigma.}\ (\rightarrow\text{i} \ - 1)$$ □

Discussion 12.5 Before we come to define the type-assignment system, we need to consider one further rule, for α-conversion. Since two α-convertible terms are intended to represent the same operation, any two such terms should be assigned exactly the same types. That is, we want an *α-invariance property*:

$$\Gamma \vdash M:\tau, \quad M \equiv_\alpha N \quad \Longrightarrow \quad \Gamma \vdash N:\tau \tag{1}$$

(where Γ is any set of formulas). If all the terms in Γ are atoms, then α-invariance will turn out to be provable by induction on the lengths of deductions. But sometimes it will be interesting to consider more general sets Γ. For example, if there is an atomic type **N** for the natural numbers, and 0 is represented by $\lambda xy.y$, we shall want to assume

$$\lambda xy.y : \mathbf{N}.$$

The α-invariance property will then fail unless we also assume

$$\lambda xz.z : \mathbf{N}, \quad \lambda uv.v : \mathbf{N}, \quad \text{etc.}$$

But this makes our set of assumptions infinite, in a rather boring way. To avoid this, we shall postulate a formal rule which, in effect, closes every set of assumptions under α-conversion. (It is tempting to simply postulate (1) as an unrestricted rule, but this would make the subject-construction property harder to state and use.)

Definition 12.6 (The type-assignment system $\mathrm{TA}_\lambda^{\rightarrow}$) $\mathrm{TA}_\lambda^{\rightarrow}$ is a Natural Deduction system. Its *formulas*, called $\mathrm{TA}_\lambda^{\rightarrow}$*-formulas*, are expressions $M:\tau$ for all λ-terms M and all types τ. (M is called the formula's *subject* and τ its *predicate*.) $\mathrm{TA}_\lambda^{\rightarrow}$ has no axioms. It has the following three rules:

(→e) $$\frac{M:\sigma\rightarrow\tau \quad N:\sigma}{MN:\tau}$$

(→i) $$\frac{\begin{matrix}[x:\sigma]\\ M:\tau\end{matrix}}{(\lambda x.M):\sigma\rightarrow\tau}$$

Condition: $x:\sigma$ is the only undischarged assumption in whose subject x occurs free. After rule (→i) is used, every occurrence of $x:\sigma$ at branch-tops above $M:\tau$ is called 'discharged' and enclosed in brackets

($\equiv'_\alpha$) $$\frac{M:\tau \quad M\equiv_\alpha N}{N:\tau}$$

Condition: $M \not\equiv N$, and $M:\tau$ is not the conclusion of a rule.

(Strictly speaking, $\mathrm{TA}_\lambda^{\rightarrow}$ also contains axioms and rules to define α-conversion, but we shall leave these to the imagination.) For any finite or infinite set Γ of formulas, the notation

$$\Gamma \ \vdash_{\mathrm{TA}_\lambda^\to} \ M:\tau$$

means that there is a deduction of $M:\tau$ whose undischarged assumptions are members of Γ. If Γ is empty, we say simply

$$\vdash_{\mathrm{TA}_\lambda^\to} \ M:\tau.$$

Example 12.7 Recall that $\mathbf{B} \equiv \lambda xyz.x(yz)$. Then, for all ρ, σ, τ,

$$\vdash_{\mathrm{TA}_\lambda^\to} \ \mathbf{B} : (\sigma\to\tau)\to(\rho\to\sigma)\to\rho\to\tau.$$

Proof

$$\dfrac{\dfrac{\dfrac{\dfrac{\overset{3}{[x:\sigma\to\tau]} \qquad \dfrac{\overset{2}{[y:\rho\to\sigma]} \qquad \overset{1}{[z:\rho]}}{yz:\sigma}\,(\to\mathrm{e})}{x(yz):\tau}\,(\to\mathrm{e})}{\lambda z.x(yz):(\rho\to\tau)}\,(\to\mathrm{i}-1)}{\lambda yz.x(yz):(\rho\to\sigma)\to\rho\to\tau}\,(\to\mathrm{i}\ -2)}{\lambda xyz.x(yz):(\sigma\to\tau)\to(\rho\to\sigma)\to\rho\to\tau.}\,(\to\mathrm{i}\ -3)$$

□

Remark 12.8 The condition in rule $(\to\mathrm{i})$ prevents the term $\lambda x.xx$ from having a type. This is because any $\mathrm{TA}_\lambda^\to$-deduction for $\lambda x.xx$ would have to begin with a deduction for xx, and then apply $(\to\mathrm{i})$, like this:

$$\dfrac{\dfrac{\overset{1}{x:\sigma\to\tau} \qquad \overset{2}{x:\sigma}}{xx:\tau}\,(\to\mathrm{e})}{\lambda x.xx:\rho\to\tau\,,}\,(\to\mathrm{i, discharging\ 1\ or\ 2\ or\ v})$$

for some ρ. But the condition in $(\to\mathrm{i})$ is that the discharged assumption is the only one whose subject is x, so neither 1 nor 2 can be discharged here, nor can a vacuous assumption $x:\rho$ be discharged. (Cf. the remark about xx in Example 11.24(c).)

Exercise 12.9 * For each of the seven terms shown on the left-hand side in the following list, give a $\mathrm{TA}_\lambda^\to$-deduction to show that it has all the types shown on the right-hand side (one type for each ρ, σ, τ). Cf. Exercise 11.8.

	Term		*Type*
(a)	$\overline{0} \equiv \lambda xy.y$	(see 4.2)	$\tau \to \sigma \to \sigma$
(b)	$\overline{\sigma} \equiv \lambda uxy.x(uxy)$	(see 4.2)	$((\sigma\to\tau)\to\rho\to\sigma)\to(\sigma\to\tau)\to\rho\to\tau$
(c)	$\mathsf{W} \equiv \lambda xy.xyy$	(see 3.2)	$(\sigma \to \sigma \to \tau) \to \sigma \to \tau$
(d)	$\lambda xyz.y$		$\rho \to \sigma \to \tau \to \sigma$
(e)	$\overline{0} \equiv \lambda xy.y$		$\mathsf{N}_\tau \;\; (\equiv (\tau\to\tau)\to\tau\to\tau)$
(f)	$\overline{\sigma} \equiv \lambda uxy.x(uxy)$		$\mathsf{N}_\tau \to \mathsf{N}_\tau$
(g)	$\overline{n} \equiv \lambda xy.x^n y$		N_τ.

12B Basic properties of $\mathrm{TA}_\lambda^{\to}$

Definition 12.10 (Kinds of assumption-sets) Let Γ be a set of $\mathrm{TA}_\lambda^{\to}$-formulas $\{U_1 : \pi_1, U_2 : \pi_2, \ldots\}$. We call Γ [β- or $\beta\eta$-] *inert* iff every U_i is a normal form [β or $\beta\eta$, respectively] which does not begin with λ.

The definition of *monoschematic basis* is the same as for CL, see 11.44.

(Every monoschematic basis is both β- and $\beta\eta$-inert.)

Lemma 12.11 (Closure under type-substitutions) *Let Γ be any set of $\mathrm{TA}_\lambda^{\to}$-formulas, and let*

$$\Gamma \vdash_{\mathrm{TA}_\lambda^{\to}} M : \tau .$$

Then, for all type-variables $a_1, \ldots, a_k$ and types $\sigma_1, \ldots, \sigma_k$,

$$[\sigma_1/a_1, \ldots, \sigma_k/a_k]\Gamma \;\; \vdash_{\mathrm{TA}_\lambda^{\to}} \;\; M : [\sigma_1/a_1, \ldots, \sigma_k/a_k]\tau .$$

Proof (Cf. Lemma 11.11.) Substitute $[\sigma_1/a_1, \ldots, \sigma_k/a_k]$ throughout the predicates in the given deduction. This substitution will change an instance of rule ($\to$e), ($\to$i) or ($\equiv'_\alpha$) into a new instance of the same rule, so the result is still a genuine deduction. □

Lemma 12.12 (α-invariance) *Let Γ be any set of $\mathrm{TA}_\lambda^{\to}$-formulas. If*

$$\Gamma \vdash_{\mathrm{TA}_\lambda^{\to}} M : \tau$$

and $M \equiv_\alpha N$, then

$$\Gamma \vdash_{\mathrm{TA}_\lambda^{\to}} N : \tau .$$

Proof [CHS72, Section 14D3, Case 1], replacing assumption (ii) in that proof by rule $(\equiv'_\alpha)$. □

Remark 12.13 (The subject-construction property) Similarly to $\mathrm{TA}_C^{\to}$, the deduction of a formula $M:\tau$ in $\mathrm{TA}_\lambda^{\to}$ closely follows the construction of M; see Examples 12.2, 12.3, 12.4 and 12.7. The only extra complication here is rule $(\equiv'_\alpha)$, and this can only be used at the top of a branch in a deduction-tree. (Indeed, if all the subjects of the assumptions are atoms, it cannot be used at all.) Just as with $\mathrm{TA}_C^{\to}$, we shall not state the property in full formal detail here, but merely give some simple examples of its use.[2]

Example 12.14 Every type assigned to $\mathbf{I}$ $(\equiv \lambda x.x)$ in $\mathrm{TA}_\lambda^{\to}$ has the form

$$\sigma \to \sigma.$$

Proof Since $\mathbf{I} \equiv \lambda x.x$, every type assigned to $\mathbf{I}$ must be compound, and the last inference in the deduction must be by $(\to \mathrm{i})$. In other words, if there is a deduction which gives

$$\vdash_{\mathrm{TA}_\lambda^{\to}} \mathbf{I} : \sigma \to \tau,$$

then removing the last inference from the deduction leaves a deduction giving

$$x:\sigma \vdash_{\mathrm{TA}_\lambda^{\to}} x:\tau.$$

But this latter deduction can only be a deduction with one step, and it follows that $\tau \equiv \sigma$. □

Exercise 12.15* Prove that every type assigned to $\mathbf{B}$ $(\equiv \lambda xyz.x(yz))$ in $\mathrm{TA}_\lambda^{\to}$ has the form

$$(\sigma \to \tau) \to (\rho \to \sigma) \to \rho \to \tau.$$

Exercise 12.16* Prove that there is no type assigned in $\mathrm{TA}_\lambda^{\to}$ to the fixed-point combinator $\mathbf{Y}_{\mathrm{Curry-Ros}}$ $(\equiv \lambda x.VV$, where $V \equiv \lambda y.x(yy)$, from Definition 3.4).

The next theorem will show that, like $\mathrm{TA}_C^{\to}$, $\mathrm{TA}_\lambda^{\to}$ preserves types

[2] The property for a system without the α-conversion rule is expressed formally in [CHS72, Section 14D2, Subject-Construction theorem].

under reductions (though here, of course, reductions will be β- and $\beta\eta$-reductions). And, as in $\mathrm{TA}_C^{\rightarrow}$, we shall need a replacement lemma before the theorem, though here the presence of bound variables will complicate the lemma's statement and proof.

Lemma 12.17 (Replacement) *Let Γ_1 be any set of $\mathrm{TA}_\lambda^{\rightarrow}$-formulas, and $\mathcal{D}$ be a deduction giving*

$$\Gamma_1 \vdash_{\mathrm{TA}_\lambda^{\rightarrow}} X:\tau\,.$$

Let V be a term-occurrence in X, and let $\lambda x_1,\ldots,\lambda x_n$ be those λ's in X whose scope contains V. Let $\mathcal{D}$ contain a formula $V:\sigma$ in the same position as V has in the construction-tree for X, and let

$$x_1:\rho_1,\ \ldots,\ x_n:\rho_n$$

be the assumptions above $V:\sigma$ that are discharged by applications of $(\rightarrow\mathrm{i})$ below it. Assume that $V:\sigma$ is not in Γ_1. Let W be a term such that $\mathrm{FV}(W)\subseteq\mathrm{FV}(V)$, and let Γ_2 be a set of $\mathrm{TA}_\lambda^{\rightarrow}$-formulas whose subjects do not contain $x_1,\ldots,x_n$ free. Let

$$\Gamma_2,\ x_1:\rho_1,\ \ldots,\ x_n:\rho_n \ \vdash_{\mathrm{TA}_\lambda^{\rightarrow}}\ W:\sigma\,.$$

Let $X^\star$ be the result of replacing V by W in X. Then

$$\Gamma_1\cup\Gamma_2 \ \vdash_{\mathrm{TA}_\lambda^{\rightarrow}}\ X^\star:\tau\,.$$

Proof A full proof requires a careful induction on X. Here is an outline. First cut off from $\mathcal{D}$ the subtree above the formula $V:\sigma$. The result is a tree $\mathcal{D}_1$ with form

$$\begin{array}{c} V:\sigma \\ \mathcal{D}_1 \\ X:\tau\,. \end{array}$$

And since $V:\sigma$ is not in Γ_1, the first step below $V:\sigma$ cannot be rule $(\equiv'_\alpha)$; in fact, that rule cannot be used anywhere below $V:\sigma$. Replace V by W in the formula $V:\sigma$, and in all formulas below it in $\mathcal{D}_1$; then take the given deduction of $W:\sigma$ and place it above. The result is a tree, leading from assumptions in $\Gamma_1\cup\Gamma_2$ to the conclusion $X^\star:\tau$. And each $(\rightarrow\mathrm{i})$-step in this tree satisfies the conditions required in this rule, because $x_1,\ldots,x_n$ do not occur in Γ_2. So the tree is a correct deduction of $X^\star:\tau$. □

Lemma 12.18 *Let* Γ *be any set of* $\mathrm{TA}_\lambda^{\to}$*-formulas such that* x *does not occur in any term of* Γ. *Let*

$$\Gamma,\ x{:}\sigma\ \vdash\ Y{:}\tau. \tag{2}$$

Then for any term U,

$$\Gamma,\ U{:}\sigma\ \vdash\ [U/x]Y : \tau, \tag{3}$$

where the number of steps in the deduction of (3) is the same as that in the deduction of (2).

Proof See [CHS72, Section 14D2 Corollary 1.1]. □

Theorem 12.19 (Subject-reduction) *Let* Γ *be a* β- $[\beta\eta$-$]$ *inert set of* $\mathrm{TA}_\lambda^{\to}$*-formulas. If*

$$\Gamma\ \vdash_{\mathrm{TA}_\lambda^{\to}}\ X{:}\tau$$

and $X \rhd_\beta X'$ $[X \rhd_{\beta\eta} X']$, *then*

$$\Gamma\ \vdash_{\mathrm{TA}_\lambda^{\to}}\ X'{:}\tau\,.$$

Proof If the step from X to X' is an α-conversion, use Lemma 12.12. Now suppose X $\beta\eta$-contracts to X'. By the replacement lemma, it is enough to take care of the case that X is a redex and X' is its contractum. By 12.12, we can assume that no variable bound in XX' occurs free in a subject in Γ.

Case 1: X is a β-redex, say $(\lambda x.M)N$, and X' is $[N/x]M$. By the assumption that the subjects in Γ are normal forms, the formula $X:\sigma$ cannot be in Γ, and cannot be the conclusion of rule $(\equiv'_\alpha)$. Hence, it is the conclusion of an inference by $(\to\mathrm{e})$, for which the premises are

$$\Gamma\ \vdash\ \lambda x.M : \sigma\to\tau, \qquad \Gamma\ \vdash\ N{:}\sigma,$$

for some σ. By the assumption that the subjects in Γ do not begin with λ, the formula $\lambda x.M : \sigma\to\tau$ cannot be in Γ and cannot be the conclusion of $(\equiv'_\alpha)$. Hence it must be the conclusion of an inference by $(\to\mathrm{i})$, the premise for which is

$$\Gamma,\ x{:}\sigma\ \vdash\ M{:}\tau,$$

where x does not occur free in any subject in Γ. The conclusion, which is

$$\Gamma\ \vdash\ [N/x]M : \tau,$$

then follows by Lemma 12.18.[3]

Case 2 ($\beta\eta$-reduction only): X is an η-redex. Then $X \equiv \lambda x.Mx$, where x does not occur free in M, and $X' \equiv M$. By the assumption that the subjects in Γ are $\beta\eta$-normal forms, the formula $X:\tau$ is not in Γ. Hence, it is the conclusion of an inference by ($\rightarrow$i), where $\tau \equiv \rho \rightarrow \sigma$ and the premise is

$$\Gamma,\ x:\rho\ \vdash\ Mx:\sigma.$$

Since x does not occur free in any subject of Γ, the formula $Mx:\sigma$ does not occur in Γ, and is not the conclusion of rule ($\equiv_\alpha'$); hence it must be the conclusion of an inference by ($\rightarrow$e) whose premises are

$$\Gamma,\ x:\rho\ \vdash\ M:\mu\rightarrow\sigma, \qquad \Gamma,\ x:\rho\ \vdash\ x:\mu,$$

for some μ. By the second of these, and the fact that x does not occur free in any subject of Γ, we have $\mu \equiv \rho$, and hence the first of these is

$$\Gamma,\ x:\rho\ \vdash\ M:\tau.$$

Since x does not occur free in M or in any subject of Γ, the assumption $x:\rho$ is not used in this deduction and can thus be omitted from the list of undischarged assumptions. Hence $\Gamma \vdash M:\tau$. □

Remark 12.20 (a) The above proof will still work if the condition on Γ is relaxed slightly, to say that every subject in Γ is in normal form and if a subject in Γ begins with a λ, then every type it receives in Γ is an atomic constant. An example of such an assumption-set is

$$\Gamma = \{\overline{1}:\mathbf{N},\ \overline{2}:\mathbf{N},\ \overline{3}:\mathbf{N},\ \ldots\},$$

where $\overline{n} \equiv \lambda xy.x^n y$. Hence the subject-reduction theorem holds for this set of assumptions.

(b) An example of an assumption-set for which the theorem's conclusion fails is

$$\{\overline{0}:\mathbf{N},\ \overline{\sigma}:\mathbf{N}\rightarrow\mathbf{N}\},$$

where $\overline{0} \equiv \lambda xy.y$ and $\overline{\sigma} \equiv \lambda uxy.x(uxy)$. Both these terms begin with λ, so the hypothesis of the theorem fails. The conclusion also fails, since from this assumption-set it is possible to prove $\overline{\sigma}\,\overline{0}:\mathbf{N}$, and $\overline{\sigma}\,\overline{0} \rhd_\beta \overline{1}$, but it is impossible to prove $\overline{1}:\mathbf{N}$.

[3] The authors would like to thank John Stone for pointing out that in [HS86] the proof of the corresponding theorem (15.17) was in error in relying on Lemma 12.17 at this point.

Remark 12.21 Theorem 12.19 cannot be reversed; it is not, in general, true that if $\vdash X:\sigma$ and $X' \rhd X$ then $\vdash X':\sigma$. For example, let

$$X \equiv \overline{0} \equiv \lambda xy.y, \qquad X' \equiv \lambda xy.\mathsf{K}y(xy).$$

Then, as indicated in Exercise 12.9(a), we have $\vdash X : \tau \to \sigma \to \sigma$ for any type τ; but it is not hard to check that $\vdash X' : \tau \to \sigma \to \sigma$ holds only if $\tau \equiv \sigma \to \mu$ for some μ.

An even stronger example is $X \equiv \mathsf{I}$ and $X' \equiv (\lambda z.zz)\mathsf{I}$, since we have $\vdash X : \sigma \to \sigma$ whereas $\mathrm{TA}_\lambda^{\to}$ assigns no type at all to X' (by Example 12.27 and the fact that $\mathrm{TA}_\lambda^{\to}$ assigns a type to a term only if it assigns a type to each of its subterms).

However, reversal is possible under certain very restricted conditions; see [CHS72, Section 14D4].

In Section 12E we shall study a system defined by adding a rule of equality-invariance to $\mathrm{TA}_\lambda^{\to}$.

12C Typable λ-terms

The notion of typable term will be the same for $\mathrm{TA}_\lambda^{\to}$ as for $\mathrm{TA}_C^{\to}$ in Section 11F. And, just as in that section, for simplicity we shall only consider pure terms.

Following Definition 11.21, a (*type-*)*context* is a finite or infinite set $\Gamma \equiv \{x_1:\rho_1, x_2:\rho_2, \dots\}$ which gives only one type to each x_i, i.e. which satisfies $x_i \equiv x_j \Longrightarrow \rho_i \equiv \rho_j$. If X is a λ-term, an FV(X)-*context* is a context whose subjects are exactly the variables occurring free in X.

If $\mathcal{D}$ is a deduction of $X:\tau$ from a context Γ, and X is a pure term, then rule $(\equiv'_\alpha)$ cannot occur in $\mathcal{D}$ (by the restriction on that rule). However, the α-invariance lemma (12.12) is still valid; its proof in [CHS72, Section 14D3] covers this situation.

Definition 12.22 (Typable pure λ-terms) A pure λ-term X, with $\mathrm{FV}(X) = \{x_1, \dots, x_n\}$, is said to be *typable* iff there exist a context $\{x_1:\rho_1, \dots, x_n:\rho_n\}$ and a type τ such that

$$x_1:\rho_1, \dots, x_n:\rho_n \quad \vdash_{\mathrm{TA}_\lambda^{\to}} \; X:\tau.$$

In particular, a closed term X is typable iff there exists τ such that

$$\vdash_{\mathrm{TA}_\lambda^{\to}} \; X:\tau.$$

Example 12.23 By 12.2, 12.3, 12.4, 12.7 and 12.9, the following λ-terms are typable:

$$\mathsf{S},\quad \mathsf{K},\quad \mathsf{I},\quad \mathsf{B},\quad \mathsf{W},\quad \overline{n}\ (\equiv \lambda xy.x^n y),\quad \overline{\sigma}\ (\equiv \lambda uxy.x(uxy)).$$

It is not hard to show that the following are also typable:

$$\mathsf{C}\ (\equiv \lambda xyz.xzy), \qquad \mathsf{D}\ (\equiv \lambda xyz.z(\mathsf{K}y)x,\ \text{cf. } 11.15(\text{b})),$$

$$\mathsf{R}_{\text{Bernays}}\ \ (\text{cf. } 11.15(\text{c})).$$

In contrast, xx is untypable in $\mathrm{TA}_\lambda^{\to}$ just as in $\mathrm{TA}_C^{\to}$ (see Example 11.24(c), which applies to both systems since it involves no axioms).

Lemma 12.24 *In* TA_λ*:*

(a) *A pure λ-term X is typable iff every subterm of X is typable.*

(b) *A pure λ-term X is typable iff there exist* closed *types $\rho_1, \ldots, \rho_n, \tau$ satisfying Definition 12.22.*

(c) *The set of all typable pure λ-terms is closed under β- and βη-reduction, but not expansion.*

(d) *The set of all typable pure λ-terms is closed under abstraction, but not under application.*

Proof (a) By the subject-construction property, 12.13.

(b) By the type-substitution lemma, 12.11.

(c) By the subject-reduction theorem (12.19), and Remark 12.21.

(d) By rule ($\to$i), and the fact that xx is not typable, 12.23. □

Definition 12.25 (Principal type, p.t.) Let X be any pure λ-term, with $\mathrm{FV}(X) = \{x_1, \ldots, x_n\}$ ($n \geq 0$).

(a) If $n = 0$: we call a type π a *p.t.* of X iff $\vdash_{\mathrm{TA}_\lambda^{\to}} X : \tau$ holds for a type τ when and only when τ is a substitution-instance of π.

(b) If $n \geq 0$: we call a pair $\langle \Gamma, \pi \rangle$ a *principal pair* (*p.p.*) of X, and π a *p.t.* of X, iff Γ is an $\mathrm{FV}(X)$-context and the relation $\Gamma' \vdash_{\mathrm{TA}_\lambda^{\to}} X : \tau$ holds for an $\mathrm{FV}(X)$-context Γ' and a type τ when and only when $\langle \Gamma', \tau \rangle$ is a substitution-instance of $\langle \Gamma, \pi \rangle$ (cf. note after 11.32).

Example 12.26 I has p.t. $a \to a$.

Proof See Example 12.14. □

Example 12.27 $\lambda x.xx$ is untypable.

Proof By Example 11.24(c), xx is untypable. The result then follows by Lemma 12.24(a). □

Just as in Chapter 11, beyond these examples lies a general *principal-type algorithm*, which will decide whether a term X is typable and, if it is, will output a p.t. and p.p. for X. This algorithm is described in several publications, for example [Mil78], [Hin97, Section 3E], and [Pie02, Chapter 22]. On it rest the following two theorems. Their proofs are omitted.

Theorem 12.28 (P.t. theorem) *Every typable pure λ-term has a p.t. and a p.p.*

Theorem 12.29 (Decidability of typability) *The set of all typable pure λ-terms is decidable.*

Now, if each CL-term in the table in 11.39 is replaced by the corresponding λ-term, it is not hard to show that the result is a table of p.t.s of λ-terms.

The fact that these corresponding terms have the same p.t.s suggests that $\mathrm{TA}_C^{\rightarrow}$ and $\mathrm{TA}_\lambda^{\rightarrow}$ are equivalent. To state the precise form of this equivalence, first define, for every assumption-set Γ in $\mathrm{TA}_C^{\rightarrow}$,

$$\Gamma_\lambda \;=\; \{\,\text{formulas } X_\lambda : \tau \;:\; X : \tau \text{ is in } \Gamma\,\}.$$

Similarly, for a set Γ of assumptions in $\mathrm{TA}_\lambda^{\rightarrow}$, and any H-transformation, define

$$\Gamma_H \;=\; \{\,\text{formulas } X_H : \tau \;:\; X : \tau \text{ is in } \Gamma\,\}.$$

Then an easy proof gives the following result.

Theorem 12.30 (Equivalence of $\mathbf{TA}_C^{\rightarrow}$ and $\mathbf{TA}_\lambda^{\rightarrow}$) *Let H be H_η, H_w, or H_β (9.10, 9.24, 9.27); then*

(a) $\Gamma \vdash_{\mathrm{TA}_C^{\rightarrow}} X : \tau \quad \Longrightarrow \quad \Gamma_\lambda \vdash_{\mathrm{TA}_\lambda^{\rightarrow}} X_\lambda : \tau,$

(b) $\Gamma \vdash_{\mathrm{TA}_\lambda^{\rightarrow}} M : \tau \quad \Longrightarrow \quad \Gamma_H \vdash_{\mathrm{TA}_C^{\rightarrow}} M_H : \tau.$

Exercise 12.31 *

(a) Prove that, for every pure CL-term X, X is typable in $\mathrm{TA}_C^{\rightarrow}$ iff X_λ is typable in $\mathrm{TA}_\lambda^{\rightarrow}$; also X and X_λ have the same p.t.

(b) Let H be H_η; find a pure λ-term M such that M_H has a different p.t. from M.
(c) What are the results for H_w and H_β corresponding to (b)?

12D Propositions-as-types and normalization

Deduction-reductions work for $\mathrm{TA}_\lambda^{\rightarrow}$ much as they do for $\mathrm{TA}_\mathrm{C}^{\rightarrow}$. Of course the **S**-, **K**- and **I**-reductions in the last chapter must be replaced by β-reductions (defined below), but this is the same sort of replacement one makes in passing from weak CL-reduction to $\lambda\beta$-reduction in the world of terms.

Definition 12.32 (Deduction-reductions for $\mathrm{TA}_\lambda^{\rightarrow}$) A *reduction* of one deduction to another consists of a sequence of replacements by the following reduction-rule:

β-reductions for deductions A deduction of the form

$$\dfrac{\dfrac{\begin{array}{c} 1 \\ [x:\sigma] \\ \mathcal{D}_1(x) \\ M:\tau \end{array}}{\lambda x.M:\sigma\to\tau}\,(\to\mathrm{i}-1) \qquad \begin{array}{c}\mathcal{D}_2 \\ N:\sigma\end{array}}{(\lambda x.M)N:\tau}\,(\to\mathrm{e})$$
$$\mathcal{D}_3$$

may be reduced to

$$\begin{array}{c} \mathcal{D}_2 \\ N:\sigma \\ \mathcal{D}_1(N) \\ [N/x]M:\tau \\ \mathcal{D}_3{}', \end{array}$$

where $\mathcal{D}_3{}'$ is obtained from $\mathcal{D}_3$ by replacing appropriate occurrences of $(\lambda x.M)N$ by $[N/x]M$.

Note that carrying out this reduction step has the effect of performing one contraction on the subject of the conclusion.

For readers who know propositional logic in Gentzen's 'Natural Deduction' version, it is worth noting that if we delete all subjects from the preceding reduction-step, the result will be a reduction of Natural Deductions in propositional logic. Such reductions were first described in [Pra65]. In fact, the proof of [Pra65, Chapter III Theorem 2] can be combined with the propositions-as-types transformation to show that every deduction in TA_λ can be reduced to a normal (irreducible) deduction; see [Sel77, Theorem 6, p. 22]. This gives us the following result.

Theorem 12.33 (WN for deductions) *Every $\mathrm{TA}_\lambda^{\rightarrow}$-deduction can be reduced to a normal deduction.*

Corollary 12.33.1 (WN for λ-terms) *Let Γ be β-inert in the sense of Definition 12.10. If $\Gamma \vdash_{\mathrm{TA}_\lambda^{\rightarrow}} M:\tau$, then M has a β-normal form.*

Proof By 12.33 we can assume the deduction of $M:\tau$ is normal. But it is easy, in the light of the proof of 12.19, to see that if a β-redex occurred in M, then the deduction could be reduced by a β-reduction; see [Sel77, Corollary 6.2 p. 23]. (This depends, of course, on the assumption that Γ is inert.) □

Remark 12.34 WN for typable pure λ-terms can be obtained from the preceding theorem and corollary by taking the special case in which Γ is a context. Also SN for these terms can probably be obtained by a similar method of proof. We have not checked the details of this, however, because SN can be proved by a slightly different method, as follows.

Theorem 12.35 (SN for λ-terms and $\triangleright_\beta$) *Every typable pure λ-term is strongly normalizable with respect to $\triangleright_\beta$.*

Proof (outline) Let M_0 be a pure λ-term and $\mathcal{D}_0$ be a $\mathrm{TA}_\lambda^{\rightarrow}$-deduction of $M_0 : \tau$ from some context Γ, say $\Gamma = \{x_1:\rho_1, \ldots, x_n:\rho_n\}$. Suppose there is a reduction of M_0 with an infinite number of β-steps:

$$M_0 \ \triangleright_{1\beta}\ M_1 \equiv_\alpha M_1' \ \triangleright_{1\beta}\ M_2 \equiv_\alpha M_2' \ \triangleright_{1\beta}\ M_3 \equiv_\alpha M_3' \ \ldots \qquad (4)$$

By the subject-reduction theorem, 12.19, for each $k \geq 0$ there exists a $\mathrm{TA}_\lambda^{\rightarrow}$-deduction $\mathcal{D}_k$ giving $\Gamma \vdash M_k:\tau$. Now the subjects in Γ are atoms, so by the restriction in rule $(\equiv_\alpha')$, that rule cannot occur in $\mathcal{D}_k$. Hence a Church-style typed term $M_k^{\star\tau}$ can be assigned to $\mathcal{D}_k$, by first assigning to each assumption $x_i : \rho_i$ in Γ a distinct Church-style typed variable with type ρ_i, then working down the deduction $\mathcal{D}_k$. Corresponding to rules ($\to$e) and ($\to$i) in Definition 12.6, one builds terms

$$\left(M^{\star\,\sigma\to\tau} N^{\star\sigma}\right)^{\tau}, \qquad \left(\lambda u^{\sigma} . M^{\star\tau}\right)^{\sigma\to\tau},$$

where u^{σ} is the typed variable assigned to the formula $x : \sigma$.

The details of the mapping from $\mathcal{D}_k$ to $M_k^{\star\tau}$ depend on the Church-style typed variables chosen to correspond to the assumptions in Γ and to the bound variables in M_0, M_1, etc. We omit those details here. But a suitable choice can be made so that the reduction (4) changes to an infinite reduction of the typed term $M_0^{\star\tau}$. This contradicts the SN theorem for typed terms, Theorem 10.15. Hence M_0 cannot have an infinite β-reduction. □

Remark 12.36 ($\beta\eta$-reduction) A deduction-reduction analogous to $\beta\eta$-reduction can be defined by adding to Definition 12.32 the following extra reduction rule.

η-reductions for deductions A deduction of the form

$$\dfrac{\dfrac{\begin{matrix}\mathcal{D}_1 \\ M : \sigma\to\tau\end{matrix} \qquad \begin{matrix}1 \\ [x : \sigma]\end{matrix}}{Mx : \tau}\,(\to\mathrm{e})}{\begin{matrix}\lambda x . Mx : \sigma\to\tau \\ \mathcal{D}_2,\end{matrix}}\,(\to\mathrm{i}-1)$$

where x does not occur free in $\mathcal{D}_1$ (and hence does not occur free in M), may be reduced to

$$\begin{matrix}\mathcal{D}_1 \\ M : \sigma\to\tau \\ \mathcal{D}_2{}',\end{matrix}$$

where $\mathcal{D}_2{}'$ is obtained from $\mathcal{D}_2$ by replacing appropriate occurrences of $\lambda x . Mx$ by M.

The weak normalization theorem for $\beta\eta$-reductions of deductions is proved in [Sel77, Corollary 6.1, p. 22]. For $\beta\eta$-reductions of terms, WN comes from WN for $\triangleright_\beta$ and the fact that a term has a $\beta\eta$-normal form iff it has a β-normal form (7.14).

12E The equality-rule Eq′

The system $\mathrm{TA}_\lambda^{\rightarrow}$ is like $\mathrm{TA}_C^{\rightarrow}$ in failing to be invariant under equality (Remark 12.21). Hence there is interest in adding the following rule:

Rule Eq′ $$\frac{X:\tau \qquad X =_\star Y}{Y:\tau\,.}$$

This is really two alternative rules: '$=_\star$' may denote $=_\beta$ or $=_{\beta\eta}$.

Definition 12.37 (The systems $\mathbf{TA}_{\lambda=}^{\rightarrow}$) These systems are obtained from $\mathrm{TA}_\lambda^{\rightarrow}$ (Definition 12.6) by adding rule Eq′. If $=_\star$ is $=_\beta$, we call the rule Eq'_β and the system $\mathrm{TA}_{\lambda=\beta}^{\rightarrow}$. If $=_\star$ is $=_{\beta\eta}$, we call the rule $\mathrm{Eq}'_{\beta\eta}$ and the system $\mathrm{TA}_{\lambda=\beta\eta}^{\rightarrow}$. The names Eq′ and $\mathrm{TA}_{\lambda=}^{\rightarrow}$ will mean either and/or both of these rules and systems, according to the context.

Remark 12.38 $\mathrm{TA}_{\lambda=}^{\rightarrow}$ is undecidable, because $=_\beta$ and $=_{\beta\eta}$ are so.

Discussion 12.39 The Eq′-postponement theorem can be proved for $\mathrm{TA}_{\lambda=}^{\rightarrow}$ by adding to the proof for $\mathrm{TA}_{C=}^{\rightarrow}$, in Discussion 11.63, the extra case in which an inference by Eq′ occurs directly above an inference by rule ($\rightarrow$i). In this case, the given deduction has the following form:

$$\dfrac{\dfrac{\begin{matrix}\overset{1}{[x:\sigma]}\\ \mathcal{D}_1(x)\\ X:\tau\end{matrix} \qquad X =_\star Y}{Y:\tau}\,(\mathrm{Eq}')}{\lambda x.Y:\sigma\rightarrow\tau}\,(\rightarrow\mathrm{i}-1)$$
$$\mathcal{D}_2\,,$$

and it can be replaced by

$$\dfrac{\dfrac{\begin{matrix}\overset{1}{[x:\sigma]}\\ \mathcal{D}_1(x)\\ X:\tau\end{matrix}}{\lambda x.X:\sigma\rightarrow\tau}\,(\rightarrow\mathrm{i}-1) \qquad \lambda x.X =_\star \lambda x.Y}{\lambda x.Y:\sigma\rightarrow\tau}\,(\mathrm{Eq}')$$
$$\mathcal{D}_2\,.$$

If this replacement is used with the others in Discussion 11.63, the result is a proof of the following theorem.

Theorem 12.40 (Eq′-postponement) *Let* $=_\star$ *be* $=_{\lambda\beta}$ *or* $=_{\lambda\beta\eta}$*. If* Γ *is any set of* $\mathrm{TA}_\lambda^{\rightarrow}$*-formulas, and*

$$\Gamma \vdash_{\mathrm{TA}_{\lambda=}^{\rightarrow}} X:\tau,$$

then there is a term Y *such that* $Y =_\star X$ *and*

$$\Gamma \vdash_{\mathrm{TA}_\lambda^{\rightarrow}} Y:\tau.$$

Corollary 12.40.1 (WN theorem for $\mathrm{TA}_{\lambda=}^{\rightarrow}$**)** *If the set* Γ *of* $\mathrm{TA}_\lambda^{\rightarrow}$*-formulas is* β*-inert, and* $\Gamma \vdash_{\mathrm{TA}_{\lambda=\beta}^{\rightarrow}} X:\tau$*, then* X *has a* β*-normal form. Similarly for* $\beta\eta$*.*

For reasons stated in Remark 11.65(b), this corollary cannot be extended to conclude that X is SN.

Corollary 12.40.2 (Principal type theorem for $\mathrm{TA}_{\lambda=}^{\rightarrow}$**)** *Let* $=_\star$ *be* $=_{\lambda\beta}$ *or* $=_{\lambda\beta\eta}$*. Then every typable pure* λ*-term has a p.t. and a p.p. in* $\mathrm{TA}_{\lambda=}^{\rightarrow}$*.*

Remark 12.41 The definitions of *typable*, *p.t.* and *p.p.* used in the above corollary are the same as for $\mathrm{TA}_\lambda^{\rightarrow}$, but with $\mathrm{TA}_{\lambda=}^{\rightarrow}$-deducibility replacing $\mathrm{TA}_\lambda^{\rightarrow}$-deducibility. Note that a term may have a p.t. in $\mathrm{TA}_{\lambda=}^{\rightarrow}$ and a different one, or none at all, in $\mathrm{TA}_\lambda^{\rightarrow}$ (cf. 11.69). The following theorem connects the two systems, and, together with the Eq′-postponement theorem, goes a long way towards reducing the study of $\mathrm{TA}_{\lambda=}^{\rightarrow}$ to that of $\mathrm{TA}_\lambda^{\rightarrow}$.

Theorem 12.42 *Let* $=_\star$ *be* $=_{\lambda\beta}$ *or* $=_{\lambda\beta\eta}$*. Then a pure* λ*-term* X *is typable in* $\mathrm{TA}_{\lambda=}^{\rightarrow}$ *iff* X *has a normal form* $X^\star$ *which is typable in* $\mathrm{TA}_\lambda^{\rightarrow}$*. Further, the types that* $\mathrm{TA}_{\lambda=}^{\rightarrow}$ *assigns to* X *are exactly those that* $\mathrm{TA}_\lambda^{\rightarrow}$ *assigns to* $X^\star$*.*

Finally, the systems $\mathrm{TA}_{\lambda=}^{\rightarrow}$ are linked to $\mathrm{TA}_{C=}^{\rightarrow}$ by the following theorem. To state it, let us say that systems $\mathrm{TA}_{C=}^{\rightarrow}$, $\mathrm{TA}_{\lambda=}^{\rightarrow}$, and an H-transformation are *compatible* iff either they are $\mathrm{TA}_{C=\beta}^{\rightarrow}$, $\mathrm{TA}_{\lambda=\beta}^{\rightarrow}$, H_β, or they are $\mathrm{TA}_{C=ext}^{\rightarrow}$, $\mathrm{TA}_{\lambda=\beta\eta}^{\rightarrow}$, H_η.

Theorem 12.43 (Equivalence of $\mathrm{TA}_{C=}^{\rightarrow}$ and $\mathrm{TA}_{\lambda=}^{\rightarrow}$) *If* $\mathrm{TA}_{\lambda=}^{\rightarrow}$, $\mathrm{TA}_{C=}^{\rightarrow}$ *and* H *are compatible, then*

(a) $\quad \Gamma \vdash_{\mathrm{TA}_{C=}^{\rightarrow}} X:\tau \iff \Gamma_\lambda \vdash_{\mathrm{TA}_{\lambda=}^{\rightarrow}} X_\lambda:\tau,$

(b) $\quad \Gamma \vdash_{\mathrm{TA}_{\lambda=}^{\rightarrow}} X:\tau \iff \Gamma_H \vdash_{\mathrm{TA}_{C=}^{\rightarrow}} X_H:\tau,$

Further reading

There is an enormous literature on types and type-assignment. A few items have already been mentioned; here are a few more. Many more can easily be found using an internet search engine.

[Pie02] is a well written comprehensive introduction to λ and types, for readers with a computing background. It covers all the material in the present book's Chapters 10–12, plus subtyping, recursive types, higher-order systems, and much more.

[Bar92] is a summary and comparison of some of the most important type systems based on λ, clearly explaining the relations between them. (The second half of the account describes *Pure Type Systems*, to which we shall give a short introduction in Section 13D.)

[BDS] is an advanced and up-to-date account of three type systems in lambda calculus – simple types (Church-style and Curry-style), intersection types, and recursive types. Besides the syntax of these systems, decidability questions and semantic aspects are treated thoroughly and in depth.

[And02, Chapter 5] develops logic and mathematics in a type-system based on Church's original system, [Chu40]. Also [And65] describes an extension of Church's system with rules which make certain types *transfinite*.

[Hin97] is a detailed account of $\mathrm{TA}_\lambda^{\rightarrow}$ focussing on three algorithms – to find the principal type of a term, to find a term for which a given type is principal, and the Ben–Yelles algorithm to count the number of closed terms with a given type.

[CDV81], [CC90, Section 3] and [Hin92] are introductions to the extension of $\mathrm{TA}_\lambda^{\rightarrow}$ called *intersection types.* This system has, besides $\sigma \rightarrow \tau$, also $\sigma \cap \tau$. Its types give more information than $\mathrm{TA}_\lambda^{\rightarrow}$; for example, it assigns to $\lambda x.xx$ the type

$$(a \cap (a \rightarrow b)) \rightarrow b\,,$$

which says that if we wanted to give two types to x, then xx would get a type, a fact not expressible in $\mathrm{TA}_\lambda^{\rightarrow}$ (which simply refuses to assign a type to $\lambda x.xx$). The standard version of the intersection system also has a *universal* type ω, which can be used to give further information (see 11.58), and to make a term's set of types invariant with respect to equality (in contrast to $TA_\lambda^{\to}$, see 12.21). Three pioneering papers on intersection types are [CD78], [Sal78] and [Pot80]. A modern advanced account is in [BDS, Part III].

[CC90, Section 2], [CC91] and [Pie02, Chapters 20 & 21] are introductions to the extension of $TA_\lambda^{\to}$ in which there are *recursively defined* types. As mentioned above, a further account of this field is in [BDS, Part II]. More information can be found by searching the internet for 'recursive types'.

[LS86] describes the close connection between $TA_\lambda^{\to}$ and *cartesian closed categories* (and includes a short introduction to the latter). Some introductions to category theory in general are [Pie91], [Cro94], [Fia05] and (for more mathematical readers) [Mac71], [AL91].

13
Generalizations of typing

13A Introduction

In programming languages, there are many applications of typing that require generalizations of the theories we have considered so far. These generalizations are the subject of this chapter.

Of course, it is easy to generalize any theory of typing by just adding new type-forming operations. For example, to relate typing to cartesian closed categories, one needs ordered pairs in which the first and second elements may have arbitrarily different types. This is impossible in $\mathrm{TA}_{\mathrm{C}}^{\rightarrow}$ and $\mathrm{TA}_{\lambda}^{\rightarrow}$ by [Bar74], so it is necessary to introduce a new type-forming operation $\times$ and to postulate

$$\begin{aligned} \mathbf{D} &: \alpha \to \beta \to (\alpha \times \beta), \\ \mathbf{D}_1 &: (\alpha \times \beta) \to \alpha, \\ \mathbf{D}_2 &: (\alpha \times \beta) \to \beta, \end{aligned}$$

where, as in Note 4.14,

$$\begin{aligned} \mathbf{D} &\equiv \lambda xyz\,.\,z(\mathbf{K}y)x, \\ \mathbf{D}_1 &\equiv \lambda x\,.\,x\overline{0}, \\ \mathbf{D}_2 &\equiv \lambda x\,.\,x\overline{1}. \end{aligned}$$

Although an extension like this adds new types and assigns new types to terms, it does not represent a major change in the way typing operates. The extensions we will consider in this chapter, however, require major changes in the foundations of the theories of type assignment.

13B Dependent function types, introduction

The main novelty in the typing systems considered in this chapter is the replacement of the function type $\sigma \to \tau$ as the main compound type by the *dependent function type* $(\Pi x : \sigma . \tau(x))$, which can be read informally as 'for all x in σ, $\tau(x)$.' Here, σ is a type, but $\tau(x)$ is a function whose values are types for arguments in type σ, so that a term of type $(\Pi x{:}\sigma . \tau(x))$ represents a function whose arguments are of type σ and whose value for an argument N is in type $\tau(N)$.

The definition of the types of the various systems will be more complicated than for the systems of Chapters 10, 11 and 12, and will have to allow for the possibility that term-variables occur free in types. In this chapter, terms and types will not be separate; a type will be just a special kind of term.

Informally speaking, in the special case that $\tau(x)$ is a constant function whose value for any argument is a type τ, $(\Pi x{:}\sigma . \tau(x))$ is the type $\sigma \to \tau$. In the systems considered below, this will occur when the variable x does not occur free in $\tau(x)$. Thus, the typing systems of Chapters 10, 11 and 12 will be subsystems of many of the systems to be considered here.

To express the idea of dependent function type we shall use variants of the following two rules, which, for convenience, are stated for Curry-style typing in λ:

$$(\Pi \text{ e}) \quad \frac{M : (\Pi x{:}\sigma . \tau(x)) \qquad N : \sigma}{MN : \tau(N);}$$

$$(\Pi \text{ i}) \quad \frac{\begin{array}{c}[x : \sigma] \\ M : \tau(x)\end{array}}{(\lambda x . M) : (\Pi x{:}\sigma . \tau(x))}$$

Condition: $x{:}\sigma$ is the only undischarged assumption in whose subject x occurs free, and x does not occur free in σ.

For reasons that will be more fully justified below, we shall also need the following rule:

$$(\text{Eq}'') \quad \frac{M : \sigma \qquad \sigma =_\beta \tau}{M : \tau}$$

(Until otherwise indicated, in this chapter conversion will be $=_\beta$ in λ-calculus.)

Notation 13.1 The type $(\Pi x : \sigma . \tau(x))$ has also appeared in the literature as $(\Pi x : \sigma)\tau(x)$, $(\Pi x \in \sigma)\tau(x)$, and $(\forall x : \sigma)\tau(x)$, the latter emphasizing the propositions-as-types aspect of the type. It is called the *cartesian product type* in [ML75].

Remark 13.2 In terms of the notion of propositions-as-types (Discussion 11.49 and the paragraph before Theorem 12.33), $(\Pi x : \sigma . \tau(x))$ not only represents implication (by its inclusion of the type $\rightarrow$), but it also represents the universal quantifier over a type. The rule (Π e) represents the elimination rule for the universal quantifier over σ, and the rule (Π i) represents the introduction rule for that same quantifier.

Remark 13.3 In this chapter we will not take up the use of dependent types in CL. The subject is far less developed for CL than it is for λ, and so the systems of this chapter will be for λ only.

To allow for dependent types, the definition of types will have to be very different from the definition of types in 11.1. As mentioned earlier, one of the main differences is that whereas the definition of types in 11.1 is completely separate from the definition of terms, in systems with the dependent function type, types cannot be completely separate from terms, and for such systems, all types will be terms. Furthermore, the definition will have to allow for variables to occur free in these terms, so we will be talking not only about types, but also about functions whose values are types. There are two alternative approaches to the definition of types for these systems:

G1. Defining types so that if a term T represents a type and contains a term-variable x, then $[N/x]T$ represents a type also, no matter what term N is and what type N has.

G2. Defining types so that $[N/x]T$ will only represent a type if N has the same type as x.

Remark 13.4 Curry introduced dependent types using the notation $\mathsf{G}\sigma\tau$ for $(\Pi x : \sigma . \tau x)$, or $\mathsf{G}\sigma(\lambda x . \tau)$ for $(\Pi x : \sigma . \tau)$. This idea first appeared in print in [CHS72, Section 15A8], and was then developed in [Sel79]; see also [HS86, Chapter 16]. This formalism requires a different form of the rules (Π e) and (Π i):

$$(\mathsf{G}\ \mathrm{e}) \quad \frac{M : \mathsf{G}\sigma\tau \quad N : \sigma}{MN : \tau N;}$$

(**G** i)

$$\frac{\begin{array}{c}[x:\sigma]\\ M:\tau\end{array}}{(\lambda x.M):\mathbf{G}\sigma(\lambda x\,.\,\tau)}$$

Condition: $x{:}\sigma$ is the only undischarged assumption in whose subject x occurs free, and x does not occur free in σ.

13C Basic generalized typing, Curry-style in $\boldsymbol{\lambda}$

We shall now define a system of dependent types using the approach G1. This will be called *basic generalized typing*, and we will define it in the Curry-style in λ. (The next section will make it clear how to modify this system for Church-style typing.) The definition assumes that we are given a set (possibly infinite) of *atomic type constants*, θ_i^n, each with a *degree* n, Each atomic type constant with degree n will represent a type function intended to take n arguments, the value of which is a type. We will begin with the definition of terms.

Definition 13.5 *Terms* are defined as follows.

- T1. Every variable is a term.
- T2. Every atomic type constant is a term.
- T3. If M and N are terms, then (MN) is a term.
- T4. If x is a variable and M is a term, then $(\lambda x\,.\,M)$ is a term.
- T5. If M and N are terms and x is a variable which does not occur free in M, then $(\Pi x{:}M\,.\,N)$ is a term.

Remark 13.6 In terms of the form $(\Pi x : M\,.\,N)$, the *scope* of Πx is said to be N, and Πx *binds* all free occurrences of x in N. Then the definition of substitution is like Definition 1.12.

We will now define for this system types and type functions, which will be denoted by lower case Greek letters.

Definition 13.7 (Type functions and types) *Type functions* of given degrees and ranks are defined in terms of *proper* type functions, which are defined as follows.

- B1. An atomic type constant of degree n is an atomic proper type function of degree n and rank 0.
- B2. If σ is a proper type function of degree $m > 0$ and rank k and M is any term, then σM is a proper type function of degree $m - 1$ and rank k.

B3. If σ is a proper type function of degree m and rank k, then $\lambda x \,.\, \sigma$ is a proper type function of degree $m+1$ and rank k.

B4. If σ and τ are proper type functions of degree 0 and ranks k and l respectively, and if $x \notin \mathrm{FV}(\sigma)$, then $(\Pi x\!:\!\sigma \,.\, \tau)$ is a proper type function of degree 0 and rank $1+k+l$.

The term σ is a *type function* of rank k and degree m iff there is a proper type function τ of rank k and degree m and such that $\sigma \triangleright_\beta \tau$.

A *type* is a type function of degree 0.

When there is a need to distinguish the types of this definition from the types defined earlier, those types will be called *simple types*.

A type function of degree m represents a function of m arguments which accepts types as inputs and produces types as outputs. The rank of a type function measures the number of occurrences of Π in the normal form of the term representing it.

Theorem 13.8 *The degree and rank of a type function are unique.*

For the proof, see [Sel79, Theorem 1.1].

Remark 13.9 The proof of [Sel79, Theorem 1.1] also shows that type functions have the following properties.

(i) *If σ is a type function of degree m and rank k, and if T is any term such that $T =_\beta \sigma$, then T is a type function of degree m and rank k.*

(ii) *If σ is a type function of degree m and rank k, then $\lambda x \,.\, \sigma$ is a type function of degree $m+1$ and rank k.*

(iii) *If σ is a type function of degree $m+1$ and rank k and if M is any term, then σM is a type function of degree m and rank k.*

(iv) *The term $\Pi x : \sigma \,.\, \tau$ is a type function of degree 0 and rank k if and only if σ is a type function of degree 0 and rank i, τ is a type function of degree 0 and rank j, and $k = 1 + i + j$.*

Remark 13.10 It turns out that in order for types to be more general than simple types, there must be at least one atomic type constant of degree greater than 0; see [Sel79, Corollary 1.1.1].

Corollary 13.10.1 *If every atomic type constant has degree 0, then every type converts to a simple type of the kind defined in Definition 10.1, where $\sigma \to \tau$ is defined as $(\Pi x\!:\!\sigma \,.\, \tau)$ when $x \notin \mathrm{FV}(\tau)$.*

Definition 13.11 (The type assignment system TAG$_\lambda$) The system TAG$_\lambda$ (*generalized type assignment to λ-terms*) is a Natural Deduction system whose formulas have the form

$$M : \sigma$$

for λ-terms M and types σ. TAG$_\lambda$ has no axioms. Its rules are the following:

$$(\Pi\ \mathrm{e})\quad \frac{M : (\Pi x{:}\sigma \,.\, \tau) \quad N : \sigma}{MN : [N/x]\tau}$$

$$(\Pi\ \mathrm{i})\quad \frac{\begin{array}{c}[x : \sigma]\\ M : \tau\end{array}}{(\lambda x.M) : (\Pi x{:}\sigma \,.\, \tau)}$$

Condition: $x{:}\sigma$ is the only undischarged assumption in whose subject x occurs free, and x does not occur free in σ

$$(\mathrm{Eq}'')\quad \frac{M : \sigma \qquad \sigma =_\beta \tau}{M : \tau}$$

$$(\equiv_\alpha')\quad \frac{M : \sigma \qquad M \equiv_\alpha N}{N : \sigma}$$

Condition: M is not identical to N.

Remark 13.12 Note that rule $(\equiv_\alpha')$ is not restricted here the way the corresponding rule is in TA$_\lambda^{\rightarrow}$, to the case in which $M{:}\sigma$ is an assumption. If this restriction were adopted here, then deductions would no longer be invariant under substitution, as the following example shows: let θ be an atomic type constant of degree 1, let x and z be distinct variables, and consider the deduction

$$\frac{\stackrel{1}{[z : \theta x]}}{(\lambda z \,.\, z) : (\Pi z{:}\theta x \,.\, \theta x).}\ (\Pi\ \mathrm{i} - 1)$$

Suppose we substitute z for x in this deduction. Since x occurs free only in the type, and since

$$[z/x](\Pi z{:}\theta x \,.\, \theta x) \equiv (\Pi u{:}\theta z \,.\, \theta z),$$

where u is the first variable (in the given list of variables) distinct from x and z, we would expect a deduction of

$$(\lambda z \,.\, z) : (\Pi u{:}\theta z \,.\, \theta z).$$

But without rule $(\equiv_\alpha')$ at the end of the deduction, this is impossible; with $(\equiv_\alpha')$ at the end, the required deduction is

$$\dfrac{\dfrac{\overset{1}{[u : \theta z]}}{(\lambda u\,.\,u) : (\Pi u{:}\theta z\,.\,\theta z)}\;\Pi\,\mathrm{i}-1}{(\lambda z\,.\,z) : (\Pi u{:}\theta z\,.\,\theta z).}\;(\equiv_\alpha')$$

It is not hard to prove that rule $(\equiv_\alpha')$ can always be pushed down to the bottom of a deduction, although at the cost of introducing some new Eq$''$-steps.

Remark 13.13 The condition on rule (Π i) implies that if a sequence of assumptions $x_1 : \sigma_1,\ \ldots,\ x_n : \sigma_n$ is to be discharged in reverse numerical order, the following condition must be satisfied: *the variable x_i does not occur free in any of the types $\sigma_1, \ldots, \sigma_i$ (but it may occur free in any of the types $\sigma_{i+1}, \ldots, \sigma_n$)*. This means that instead of sets of assumptions, we will be interested in *sequences* of assumptions that assign types to variables.

Definition 13.14 A *context* is a finite sequence of formulas of form $x_1 : \sigma_1,\ \ldots,\ x_n : \sigma_n$, such that $x_1, \ldots, x_n$ are all distinct. (Cf. Definition 11.21.) It is *legal for* TAG$_\lambda$ iff it also satisfies

L1 For each i $(1 \le i \le n)$, x_i does not occur free in any of the types $\sigma_1, \ldots, \sigma_i$ (but it may occur free in any of $\sigma_{i+1}, \ldots, \sigma_n$).

Note that contexts do not assign types to terms other than variables. In systems of generalized typing, assigning types to atomic constants will be done by *axioms*. (We will not be interested in axioms assigning types to compound terms.) This leads to the following alternative formulation of TAG$_\lambda$.

Definition 13.15 The system TAG$_\lambda^a$, the *alternative formulation of generalized typing*, is a system with statements of the form

$$\Gamma \vdash M : \sigma,$$

where M is a term, σ is a type (in the sense of Definition 13.7), and Γ is a context. There may be a set $\mathcal{A}$ of *axioms* of the form $c{:}\sigma$, where c is an atomic constant and σ is a type. The rules of TAG$_\lambda^a$ are as follows:

(axiom) $$\frac{}{\vdash\ c:\sigma}$$ *Condition:* $c{:}\sigma \in \mathcal{A}$

(start) $$\frac{}{\Gamma,\ x{:}\sigma\ \vdash\ x{:}\sigma}$$ *Condition:* $x \notin \mathrm{FV}(\Gamma, \sigma)$

(weakening) $$\frac{\Gamma\ \vdash\ M{:}\tau}{\Gamma,\ x{:}\sigma\ \vdash\ M : \tau}$$ *Condition:* $x \notin \mathrm{FV}(\Gamma, \sigma)$

(application) $$\frac{\Gamma\ \vdash\ M : (\Pi x{:}\sigma\,.\,\tau) \quad \Gamma\ \vdash\ N : \sigma}{\Gamma\ \vdash\ MN : [N/x]\tau}$$

(abstraction) $$\frac{\Gamma,\ x{:}\sigma\ \vdash\ M{:}\tau}{\Gamma\ \vdash\ (\lambda x{:}M) : (\Pi x{:}\sigma\,.\,\tau)}$$ *Condition:* $x \notin \mathrm{FV}(\Gamma, \sigma)$

(conversion) $$\frac{\Gamma\ \vdash\ M : \sigma \quad \sigma =_\beta \tau}{\Gamma \vdash M : \tau}$$

(α-conv) $$\frac{\Gamma\ \vdash\ M : \sigma \qquad M \equiv_\alpha N}{\Gamma\ \vdash\ N : \sigma}$$ *Condition:* M is not identical to N.

Note 13.16 With these rules, the assumptions to the left of the symbol '$\vdash$' are automatically built up as legal contexts.

13D Deductive rules to define types

We now turn to systems using the approach G2, systems in which a substitution instance of a type is only a type if the terms substituted for variables match the types of the variables. In such systems, a statement that a term is a type is not part of the syntax, but must be proved by the deductive typing rules. To formulate the rules adequately, the system must contain at least one type of types.

As an example of how this might work, let us digress for a short space from dependent types to arrow types. Suppose we modify the system $\mathrm{TA}_\lambda^\to$ by adding a new atomic constant $\star$ to represent the type of types (not including $\star$ itself).[1] This would give us the following system, called $\lambda\!\to$ in the literature.[2]

[1] It is necessary to specify that $\star$ is not the type of $\star$ itself, since $\star : \star$ leads to a contradiction.

[2] See, for example, [Bar92, Definition 5.1.10] or [BDS, Section 1.1].

Definition 13.17 The typing system $\lambda \to$ is defined by adding to $\mathrm{TA}_{\lambda}^{\to}$ (see Definition 12.6) the constant $\star$, the axioms

$$\theta : \star$$

for each type-constant θ, and the rule

$$(\to \mathrm{f}) \quad \frac{\sigma : \star \quad \tau : \star}{(\sigma \to \tau) : \star}$$

and then modifying rule $(\to \mathrm{i})$ as follows:

$$(\to \mathrm{i}) \quad \frac{\begin{array}{ll}[x:\sigma] & \\ M : \tau & (\sigma \to \tau) : \star\end{array}}{(\lambda x \,.\, M) : (\sigma \to \tau)}$$

Condition: $x{:}\sigma$ is the only undischarged assumption in whose subject x occurs free, and x does not occur free in σ.

If we wanted to extend the system $\lambda\to$ to include the parametric types of Definition 11.1, then we would need to add assumptions of the form $v{:}\star$ for each type-variable v. This would mean that we would have

$$\Gamma \vdash_{\mathrm{TA}_{\lambda}^{\to}} M : \sigma$$

if and only if

$$\Gamma,\ v_1{:}\star,\ \ldots,\ v_n{:}\star \ \vdash_{\lambda\to}\ M : \sigma,$$

where $v_1, \ldots, v_n$ are the type variables which occur in Γ and σ.

In the system $\lambda \to$, a term M is a type iff either M has type $\star$ or else M is $\star$; see [Bar92, Corollary 5.2.14, part 1].[3] Types which play the role of $\star$ are called *sorts*. As we shall see below, a system can have more than one sort.

Definition 13.18 In systems of type assignment in which being a type is determined by the deductive axioms and rules, the types whose terms are all types are called *sorts*.

In some systems rule $(\to \mathrm{i})$ is modified as follows:

$$(\to \mathrm{i}) \quad \frac{\begin{array}{ll}[x:\sigma] & \\ M : \tau & \sigma : \star\end{array}}{(\lambda x \,.\, M) : (\sigma \to \tau)}$$

Condition: $x{:}\sigma$ is the only undischarged assumption in whose subject x occurs free, and x does not occur free in σ.

[3] This corollary actually applies to pure type systems, or PTSs, which are discussed below in Definition 13.34. It applies to this system because it is a PTS.

If this rule together with the other rules of the system guarantee that every term on the right of the colon in every step of a deduction is a type, then this modification does not change the provable formulas in this system. However, in some systems, it makes a difference. We shall see more about this below.

Rule ($\to$ f) is sometimes generalized as follows:

($\to$ g)
$$\dfrac{\sigma : \star \qquad \begin{matrix}[x:\sigma] \\ \tau : \star\end{matrix}}{(\sigma \to \tau) : \star}$$

Condition: $x{:}\sigma$ is the only undischarged assumption in whose subject x occurs free, and x does not occur free in σ.

With this rule, the condition for being able to discharge assumptions $x_1{:}\sigma_1, \ldots, x_n{:}\sigma_n$ in reverse order is as follows: *the variables* $x_1, \ldots, x_n$ *are all distinct and for each* i,

$$\Gamma,\ x_1{:}\sigma_1,\ \ldots,\ x_{i-1}{:}\sigma_{i-1} \quad \vdash \quad \sigma_i{:}\star.$$

Note that here, variables do not occur in types. If they could occur in types, we would have to specify that each x_i does not occur free in $\sigma_1, \ldots, \sigma_i$, but may occur free in $\sigma_{i+1}, \ldots, \sigma_n$. This condition will be included in the following definition for later comparison, although it will have no application here.

Definition 13.19 A *legal context for* $\lambda\to$ is a context (i.e. a finite sequence $x_1{:}\sigma_1, \ldots, x_n{:}\sigma_n$ with $x_1, \ldots, x_n$ distinct) which satisfies

L1. For each i $(1 \le i \le n)$, x_i does not occur free in any of $\sigma_1, \ldots, \sigma_i$ (but it may occur free in $\sigma_{i+1}, \ldots, \sigma_n$),

L2. For each i $(1 \le i \le n)$, either $\sigma_i \equiv \star$ or

$$x_1{:}\sigma_1,\ \ldots,\ x_{i-1}{:}\sigma_{i-1} \quad \vdash \quad \sigma_i : \star.$$

Then the alternative version of $\lambda\to$ corresponding to TAG^a_λ is defined as follows.

Definition 13.20 Assume that there is a sequence $\theta_1, \ldots, \theta_n, \ldots$, possibly infinite, of *atomic types*, and assume that there is a symbol $\star$, called a *sort*, distinct from $\theta_1, \ldots, \theta_n, \ldots$. The typing system $\lambda\to^a$, the alternative formulation of $\lambda\to$, is a system with statements of the form

$$\Gamma \vdash M : \sigma,$$

where M and σ are λ-terms and Γ is a context. There is a set $\mathcal{A}$ of axioms, which consists of $\theta_n{:}\star$ for each n. The rules are as follows:

(axiom) $$\frac{}{\vdash\ \theta_i : \star}$$ *Condition:* $\theta_i : \star \in \mathcal{A}$

(start1) $$\frac{\Gamma\ \vdash\ \sigma : \star}{\Gamma,\ x{:}\sigma\ \vdash\ x{:}\sigma}$$ *Condition:* $x \notin \mathrm{FV}(\Gamma, \sigma)$

(start2) $$\frac{}{x{:}\star\ \vdash\ x{:}\star}$$ *Condition:* $x \notin \mathrm{FV}(\Gamma)$

(weakening1) $$\frac{\Gamma\ \vdash\ M : \tau \quad \Gamma\ \vdash\ \sigma : \star}{\Gamma,\ x{:}\sigma\ \vdash\ M : \tau}$$ *Condition:* $x \notin \mathrm{FV}(\Gamma, \sigma)$

(weakening2) $$\frac{\Gamma\ \vdash\ M : \tau}{\Gamma,\ x{:}\star\ \vdash\ M : \tau}$$ *Condition:* $x \notin \mathrm{FV}(\Gamma, \sigma)$

(application) $$\frac{\Gamma\ \vdash\ M : \sigma \to \tau \quad \Gamma\ \vdash\ N : \sigma}{\Gamma\ \vdash\ MN : \tau}$$

(abstraction) $$\frac{\Gamma,\ x{:}\sigma\ \vdash\ M{:}\tau \quad \Gamma\ \vdash\ (\sigma \to \tau) : \star}{\Gamma\ \vdash\ (\lambda x{:}M) : \sigma \to \tau}$$ *Condition:* $x \notin \mathrm{FV}(\Gamma, \sigma)$

(product) $$\frac{\Gamma\ \vdash\ \sigma : \star \quad \Gamma,\ x{:}\sigma\ \vdash\ \tau : \star}{\Gamma\ \vdash\ (\sigma \to \tau) : \star}$$ *Condition:* $x \notin \mathrm{FV}(\Gamma, \sigma)$

(conversion) $$\frac{\Gamma\ \vdash\ M : \sigma \quad \sigma =_\beta \tau \quad \Gamma\ \vdash\ \tau : \star}{\Gamma\ \vdash\ M : \tau}$$

(α-conv) $$\frac{\Gamma\ \vdash\ M : \sigma \qquad M \equiv_\alpha N}{\Gamma\ \vdash\ N : \sigma}$$ *Condition:* M is not identical to N.

It can be shown that, with these rules, only a legal context can occur to the left of the symbol '$\vdash$' in a deduction in $\lambda\!\to^a$.

Discussion 13.21 Let us now extend the G2 approach to types from $\to$-types to Π-types. To do this, a rule is needed that corresponds to ($\to$f) in Definition 13.17, and rule (Π i) in Definition 13.11 needs to be modified. The rule corresponding to ($\to$f) for a system with a dependent function type would be

(Π f) $$\frac{\sigma : \star \qquad \begin{matrix}[x : \sigma]\\ \tau : \star\end{matrix}}{(\Pi x{:}\sigma\,.\,\tau) : \star}$$ *Condition:* $x : \sigma$ is the only undischarged assumption in whose subject x occurs free, and x does not occur free in σ;

and the modified form of rule (Π i) would be

$$(\Pi\ \mathrm{i})\quad \frac{\begin{array}{l}[x:\sigma]\\ M:\tau \qquad (\Pi x\!:\!\sigma\,.\,\tau):\star\end{array}}{(\lambda x.M):(\Pi x\!:\!\sigma\,.\,\tau)}$$

Condition: $x\!:\!\sigma$ is the only undischarged assumption in whose subject x occurs free, and x does not occur free in σ.

In terms of the definition of types, if the only axioms were of the form $\theta_i : \star$, then it would not be difficult to see that with these two rules and (Π e), (Eq″) and ($\equiv'_\alpha$) as in Definition 13.11, we would not get a system any more general than $\lambda\!\rightarrow^a$, and in all occurrences of types of the form $(\Pi x:\sigma\,.\,\tau)$ we would get $x \notin \mathrm{FV}(\tau)$, so that, as indicated in the third paragraph of Section 13B, this type would really be $\sigma \rightarrow \tau$. Thus, if these were all the changes we made, the system would be no more general than $\lambda\!\rightarrow^a$.

We could try to obtain a more general system by postulating type functions of degree 1 or more. But the axioms for such type functions would have to take the form

$$\theta : (\Pi x_1\!:\!\sigma_1\,.\,\Pi x_2\!:\!\sigma_2\,.\,\ldots\,.\,\Pi x_n\!:\!\sigma_n\,.\,\star).$$

But with the rules we have so far, it is impossible to prove that

$$(\Pi x_1\!:\!\sigma_1\,.\,\Pi x_2\!:\!\sigma_2\,.\,\ldots\,.\,\Pi x_n\!:\!\sigma_n\,.\,\star):\star,$$

and so we would lose an important property: that every term occurring to the right of a colon in a proof is either a term of type $\star$ or else converts to $\star$. We need another form of generalization.

The other form of generalization which has become standard today is to have more than one sort, and to adopt axioms that allow some sorts to be terms of the type of another sort. For example, we can take the sorts to be $\star$ and $\square$, and postulate as an axiom $\star : \square$.

The systems we consider in the rest of this chapter will be of this kind.

13E Church-style typing in λ

Most of the generalized systems considered today are really systems of Church typing.

In Chapter 10, abstractions were written in the form $\lambda x^\sigma . M$. This was fine for these systems because the types were formed in such a simple way. However, in the generalized systems we are considering here, where types are terms which may contain variables and where the deduction rules determine which of these terms are really types, this turns out to be inconvenient. Thus, in these systems, abstraction terms are written

$$\lambda x{:}\sigma\,.\,M.$$

For the systems in the present section, the definition of the terms will be in two stages: first, expressions called *pseudoterms* will be defined, and then the deduction rules of each system will determine when a pseudoterm is a proper term in that system. For example, in an abstraction $\lambda x{:}\sigma\,.\,M$, σ may be a pseudoterm or a term that is not a type, and the whole expression may be just a pseudoterm.

Since the types are just terms of a certain kind, from now on we shall use A, B, etc. for σ, τ. When the types are variables, we shall use lower-case Roman letters, such as x, y, z, etc.

Definition 13.22 *Pseudoterms* are defined as follows.

PT1. Every variable is a pseudoterm.
PT2. Every atomic type constant is a pseudoterm.
PT3. If M and N are pseudoterms, then (MN) is a pseudoterm.
PT4. If x is a variable and M and N are pseudoterms, then $(\lambda x{:}M\,.\,N)$ is a pseudoterm.
PT5. If M and N are pseudoterms and x is a variable which does not occur free in M, then $(\Pi x{:}M\,.\,N)$ is a pseudoterm.

For pseudoterms, reduction is defined by replacing ordinary β-contractions by contractions of the form

$$(\lambda x{:}A\,.\,M)N \;\rhd\; [N/x]M.$$

In his survey paper [Bar92, Section 5], Henk Barendregt introduced a group of eight typing systems which he called the 'λ-*cube*.' All are based on the dependent function type, and all are based on two sorts, $\star$ and $\Box$. These systems have only one axiom: $\star : \Box$. The rules are like those of $\lambda\!\rightarrow^{a}$. Here is the formal definition.

Definition 13.23 (λ-cube) The eight typing systems of the λ-*cube* are all based on *pseudoterms*. The systems all have two special constants, $\star$ and $\Box$, which are called *sorts*. Each system has one axiom, namely $\star : \Box$. Each system also has a set $\mathcal{R}$ of *special rules*, each of which is of the form (s_1, s_2), where s_1 and s_2 are sorts; i.e., each of s_1 and s_2 is one of $\star$ and $\Box$. The deduction rules of the system are as follows:

(axiom) $$\frac{}{\vdash \star : \square}$$

(start) $$\frac{\Gamma \vdash A : s}{\Gamma,\ x{:}A \vdash x{:}A}$$ *Condition:* $x \notin \mathrm{FV}(\Gamma, A)$ and s is a sort

(weakening) $$\frac{\Gamma \vdash M{:}B \quad \Gamma \vdash A{:}s}{\Gamma,\ x{:}A \vdash M{:}B}$$ *Condition:* $x \notin \mathrm{FV}(\Gamma, A)$ and s is a sort

(application) $$\frac{\Gamma \vdash M{:}(\Pi x{:}A\,.\,B) \quad \Gamma \vdash N{:}A}{\Gamma \vdash MN{:}[N/x]B}$$

(abstraction) $$\frac{\Gamma,\ x{:}A \vdash M{:}B \quad \Gamma \vdash (\Pi x{:}A\,.\,B){:}s}{\Gamma \vdash (\lambda x{:}A\,.\,M) : (\Pi x{:}A\,.\,B)}$$ *Condition:* $x \notin \mathrm{FV}(\Gamma, A)$ and s is a sort

(product) $$\frac{\Gamma \vdash A{:}s_1 \quad \Gamma,\ x{:}A \vdash B{:}s_2}{\Gamma \vdash (\Pi x{:}A\,.\,B){:}s_2}$$ *Condition:* $x \notin \mathrm{FV}(\Gamma, A)$ and s_1 and s_2 are sorts, and $(s_1, s_2) \in \mathcal{R}$

(conversion) $$\frac{\Gamma \vdash M{:}A \quad A =_\beta B \quad \Gamma \vdash B{:}s}{\Gamma \vdash M{:}B}$$ *Condition:* s is a sort

(α-conv) $$\frac{\Gamma \vdash M{:}A \qquad M \equiv_\alpha N}{\Gamma \vdash N{:}A}$$ *Condition:* M is not identical to N.

A *pseudocontext* is a sequence of formulas of the form $x_1 : A_1, \ldots, x_n : A_n$, where $x_1, \ldots, x_n$ are distinct variables and $A_1, \ldots, A_n$ are pseudoterms. A pseudocontext is a *legal context* iff the following two conditions are satisfied.

L1. The variable x_i does not occur free in $A_1, \ldots, A_i$ (although it may occur free in $A_{i+1}, \ldots, A_n$);

L2. For each i ($1 \le i \le n$), either $A_i \equiv s$ or

$$x_1 : A_1,\ \ldots,\ x_{i-1} : A_{i-1} \quad \vdash \quad A_i : s$$

for some sort s (depending on i).

A pseudoterm M is a *term* iff there are a legal context Γ and a pseudoterm A such that

$$\Gamma \vdash M : A.$$

A pseudoterm A is a *type* iff there are a legal context Γ and a pseudoterm M such that

$$\Gamma \vdash M : A.$$

The eight specific systems are determined by the set $\mathcal{R}$ of special rules, as indicated by the following table (from [Bar92, p. 205]):

System	$\mathcal{R}$			
$\lambda\!\rightarrow$	$(\star,\star)$			
$\lambda 2$	$(\star,\star)$	$(\Box,\star)$		
λP	$(\star,\star)$		$(\star,\Box)$	
λP2	$(\star,\star)$	$(\Box,\star)$	$(\star,\Box)$	
$\lambda\underline{\omega}$	$(\star,\star)$			$(\Box,\Box)$
$\lambda\omega$	$(\star,\star)$	$(\Box,\star)$		$(\Box,\Box)$
λP$\underline{\omega}$	$(\star,\star)$		$(\star,\Box)$	$(\Box,\Box)$
λP$\omega = \lambda$C	$(\star,\star)$	$(\Box,\star)$	$(\star,\Box)$	$(\Box,\Box)$

The λ-cube is often represented by the diagram in Figure 13:1.

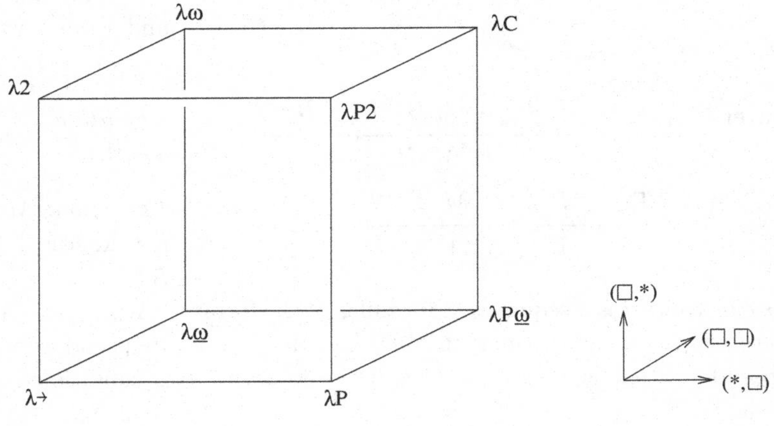

Fig. 13:1 Barendregt's λ-cube

Remark 13.24 It can be proved that the rules of these systems guarantee that only legal contexts can appear on the left of the symbol '$\vdash$' in any deduction. Furthermore, for Γ to be a legal context is equivalent to $\Gamma \vdash \star : \Box$ being derivable in the system, [Sel97, Theorem 14]. And if $\Gamma \vdash \star : \Box$ is derivable in any of these systems, then for any initial segment Γ' of Γ, $\Gamma' \vdash \star : \Box$ is also derivable, [Sel97, Lemma 9]. (The proofs in [Sel97] are for λC, but they apply to all the systems of the λ-cube.)

Definition 13.25 The *arrow type* $A \to B$ is defined to be $(\Pi x : A . B)$ where $x \notin \mathrm{FV}(B)$.

Remark 13.26 Given the above definition of $\to$, the system called $\lambda\!\to$ in the λ-cube is really the same as $\lambda\!\to^{a}$ in Definition 13.20. This is because, by [Bar92, Lemma 5.1.14], if $\Gamma \vdash A : \star$ can be proved in the λ-cube version of $\lambda\!\to$, then A is built up from the set of all terms B such that $B : \star$ occurs in Γ, using only $\to$.

The following are some examples of what can can be derived in $\lambda\!\to$:[4]

$$\begin{array}{rcl}
u:\star & \vdash & (u \to u):\star \\
u:\star,\ v:\star & \vdash & (u \to v):\star \\
u:\star & \vdash & (\lambda x{:}u\,.\,x):(u \to u) \\
u:\star,\ v:\star,\ y:v & \vdash & (\lambda x{:}u\,.\,y):(u \to v) \\
u:\star,\ y:u & \vdash & ((\lambda x{:}u\,.\,x)y):u \\
u:\star,\ v:\star,\ y:v,\ z:u & \vdash & ((\lambda x{:}u\,.\,y)z):v \\
u:\star,\ v:\star & \vdash & (\lambda x{:}u\,.\,\lambda y{:}v\,.\,x):(u \to (v \to u)).
\end{array}$$

For example, the first of these can be derived as follows:

$$\dfrac{\dfrac{\dfrac{}{\vdash \star:\Box}\,(\text{axiom})}{u{:}\star \vdash u{:}\star}\,(\text{start}) \qquad \dfrac{\dfrac{\dfrac{}{\vdash \star:\Box}\,(\text{axiom})}{u{:}\star \vdash u{:}\star}\,(\text{start}) \quad \dfrac{\dfrac{}{\vdash \star:\Box}\,(\text{axiom})}{u{:}\star \vdash u{:}\star}\,(\text{start})}{u{:}\star,\ x{:}u \vdash u{:}\star}\,(\text{weakening})}{u{:}\star \vdash (u \to u){:}\star.}\,(\text{product})$$

Note that the only special rule in this system is $(\star, \star)$, which occurs in all the systems of the λ-cube. It allows the system to say that certain terms are types, but, in a sense to be explained below, it does not allow quantification over types.

Remark 13.27 The system λ2 has, besides $(\star, \star)$, the special rule $(\Box, \star)$ (and it is the weakest system in the λ-cube which has this rule). This rule makes it possible to quantify over $\star$, as the following example will

[4] The examples in this and the following remarks come from [Bar92, Exs. 5.1.15].

show. From

$$u:\star \ \vdash \ (u \to u):\star,$$

which can be derived in $\lambda\!\to$, and from the axiom

$$\vdash \ \star:\square,$$

we can use the rule (product) to derive

$$\vdash \ (\Pi u\!:\!\square\,.\,u \to u):\star.$$

From this and

$$u:\star \ \vdash \ (\lambda x\!:\!u\,.\,x):u \to u$$

(which can already be derived in $\lambda\to$), we can now derive by the rule (abstraction),

$$\vdash \ (\lambda u\!:\!\star\,.\,\lambda x\!:\!u\,.\,x):(\Pi u\!:\!\star\,.\,u \to u). \qquad (1)$$

Now $(\lambda x\!:\!u\,.\,x)$ is the identity function on type u, or what was called $\mathbf{I}_u$ in Chapter 10. Hence

$$(\lambda u\!:\!\star\,.\,\lambda x\!:\!u\,.\,x)$$

is a function which, when applied to any type in sort $\star$, gives the identity function over that type. Thus in $\lambda 2$ we have quantification over types.

Note that (1) implies

$$v:\star \ \ \vdash \ \ (\lambda u\!:\!\star\,.\,\lambda x\!:\!u\,.\,x)v:(v \to v),$$

and hence

$$v:\star,\ y:v \ \ \vdash \ \ (\lambda u\!:\!\star\,.\,\lambda x\!:\!u\,.\,x)vy:v.$$

We also have the following reduction:

$$\begin{aligned}(\lambda u\!:\!\star\,.\,\lambda x\!:\!u\,.\,x)vy \ \ &\rhd_\beta \ \ (\lambda x\!:\!v\,.\,x)y \\ &\rhd_\beta \ \ y.\end{aligned}$$

Another example shows the connection with second-order logic. Let $\bot \equiv (\Pi u:\star\,.\,u)$. Then $\bot$ represents the usual definition of falsum (a generalized contradiction, usually taken to be $(\forall u)u$ in second-order logic). We can derive

$$\vdash \ (\lambda v\!:\!\star\,.\,\lambda x\!:\!\bot\,.\,xv):(\Pi v\!:\!\star\,.\,\bot \to v).$$

When this is considered under the propositions-as-types interpretation, it says that anything follows from a contradiction, the principle of *ex falso quodlibet*.

The system λ2 is a slightly modified form of the *second-order polymorphic λ-calculus*, or *System F*, originally introduced independently by Girard in [Gir71, Gir72] and Reynolds in [Rey74]. In Reynold's notation, types are obtained from the types of Definition 11.1 by adding a new abstraction operator Δ for type variables, so that the type we are writing as $(\Pi u : \star \,.\, \sigma)$ is written $\Delta u \,.\, \sigma$. Then, for terms, in addition to the term abstraction $\lambda x : \sigma \,.\, M$, there is a term abstraction for type variables of the form $\Lambda u \,.\, M$. Then the term we have written as $(\lambda u{:}\star \,.\, \lambda x{:}u \,.\, x)$ would be written $(\Lambda u \,.\, \lambda x{:}u \,.\, x)$. Thus, although there is some interplay between the terms and the types, types can still be defined separately from the terms.

Note that from the viewpoint of the propositions-as-types idea, $\star$ is a sort of propositions. In some works, $\star$ is written as Prop, and in many of these same works, $\Box$ is written as Type.

Remark 13.28 The system $\lambda\underline{\omega}$ is closely related to POLYREC, a language with polymorphic and recursive types (see [RdL92]). A recursive type is one defined by initial elements and constructor functions. In a language such as ML, the natural number type `nat` is a recursive type with initial element `0` and constructor `succ` (for successor). (The type `nat` has the property that only natural numbers inhabit it.) For such a system, we need type constructors, and the special rule $(\Box, \Box)$ allows for them. For we have the following derivation:

$$\dfrac{\dfrac{}{\vdash \star : \Box}\,(\text{axiom}) \qquad \dfrac{\dfrac{}{\vdash \star : \Box}\,(\text{axiom}) \quad \dfrac{}{\vdash \star : \Box}\,(\text{axiom})}{x : \star \vdash \star : \Box}\,(\text{weakening})}{\vdash (\star \to \star) : \Box.}\,(\text{product})$$

The type $(\star \to \star)$ is the type of type constructors and it is the result of the above derivation that allows the use of this type in this system. We can also derive the following examples:

$$\begin{array}{rcl}
 & \vdash & (\lambda u{:}\star \,.\, (u \to u)) : (\star \to \star) \\
v : \star & \vdash & (\lambda u{:}\star \,.\, u \to u)v \\
v : \star,\ x : v & \vdash & (\lambda y{:}v \,.\, x) : (\lambda u{:}\star \,.\, u \to u)v \\
u : \star,\ f : \star \to \star & \vdash & f(fu) : \star \\
u : \star & \vdash & (\lambda f{:}(\star \to \star) \,.\, f(fu)) : (\star \to \star) \to \star \,.
\end{array}$$

The term in the last example, $(\lambda f{:}(\star \to \star) \,.\, f(fu))$, is an example of a higher-order type constructor: it takes as its argument a type constructor f, and its value is a type.

Remark 13.29 The system λP has the special rule $(\star, \Box)$, which allows for types which depend on terms. For example, we have the following derivation:

$$\dfrac{\dfrac{D}{u:\star \vdash u:\star}\,(\text{start}) \qquad \dfrac{\dfrac{D \qquad D}{u:\star \vdash \star:\Box}\,(\text{wk}) \qquad \dfrac{D}{u:\star \vdash u:\star}\,(\text{start})}{u:\star,\ x:u \vdash \star:\Box}\,(\text{wk})}{u:\star \vdash (u \to \star):\Box}\,(\text{product})$$

where D is

$$\dfrac{}{\vdash \star:\Box}\,(\text{axiom})$$

and (wk) is (weakening). The type $(u \to \star)$ is a type of types which depend on terms. Then using rule (application) we can derive

$$u:\star,\ p:(u \to \star),\ x:u \ \vdash\ px:\star,$$

so px is a type which depends on the term x.[5] If we think of u as a set with $x \in u$, and think of p as a predicate on u, then px is a proposition, which is true if it is inhabited[6] and false otherwise. We can also derive

$$u:\star,\ p:(u \to u \to \star) \ \vdash\ (\Pi x\!:\!u\,.\,pxx):\star,$$

and under an informal propositions-as-types interpretation this says that if p is a binary predicate on u then $(\forall x \in u)pxx$ is a proposition. We can also derive

$$u:\star,\ p:(u \to \star),\ q:(u \to \star) \ \vdash\ (\Pi x\!:\!u\,.\,(px \to qx)):\star,$$

and the type $(\Pi x:u\,.\,(px \to qx))$ is interpreted as the proposition which states that the predicate p is included in the predicate q. We can also derive the following:

$$u:\star,\ p:(u \to \star) \ \vdash\ (\Pi x\!:\!u\,.\,(px \to px)):\star,$$

where $(\Pi x\!:\!u\,.\,(px \to px))$ is the type which is interpreted as the reflexivity of inclusion, and from this we can derive

$$u:\star,\ p:(u \to \star) \ \vdash\ (\lambda x\!:\!u\,.\,\lambda y\!:\!pa\,.\,x):(\Pi x\!:\!u\,.\,(px \to px)),$$

[5] Of course, here p and x are variables, but arbitrary terms could be substituted for them, so that this implies that if $\Gamma \vdash U:\star$, $\Gamma \vdash P:(U \to \star)$, and $\Gamma \vdash M:U$, then $\Gamma \vdash PM:\star$, and then PM is a type which depends on the term M.

[6] In the sense of Definition 11.50.

and $(\lambda x : u \,.\, \lambda y : pa \,.\, x)$ is interpreted as the proof that inclusion is reflexive. Finally, we can derive

$$u : \star,\ p : (u \to \star),\ q : \star \quad \vdash \quad \big((\Pi x : u \,.\, px \to q) \to (\Pi x : u \,.\, px) \to q\big) : \star,$$

$$\begin{aligned} u : \star,\ p : (u \to \star),\ q : \star,\ z : u \quad \vdash \quad & \\ & \big(\lambda v : (\Pi x : u \,.\, px \to q) \,.\, \lambda w : (\Pi x : u \,.\, px) \,.\, vz(wz)\big) : \\ & \big(\Pi v : (\Pi x : u \,.\, px \to q) \,.\, \Pi w : (\Pi x : u \,.\, px) \,.\, q\big), \end{aligned}$$

where the last type is equivalent to

$$(\Pi x : u \,.\, (px \to q) \to (\Pi x : u \,.\, px) \to q),$$

which is interpreted as saying that the formula

$$(\forall x \in u)(px \to q) \to (\forall x \in u)(px) \to q$$

is true in a non-empty structure u.

The system λP is related to the system AUT-QE of [Bru70][7] and the system LF of [HHP87]. For a more exact description of the relationship, see [KLN04, Section 4c1, p. 121, footnotes 3 and 4].

Remark 13.30 The system $\lambda\omega$, which includes the rules $(\square, \star)$ and $(\square, \square)$ as well as $(\star, \star)$, combines features of $\lambda\underline{\omega}$ and $\lambda 2$ and is related to the system $F\omega$ of [Gir72]. To see its strength, for $u{:}\star$ and $v{:}\star$, define

$$u \wedge v \quad \equiv \quad \Pi w{:}\star \,.\, (u \to v \to w) \to w.$$

This is the standard second-order definition of conjunction, as we shall see in Section 13G, and can be defined in λ2. Then, as can also be done in λ2, we can derive

$$u : \star,\quad v : \star \quad \vdash \quad u \wedge v : \star. \tag{2}$$

If we now define

$$\text{AND} \ \equiv \ \lambda u{:}\star \,.\, \lambda v{:}\star \,.\, u \wedge v,$$

and

$$K \ \equiv \ \lambda u{:}\star \,.\, \lambda v{:}\star \,.\, \lambda x{:}u \,.\, \lambda y{:}v \,.\, x,$$

then we can derive

$$\vdash \ \text{AND} : (\star \to \star \to \star) \tag{3}$$

and

$$\vdash \ K : (\Pi u{:}\star \,.\, \Pi v{:}\star \,.\, u \to v \to u). \tag{4}$$

[7] See also [NG94], [Daa94] and [NGdV94].

Here, (4) can be derived in $\lambda 2$, but (3) cannot, since rule $(\Box, \Box)$ is needed to obtain it by (abstraction) from (2). Also, we can derive

$$u : \star, \quad v : \star \quad \vdash \quad (\lambda x : \mathrm{AND}uv\,.\,xu(Kuv)) : (\mathrm{AND}uv \to u)$$

and

$$u : \star, \quad v : \star \quad \vdash \quad (\mathrm{AND}uv \to u) : \star.$$

Here, the term $(\lambda x : \mathrm{AND}uv\,.\,xu(Kuv))$ can be interpreted as a proof that $\mathrm{AND}uv \to u$ is a tautology.

Remark 13.31 The system λP2, which includes the rules $(\Box, \star)$ and $(\star, \Box)$ as well as $(\star, \star)$, combines features of $\lambda 2$ and λP, and is related to a system in [LM91]. Informally speaking, it corresponds to second order predicate logic. In it, the following can be derived:

$$u : \star, \quad p : u \to \star \quad \vdash \quad (\lambda x{:}u\,.\,px \to \bot) : (u \to \star)$$

and

$$u : \star, \quad p : u \to u \to \star \quad \vdash$$
$$((\Pi x{:}u\,.\,\Pi y{:}u\,.\,pxy \to pyx \to \bot) \to (\Pi x{:}u\,.\,puu \to \bot)) : \star.$$

The second of these says that a binary relation which is asymmetric is irreflexive.

Remark 13.32 The system $\lambda\mathrm{P}\underline{\omega}$, which has the rules $(\star, \Box)$ and $(\Box, \Box)$ as well as $(\star, \star)$, has features of both λP and $\lambda\underline{\omega}$. In this system, it is possible to derive

$$u : \star \ \vdash \ (\lambda p : u \to u \to \star\,.\,\lambda x{:}u\,.\,pxx) : ((u \to u \to \star) \to (u \to \star))$$

and

$$u : \star \ \vdash \ ((u \to u \to \star) \to (u \to \star)) : \Box.$$

The term $(\lambda p : u \to u \to \star\,.\,\lambda x{:}u\,.\,pxx)$ is a constructor which assigns to a binary relation its 'diagonalization'. This can be extended so that it does the same thing uniformly on u:

$$\vdash \ (\lambda u{:}\star\,.\,\lambda p{:}u \to u \to \star\,.\,\lambda x{:}u\,.\,pxx) :$$
$$(\Pi u{:}\star\,.\,\Pi p : u \to u \to \star\,.\,\Pi x{:}u\,.\,\star)$$

and

$$\vdash \ (\Pi u{:}\star\,.\,\Pi p : u \to u \to \star\,.\,\Pi x{:}u\,.\,\star) : \Box.$$

Remark 13.33 The system λC, which includes the rules $(\Box, \star)$, $(\star, \Box)$ and $(\Box, \Box)$ as well as $(\star, \star)$, is the *calculus of constructions* of [CH88], which under the propositions-as-types interpretation is higher-order intuitionistic logic, and is the basis of the proof assistant Coq. This system includes features of all the systems of the λ-cube. In it, for example, the following can be derived:

$$\vdash\ (\lambda u{:}\star\,.\,\lambda p{:}(u \to \star)\,.\,\lambda x{:}u\,.\,x \to \bot) : (\Pi u{:}\star\,.\,(u \to \star) \to (u \to \star))$$

and

$$\vdash\ (\Pi u{:}\star\,.\,(u \to \star) \to (u \to \star)) : \Box.$$

The term $(\lambda u : \star\,.\,\lambda p : (u \to \star)\,.\,\lambda x : u\,.\,x \to \bot)$ is a constructor which assigns to a type u and a predicate p on u the negation of p. We can also do universal quantification uniformly by defining

$$\text{ALL}\ \equiv\ (\lambda u{:}\star\,.\,\lambda p{:}(u \to \star)\,.\,\Pi x{:}u\,.\,px);$$

then we have

$$A : \star,\ \ P : A \to \star\ \ \vdash\ \ \text{ALL}AP : \star$$

and

$$\text{ALL}AP\ =_\beta\ (\Pi x{:}A\,.\,Px).$$

The systems of the λ-cube can be generalized to *pure type systems*:

Definition 13.34 (Pure type systems) *Pure type systems* (PTSs) are defined by modifying Definition 13.23 as follows: arbitrary constants different from all other constants in the system are now allowed as sorts, there is a set $\mathcal{A}$ of *axioms* of the form $s_1 : s_2$, where s_1 and s_2 are sorts, the rule (axiom) now has the form

$$\overline{s_1 : s_2},$$

for every axiom $s_1 : s_2 \in \mathcal{A}$, the special rules in $\mathcal{R}$ are now to be taken in the form (s_1, s_2, s_3), and the rule (product) is now to be taken in the following form:

(product) $$\frac{\Gamma \vdash A : s_1 \qquad \Gamma,\ x : A \vdash B : s_2}{\Gamma \vdash (\Pi x{:}A\,.\,B) : s_3}$$

Condition: $x \notin \text{FV}(\Gamma, A)$, s_1, s_2 and s_3 are sorts, and $(s_1, s_2, s_3) \in \mathcal{R}$.

In these systems, (s_1, s_2) is taken to be an abbreviation for the rule (s_1, s_2, s_2).

The set of sorts is denoted by $\mathcal{S}$, and the pure type system is said to be *determined* by $\mathcal{S}, \mathcal{A}$, and $\mathcal{R}$.

Clearly, the systems of Barendregt's λ-cube are all pure type systems. Another important pure type system is Luo's extended calculus of constructions [Luo90].

Example 13.35 Luo's *extended calculus of constructions*, ECC, is the PTS determined by the following sets:

$$
\begin{aligned}
\mathcal{S} &= \{\star\} \cup \{\square_n : n \text{ a non-negative integer}\}, \\
\mathcal{A} &= \{\star : \square_0\} \cup \{\square_n : \square_{n+1} : n \text{ a non-negative integer}\}, \\
\mathcal{R} &= \{(\star,\star,\star), (\star,\star,\square_n), (\square_n,\star,\star), (\square_n,\star,\square_m) : 0 \le n \le m\} \\
&\quad \cup \{(\star,\square_n,\square_m) : n \le m\} \\
&\quad \cup \{(\square_n,\square_m,\square_r) : 0 \le n \le r \text{ and } 0 \le m \le r\}.
\end{aligned}
$$

13F Normalization in PTSs

In this section we will take up the basic meta-theory of PTSs. Note that we have already stated in Definition 13.23 that the systems of the λ-cube are based on *pseudoterms* as defined in Definition 13.22. This is also true of PTSs. In what follows, we assume that we are dealing with a particular PTS.

The definitions of *pseudocontext* and *legal context* are the same for PTSs in general as for the eight systems of the λ-cube. We re-state them here for ease of reference.

Definition 13.36 A *pseudocontext* is a sequence of the form

$$\Gamma \equiv x_1 : A_1, \ \ldots, \ x_n : A_n,$$

where the variables $x_1, \ldots, x_n$ are all distinct. It is said to be a *legal context* (for a given PTS) iff there are pseudoterms M and A such that

$$\Gamma \vdash M : A.$$

In the rest of this chapter 'Γ' denotes an arbitrary pseudocontext.

Definition 13.37 If $\Gamma \equiv x_a : A_1, \ldots, x_n : A_n$, we say that a formula $x : A$ is *in* Γ, or $(x : A) \in \Gamma$, iff $x \equiv x_i$ and $A \equiv A_i$ for some i, $1 \leq i \leq n$.

Definition 13.38 Let $\Delta \equiv u_1 : B_1, \ldots, u_m : B_m$ be a pseudocontext with $m > 1$. Then $\Gamma \vdash \Delta$ means

$$\Gamma \vdash u_1 : B_1 \text{ and } \ldots \text{ and } \Gamma \vdash u_m : B_m.$$

Lemma 13.39 (Restricted weakening) *If* $\Gamma \vdash M : A$, *we may assume that the only applications of the rule (weakening) in the derivation of* $\Gamma \vdash M : A$ *are of the form*

$$\frac{\Gamma \vdash a : B \qquad \Gamma \vdash B : s}{\Gamma,\, x : B \vdash a : B,}$$

where s *is a sort and* a *is either a variable or a constant.*

Proof [Geu93, Lemma 4.4.21]. □

Lemma 13.40 (Free variable lemma) *Let* $\Gamma \equiv x_1 : A_1, \ldots, x_n : A_n$, *and suppose* $\Gamma \vdash M : A$. *Then*

(i) *every variable occurring free in* M *or in* A *is in* $\{x_1, \ldots, x_n\}$;

(ii) *for* $1 \leq i \leq n$, *the variables occurring free in* A_i *are among* $x_1, \ldots, x_{i-1}$.

Proof [Bar92, Lemma 5.2.8]. □

Lemma 13.41 (Start lemma) *Let* $\Gamma \equiv x_1 : A_1, \ldots, x_n : A_n$ *be legal for a PTS whose set of axioms is* $\mathcal{A}$. *Then*

(i) $\Gamma \vdash s_1 : s_2$ *for all* $(s_1 : s_2) \in \mathcal{A}$;

(ii) *for each* $i = 1, \ldots, n$, $\Gamma \vdash x_i : A_i$.

Proof [Bar92, Lemma 5.2.9]. □

Lemma 13.42 (Transitivity lemma) *Let* Γ *and* Δ *be pseudocontexts. If* $\Gamma \vdash \Delta$ *and* $\Delta \vdash M : A$, *then*

$$\Gamma \vdash M : A.$$

Proof [Bar92, Lemma 5.2.10]. □

Lemma 13.43 (Substitution lemma) *If* Γ *and* Δ *are pseudocontexts with no subjects in common, and* $x \notin \mathrm{FV}(\Gamma)$ *and* x *is not a subject in* Δ, *and*

$$\Gamma,\ x : A,\ \Delta\ \vdash\ M : B \qquad \textit{and} \qquad \Gamma \vdash N : A,$$

then

$$\Gamma,\ [N/x]\Delta\ \vdash\ [N/x]M : [N/x]B.$$

Proof [Bar92, Lemma 5.2.11]. Note that it follows from that proof that the derivation of the conclusion does not introduce any new inferences by (product) that use a special rule (as defined in Definition 13.23) not already present in the derivation of the first premise of the lemma. We shall use this fact below. □

Lemma 13.44 (Thinning lemma) *If* Γ *and* Δ *are legal, and every* $(x : A) \in \Gamma$ *is also in* Δ, *and* $\Gamma\ \vdash\ M : A$, *then*

$$\Delta\ \vdash\ M : A.$$

Proof [Bar92, Lemma 5.2.12]. □

Lemma 13.45 (Generation lemma)

(i) *If* $\Gamma\ \vdash\ s : C$, *where* s *is a sort, then there is a sort* s' *such that* $C =_\beta s'$ *and* $s\!:\!s' \in \mathcal{A}$.

(ii) *If* $\Gamma\ \vdash\ x : C$, *then there are a sort* s *and a pseudoterm* B *such that*

$$B =_\beta C, \quad \Gamma\ \vdash\ B : s, \quad (x\!:\!B) \in \Gamma.$$

(iii) *If* $\Gamma\ \vdash\ (\Pi x\!:\!A\,.\,B) : C$, *then there are sorts* s_1, s_2, *and* s_3 *such that* $(s_1, s_2, s_3) \in \mathcal{R}$ *and*

$$\Gamma\ \vdash\ A : s_1, \quad \Gamma,\ x : A \vdash\ B : s_2, \quad C =_\beta s_3.$$

(iv) *If* $\Gamma\ \vdash\ (\lambda x\!:\!A\,.\,M) : C$, *then there are a sort* s *and a pseudoterm* B *such that*

$$\Gamma\ \vdash\ (\Pi x\!:\!A\,.\,B) : s, \quad \Gamma,\ x : A\ \vdash\ M : B, \quad C =_\beta (\Pi x\!:\!A\,.\,B).$$

(v) *If* $\Gamma\ \vdash\ MN : C$, *then there are pseudoterms* A *and* B *such that*

$$\Gamma\ \vdash\ M : (\Pi x\!:\!A\,.\,B), \quad \Gamma\ \vdash\ N : A, \quad C =_\beta [N/x]B.$$

Proof [Bar92, Lemma 5.2.13]. □

Remark 13.46 In a sense, this lemma corresponds to the subject-construction property discussed in Section 11C, and to Curry's *Subject-construction theorem*, [CF58, Theorem 9B1].

Lemma 13.47 (Correctness of types) *If* $\Gamma \vdash M : A$, *then there is a sort* s *such that* $A =_\beta s$ *or* $\Gamma \vdash A : s$.

Proof [Bar92, Corollary 5.2.14, part 1]. □

Lemma 13.48 *If* $\Gamma \vdash M : (\Pi x : B_1 . B_2)$, *then there are sorts* s_1 *and* s_2 *such that* $\Gamma \vdash B_1 : s_1$ *and* $\Gamma, x : B_1 \vdash B_2 : s_2$.

Proof [Bar92, Corollary 5.2.14, part 2]. □

Lemma 13.49 *If* $\Gamma \vdash A : B$ *or* $\Gamma \vdash B : A$, *then either (i) there is a sort* s *such that* $A =_\beta s$, *or (ii) there is a sort* s *such that* $\Gamma \vdash A : s$, *or (iii) there are a sort* s *and a pseudoterm* C *such that* $\Gamma \vdash A : C$ *and* $\Gamma \vdash C : s$.

Proof [Bar92, Corollary 5.2.14, part 3]. □

Definition 13.50 A pseudoterm A for which there are an environment Γ and a pseudoterm B such that either $\Gamma \vdash A : B$ or $\Gamma \vdash B : A$ is said to be *legal*.

Thus, the hypothesis of Lemma 13.49 is that A be legal.

Lemma 13.51 (Subterm lemma) *If* A *is legal and* B *is a subterm of* A, *then* B *is legal.*

Proof [Bar92, Corollary 5.2.14, part 4]. □

Theorem 13.52 (Subject-reduction theorem) *If*

$$\Gamma \vdash M : A \qquad \textit{and} \qquad M \rhd_\beta M',$$

then

$$\Gamma \vdash M' : A.$$

Proof [Bar92, Theorem 5.2.15]. □

Corollary 13.52.1 *If* $\Gamma \vdash M : A$ *and* $A \rhd_\beta A'$, *then* $\Gamma \vdash M : A'$.

Proof [Bar92, Corollary 5.2.16, part 1]. □

Lemma 13.53 (Strengthening lemma) *If* $\Gamma,\ x\!:\!A,\ \Delta$ *is a pseudocontext and*

$$\Gamma,\ x : A,\ \Delta\ \vdash\ M : B$$

and $x \notin \mathrm{FV}(\Delta) \cup \mathrm{FV}(M) \cup \mathrm{FV}(B)$, *then*

$$\Gamma,\ \Delta \vdash M : B.$$

Proof [vBJ93, Lemma 6.2]. □

Corollary 13.53.1 *For a PTS with a finite set of sorts, with the property that every legal term is weakly or strongly normalizing, the questions of type checking and typability are decidable.*

Proof [vBJ93, Theorem 7.5]. □

Definition 13.54 A PTS given by $\mathcal{S}$, $\mathcal{A}$, and $\mathcal{R}$ is *singly sorted* iff

(i) if $(s_1, s_2), (s_1, s_2') \in \mathcal{A}$, then $s_2 \equiv s_2'$;
(ii) if $(s_1, s_2, s_3), (s_1, s_2, s_3') \in \mathcal{R}$, then $s_3 \equiv s_3'$.

Example 13.55

(i) The PTSs of the λ-cube are singly sorted.
(ii) The PTS specified by

$$\begin{array}{rcl} \mathcal{S} & = & \{\star, \square,\ \diamond\} \\ \mathcal{A} & = & \{\star\!:\!\square,\ \star\!:\!\diamond\} \\ \mathcal{R} & = & \{(\star,\star),\ (\star,\square)\} \end{array}$$

is not singly sorted.

Lemma 13.56 (Unicity of types) *In a singly sorted PTS, if*

$$\Gamma \vdash M : A \qquad \text{and} \qquad \Gamma \vdash M : A',$$

then $A =_\beta A'$.

Proof [Bar92, Lemma 5.2.21]. □

Lemma 13.57 (Strong permutation lemma) *If* $\Gamma, x\!:\!A, y\!:\!B$ *is a pseudocontext, and*

$$\Gamma,\ x : A,\ y : B\ \vdash\ M : C,$$

and $x \notin \mathrm{FV}(B)$, *then*

$$\Gamma,\ y : B,\ x : A\ \vdash\ M : C.$$

See [KLN04, Lemma 4.37, page 122].

Definition 13.58 (Topsort) A sort s is a *topsort* iff there is no sort s' such that $(s, s') \in \mathcal{A}$.

Lemma 13.59 (Topsort lemma) *If* s *is a topsort and* $\Gamma \vdash A\!:\!s$, *then* A *is not of the form* $A_1 A_2$ *or* $\lambda x\!:\!A_1 \,.\, A_2$.

See [KLN04, Lemma 4.39, page 123].

Theorem 13.60 (Strong normalization theorem for the λ-cube) *For systems of the λ-cube,*

(i) *if* $\Gamma \vdash M : A$, *then* M *and* A *are SN;*

(ii) *if* $x_1 : A_1,\ \ldots,\ x_n : A_n \vdash M : B$, *then* $A_1, \ldots, A_n$, M *and* B *are SN.*

Proof [Bar92, Theorems 5.3.32 and 5.3.33]. Note that the theorem is proved for λC, the strongest system of the cube, from which it follows for all the other systems. □

Remark 13.61 The theorem also holds for Luo's ECC of Example 13.35; see [Luo90, Corollary 5.12.14]. Since λC is a subsystem of ECC, the above theorem follows from Luo's result.

Remark 13.62 The proof of Theorem 13.60 in [Bar92] does not follow the form of Theorems 11.56 and 12.33 in reducing deductions. The proof can be carried out this way by defining reductions of deductions as follows.

Deduction reduction A deduction of the form

$$\dfrac{\dfrac{\dfrac{\Gamma,\ x\!:\!A \ \vdash\ M\!:\!B \quad \Gamma\ \vdash\ (\Pi x\!:\!A\,.\,B) : s}{\Gamma\ \vdash\ (\lambda x\!:\!A\,.\,M) : (\Pi x\!:\!A\,.\,B)}\ \text{(abstraction)}}{\Gamma\ \vdash\ (\lambda x\!:\!A\,.\,M) : (\Pi x\!:\!C\,.\,D)}\ \text{(conversion)} \qquad \Gamma\ \vdash\ N\!:\!C}{\Gamma\ \vdash\ (\lambda x\!:\!A\,.\,M)N : [N/x]D}\ \text{(a)}$$

where (a) is the rule (application), $x \notin \mathrm{FV}(\Gamma, A)$, $A =_\beta C$, and $B =_\beta D$, reduces to

$$\dfrac{\dfrac{\Gamma,\ x\!:\!A\ \vdash\ M\!:\!B \qquad \dfrac{\Gamma\ \vdash\ N\!:\!C}{\Gamma\ \vdash\ N\!:\!A}\ \text{(conversion)}}{\Gamma\ \vdash\ [N/x]M : [N/x]B}\ \text{(substitution lemma, 13.43)}}{\Gamma\ \vdash\ [N/x]M : [N/x]D.}\ \text{(conversion)}$$

A proof that every deduction can be strongly normalized with respect to this reduction rule is given for λC in [Sel97, Theorem 11]. As noted above in the proof of Lemma 13.43, the transformation of the proof using that lemma does not introduce any inferences by (product) using a special rule not already present in the deduction before the substitution, and hence it follows that the result holds for all systems of the λ-cube. We conjecture that it also holds for Luo's ECC, but we have not checked the details.

Warning 13.63 ($\beta\eta$-conversion) In simply typed λ-calculus it was easy to add a rule for η-conversion, as in Definition 10.16. But in a PTS the syntax of terms is more complex, and if η-reductions were allowed, the Church–Rosser theorem would fail. This is shown by the following example, due to Nederpelt [NGdV94, Chapter C.3, Section 7]. Let x, y, and z be distinct variables, and consider the term $\lambda x : y\,.\,(\lambda x : z\,.\,x)x$. We would have

$$\lambda x\!:\!y\,.\,(\lambda x\!:\!z\,.\,x)x \ \ \triangleright_\beta\ \ \lambda x\!:\!y\,.\,x$$

by contracting the β-redex $(\lambda x\!:\!z\,.\,x)x$, and we would also have

$$\lambda x\!:\!y\,.\,(\lambda x\!:\!z\,.\,x)x \ \ \triangleright_\eta\ \ \lambda x\!:\!z\,.\,x$$

by contracting the η-redex $\lambda x\!:\!y\,.\,(\lambda x\!:\!z\,.\,x)x$. But $\lambda x\!:\!y\,.\,x$ and $\lambda x\!:\!z\,.\,x$ are both irreducible, and they are distinct normal forms.

13G Propositions-as-types

Logical connectives and quantifiers can be represented in many systems of the λ-cube.[8] These systems can be viewed either as systems of type-theory, in which an expression $M\!:\!A$ says that M has type A, or systems of logic, in which the A in $M\!:\!A$ is interpreted as a logical formula and M is thought of as encoding a proof of A. When the systems are seen from the second viewpoint, the logic that they express turns out to be, not the classical logic of two-valued truth-tables, but the logic of the intuitionists that was mentioned in Discussion 11.49, and is important in the theoretical foundations of computing.

The discussion in the present section will apply to $\lambda 2$ and those systems stronger than it, namely λP2, $\lambda\omega$ and λC.

Definition 13.64 The term F is defined as follows:

$$\mathsf{F} \equiv \lambda u\!:\!\star\,.\,\lambda v\!:\!\star\,.\,(\Pi x\!:\!u\,.\,v).$$

We use either '$A \to B$' (see Definition 13.25) or '$A \supset B$', as an abbreviation for $\mathsf{F}AB$, depending on whether we wish to emphasize a particular expression's role as a type or a logical formula.

It is easy to show that in $\lambda 2$ and all stronger systems, $\to$ satisfies the rules

$$\frac{\Gamma \vdash A:\star \qquad \Gamma \vdash B:\star}{\Gamma \vdash (A \to B):\star,}$$

$$\frac{\Gamma \vdash M: A \to B \qquad \Gamma \vdash N:A}{\Gamma \vdash MN:B,}$$

and, if $x \notin \mathrm{FV}(B)$,

$$\frac{\Gamma,\, x:A \vdash M:B \qquad \Gamma \vdash A \to B:\star}{\Gamma \vdash (\lambda x\!:\!A\,.\,M): A \to B.}$$

This means, of course, that $\supset$ satisfies rules

$$\frac{\Gamma \vdash A:\star \qquad \Gamma \vdash B:\star}{\Gamma \vdash (A \supset B):\star,}$$

$$\frac{\Gamma \vdash M: A \supset B \qquad \Gamma \vdash N:A}{\Gamma \vdash MN:B,}$$

[8] The material of this section is a revision of the material of [Sel97, Sections 6, 9].

and, if $x \notin \mathrm{FV}(B)$,

$$\frac{\Gamma,\ x:A\ \vdash\ M:B \qquad \Gamma \vdash A \supset B : \star}{\Gamma\ \vdash\ (\lambda x\!:\!A\,.\,M) : A \supset B.}$$

Definition 13.65 The *conjunction proposition operator* and its associated pairing and projection operators are defined as follows:

(a) $\mathsf{\Lambda} \equiv \lambda u\!:\!\star\,.\,\lambda v\!:\!\star\,.\,(\Pi w\!:\!\star\,.\,(u \to v \to w) \to w)$;

(b) $\mathbf{D} \equiv \lambda u\!:\!\star\,.\,\lambda v\!:\!\star\,.\,\lambda x\!:\!u\,.\,\lambda y\!:\!v\,.\,\lambda w\!:\!\star\,.\,\lambda z\!:\!(u \to v \to w)\,.\,zxy$;

(c) $\mathsf{fst} \equiv \lambda u\!:\!\star\,.\,\lambda v\!:\!\star\,.\,\lambda x\!:\!(\mathsf{\Lambda} uv)\,.\,xu(\lambda y\!:\!u\,.\,\lambda z\!:\!v\,.\,y)$;

(d) $\mathsf{snd} \equiv \lambda u\!:\!\star\,.\,\lambda v\!:\!\star\,.\,\lambda x\!:\!(\mathsf{\Lambda} uv)\,.\,xv(\lambda y\!:\!u\,.\,\lambda z\!:\!v\,.\,z)$.

We use '$A \wedge B$' and '$A \times B$' as abbreviations for $\mathsf{\Lambda} AB$, the former in logic and the latter in type-theory. (For $\mathbf{D}$, fst and snd, cf. $\mathbf{D}$, $\mathbf{D}_1$ and $\mathbf{D}_2$ in the answer to Exercise 2.34(a).)

It is not at all difficult to prove from these definitions that in $\lambda 2$ and stronger systems,

$$u:\star,\ v:\star\ \vdash\ \mathbf{D}uv : u \to v \to (u \wedge v),$$

$$u:\star,\ v:\star\ \vdash\ \mathsf{fst}uv : (u \wedge v) \to u,$$

$$u:\star,\ v:\star\ \vdash\ \mathsf{snd}uv : (u \wedge v) \to v.$$

Furthermore, it is easy to prove

$$u:\star,\ v:\star,\ x:u,\ y:v\ \vdash\ \mathsf{fst}uv(\mathbf{D}uvxy) : u,$$

$$u:\star,\ v:\star,\ x:u,\ y:v\ \vdash\ \mathsf{snd}uv(\mathbf{D}uvxy) : v$$

and

$$\mathsf{fst}uv(\mathbf{D}uvxy) =_\beta x, \qquad \mathsf{snd}uv(\mathbf{D}uvxy) =_\beta y.$$

Definition 13.66 The *disjunction proposition operator* and its associated injection and case operators are defined as follows:

(a) $\mathsf{V} \equiv \lambda u\!:\!\star\,.\,\lambda v\!:\!\star\,.\,(\Pi w\!:\!\star\,.\,(u \to w) \to ((v \to w) \to w))$;

(b) $\mathsf{inl} \equiv \lambda u\!:\!\star\,.\,\lambda v\!:\!\star\,.\,\lambda x\!:\!u\,.\,\lambda w\!:\!\star\,.\,\lambda f\!:\!(u \to w)\,.\,\lambda g\!:\!(v \to w)\,.\,fx$;

(c) $\mathsf{inr} \equiv \lambda u\!:\!\star\,.\,\lambda v\!:\!\star\,.\,\lambda y\!:\!v\,.\,\lambda w\!:\!\star\,.\,\lambda f\!:\!(u \to w)\,.\,\lambda g\!:\!(v \to w)\,.\,gy$;

(d) $\mathsf{case} \equiv$

$$\lambda u\!:\!\star\,.\,\lambda v\!:\!\star\,.\,\lambda z\!:\!(\mathsf{V}uv)\,.\,\lambda w\!:\!\star\,.\,\lambda f\!:\!(u \to w)\,.\,\lambda g\!:\!(v \to w)\,.\,zwfg.$$

We use '$A \vee B$' as an abbreviation for $\mathsf{V}AB$.

It is easy to show that in $\lambda 2$ and stronger systems,

$$u:\star,\ v:\star\ \vdash\ \mathsf{inl}uv : u \to u \vee v,$$

$$u:\star,\ v:\star\ \vdash\ \mathsf{inr}uv : v \to u \vee v,$$

$$u:\star,\ v:\star\ \vdash\ \mathsf{case}uv :\ u \vee v \to (\Pi w{:}\star)\big((u \to w) \to ((v \to w) \to w)\big).$$

Furthermore, it is easy to prove

$$u:\star,\ v:\star,\ w:\star,\ x:u,\ y:v,\ f:u \to w,\ g:v \to w \\ \vdash\ \mathsf{case}uv(\mathsf{inl}uvx)wfg : w,$$

$$u:\star,\ v:\star,\ w:\star,\ x:u,\ y:v,\ f:u \to w,\ g:v \to w \\ \vdash\ \mathsf{case}uv(\mathsf{inr}uvy)wfg : w,$$

and

$$\mathsf{case}uv(\mathsf{inl}uvx)wfg\ =_\beta\ fx,$$

$$\mathsf{case}uv(\mathsf{inr}uvy)wfg\ =_\beta\ gy.$$

Definition 13.67 $\mathsf{void} \equiv \perp \equiv (\Pi u{:}\star\,.\,u)$.

We shall use '$\perp$' when we are thinking of the proposition and 'void' when we are thinking of the type. It is easy to prove in $\lambda 2$ and stronger systems that

$$\vdash\ \perp : \star$$

and

$$x:\perp,\ u:\star\ \vdash\ xu : u.$$

It follows from the second of these that if there is a closed term in $\perp$, then there is a proof of every proposition. Hence, in terms of propositions, $\perp$ represents a generalized contradiction. However, in systems of the λ-cube, there is no closed term in $\perp$:

Theorem 13.68 (Consistency) *In systems of the λ-cube, there is no closed term M such that $\vdash M{:}\perp$.*

Proof Suppose there is such a term M. Then the proof of $\vdash M{:}\perp$ can be extended as follows:

$$\frac{\vdash\ M:\perp \qquad u:\star\ \vdash\ u:\star}{u:\star\ \vdash\ Mu:u.}\ \text{(application)}$$

By Theorem 13.60, Mu has a normal form, say N. By Lemma 13.45 and the fact that u is a variable, N does not have the form $\lambda x : A \,.\, P$. Hence, N must have the form $aN_1 \ldots N_n$, where a is a variable or a constant, and

$$u : \star \;\vdash\; a : (\Pi y_1 : A_1 \,.\; \ldots \;.\, \Pi y_n : A_n \,.\, \star), \tag{5}$$

and for $i = 1, \ldots, n$,

$$u : \star \;\vdash\; N_i : A_i.$$

In the proof of $\vdash N : u$, if a is a constant, (5) must be an axiom, and the only axiom is $\star : \Box$, which does not have the right form. If a is a variable, it must be u, in which case $n = 0$ and $N \equiv u$; but the only provable type for u is $\star$, not u. Hence, in these systems, there is no way to prove (5). □

Remark 13.69 The above proof will also apply to PTSs not in the λ-cube for which Theorem 13.60 holds and for which the axioms are sufficiently limited.

Some axioms which would preserve consistency if added are discussed in [Sel97, Section 7].

Definition 13.70 The *negation proposition operator* is defined thus:

$$\neg \;\equiv\; \lambda x{:}\star \,.\, x \to \bot.$$

It is easy to show that if $\Gamma \;\vdash\; A{:}\star$, then in $\lambda 2$ and stronger systems,

$$\frac{\Gamma \vdash M : \neg A \qquad \Gamma \vdash N : A}{\Gamma \vdash MN : \bot}$$

and

$$\frac{\Gamma,\ x{:}A \vdash M : \bot \qquad \Gamma \vdash \neg A : \star}{\Gamma \vdash (\lambda x : A \,.\, M) : \neg A.}$$

Definition 13.71 The *existential quantifier operator* and its associated pairing and projection functions are defined as follows:

(a) $\boldsymbol{\Sigma} \equiv \lambda u{:}\star \,.\, \lambda v{:}(u \to \star) \,.\, (\Pi w{:}\star \,.\, (\Pi x : u \,.\, vx \to w) \to w)$;

(b) $\mathsf{D}' \equiv$
$\lambda u{:}\star \,.\, \lambda v{:}(u \to \star) \,.\, \lambda x{:}u \,.\, \lambda y{:}vx \,.\, \lambda w{:}\star \,.\, \lambda z{:}(\Pi x : u \,.\, vx \to w) \,.\, zxy$;

(c) $\mathsf{proj} \equiv$
$\lambda u{:}\star \,.\, \lambda v{:}(u \to \star) \,.\, \lambda w{:}\star \,.\, \lambda z{:}(\Pi x : u \,.\, vx \to w) \,.\, \lambda y{:}(\Pi x : u \,.\, vx) \,.\, ywz.$

We use '$(\exists x\!:\!A\,.\,B)$' as an abbreviation for $\Sigma A(\lambda x\!:\!A\,.\,B)$.

It is not hard to show that in $\lambda 2$ and stronger systems,

$$u:\star,\ v:u\to\star \ \vdash\ (\exists x\!:\!u\,.\,vx):\star,$$

$$u:\star,\ v:u\to\star \ \vdash\ \mathbf{D}'uv:(\Pi t\!:\!u\,.\,vt\supset(\exists x\!:\!u\,.\,vx)),$$

and

$$u:\star,\ v:u\to\star \ \vdash$$
$$\mathsf{proj}uv:\big(\Pi w\!:\!\star\,.\,(\Pi y\!:\!u\,.\,vy\to w)\supset(\exists x\!:\!u\,.\,vx)\supset w\big).$$

Furthermore, it is easy to prove

$$u:\star,\ v:u\to\star,\ w:\star,\ x:u,\ y:vx,\ z:(\Pi x\!:\!u\,.\,vx\to w)\ \vdash$$
$$\mathsf{proj}uvwz(\mathbf{D}'uvxy):w$$

and

$$\mathsf{proj}uvwz(\mathbf{D}'uvxy)\ =_\beta\ zxy.$$

Note that $\mathbf{D}'$ differs from $\mathbf{D}$ only in the types postulated for some of the bound variables. But this difference is enough to make it impossible to define a right projection for $\mathbf{D}'$ that is correctly typed: this point is discussed in [Car86]. However, a modified version of fst works as a left projection function for $\mathbf{D}'$:

$$\mathsf{fst}'\ \equiv\ \lambda u\!:\!\star\,.\,\lambda v\!:\!(u\to\star)\,.\,\lambda x\!:\!(\Sigma uv)\,.\,xu(\lambda y\!:\!u\,.\,\lambda z\!:\!v\,.\,y).$$

These definitions give us the logical connectives and quantifiers. We can also define equality over any type:

Definition 13.72 The *equality proposition*

$$M=_A N,$$

is defined to be

$$\mathbf{Q}AMN,$$

where

$$\mathbf{Q}\ \equiv\ \lambda u\!:\!\star\,.\,\lambda x\!:\!u\,.\,\lambda y\!:\!u\,.\,(\Pi z\!:\!(u\to\star)\,.\,zx\supset zy).$$

This definition will only be used when $A : \star$ has already been proved or assumed in a context.

It is not hard to show that in $\lambda 2$ and stronger systems,

$$\vdash \mathsf{Q} : (\Pi u{:}\star . u \to u \to \star),$$

$$u : \star,\ x : u \ \vdash\ \big(\lambda z{:}(u \to \star) . (\lambda w{:}zx . w)\big) : x =_u x,$$

and

$$u : \star,\ x : u,\ y : u,\ m : (x =_u y),\ z : u \to \star,\ n : zx \ \vdash\ mzn : zy.$$

This gives us the reflexivity and substitution properties of equality; these two properties are well known to imply all the usual properties of equality.

We can also interpret arithmetic in $\lambda 2$ and stronger systems. The interpretation is based on the representation of arithmetic in Chapter 4, with suitable modifications for the types.

Definition 13.73 (Basic arithmetic operators) The *natural-numbers type* and basic *arithmetical operators* are defined as follows:[9]

(a) $\mathsf{N} \equiv (\Pi u{:}\star . (u \to u) \to (u \to u))$;

(b) $\mathbf{0} \equiv \lambda u{:}\star . \lambda x{:}u{\to}u . \lambda y{:}u . y$;

(c) $\boldsymbol{\sigma} \equiv \lambda v{:}\mathsf{N} . \lambda u{:}\star . \lambda x{:}u{\to}u . \lambda y{:}u . x(vuxy)$;

(d) $\boldsymbol{\pi} \equiv \lambda u{:}\mathsf{N} . \mathsf{snd}\,\mathsf{N}\,\mathsf{N}\,\big(u(\mathsf{N} \times \mathsf{N})Q\,(\mathsf{D}\,\mathsf{N}\,\mathsf{N}\,\mathbf{0}\,\mathbf{0})\big)$,
where $Q \equiv \lambda v{:}(\mathsf{N} \times \mathsf{N}) . \mathsf{D}\,\mathsf{N}\,\mathsf{N}\,(\boldsymbol{\sigma}(\mathsf{fst}\,\mathsf{N}\,\mathsf{N}v))(\mathsf{fst}\,\mathsf{N}\,\mathsf{N}v)$;

(e) $\mathsf{R} \equiv \lambda u{:}\star . \lambda x{:}u . \lambda y{:}\mathsf{N}{\to}u{\to}u . \lambda z{:}\mathsf{N} . z(\mathsf{N} \to u)P(\lambda w{:}\mathsf{N} . x)z$,
where $P \equiv \lambda v{:}\mathsf{N} \to u . \lambda w{:}\mathsf{N} . y(\boldsymbol{\pi} w)(v(\boldsymbol{\pi} w))$.

The term n, which represents the natural number n, is defined as usual by

$$\mathsf{n} \ \equiv\ \boldsymbol{\sigma}^n\mathbf{0} \ \equiv\ \underbrace{\boldsymbol{\sigma}(\boldsymbol{\sigma}(...(\boldsymbol{\sigma}}_{n}\,\mathbf{0})...)).$$

It is not hard to show that in $\lambda 2$ and stronger systems

$$\vdash \mathbf{0} : \mathsf{N},$$

[9] For (a), cf. N_τ in 11.2. For (b), cf. the Church numeral $\overline{0}$ in 4.2. For (c), cf. $\overline{\sigma}$ in 4.6. For (d), cf. $\overline{\pi}_{\text{Bernays}}$ in 4.13. For (e), cf. R and $(M_\tau y)$ in Appendix A3's A3.21(8) and (9).

$$\vdash \boldsymbol{\sigma} : \mathsf{N} \to \mathsf{N},$$

$$\vdash \boldsymbol{\pi} : \mathsf{N} \to \mathsf{N}$$

and

$$\vdash \mathsf{R} : (\Pi u{:}\star\,.\,u \to (\mathsf{N} \to u \to u) \to \mathsf{N} \to u).$$

It is also easy to show that

$$\mathsf{n} \;=_\beta\; \lambda u{:}\star\,.\,\lambda x{:}u \to u\,.\,\lambda y{:}u\,.\,x^n y,$$

$$\boldsymbol{\pi}\mathbf{0} \;=_\beta\; \mathbf{0},$$

$$\boldsymbol{\pi}(\boldsymbol{\sigma}\mathsf{n}) \;=_\beta\; \mathsf{n};$$

and

$$\mathsf{R}AMN\mathbf{0} \;=_\beta\; M,$$

$$\mathsf{R}AMN(\boldsymbol{\sigma}\mathsf{n}) \;=_\beta\; N\mathsf{n}(\mathsf{R}AMN\mathsf{n}),$$

for all A, M, N such that $A : \star$, $M : A$ and $N : \mathsf{N} \to A \to A$ have been previously proved. It is also not hard to show that

$$\vdash \mathsf{N} : \star.$$

It can be shown that Definition 13.73 is an appropriate way to represent arithmetic if all we want to do is define the primitive recursive functions.

But if we go further, to consider the Peano axioms, we find that it is not possible to prove all the formulas representing these axioms as theorems.

Four of the Peano axioms are no problem: they are essentially just the defining equations for $+$ and $\times$, and follow from the reduction properties of R and rule (conversion), given suitable λ-representations of $+$ and $\times$, cf. Exercise 4.16(b).

The other Peano axioms can be translated most easily and directly into $\lambda 2$ as:

(i) $\mathsf{Peano1} \;\equiv\; (\Pi n{:}\mathsf{N}\,.\,\neg(\boldsymbol{\sigma} n =_{\mathsf{N}} \mathbf{0}))$;

(ii) $\mathsf{Peano2} \;\equiv\; (\Pi m{:}\mathsf{N}\,.\,\Pi n{:}\mathsf{N}\,.\,(\boldsymbol{\sigma} m =_{\mathsf{N}} \boldsymbol{\sigma} n \;\supset\; m =_{\mathsf{N}} n))$;

(iii) $\mathsf{Peano3} \;\equiv\; (\Pi u{:}\mathsf{N} \to \star\,.$
$(\Pi m{:}\mathsf{N}\,.\,um \supset u(\boldsymbol{\sigma} m)) \supset u\mathbf{0} \supset (\Pi n{:}\mathsf{N}\,.\,un))$.

However, Peano3 in this simple version cannot be derived in $\lambda 2$. This rests on the the fact that there is a term with type $\mathbf{N}$ in this system which is not a representative of a natural number:

$$\lambda A : \star\,.\, \lambda x : A \to A\,.\, x. \tag{6}$$

True, this term η-converts to $\mathbf{1}$, but it does not β-convert to n for any n. It may appear that the problem is the way we have chosen to represent the natural numbers, but that is not the case. Geuvers [Geu01] shows that it is not possible to prove induction in the simple form shown.

To get round this problem we must define a predicate which will say, in effect, that an object is a natural number. One suitable definition, which, in a sense, goes back to Dedekind [Ded87], is as follows:

$$\mathcal{N} \equiv \lambda n{:}\mathbf{N}\,.\,(\Pi u : \mathbf{N} \to \star)\big((\Pi m{:}\mathbf{N}\,.\,um \supset u(\boldsymbol{\sigma} m)) \supset u\mathbf{0} \supset un\big). \tag{7}$$

It is easy to prove in $\lambda 2$ and stronger systems that

$$\begin{array}{ll} \vdash & \mathcal{N} : \mathbf{N} \to \star, \\ \vdash & M : \mathcal{N}\mathbf{0}, \\ \vdash & N : (\Pi n{:}\mathbf{N}\,.\,\mathcal{N}n \supset \mathcal{N}(\boldsymbol{\sigma} n)), \end{array}$$

for some suitable closed terms M and N. Furthermore, we can prove induction in the following form: there is a closed term P such that

$$\begin{aligned} \vdash P : \big(&\Pi u{:}\mathbf{N} \to \star\,. \\ &(\Pi m{:}\mathbf{N}\,.\,um \supset u(\boldsymbol{\sigma} m)) \supset u\mathbf{0} \supset (\Pi n{:}\mathbf{N}\,.\,\mathcal{N}n \supset un)\big). \end{aligned} \tag{8}$$

This gives us induction within the logic.

This leaves us with the axioms Peanol and Peano2 as unproved assumptions. However, Peano2 is not really needed, as the second of the following two lemmas shows that a version of Peano2 involving $\mathcal{N}$ can be proved in $\lambda 2$.

Lemma 13.74 *In $\lambda 2$ there exists a closed term Q such that*

$$\vdash Q : \big(\Pi n{:}\mathbf{N}\,.\,\mathcal{N}n \to \boldsymbol{\pi}(\boldsymbol{\sigma} n) =_{\mathbf{N}} n\big).$$

Proof A direct calculation gives that $\boldsymbol{\pi}(\boldsymbol{\sigma}(\boldsymbol{\sigma} n)) =_\beta \boldsymbol{\sigma}(\boldsymbol{\pi}(\boldsymbol{\sigma} n))$. Hence, there is a term Q_1 such that

$$n : \mathbf{N},\ x : (\boldsymbol{\pi}(\boldsymbol{\sigma} n) =_{\mathbf{N}} n) \ \vdash\ Q_1 : (\boldsymbol{\pi}(\boldsymbol{\sigma}(\boldsymbol{\sigma} n)) =_{\mathbf{N}} \boldsymbol{\sigma} n).$$

Hence, by (abstraction), there is a term Q_2 such that

$$\vdash\ Q_2 : \Big(\Pi n{:}\mathsf{N}\,.\,(\boldsymbol{\pi}(\boldsymbol{\sigma} n) =_{\mathsf{N}} n) \to (\boldsymbol{\pi}(\boldsymbol{\sigma}(\boldsymbol{\sigma} n)) =_{\mathsf{N}} \boldsymbol{\sigma} n)\Big).$$

This is the induction step. The basis is easy, since $\boldsymbol{\pi}(\boldsymbol{\sigma}\mathbf{0}) =_\beta \mathbf{0}$. Then induction (which follows from the definition of $\mathcal{N}$) gives us the lemma. □

Lemma 13.75 *In* $\lambda 2$ *there exists a closed term* R *such that*

$$\vdash\ R : \Big(\Pi n{:}\mathsf{N}\,.\,\Pi m{:}\mathsf{N}\,.\,\mathcal{N} n \to \mathcal{N} m \to (\boldsymbol{\sigma} n =_{\mathsf{N}} \boldsymbol{\sigma} m) \to (n =_{\mathsf{N}} m)\Big).$$

Proof We can easily formalize in this logic the following argument, where $n = m$ represents $n =_{\mathsf{N}} m$: if $\boldsymbol{\sigma} n = \boldsymbol{\sigma} m$, then $\boldsymbol{\pi}(\boldsymbol{\sigma} n) = \boldsymbol{\pi}(\boldsymbol{\sigma} m)$, and so $n = m$. □

Thus, to obtain the Peano postulates in the weakest possible extension of $\lambda 2$, it is sufficient to add as an assumption

$$c : \mathsf{Peano1}, \tag{9}$$

for a new atomic constant c. In [Sel97, Theorem 21], it is shown that if this unproved assumption is added to a certain kind of consistent context, the result is a consistent context.

This approach to arithmetic can be extended to other inductively defined data types. This is done for λC in [Ber93, Sel00b].

We can make the logic classical logic by adding an unproved assumption of the form

$$\mathsf{cl} : (\Pi u{:}\star\,.\,\neg\neg u \supset u), \tag{10}$$

where cl is a new constant. In [Sel97, Theorem 23], it is shown that if

$$\mathsf{cl} : (\Pi u{:}\star\,.\,\neg\neg u \supset u), \qquad c : \mathsf{Peano1} \tag{11}$$

are added to a certain kind of consistent context, the result is still a consistent context.

13H PTSs with equality

As in the systems of Chapters 11 and 12, typing in PTSs is not invariant of conversion. Conversion of types is allowed by the rules in Definition 13.23, but not conversion of terms in general. This suggests that we add a rule corresponding to Eq′. In keeping with the names of the rules of PTSs, we should probably call it (conversion′). The rule would be the following:

$$\text{(conversion}')\qquad \frac{\Gamma \vdash M : A \quad M =_\beta N}{\Gamma \vdash N : A.}$$

Note that this makes the rule (α-conv) redundant. Note that it also makes the third premise of the rule (conversion) redundant, since if $A =_\beta B$ then rule (conversion′) permits an inference from $A : s$ to $B : s$. Thus, the rule (conversion) should be replaced by the rule

$$\text{(conversion}'')\qquad \frac{\Gamma \vdash M : A \quad A =_\beta B}{\Gamma \vdash M : B.}$$

Definition 13.76 For every PTS S, the corresponding *PTS with equality*, $S^=$, is defined by deleting the rule (α-conv), adding in its place the rule (conversion′), and replacing the rule (conversion) by the rule (conversion″).

Because of Theorems 11.64 and 12.40, it might be expected that a theorem on the postponement of (conversion′) can be proved for PTSs with equality. Indeed, Seldin presented such a proof for a formulation of the calculation of constructions in [Sel00a, Theorem 1]. But the method of proof, pushing inferences by (conversion″) followed by another inference down past that inference, will not work without modification in the formulation given here, for there are cases that cause problems. The most important of these occurs when the inference by (conversion′) occurs above the right premise for an inference by (abstraction):

$$\dfrac{\Gamma, x : A \vdash M : B \qquad \dfrac{\Gamma \vdash C : s \quad C =_\beta (\Pi x{:}A\,.\,B)}{\Gamma \vdash (\Pi x{:}A\,.\,B) : s}\,\text{(conversion}')}{\Gamma \vdash (\lambda x{:}A\,.\,M) : (\Pi x{:}A\,.\,B).}\,\text{(abstraction)}$$

It is hard to see how to push this inference down from here. So no proof of postponement of (conversion′) will be given here.

Another difference between PTSs with equality and ordinary PTSs is that there are algorithms for type-checking for many PTSs, but because conversion is undecidable there are no such algorithms for PTSs with equality.

On the other hand, PTSs with equality seem to be better suited for representing systems of logic via propositions-as-types.

Furthermore, PTSs with equality seem better suited to express the idea that one type is a subtype of another. The statement that every term of type A is also a term of type B can be expressed by the statement

$$(\lambda x\!:\!A\,.\,x) : A \to B. \tag{12}$$

The term $(\lambda x : A\,.\,x)$ is called a *coercion*, because it coerces terms of type A into terms in type B. However, to use (12) in constructing a formal inference requires rule (conversion′):

$$\dfrac{\dfrac{\Gamma \vdash (\lambda x\!:\!A\,.\,x) : A \to B \quad \Gamma \vdash M : A}{\Gamma \vdash (\lambda x\!:\!A\,.\,x)M : B}\,(\text{application})}{\Gamma \vdash M : B.}\,(\text{conversion}')$$

Note that it follows from this that if $\Gamma \vdash (\lambda x\!:\!B\,.\,M) : B \to C$, then for a variable $y \notin \mathrm{FV}(M)$,

$$\Gamma \vdash (\lambda y\!:\!A\,.\,(M((\lambda x\!:\!A\,.\,x)y))) : A \to C.$$

The term $(\lambda y : A\,.\,(M((\lambda x : A\,.\,x)y)))$ represents the *restriction* of the function represented by M to A. It can be β-reduced as follows:

$$(\lambda y\!:\!A\,.\,(M((\lambda x\!:\!A\,.\,x)y))) \;\triangleright_\beta\; (\lambda y\!:\!A\,.\,My),$$

so $(\lambda y\!:\!A\,.\,My)$ also represents the restriction of M to A.

Remark 13.77 Note that $(\lambda y : A\,.\,My)$ resembles an η-redex which would η-reduce to M; in fact, it corresponds to an ordinary η-redex the way $(\lambda x : A\,.\,M)N$ corresponds to an ordinary β-redex. For the reason stated in Remark 13.63, we have not been using $\beta\eta$-reduction in this chapter. The above discussion shows that if we were to find a solution to the problem of the failure of CR discussed in Remark 13.63 and adopt $\beta\eta$-reduction for PTSs with subtyping, we would wind up with systems which cannot distinguish functions from their restrictions.

14
Models of CL

14A Applicative structures

In first-order logic, a common question to ask about a formal theory is 'what are its models like?'. For the theories $\lambda\beta$ and CLw the first person to ask this was Dana Scott in the 1960s, while he was working on extending the concept of 'computable' from functions of numbers to functions of functions. The first non-trivial model, D_∞, was constructed by Scott in 1969.

Since then many other models have been made. The present chapter will set the scene by introducing a few basic general properties of models of CLw, and the next will do the same for $\lambda\beta$, whose concept of model is more complicated. Then Chapter 16 will describe the model D_∞ in detail and give outlines and references for some other models. Scott's D_∞ is not the simplest model known, but it is a good introduction, as the concepts used in building it are also involved in discussions of other models.

But first, a comment: although λ-calculus and combinatory logic were invented as long ago as the 1920s, there was a 40-year gap before their first model was constructed; why was there this long delay?

There are two main reasons. The first is the origin of $\lambda\beta$ and CLw. Both Church and Curry viewed these theories, not from within the semantics that most post-1950 logicians were trained in, but from the alternative viewpoint described in Discussion 3.27. Their aim was to formalize a concept of operator which was independent of the concept of set, and which did not necessarily correspond to the function-concept in the usual set-theories (e.g. Zermelo–Fraenkel set theory, ZF). In contrast, the semantics usually taught today presupposes the set-concept, so to ask for a model of the theory CLw is really asking for an interpretation of CLw in ZF. From the Church–Curry point of view this question was of course interesting, but it was not primary.

The second reason was the complexity of the models. The problem of constructing set-theoretic objects which behaved like combinators was far from easy and the resulting structure was not simple (although simpler models were later found).

Notation 14.1 In this chapter, 'term' will mean 'CL-term'. The formal theories whose models will be studied are:

CLw (see 6.5), which determines weak equality $=_w$;
CLext_{ax} (see 8.10), determining extensional equality $=_{C\,ext}$;
CLβ_{ax} (see 9.38), determining β-equality $=_{C\beta}$ (see 9.29).

(Details of the axioms in CLβ_{ax} will not be needed.)

Identity will, as usual, be written as '$\equiv$' for terms, and '$=$' for all other objects, in particular for members of a model.

Vars will be the class of all variables. As usual, 'x', 'y', 'z', 'u', 'v', 'w' will denote variables.

In contrast, 'a', 'b', 'c', 'd', 'e' will denote arbitrary members of a given set D (see later). If $\bullet$ is a mapping from D^2 to D, expressions such as

$$(((a \bullet b) \bullet c) \bullet d)$$

will be shortened to $a \bullet b \bullet c \bullet d$ (the convention of *association to the left*).

Any mapping ρ from *Vars* to D will be called a *valuation* (*of variables*). For $d \in D$ and $x \in$ *Vars*, the notation

$$[d/x]\rho$$

will be used for the valuation $\rho^\star$ which is the same as ρ except that $\rho^\star(x) = d$. (In the special case that $\rho(x) = d$, we have $[d/x]\rho = \rho$.)

The reader who has already met the usual definition of model of a first-order theory will find it helpful as an analogy and a source of ideas, though this chapter will not depend formally on it. (The usual definition can be found in textbooks such as [Men97, Chapter 2, Sections 2, 3, 8], [Dal97, Section 2.4] and [End00, Sections 2.2, 2.6].)

Models will here be described in the usual informal set-theory in which mathematics is commonly written. (If desired, this could be formalized in Zermelo–Fraenkel set theory with the axiom of choice added.) In particular, recall that, as usual, '*function*', '*mapping*' and '*map*' mean 'a set of ordered pairs such that no two pairs have the same first member'.

Definition 14.2 An *applicative structure* is a pair $\langle D, \bullet \rangle$ where D is a set (called the *domain* of the structure) with at least two members, and $\bullet$ is any mapping from D^2 to D.

A model of a theory such as CLw or $\lambda\beta$ will be an applicative structure with certain extra features, and such that $\bullet$ has some of the properties of function-application. The 2-member condition is just to prevent triviality.

Definition 14.3 Let $\langle D, \bullet \rangle$ be an applicative structure and let $n \geq 1$. A function $\theta : D^n \to D$ is *representable in* D iff D has a member a such that

$$(\forall d_1, \ldots, d_n \in D) \qquad a \bullet d_1 \bullet d_2 \bullet \ldots \bullet d_n \;=\; \theta(d_1, \ldots, d_n).$$

By the association-to-the-left convention this equation really says

$$(\ldots((a \bullet d_1) \bullet d_2) \bullet \ldots) \bullet d_n \;=\; \theta(d_1, \ldots, d_n)\,.$$

Each such a is called a *representative* of θ. The set of all representable functions from D^n to D is called

$$\big(D^n \to D\big)_{\text{rep}}.$$

Note A representable function may have several representatives. On the other hand, in general, very few functions on D are representable, because there are far more functions on a given set than there are members to serve as representatives.

Also, every $a \in D$ represents a function; indeed, for every $n \geq 1$, a represents a function of n arguments.

Definition 14.4 For every $a \in D$, Fun(a) is the unique one-argument function that a represents: i.e.

$$(\forall d \in D) \qquad \text{Fun}(a)(d) \;=\; a \bullet d.$$

Conversely, for every one-argument function $\theta \in (D \to D)_{\text{rep}}$, the set of all θ's representatives in D is called

$$\text{Reps}(\theta).$$

Definition 14.5 For all $a, b \in D$: we say a *is extensionally equivalent to* b (notation $a \sim b$) iff

$$(\forall d \in D) \qquad a \bullet d \;=\; b \bullet d.$$

For every $a \in D$, the *extensional-equivalence-class* containing a is

$$\widetilde{a} \;=\; \{b \in D : b \sim a\}.$$

The set of all these classes is called $D/\!\sim$:

$$D/\!\sim \;=\; \{\widetilde{a} : a \in D\}.$$

Lemma 14.6 *Let $\langle D, \bullet \rangle$ be an applicative structure. Then*

(a) $a \sim b \iff \mathrm{Fun}(a) = \mathrm{Fun}(b)$;

(b) $a \sim b \iff \widetilde{a} = \widetilde{b}$;

(c) *the members of $D/\!\sim$ are non-empty, non-overlapping, and their union is D;*

(d) *$(D \to D)_{\mathrm{rep}}$ corresponds one-to-one with $D/\!\sim$ by the map* Reps.

Definition 14.7 (Extensionality) An applicative structure $\langle D, \bullet \rangle$ is called *extensional* iff, for all $a, b \in D$,

$$\Big((\forall d \in D) \;\; a \bullet d = b \bullet d \Big) \quad \Longrightarrow \quad a = b.$$

Lemma 14.8 *Extensionality is equivalent to any one of:*

(a) $(\forall a, b \in D) \;\; a \sim b \Longrightarrow a = b$;

(b) $(\forall a \in D) \;\; \widetilde{a}$ *is a singleton;*

(c) $\big(\forall \theta \in (D \to D)_{\mathrm{rep}}\big)$ $\mathrm{Reps}(\theta)$ *is a singleton;*

(d) *D corresponds one-to-one with $(D \to D)_{\mathrm{rep}}$ by the map* Fun.

14B Combinatory algebras

Definition 14.9 A *combinatory algebra* is a pair $\mathbb{D} = \langle D, \bullet \rangle$ where D is a set with at least two members, $\bullet$ maps D^2 to D, and D has members k and s such that

(a) $(\forall a, b \in D) \;\; k \bullet a \bullet b \;=\; a$;

(b) $(\forall a, b, c \in D) \;\; s \bullet a \bullet b \bullet c \;=\; a \bullet c \bullet (b \bullet c)$.

A *model of* CLw is a quintuple $\langle D, \bullet, i, k, s \rangle$ such that $\langle D, \bullet \rangle$ is a combinatory algebra and k, s satisfy (a), (b), and

$$i = s \bullet k \bullet k.$$

The definition of 'combinatory algebra' is from [Bar84, Section 5.1]. That of 'model of CLw' is very similar and keeps as close as possible to the usual definition of 'model' in first-order logic.

Exercise 14.10 * Prove that in every combinatory algebra $\mathbb{D}$,

$$i \neq k \neq s \neq i.$$

Definition 14.11 (Interpretation of a term) Let $\mathbb{D} = \langle D, \bullet, i, k, s \rangle$ where $\langle D, \bullet \rangle$ is an applicative structure and $i, k, s \in D$. Let ρ be a valuation of variables. Using ρ, we assign to every term X a member of D called its *interpretation* or $[\![X]\!]^{\mathbb{D}}_{\rho}$, thus:

(a) $[\![x]\!]^{\mathbb{D}}_{\rho} = \rho(x)$;

(b) $[\![\mathsf{I}]\!]^{\mathbb{D}}_{\rho} = i, \quad [\![\mathsf{K}]\!]^{\mathbb{D}}_{\rho} = k, \quad [\![\mathsf{S}]\!]^{\mathbb{D}}_{\rho} = s$;

(c) $[\![XY]\!]^{\mathbb{D}}_{\rho} = [\![X]\!]^{\mathbb{D}}_{\rho} \bullet [\![Y]\!]^{\mathbb{D}}_{\rho}$.

When no confusion is likely, $[\![X]\!]^{\mathbb{D}}_{\rho}$ will be called just

$$[\![X]\!]_{\rho} \quad \text{or} \quad [\![X]\!].$$

Example If $a, b \in D$ and $\rho(x) = a$ and $\rho(y) = b$, then

$$[\![\mathsf{S}x(y\mathsf{K})]\!]^{\mathbb{D}}_{\rho} \;=\; s \bullet a \bullet (b \bullet k), \;\in D.$$

Lemma 14.12 *If $\rho(x) = \sigma(x)$ for all $x \in \mathrm{FV}(X)$, then*

$$[\![X]\!]_{\rho} = [\![X]\!]_{\sigma} .$$

Corollary 14.12.1 *For closed terms X, $[\![X]\!]_{\rho}$ is independent of ρ.*

Lemma 14.13 *Interpretation commutes with substitution; i.e.*

$$[\![[Z/x]X]\!]_{\rho} = [\![X]\!]_{[b/x]\rho} \quad \textit{where } b = [\![Z]\!]_{\rho} .$$

Definition 14.14 (Satisfaction) Let $\mathbb{D} = \langle D, \bullet, i, k, s \rangle$ where $\langle D, \bullet \rangle$ is an applicative structure and $i, k, s \in D$. Let ρ be a valuation of variables. Define *satisfies* (notation '$\models$') thus: for every equation $X = Y$,

$$\mathbb{D}, \rho \models X = Y \iff [\![X]\!]^{\mathbb{D}}_{\rho} = [\![Y]\!]^{\mathbb{D}}_{\rho} ;$$

$$\mathbb{D} \models X = Y \iff (\forall \rho)\big(\mathbb{D}, \rho \models X = Y\big) .$$

Warning The symbol '=' has been used in two senses here; as a formal symbol in the theory CLw (e.g. '$X = Y$'), and as a symbol in the meta-language, for identity (e.g. '$[\![X]\!]^{\mathbb{D}}_{\rho} = [\![Y]\!]^{\mathbb{D}}_{\rho}$').

Definition 14.15 A *model of the theory* CLβ_{ax} is a model $\langle D, \bullet, i, k, s\rangle$ of CLw that satisfies the β-axioms mentioned in 9.38.[1]

Definition 14.16 A *model of* CLext_{ax} is a model $\langle D, \bullet, i, k, s\rangle$ of CLw that satisfies the extensionality axioms in 8.10.[2]

Lemma 14.17 *Each model of* CLw*,* CLβ_{ax} *or* CLext_{ax} *satisfies all the provable equations of the corresponding theory.*

Proof The axioms are satisfied, by definition. And each rule of inference is a property of identity. □

Remark 14.18 As noted in 6.9–6.11, CLw is not quite a first-order theory in the usual sense, but the difference is trivial and it can be changed into a first-order theory CLw^+ without changing its set of provable equations. The models of CLw are exactly the normal models of CLw^+ in the usual first-order-logic sense. (A model of a first-order theory is called 'normal' when its interpretation of '=' is the identity relation.)

A similar remark holds for CLβ_{ax} and CLext_{ax}.

Remark 14.19 We now have enough material to build a simple model. First, CLw^+ is consistent, because by the Church–Rosser theorem there are equations such as $\mathsf{S} = \mathsf{K}$ that have no proofs in CLw, and hence none in CLw^+. And a general theorem in logic says that every consistent first-order theory has a model. (See, e.g. [Men97, Proposition 2.17], [Dal97, Lemma 3.1.11] or [End00, Section 2.5].) In the context of CL, a model like the one produced by the usual proofs of this theorem can be constructed directly as follows.

Definition 14.20 (Term models) Let $\mathcal{T}$ be CLw or CLβ_{ax} or CLext_{ax}. For each CL-term X, define

$$[X] = \{Y : \mathcal{T} \vdash X = Y\}.$$

[1] These models (with a little extra structure) were called 'λ-algebras' in [Bar84] and 'pseudo-models' in [HL80]; see [HL80, Proposition 8.9].

[2] These models were called 'Curry algebras' in [Lam80].

The *term model of* $\mathcal{T}$, called $\mathbb{TM}(\mathcal{T})$, is $\langle D, \bullet, i, k, s\rangle$, where

$$D = \{[X] : X \text{ is a CL-term}\},$$
$$[X] \bullet [Y] = [XY],$$
$$i = [\mathbf{I}], \quad k = [\mathbf{K}], \quad s = [\mathbf{S}].$$

Remark 14.21 It is routine to prove that $\bullet$ is well-defined, i.e. that

$$[X] = [X'],\ [Y] = [Y'] \quad \Longrightarrow \quad [XY] = [X'Y'],$$

and that $\mathbb{TM}(\mathcal{T})$ is indeed a model of $\mathcal{T}$.

It is also routine to prove that in this model, interpretation is the same as substitution; i.e. that if $\mathrm{FV}(X) = \{x_1, \ldots, x_n\}$ and $\rho(x_i) = [Y_i]$ for each i, then

$$[\![X]\!]_\rho = \big[\, [Y_1/x_1, \ldots, Y_n/x_n]X \,\big].$$

Thus $\mathbb{TM}(\mathcal{T})$ is in a sense trivial: it is really just a reflection of the syntax of $\mathcal{T}$ and tells us very little new about combinators. The models in Chapter 16 will be much deeper.

Remark 14.22 The following theorem is a standard result from the model-theory of algebra. It is easy to prove for CL but will fail for λ, and this will be an interesting way of expressing the difference between them (cf. Remark 15.25).

Theorem 14.23 (Submodel theorem) *Let* $\mathcal{T}$ *be* CLw *or* CLβ_{ax} *or* CLext_{ax}. *If* $\langle D, \bullet, i, k, s\rangle$ *is a model of* $\mathcal{T}$, *and* D' *is a subset of* D *which contains* i, k *and* s *and is closed under* $\bullet$, *then* $\langle D', \bullet, i, k, s\rangle$ *is a model of* $\mathcal{T}$.

Proof By assumption, D' has at least two members (for example s and k). Next, if the axioms 14.9(a) and (b) hold in D, they must also hold in D' since $D' \subseteq D$. Finally the β- and extensionality axioms are just equations between constants, so they also hold in D' if they hold in D. □

(The above proof depends on the very simple form of 14.9(a) and (b); if an axiom contained an existential quantifier the proof would fail.)

Definition 14.24 (Interiors) Let $\mathcal{T}$ be CLw, CLβ_{ax} or CLext_{ax}, and $\mathbb{D} = \langle D, \bullet, i, k, s\rangle$ be a model of $\mathcal{T}$. The *interior* of $\mathbb{D}$ is $\mathbb{D}^\circ = \langle D^\circ, \bullet, i, k, s\rangle$, where

$$D^\circ \;=\; \{[\![X]\!] : X \text{ closed}\}.$$

The interior of a model of $\mathcal{T}$ is also a model of $\mathcal{T}$, by Theorem 14.23.

Remark 14.25 (Extensionality) How does the concept of extensional structure or model defined in 14.7 relate to the theories of extensional equality in Chapter 8? It would be nice to prove that a model of CLw is extensional iff it is a model of CLext_{ax}.

Part of this conjecture is reasonably easy. (*Exercise*: prove that every extensional model of CLw is a model of CLext_{ax}.)

But unfortunately the converse part is false. For a counterexample take $(\mathbb{TM}(\text{CL}ext_{ax}))^\circ$, the interior of the term model of CLext_{ax}. This is a model of CLext_{ax} by above. But extensionality demands that, for all closed X and Y,

$$\big((\forall \text{ closed CL-terms } Z)\ \ [XZ] = [YZ]\,\big) \quad\Longrightarrow\quad [X] = [Y].$$

That is,

$$\big((\forall \text{ closed CL-terms } Z)\ \ \text{CL}ext_{ax} \ \vdash\ XZ = YZ\,\big) \quad\Longrightarrow$$

$$\big(\text{CL}ext_{ax} \ \vdash\ X = Y\,\big).$$

By Theorem 9.15 this is equivalent to

$$\big((\forall \text{ closed } \lambda\text{-terms } Q)\ X_\lambda Q =_{\lambda ext} Y_\lambda Q\,\big) \quad\Longrightarrow\quad X_\lambda =_{\lambda ext} Y_\lambda.$$

And this is false, by Plotkin's example mentioned in Remark 7.3.

Thus the 'extensionality' expressed by the theory CLext_{ax} is weaker than the extensionality concept in Definition 14.7.

Fuller discussions of extensional models are in [HL80] and [Bar84, Chapter 20].

Remark 14.26 Recall the concept of 'combinatory algebra' that was defined in 14.9 along with 'model of CLw': the only difference between these two concepts is that the latter is tied to a particular formalization of combinatory logic. For example, if **I** was not an atom in the language of CLw, then a 'model' would have to be re-defined as a quadruple $\langle D, \bullet, k, s\rangle$ instead of a quintuple.

In contrast, 'combinatory algebra' is independent of the formalism.

This might not be immediately obvious from its definition, so let us try to rewrite that definition to avoid mentioning k, s.

The characteristic property of combinatory algebras is called *combinatory completeness*; it is defined as follows.

Definition 14.27 A *combination* of $x_1, \ldots, x_n$ is any CL-term X whose only atoms are $x_1, \ldots, x_n$. (X need not contain all of $x_1, \ldots, x_n$, but must not contain **S**, **K** or **I**.)

If X is a combination of $x_1, \ldots, x_n$ and ρ is any valuation of variables, we can interpret X in the natural way, using 14.11(a) and (c) to define $[\![X]\!]_\rho$. (Lemmas 14.12 and 14.13 will still hold.)

Definition 14.28 An applicative structure $\mathbb{D} = \langle D, \bullet \rangle$ is called *combinatorially complete* iff: for every sequence $u, x_1, \ldots, x_n$ of distinct variables, and every combination X of $x_1, \ldots, x_n$ only, the formula

$$(\exists u)(\forall x_1, \ldots, x_n)\big(ux_1 \ldots x_n = X\,\big)$$

is true in $\mathbb{D}$. That is, iff there exists $a \in D$ such that, for all $d_1, \ldots, d_n \in D$,

$$a \bullet d_1 \bullet \ldots \bullet d_n \;\;=\;\; [\![X]\!]_{[d_1/x_1]\ldots[d_n/x_n]\rho},$$

where ρ is arbitrary.

Theorem 14.29 *An applicative structure $\langle D, \bullet \rangle$ is combinatorially complete iff it is a combinatory algebra.*

Proof Combinatory completeness follows from the existence of k and s by an analogue of the algorithm for constructing $[x].M$ in 2.18. Conversely, the existence of k and s follows from combinatory completeness as a special case. □

Thus combinatory completeness gives us a way of defining combinatory algebras without mentioning i, k or s. But it is not so easy a property to handle as the axioms for k and s. For example, in practice, the quickest way to show that a particular structure is combinatorially complete is usually to find members k and s which satisfy these two axioms. And standard results in the model theory of algebra (e.g. Theorem 14.23) are harder to deduce directly from the combinatory completeness definition.

15
Models of λ-calculus

15A The definition of λ-model

The discussion of models in the last chapter was almost too easy, so simple was the theory CLw. In contrast, the theory $\lambda\beta$ has bound variables and rule (ξ), and these make its concept of model much more complex. This chapter will look at that concept from three different viewpoints. The definition of λ-model will be given in 15.3, and two other approaches will be described in Section 15B to help the reader understand the ideas lying behind this definition.

Notation 15.1 In this chapter we shall use the same notation as in 14.1, except that 'term' will now mean 'λ-term'.

The *identity-function* on a set S will be called I_S here.

The *composition*, $\phi \circ \psi$, of given functions ϕ and ψ, is defined as usual by the equation

$$(\phi \circ \psi)(a) \;=\; \phi(\psi(a)),$$

and its domain is $\{a : \psi(a)$ is defined and in the domain of $\phi\}$.

If S and S' are sets, and functions $\phi : S \to S'$ and $\psi : S' \to S$ satisfy

(a) $\psi \circ \phi \;=\; I_S$,

then ψ is called a *left inverse* of ϕ, and S is called a *retract of S' by ϕ and ψ*, and the pair $\langle \phi, \psi \rangle$ is called a *retraction*; see Figure 15:1.

From (a) the following are easy to deduce:

(b) $(\phi \circ \psi) \circ (\phi \circ \psi) \;=\; \phi \circ \psi$,

(c) ψ is onto S (i.e. its range is the whole of S),

(d) ϕ is one-to-one; thus ϕ maps S one-to-one onto a subset of S', which is called $\phi(S)$.

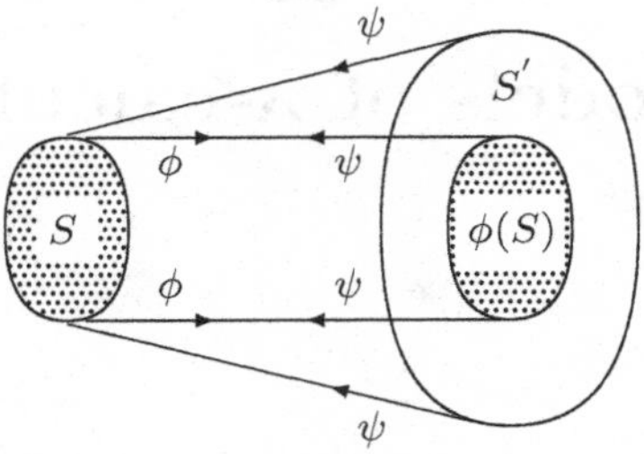

Fig. 15:1

By the way, in 15.1, (b)–(d) together imply (a). Also, Figure 9:1 in Remark 9.12 is an example of a retraction. There, ϕ is the λ-map, ψ is the H_η-map, S is $\mathcal{C}$, and S' is Λ.

Remark 15.2 Before defining 'model of $\lambda\beta$', let us look at one temptation and dismiss it. Why not simply identify 'model of $\lambda\beta$' with 'model of $\mathrm{CL}\beta_{ax}$'? After all, by 9.37 and 9.38 the theories $\lambda\beta$ and $\mathrm{CL}\beta_{ax}$ have the same set of provable equations (modulo the λ- and H_β-maps), so why should they not have the same models?

The snag is as follows. In the theory $\lambda\beta$ we can make deductions by rule (ξ), for example

$$\lambda x.yx = y \;\vdash\; \lambda yx.yx = \lambda y.y.$$

So any reasonable definition of 'model of $\lambda\beta$' should have the property that if $\mathbb{D}$ is such a model, then

$$(\mathbb{D} \models \lambda x.yx = y) \quad\Longrightarrow\quad (\mathbb{D} \models \lambda yx.yx = \lambda y.y).$$

But this implication fails for models of $\mathrm{CL}\beta_{ax}$. Two counterexamples can be found in [HL80, Section 7]; one is the interior of $\mathbb{TM}(\lambda\beta)$, and comes from Plotkin's example mentioned in Remarks 7.3 and 14.25.

This failure is only surprising if we think of $\mathrm{CL}\beta_{ax}$ as satisfying (ξ) in some sense. But it does not. True, it is equivalent to a theory in which a form of (ξ) is derivable (the theory $\mathrm{CL}\zeta_\beta$ in 9.32 and 9.39), but the equivalence is only theorem-equivalence, and the above-mentioned counterexamples show that it cannot be rule-equivalence.

So, the concept of model of $\lambda\beta$ is more complicated than that of model of $\mathrm{CL}\beta_{ax}$.

Three alternative definitions of model will be given in this chapter. We shall give them different names to distinguish them, but they will really just be the same idea seen from three different viewpoints, and they will be turn out to be equivalent.

The first definition will demand the least prior insight from the reader; in fact its clauses will correspond very closely to the axioms and rules of $\lambda\beta$. The second will define 'model' entirely in terms of internal structure and will not mention $\lambda\beta$ at all. The third will be by far the simplest, though to see why it has any connection to $\lambda\beta$ we shall need both the first and the second.

Definition 15.3 (λ-models) A *λ-model*, or *model of* $\lambda\beta$, is a triple $\mathbb{D} = \langle D, \bullet, [\![\ ]\!] \rangle$, where $\langle D, \bullet \rangle$ is an applicative structure and $[\![\ ]\!]$ is a mapping which assigns, to each λ-term M and each valuation ρ, a member $[\![M]\!]_\rho$ of D such that

(a) $[\![x]\!]_\rho = \rho(x)$;

(b) $[\![PQ]\!]_\rho = [\![P]\!]_\rho \bullet [\![Q]\!]_\rho$;

(c) $[\![\lambda x.P]\!]_\rho \bullet d = [\![P]\!]_{[d/x]\rho}$ for all $d \in D$;

(d) $[\![M]\!]_\rho = [\![M]\!]_\sigma$ if $\rho(x) = \sigma(x)$ for all $x \in \mathrm{FV}(M)$;

(e) $[\![\lambda x.M]\!]_\rho = [\![\lambda y.[y/x]M]\!]_\rho$ if $y \notin \mathrm{FV}(M)$;

(f) if $(\forall d \in D)\Big([\![P]\!]_{[d/x]\rho} = [\![Q]\!]_{[d/x]\rho}\Big)$,
then $[\![\lambda x.P]\!]_\rho = [\![\lambda x.Q]\!]_\rho$.

Notation $[\![M]\!]_\rho$ may also be called $[\![M]\!]^{\mathbb{D}}_\rho$, or simply $[\![M]\!]$ when it is known to be independent of ρ.

Some writers call the above models '*environment λ-models*' or '*syntactical λ-models*', but we shall avoid these notations as the words 'environment' and 'syntactical' have too many other meanings.

Comments 15.4 Each of (a)–(f) above is a condition that we might naturally expect a model of $\lambda\beta$ to satisfy, if the model is to imitate the behaviour of λ-terms.

First, a model of $\lambda\beta$ should allow us to interpret every term, i.e. to define $[\![M]\!]_\rho$ for all M and ρ. In first-order logic an interpretation-mapping $[\![\ ]\!]$ is often included as part of the definition of 'model', so we do the same here.

Clauses (a) and (b) are in fact the definition of $[\![M]\!]_\rho$ in the cases

$M \equiv x$ and $M \equiv PQ$. The case $M \equiv \lambda x.P$ is more difficult, which is why we need (c)–(f).

Clause (c) expresses in model-theory language the intuitive meaning behind the λ-notation: it says that $[\![\lambda x.P]\!]_\rho$ acts like a function whose value is calculated by interpreting x as d.

Clause (d) is a standard property in model theory, compare also Lemma 14.12.

Clause (e) says that the interpretation of a term is independent of changes of bound variables.

Clause (f) is the interpretation of rule (ξ).

Finally, clauses 15.3(a)–(f) together ensure that every λ-model satisfies all the provable equations of $\lambda\beta$. This will be proved in Theorem 15.12 after four lemmas.

Remark 15.5 By the way, clauses 15.3(c) and (f) together imply that

$$(\forall d \in D)\Big([\![\lambda x.P]\!]_\rho \bullet d \;=\; [\![\lambda x.Q]\!]_\rho \bullet d\Big) \quad\Longrightarrow\quad [\![\lambda x.P]\!]_\rho = [\![\lambda x.Q]\!]_\rho\,,$$

or, using the notation '$\sim$' introduced in Definition 14.5,

$$[\![\lambda x.P]\!]_\rho \;\sim\; [\![\lambda x.Q]\!]_\rho \qquad\Longrightarrow\qquad [\![\lambda x.P]\!]_\rho \;=\; [\![\lambda x.Q]\!]_\rho\,.$$

This says that objects of form $[\![\lambda x.P]\!]_\rho$ have the extensionality property, 14.7, and (f) is sometimes called the *weak extensionality* condition (see near the end of Remark 8.7).

Lemma 15.6 *Let* $\mathbb{D} = \langle D, \bullet, [\![\;]\!]\rangle$ *be a* λ*-model. If* $y \notin \mathrm{FV}(M)$ *and* $\rho(y) = \rho(x)$*, then*

$$[\![\,[y/x]M\,]\!]_\rho \;=\; [\![M]\!]_\rho\,.$$

Proof Let $d = \rho(y) = \rho(x)$. Then $[d/x]\rho = [d/y]\rho = \rho$, and

$$\begin{aligned} [\![M]\!]_\rho \;=\; [\![M]\!]_{[d/x]\rho} &= [\![\lambda x.M]\!]_\rho \bullet d && \text{by 15.3(c)},\\ &= [\![\lambda y.[y/x]M]\!]_\rho \bullet d && \text{by 15.3(e)},\\ &= [\![[y/x]M]\!]_\rho && \text{by 15.3(c)}. \end{aligned}$$

□

Lemma 15.7 *Let* $\mathbb{D} = \langle D, \bullet, [\![\;]\!]\rangle$ *be a* λ*-model. Let* $\mathrm{FV}(M) \subseteq \{x_1, \ldots, x_n\}$ *and let* $y_1, \ldots, y_n, x_1, \ldots, x_n$ *be distinct. If* ρ, σ *are valuations with* $\sigma(y_i) = \rho(x_i)$ *for* $i = 1, \ldots, n$*, then*

$$[\![\,[y_1/x_1]\ldots[y_n/x_n]M\,]\!]_\sigma \;=\; [\![M]\!]_\rho\,.$$

Proof Let $d_i = \rho(x_i) = \sigma(y_i)$. Let $\tau = [d_1/y_1]\dots[d_n/y_n]\rho$. Then

$$\begin{aligned}
[\![M]\!]_\rho &= [\![M]\!]_\tau && \text{by 15.3(d),}\\
&= [\![[y_1/x_1]\dots[y_n/x_n]M]\!]_\tau && \text{by 15.6 repeated,}\\
&= [\![[y_1/x_1]\dots[y_n/x_n]M]\!]_\sigma && \text{by 15.3(d).}
\end{aligned}$$

□

The next lemma is a small but significant strengthening of the weak extensionality property in Remark 15.5, and will be the key to the syntax-free analysis of models given later. It is due to Gérard Berry.

Lemma 15.8 (Berry's extensionality property) *Let* $\mathbb{D} = \langle D, \bullet, [\![\ ]\!]\rangle$ *be a λ-model. Then, for all* P, Q, ρ, σ, *and all* x, y *(not necessarily distinct),*

(a) *if* $(\forall d \in D)\Big([\![P]\!]_{[d/x]\rho} = [\![Q]\!]_{[d/y]\sigma}\Big)$, *then* $[\![\lambda x.P]\!]_\rho = [\![\lambda y.Q]\!]_\sigma$;

(b) $[\![\lambda x.P]\!]_\rho \sim [\![\lambda y.Q]\!]_\sigma \implies [\![\lambda x.P]\!]_\rho = [\![\lambda y.Q]\!]_\sigma$.

Proof Part (b) is equivalent to (a) by 15.3(c). To prove (a), assume that $[\![P]\!]_{[d/x]\rho} = [\![Q]\!]_{[d/y]\sigma}$ for all $d \in D$. Suppose

$$\mathrm{FV}(P) - \{x\} = \{x_1,\dots,x_m\}, \quad \mathrm{FV}(Q) - \{y\} = \{y_1,\dots,y_n\}.$$

(The x's need not be distinct from the ys.) Let $a_i = \rho(x_i)$ and $b_j = \sigma(y_j)$ for $1 \le i \le m$ and $1 \le j \le n$. Choose distinct new variables z, $u_1,\dots,u_m$, $v_1,\dots,v_n$ not in any term mentioned above. Define

$$\begin{aligned}
P' &\equiv [u_1/x_1]\dots[u_m/x_m][z/x]P,\\
Q' &\equiv [v_1/y_1]\dots[v_n/y_n][z/y]Q,\\
\tau &= [a_1/u_1]\dots[a_m/u_m][b_1/v_1]\dots[b_n/v_n]\rho.
\end{aligned}$$

Then, for all $d \in D$,

$$\begin{aligned}
[\![P']\!]_{[d/z]\tau} &= [\![P]\!]_{[d/x]\rho} && \text{by 15.7,}\\
&= [\![Q]\!]_{[d/y]\sigma} && \text{by assumption,}\\
&= [\![Q']\!]_{[d/z]\tau} && \text{by 15.7.}
\end{aligned}$$

Hence, by 15.3(f),

$$[\![\lambda z.P']\!]_\tau = [\![\lambda z.Q']\!]_\tau . \tag{1}$$

Then

$$\begin{aligned}
[\![\lambda x.P]\!]_\rho &= [\![\lambda z.[z/x]P]\!]_\rho && \text{by 15.3(e),}\\
&= [\![\lambda z.P']\!]_\tau && \text{by 15.7,}\\
&= [\![\lambda z.Q']\!]_\tau && \text{by Equation (1),}\\
&= [\![\lambda y.Q]\!]_\sigma && \text{by 15.7 and 15.3(e).}
\end{aligned}$$

□

Exercise 15.9* Prove that the three clauses (d)–(f) in Definition 15.3 could have been replaced by just one clause, Berry's extensionality property 15.8(a). That is, deduce 15.3(d)–(f) from 15.3(a)–(c) and 15.8(a) (or, equivalently, 15.8(b)).

Lemma 15.10 *Let $\mathbb{D} = \langle D, \bullet, [\![\ ]\!]\rangle$ be a λ-model. Then, for all M, N, x and ρ,*

(a) $[\![\,[N/x]M\,]\!]_\rho = [\![M]\!]_{[b/x]\rho}$ *where* $b = [\![N]\!]_\rho$*;*

(b) $[\![\,(\lambda x.M)N\,]\!]_\rho = [\![[N/x]M]\!]_\rho$.

Proof (a) We use induction on M. The only non-trivial case is $M \equiv \lambda y.P$ with $y \not\equiv x$. By 15.3(e) we can assume $y \notin \mathrm{FV}(N)$, so $[N/x]M \equiv \lambda y.[N/x]P$. For all $d \in D$, the induction hypothesis applied to P and $[d/y]\rho$ implies that

$$[\![\,[N/x]P\,]\!]_{[d/y]\rho} = [\![\,P\,]\!]_{[b/x][d/y]\rho}.$$

And $[b/x][d/y]\rho = [d/y][b/x]\rho$ since $x \not\equiv y$. Hence, by Lemma 15.8(a) applied with $\sigma = [b/x]\rho$,

$$[\![\,\lambda y.[N/x]P\,]\!]_\rho = [\![\,\lambda y.P\,]\!]_{[b/x]\rho}.$$

This proves (a) in the case $M \equiv \lambda y.P$.

$$\begin{aligned}
\text{(b)}\quad [\![\,(\lambda x.M)N\,]\!]_\rho &= [\![(\lambda x.M)]\!]_\rho \bullet b && \text{by 15.3(b),}\\
&= [\![M]\!]_{[b/x]\rho} && \text{by 15.3(c),}\\
&= [\![\,[N/x]M\,]\!]_\rho && \text{by (a) above.}
\end{aligned}$$

□

Definition 15.11 Let $\mathbb{D} = \langle D, \bullet, [\![\ ]\!]\rangle$ be a λ-model, ρ a valuation, and M, N be any terms. Iff $[\![M]\!]_\rho = [\![N]\!]_\rho$, we say ρ *satisfies the equation* $M = N$, or

$$\mathbb{D}, \rho \models M = N.$$

Iff every valuation in $\mathbb{D}$ satisfies $M = N$, we say $\mathbb{D}$ *satisfies* $M = N$, or

$$\mathbb{D} \models M = N.$$

Theorem 15.12 *Every λ-model satisfies all the provable equations of the formal theory $\lambda\beta$.*

Proof We use induction on the clauses defining $\lambda\beta$ in 6.2. Case (α) is 15.3(e). Case (β) is 15.10(b). Case (ξ) is 15.3(f). The rest are trivial. □

Corollary 15.12.1 *If $\langle D, \bullet, [\![\ ]\!]\rangle$ is a λ-model, then $\langle D, \bullet\rangle$ is a combinatory algebra, and hence is combinatorially complete.*

Proof (See 14.9 for 'combinatory algebra' and 14.28 for 'combinatorially complete'.) Define $k = [\![\lambda xy.x]\!]$, $s = [\![\lambda xyz.xz(yz)]\!]$. □

Corollary 15.12.2 *If $\langle D, \bullet, [\![\ ]\!]\rangle$ is a λ-model, then $\langle D, \bullet, i, k, s\rangle$ is a model of the theory $CL\beta_{ax}$, where k and s are defined as above and $i = [\![\lambda x.x]\!]$.*

Proof (For 'model of $\mathrm{CL}\beta_{ax}$' see 14.15.) Use the correspondence between the theories $\lambda\beta$ and $\mathrm{CL}\beta_{ax}$ given in 9.37 and 9.38. □

Remark 15.13 The converses to both these corollaries are false; there exist combinatory algebras, even models of $\mathrm{CL}\beta_{ax}$, which cannot be made into λ-models by any definition of $[\![\ ]\!]$; one is given in [BK80, Section 3]. Thus the concept of λ-model is strictly stronger than that of model of $\mathrm{CL}\beta_{ax}$, even though the formal theories $\lambda\beta$ and $\mathrm{CL}\beta_{ax}$ have the same provable equations. This agrees with our discussion in Remark 15.2.

Definition 15.14 (Models of $\lambda\beta\eta$) A *model of* $\lambda\beta\eta$ is a λ-model that satisfies the equation $\lambda x.Mx = M$ for all terms M and all $x \notin \mathrm{FV}(M)$.

It is easy to see that every model of $\lambda\beta\eta$ satisfies all the provable equations of the formal theory $\lambda\beta\eta$; compare Theorem 15.12 and its proof.

Theorem 15.15 *A λ-model $\mathbb{D}$ is extensional iff it is a model of $\lambda\beta\eta$.*

Proof Exercise*. □

The above theorem contrasts with combinatory algebras: as Remark 14.25 showed, a combinatory algebra can be a model of $\mathrm{CL}\beta\eta_{ax}$ without being extensional.

Definition 15.16 (Term models) Let $\mathcal{T}$ be either of the formal theories $\lambda\beta$, $\lambda\beta\eta$. For every λ-term M, define

$$[M] = \{N : \mathcal{T} \vdash M = N\}.$$

The *term model of* $\mathcal{T}$, called $\mathbb{TM}(\mathcal{T})$, is defined to be $\langle D, \bullet, [\![\ ]\!]\rangle$, where

$$\begin{aligned} D &= \{[M] : M \text{ is a } \lambda\text{-term}\}, \\ [P] \bullet [Q] &= [PQ], \\ [\![M]\!]_\rho &= [\,[N_1/x_1, \ldots, N_n/x_n]M\,], \end{aligned}$$

where $\mathrm{FV}(M) = \{x_1, \ldots, x_n\}$ and $\rho(x_i) = [N_i]$, and $[N_1/x_1, \ldots, N_n/x_n]$ is simultaneous substitution, compare Remark 1.23.

Remark 15.17 It is routine to prove that $\bullet$ and $[\![\ ]\!]$ are well-defined and that $\mathbb{TM}(\mathcal{T})$ is genuinely a model of $\mathcal{T}$. As noted in Remark 14.21, term models are just reflections of the syntax, so they are in a sense trivial.

But in fact this very triviality makes them one of the tests for a good definition of 'λ-model'; if the term model of $\lambda\beta$ had not satisfied the conditions of Definition 15.3, those conditions would have had to be changed. Fortunately they pass the test.

Some non-trivial λ-models will be described in Chapter 16.

15B Syntax-free definitions

In this section we shall look at two alternative definitions of 'λ-model'. They will be equivalent to Definition 15.3, but neither of them will mention λ-terms or the theory $\lambda\beta$. The first will be simpler than Definition 15.3, and the second much simpler, and they will show very neatly the difference between λ-models and combinatory algebras. However, they will not be able to completely replace Definition 15.3; experience has shown that if one wants to prove that a particular structure is a λ-model, it is often more convenient to use that definition.

Discussion 15.18 (The mapping Λ) Let $\mathbb{D} = \langle D, \bullet, [\![\ ]\!] \rangle$ be a λ-model. A relation $\sim$ called *extensional equivalence* was defined in 14.5, namely

$$a \sim b \iff (\forall d \in D)(a \bullet d = b \bullet d).$$

For each $a \in D$, the *extensional-equivalence class* $\widetilde{a}$ is a set defined by

$$\widetilde{a} = \{b \in D : b \sim a\}.$$

Obviously $\widetilde{a} \subseteq D$. Just as with any equivalence relation, the extensional-equivalence classes partition D into non-overlapping subsets, and $\widetilde{a} = \widetilde{b} \iff a \sim b$.

Now, for each $a \in D$, there exist M, x, ρ such that $[\![\lambda x . M]\!]_\rho \in \widetilde{a}$. For example, take $M \equiv ux$ and $\rho = [a/u]\sigma$ for any valuation σ; then $\rho(u) = a$, and $[\![\lambda x . ux]\!]_\rho$ is extensionally equivalent to a, because, for all $d \in D$,

$$\begin{aligned} [\![\lambda x . ux]\!]_\rho \bullet d &= [\![ux]\!]_{[d/x]\rho} && \text{by 15.3(c),} \\ &= a \bullet d && \text{by 15.3(a), (b).} \end{aligned}$$

There are an infinity of other examples M, x, ρ with $[\![\lambda x . M]\!]_\rho \in \widetilde{a}$. But whatever such M, x, ρ we take, the value of $[\![\lambda x . M]\!]_\rho$ is always the same (by Berry's extensionality property, Lemma 15.8(b)).

In effect, just one member of $\widetilde{a}$ is chosen to be the value of $[\![\lambda x . M]\!]_\rho$ for all M, x, ρ such that $[\![\lambda x . M]\!]_\rho \in \widetilde{a}$. Call this member $\Lambda(a)$:

$$\Lambda(a) = [\![\lambda x . ux]\!]_{[a/u]\sigma} \text{ for any } \sigma. \tag{2}$$

We have thus defined a mapping Λ from D to D.[1] Its properties include:

(i) $\Lambda(a) \sim a$ (by above),

(ii) $\Lambda(a) \sim \Lambda(b) \implies \Lambda(a) = \Lambda(b)$ (by 15.8(b)),

(iii) $a \sim b \iff \Lambda(a) = \Lambda(b)$ (by (i), (ii)),

(iv) $\Lambda(\Lambda(a)) = \Lambda(a)$ (by (i), (iii)).

Moreover, the map Λ is representable in D; i.e. there exists $e \in D$ such that

(v) $e \bullet a = \Lambda(a)$ for all $a \in D$.

One suitable such e is the member of D corresponding to the Church numeral $\overline{1}$:

$$e = [\![\overline{1}]\!] = [\![\lambda xy . xy]\!]_\sigma \quad \text{(for any } \sigma\text{);}$$

[1] $\Lambda(a)$ is sometimes called '$\lambda x . ax$', but that notation mixes the formal λ-calculus language with its meta-language, so we shall not use it here.

this e works because

$$\begin{aligned} [\![\lambda xy.xy]\!]_\sigma \bullet a &= [\![\lambda y.xy]\!]_{[a/x]\sigma} && \text{by 15.3(c)} \\ &= \Lambda(a) && \text{by (2) above and 15.3(e).} \end{aligned}$$

Using Λ, the definition of λ-model can be re-written as follows.

Definition 15.19 (Syntax-free λ-models) A *syntax-free λ-model* is a triple $\langle D, \bullet, \Lambda\rangle$ where $\langle D, \bullet\rangle$ is an applicative structure, Λ maps D to D, and

(a) $\langle D, \bullet\rangle$ is combinatorially complete (see 14.28–14.29),

(b) $(\forall a \in D) \quad \Lambda(a) \sim a$,

(c) $(\forall a, b \in D) \quad a \sim b \implies \Lambda(a) = \Lambda(b)$,

(d) $(\exists e \in D)(\forall a \in D) \quad e \bullet a = \Lambda(a)$.

Theorem 15.20 *$\langle D, \bullet, \Lambda\rangle$ is a syntax-free λ-model iff $\langle D, \bullet, [\![\ ]\!]\rangle$ is a λ-model in the sense of Definition 15.3. Here $[\![\ ]\!]$ is defined from Λ by*

(a) $[\![x]\!]_\rho = \rho(x)$,

(b) $[\![PQ]\!]_\rho = [\![P]\!]_\rho \bullet [\![Q]\!]_\rho$,

(c) $[\![\lambda x.P]\!]_\rho = \Lambda(a)$, *where* $(\forall d \in D)(a \bullet d = [\![P]\!]_{[d/x]\rho})$.

And conversely, Λ is defined from $[\![\ ]\!]$ by

(d) $\Lambda(a) = [\![\lambda x.ux]\!]_{[a/u]\sigma}$ *for any* σ.

Proof For 'if', see Discussion 15.18.

For 'only if': let $\langle D, \bullet, \Lambda\rangle$ be a syntax-free λ-model. We must first prove that (a)–(c) define $[\![M]\!]_\rho$ for all M and ρ, and to do this the only problem is to prove that the object a mentioned in (c) actually exists. In fact we shall prove the following simultaneously:

(i) clauses (a)–(c) define $[\![M]\!]_\rho$ for all ρ;

(ii) $[\![M]\!]_\rho$ is independent of $\rho(z)$ if $z \notin \mathrm{FV}(M)$;

(iii) for each sequence $y_1, \ldots, y_n \supseteq \mathrm{FV}(M)$ there exists $b \in D$ such that, for all $d_1, \ldots, d_n \in D$,

$$b \bullet d_1 \bullet \ldots \bullet d_n = [\![M]\!]_{[d_1/y_1]\ldots[d_n/y_n]\rho}.$$

The proof of (i)–(iii) is by induction on M.

Case 1: M is a combination of variables. Then (i) and (ii) are trivial, and (iii) holds by combinatory completeness.

Case 2: $M \equiv PQ$. Then (i) and (ii) are trivial. For (iii), let b_P, b_Q satisfy (iii) for P, Q and the given $y_1, \dots, y_n$. Define

$$g = [\![\lambda uvy_1 \dots y_n . (uy_1 \dots y_n)(vy_1 \dots y_n)]\!].$$

(This g exists by combinatory completeness.) Then $b = g \bullet b_P \bullet b_Q$ satisfies (iii).

Case 3: $M \equiv \lambda x.P$. By induction-hypothesis (iii) applied to P and $y_1, \dots, y_n, x$, there exists $b_P \in D$ such that, for all $d_1, \dots, d_n, d \in D$,

$$b_P \bullet d_1 \bullet \dots \bullet d_n \bullet d = [\![P]\!]_{[d/x][d_1/y_1]\dots[d_n/y_n]\sigma}$$

where σ is arbitrary. (The right side is independent of σ by induction hypothesis (ii).)

To prove (i), it is enough to show that the a in (c) exists. Take any ρ, let $d_i = \rho(y_i)$, and define

$$a = b_P \bullet d_1 \bullet \dots \bullet d_n.$$

Then $a \bullet d = [\![P]\!]_{[d/x]\rho}$ by the equation for b_P. This proves (i). Also (ii) is obvious from this proof of (i).

To prove (iii) for $\lambda x.P$: take any $e \in D$ that represents Λ, and define $b = f \bullet e \bullet b_P$, where

$$f = [\![\lambda uvy_1 \dots y_n . u(vy_1 \dots y_n)]\!].$$

(This f exists by combinatory completeness.) For any $d_1, \dots, d_n \in D$, we can define

$$a = b_P \bullet d_1 \bullet \dots \bullet d_n.$$

Then for all $d \in D$ we have $a \bullet d = [\![P]\!]_{[d/x]\rho}$, where ρ is defined by setting $\rho(y_i) = d_i$. Hence, by (c),

$$[\![\lambda x.P]\!]_\rho = \Lambda(a).$$

So

$$\begin{aligned} b \bullet d_1 \bullet \dots \bullet d_n &= e \bullet a && \text{by definition of } b \text{ and } f, \\ &= \Lambda(a) && \text{since } e \text{ represents } \Lambda, \\ &= [\![\lambda x.P]\!]_\rho && \text{by above.} \end{aligned}$$

This ends the proof of (i)–(iii). To complete the theorem, we need only check that $[\![\ ]\!]$ satisfies 15.3(a)–(f). This is straightforward. □

Corollary 15.20.1 *The constructions of $[\![\ ]\!]$ and Λ in Theorem 15.20 are mutual inverses. That is: if $\langle D, \bullet, [\![\ ]\!]' \rangle$ is a λ-model in the sense of 15.3, and we first define Λ from $[\![\ ]\!]'$ by 15.20(d) and then define $[\![\ ]\!]$ by 15.20(a)–(c), we shall get $[\![\ ]\!] = [\![\ ]\!]'$; and, conversely, if we start with a syntax-free λ-model $\langle D, \bullet, \Lambda' \rangle$ and define first $[\![\ ]\!]$ and then Λ, we shall get $\Lambda = \Lambda'$.*

Proof Straightforward. □

Remark 15.21 The above corollary says that the two given definitions of λ-model are equivalent in a very strong sense.

Definition 15.19 is clearly independent of the λ-syntax. Even better, in contrast to the earlier definition in 15.3, it is essentially just a finite set of first-order axioms. In fact, its clause (a) is equivalent to

(a′) $(\exists k, s \in D)(\forall a, b, c \in D)\big(k \bullet a \bullet b = a \ \wedge \ s \bullet a \bullet b \bullet c = a \bullet c \bullet (b \bullet c)\big)$,

and (b) and (c) are equivalent to

(b′) $(\forall a, b \in D)\ \big(\Lambda(a) \bullet b = a \bullet b\big)$,

(c′) $(\forall a, b \in D)\ \big((\forall d \in D)(a \bullet d = b \bullet d) \quad \Longrightarrow \quad \Lambda(a) = \Lambda(b)\big)$.

But the following definition is simpler still. It is due to Dana Scott [Sco80b, pp. 421–425] and Albert Meyer [Mey82, Definition 1.3], and instead of focussing on Λ it focusses on one of its representatives in D. By this means it avoids the need for the function-symbol 'Λ'.

Definition 15.22 (Scott–Meyer $\boldsymbol{\lambda}$-models) A *loose Scott–Meyer λ-model* is a triple $\langle D, \bullet, e \rangle$ where $\langle D, \bullet \rangle$ is an applicative structure, $e \in D$, and

(a) $\langle D, \bullet \rangle$ is combinatorially complete,

(b) $(\forall a, b \in D)\ \big(e \bullet a \bullet b = a \bullet b\big)$,

(c) $(\forall a, b \in D)\ \big((\forall d \in D)(a \bullet d = b \bullet d) \quad \Longrightarrow \quad e \bullet a = e \bullet b\big)$.

A *strict Scott–Meyer λ-model* is a loose model such that also

(d) $e \bullet e = e$.

Discussion 15.23 Suppose we take a Scott–Meyer model $\langle D, \bullet, e \rangle$, strict or loose, and define Λ to be the function that e represents, i.e.

$$\Lambda \ = \ \mathrm{Fun}(e) \tag{3}$$

in the notation of Definition 14.4; then $\langle D, \bullet, \Lambda \rangle$ is easily seen to be a syntax-free λ-model in the sense of Definition 15.19.

Conversely, if we take a syntax-free λ-model $\langle D, \bullet, \Lambda \rangle$ and let e be any representative of Λ, then $\langle D, \bullet, e \rangle$ is a loose Scott–Meyer model. So the loose Scott–Meyer definition of model is essentially equivalent to the earlier definitions, 15.3 and 15.19.

However, one mapping Λ may have many representatives, so one model in the sense of 15.19 may give rise to many loose Scott–Meyer models. But only one of these is strict. To find it, choose

$$e_0 \;=\; [\![\,\bar{1}\,]\!] \;=\; [\![\lambda xy.xy]\!], \tag{4}$$

where $[\![\;]\!]$ is defined from Λ by 15.20(a)–(c). This e_0 represents Λ, by the end of Discussion 15.18, and we also have

$$e_0 \bullet e_0 \;=\; [\![\,\bar{1}\,]\!] \bullet [\![\,\bar{1}\,]\!] \;=\; [\![\,\bar{1}\,\bar{1}\,]\!] \;=\; [\![\,\bar{1}\,]\!] \;=\; e_0, \tag{5}$$

so $\langle D, \bullet, e_0 \rangle$ is a strict model.

No other representative of Λ gives a strict model. Because if e' represents Λ and $\langle D, \bullet, e' \rangle$ is a strict model, we get $e' = e_0$. In detail:

$$\begin{aligned}
e' &= e' \bullet e' && \text{by 15.22(d) for } e', \\
&= \Lambda(e') && \text{since } e' \text{ represents } \Lambda, \\
&= e_0 \bullet e' && \text{since } e_0 \text{ represents } \Lambda, \\
&= e_0 \bullet e_0 && \text{by 15.22(c) for } e_0 \text{ since } e' \sim e_0, \\
&= e_0 && \text{by 15.22(d) for } e_0.
\end{aligned}$$

This discussion can be summed up as follows.

Theorem 15.24 *The constructions* $\Lambda = \mathrm{Fun}(e)$ *and* $e_0 = [\![\,\bar{1}\,]\!]$ *are mutual inverses. That is: if* $\langle D, \bullet, \Lambda \rangle$ *is a syntax-free* λ*-model in the sense of Definition 15.19, and* $e_0 = [\![\,\bar{1}\,]\!]$*, then* $\langle D, \bullet, e_0 \rangle$ *is a strict Scott–Meyer* λ*-model and* $\mathrm{Fun}(e_0) = \Lambda$*; and, conversely, if* $\langle D, \bullet, e \rangle$ *is a strict Scott–Meyer* λ*-model and* $\Lambda = \mathrm{Fun}(e)$*, then* $\langle D, \bullet, \Lambda \rangle$ *is a syntax-free* λ*-model and* $[\![\,\bar{1}\,]\!] = e$.

Remark 15.25 The Scott–Meyer definition of model is clearly simpler than both the previous definitions, in fact it is almost as simple as the definition of 'combinatory algebra' in 14.9. All its clauses except (c) can be expressed in the form

$$(\exists x_1, \ldots, x_m)(\forall y_1, \ldots, y_n)\,(P = Q) \qquad (m, n \geq 0). \tag{6}$$

But the exception is very important. If every clause had form (6), then an analogue of the submodel theorem could be proved (Theorem 14.23), and in particular the interior of every λ-model would be a λ-model. But the latter is not true. (Two counter-examples are given in [HL80, Section 7]; one is the interior of $\mathbb{TM}(\lambda\beta\eta)$.) So we have gone about as far as we can go in simplifying the definition of λ-model.

This fact can be seen from another point of view: every combinatory algebra contains members e satisfying (b) and (d) of Definition 15.22, but there need not be one satisfying (c) as well. In other words, as noted in Remark 15.13, not all combinatory algebras can be made into λ-models.

15C General properties of λ-models

Discussion 15.26 By concentrating on Λ and its representatives we came very quickly to a rather simple, almost algebraic, definition of λ-model. But λ-calculus is function-theory, not algebra, so a more function-oriented view seems also desirable. Here is one such view.

Consider an arbitrary syntax-free λ-model $\langle D, \bullet, \Lambda\rangle$. In the notation of 14.3 and 14.4, $(D \to D)_{\mathrm{rep}}$ is the set of all its representable one-place functions, $\mathrm{Reps}(\theta)$ is the set of all representatives of a function $\theta \in (D \to D)_{\mathrm{rep}}$, and $\mathrm{Fun}(a)$ is the one-place function represented by $a \in D$.

Of course $\mathrm{Reps}(\theta)$ may have many members. But Λ gives us a way of choosing a 'canonical' one, which will be called $\mathrm{Rep}(\theta)$:

$$\mathrm{Rep}(\theta) \;=\; \Lambda(a) \quad \text{for any } a \in \mathrm{Reps}(\theta). \tag{7}$$

(This definition is independent of a by 14.6 and 15.18.) We clearly have

$$\mathrm{Fun}(\mathrm{Rep}(\theta)) \;=\; \theta. \tag{8}$$

Thus Fun is a left inverse of Rep, so by 15.1, Rep is a one-to-one embedding of $(D \to D)_{\mathrm{rep}}$ into D, and $(D \to D)_{\mathrm{rep}}$ is a retract of D. (Figure 15:2.)

It is possible to reverse the above discussion and define application in terms of representability. Let D be any set, S be any set of one-place functions from D to D, and let $\mathrm{Rep} : S \to D$, $\mathrm{Fun} : D \to S$ be any pair of functions that form a retraction (Notation 15.1). That is, let

$$\mathrm{Fun} \circ \mathrm{Rep} \;=\; I_S, \tag{9}$$

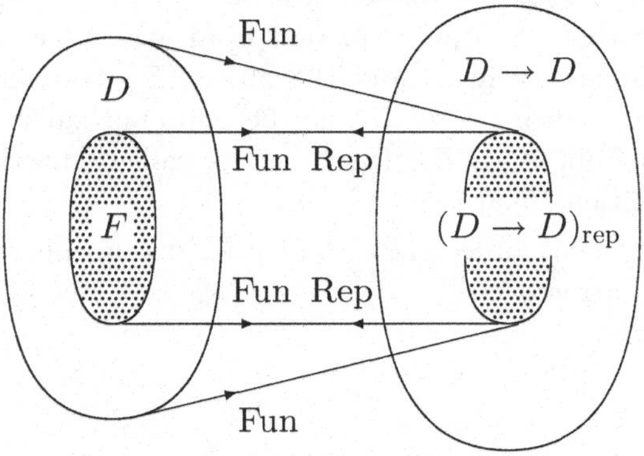

Fig. 15:2

where $\circ$ is function-composition and I_S is the identity-function on S. Then we can define application for all $a, b \in D$ thus:

$$a \bullet b \;=\; (\mathrm{Fun}(a))(b). \tag{10}$$

It is easy to show that S becomes exactly the set of all functions representable in $\langle D, \bullet \rangle$, when $\bullet$ is defined in this way. Next, define

$$\Lambda \;=\; \mathrm{Rep} \circ \mathrm{Fun}. \tag{11}$$

This Λ is easily seen to satisfy (b) and (c) in the definition of syntax-free λ-model, 15.19. Now, in the present language the other conditions in that definition say:

(i) D has at least two members;
(ii) $\langle D, \bullet \rangle$ is combinatorially complete, if $\bullet$ is defined by (10);
(iii) $\mathrm{Rep} \circ \mathrm{Fun} \;\in\; S$.

Hence any retraction that satisfies (i)–(iii) gives rise to a λ-model.

Discussion 15.27 For the reader who knows some category theory, the above conditions can be expressed rather neatly. (The classic introduction to category theory is [Mac71]; there are also many others, for example [LS86], [Pie91] and [AL91].)

Let $\mathcal{C}$ be a cartesian closed category ([Mac71, Chapter IV, Section 6], [Bar84, Definition 5.5.1], [LS86, Part 0 Section 7] or [AL91, Definition 2.3.3]). Suppose also that the objects of $\mathcal{C}$ are sets, the arrows of $\mathcal{C}$ are functions, and that the cartesian product, exponentiation, etc. in the definition of 'cartesian closed' are the usual set-theoretic constructions, except that not every function from an object A to an object B need be an arrow in $\mathcal{C}$, and the object B^A corresponding to the set of all arrows from A to B may be a proper subset of the set of all functions from A to B. (Such a $\mathcal{C}$ is called 'strictly concrete' in [Bar84, Definition 5.5.8].)

Suppose $\mathcal{C}$ has an object D with at least two members, and suppose there are two arrows

$$\text{Fun} : D \to D^D, \qquad \text{Rep} : D^D \to D,$$

such that $\langle \text{Rep}, \text{Fun} \rangle$ is a retraction (i.e. $\text{Fun} \circ \text{Rep} = I_{D^D}$). Then all the conditions in the preceding discussion are satisfied. In fact 15.26(9) and (i) are given assumptions, (iii) follows from the fact that categories are always 'closed' with respect to composition, and (ii) comes from the definition of 'cartesian closed', [Bar84, Proposition 5.5.7(ii) and the note after 5.5.8].

So every retraction in a strictly concrete cartesian closed category gives rise to a λ-model, provided its domain has at least two members. Conversely, every λ-model can be described as a retraction in some strictly concrete cartesian closed category.

Further, the model is extensional iff the retraction is an isomorphism (between D and D^D).

More about a category-theoretic view of λ-models can be found in [Koy82], [Bar84, Section 5.5], [LS86, Part 1 Sections 15–18], [AL91, Chapters 8–9] and [Plo93]. For a more general category-theoretic approach to λ, perhaps the best source is [LS86]. Cartesian closed categories are also closely related to type-theory; see, for example, [LS86, Part 1 Section 11], [Cro94] and [Jac99].

Remark 15.28 (The set F) If $\langle D, \bullet, \Lambda \rangle$ is a syntax-free λ-model, the range of Λ is called F. By Discussion 15.18, F has exactly one member in each extensional-equivalence-class in D, and corresponds one-to-one with $(D \to D)_{\text{rep}}$ by the map Rep (see Figure 15:2). An alternative characterization of F is

$$\text{(a)} \quad F = \big\{ d \in D : \ (\exists M, x, \rho) \, (d = [\![\lambda x . M]\!]_\rho) \big\}.$$

(Compare Discussion 15.18.) Finally, by Lemma 14.8(b), a λ-model is extensional iff $F = D$.

Remark 15.29 (Combinatory algebras and λ-models) Suppose we have a combinatory algebra $\langle D, \bullet \rangle$: how many maps Λ exist such that $\langle D, \bullet, \Lambda \rangle$ is a λ-model? The answer depends on the given algebra.

(a) There are examples with none. (See Remark 15.13.)

(b) There are examples with just one. (E.g. any extensional λ-model, by 15.30 below; also the non-extensional model $P\omega$ in 16.65 later, by [BL84, Section 2].) A $\langle D, \bullet \rangle$ with just one is called *lambda-categorical.*

(c) There are examples with more than one. [Lon83, Theorem 4.1 and remarks after 4.3].

More on changing combinatory algebras into λ-models can be found in [BK80], [Mey82], [Lon83, Section 4], [BL84] and [Bar84, Section 5.2]. If the given algebra is extensional, the task is easy, as the following theorem shows.

Theorem 15.30 *Every extensional combinatory algebra* $\langle D, \bullet \rangle$ *can be made into a λ-model* $\langle D, \bullet, \Lambda \rangle$ *in exactly one way, namely by defining* $\Lambda(a) = a$ *for all* $a \in D$*. And* $\langle D, \bullet, \Lambda \rangle$ *is a model of the theory* $\lambda\beta\eta$*.*

Proof By extensionality, each set $\widetilde{a}$ has only one member, so $\Lambda(a) = a$ is the only way to define Λ such that $\lambda(a) \in \widetilde{a}$. And if Λ is defined thus, it does satisfy Definition 15.19(a)–(d). □

Remark 15.31 In an extensional combinatory algebra, how do we extend the definition of $[\![\ ]\!]$ from CL-terms to λ-terms? The above theorem's proof gives an indirect method, when combined with Theorem 15.20, but the following is a direct method. (It looks very different, but, by extensionality, all definitions of $[\![\ ]\!]$ that satisfy the conditions of Definition 15.3 will give the same value to $[\![M]\!]_\rho$.)

First, find $s, k, i \in D$ satisfying the axioms of the theory CLw, and define $[\![\ ]\!]$ for CL-terms in the usual way (14.11). Then define $[\![\ ]\!]$ for λ-terms via the H-transformation, namely:

$$[\![M]\!]_\rho = [\![M_H]\!]_\rho . \tag{12}$$

It is straightforward to check that this definition satisfies 15.3(a)–(f). For example, here is the proof of 15.3(c):

$$\begin{aligned}
[\![\lambda x.P]\!]_\rho \bullet d &= [\![[x].(P_H)]\!]_\rho \bullet d && \text{by (12) above}\\
&= [\![([x].(P_H))x]\!]_{[d/x]\rho} && \text{by 14.11(c), (a)}\\
&= [\![P_H]\!]_{[d/x]\rho} && \text{by 2.21 and 14.17}\\
&= [\![P]\!]_{[d/x]\rho} && \text{by (12) above.}
\end{aligned}$$

Summary 15.32 Five main classes of models have been defined in this chapter and the previous one. We shall denote them as follows:

$\overline{\mathrm{CL}w}$: combinatory algebras (defined in 14.9, and essentially the same as models of the theory CLw which was defined in 6.5);

$\overline{\mathrm{CL}\beta_{ax}}$: models of the theory CLβ_{ax} (defined in 14.15 and 9.38, and essentially the same as the 'λ-algebras' of [Bar84]);

$\overline{\mathrm{CL}ext_{ax}}$: models of the theory CLext_{ax} which was defined in 8.10;

$\overline{\lambda\beta}$: λ-models, as defined in 15.3 (or equivalently, syntax-free λ-models in 15.19 or Scott–Meyer λ-models in 15.22);

$\overline{\lambda\beta\eta}$: extensional combinatory algebras (where extensionality was defined in 14.7).

By 15.30 we can say $\overline{\lambda\beta\eta} \subseteq \overline{\lambda\beta}$, in the sense that every extensional combinatory algebra can be made into a λ-model by adding some extra structure (namely Λ or $[\![\;]\!]$). In a similar sense, by 15.12–15.12.2:

(i) $\overline{\lambda\beta\eta} \subseteq \overline{\mathrm{CL}ext_{ax}} \subseteq \overline{\mathrm{CL}\beta_{ax}} \subseteq \overline{\mathrm{CL}w}$,

(ii) $\overline{\lambda\beta\eta} \subseteq \overline{\lambda\beta} \subseteq \overline{\mathrm{CL}\beta_{ax}}$.

All these inclusions except the second one in (i) are known to be proper, in the sense that there is a model in the right-hand class which is not in the left-hand class and cannot be made so by an acceptably small change. (See 14.25 for the first one in (i), and [BK80] for the rest. The second one in (i) lacks an obvious definition of 'acceptably small change'.)

Further reading

A fuller account of the general concept of λ-model is in [Bar84, Chapter 5]. Short outline accounts can be found in several books, for example [Han04, Chapter 5] and [Kri93, Chapter 7]. The basic ideas behind the concept were explored in a cluster of papers around 1980; these included [HL80], [BK80], [Sco80a], [Mey82], [Koy82] and [BL84].

However, much of the concept of λ-model goes back 30 years further. Leon Henkin defined two versions of it in [Hen50, p. 83 'standard model' and p. 84 'general model'], and, although his λ-system was limited by type-restrictions and contained an extensionality axiom (which simplifies the definition of model considerably, as we have seen), many of the key ideas in the present chapter can be traced back to him.

But we have spent long enough studying the general concept of λ-model without seeing any particular examples. The next chapter will describe three particular λ-models in detail.

16
Scott's D_∞ and other models

16A Introduction: complete partial orders

Having looked at the abstract definition of 'model' in the last two chapters, let us now study one particular model in detail. It will be a variant of Dana Scott's D_∞, which was the first non-trivial model invented, and has been a dominant influence on the semantics of λ-calculus and programming languages ever since.

Actually, D_∞ came as quite a surprise to all workers in λ – even to Scott. In autumn 1969 he wrote a paper which argued vigorously that an interpretation of all untyped λ-terms in set theory was highly unlikely, and that those who were interested in making models of λ should limit themselves to the typed version. (For that paper, see [Sco93].) The paper included a sketch of a new interpretation of typed terms. Then, only a month later, Scott realized that, by altering this new interpretation only slightly, he could make it into a model of untyped λ; this was D_∞.

D_∞ is a model of both CLw and $\lambda\beta$, and is also extensional. The description below will owe much to accounts by Dana Scott and Gordon Plotkin, and to the well-presented account in [Bar84], but it will give more details than these and will assume the reader has a less mathematical background.

The construction of D_∞ involves notions from topology. These will be defined below. They are very different from the syntactical techniques used in this book so far, but they are standard tools in the semantics of programming languages. The reader who wishes to study semantics further will find them essential, and will see in D_∞ the place where they were first introduced.

At the end of the chapter some other models will be defined in outline, with references. These are simpler than D_∞, and the reader who only wishes to see a model without looking any deeper should go straight to Section 16F. (But be warned, they are not as simple as they look!)

Notation 16.1 In this chapter, $\mathbb{N}$ will be the set of all natural numbers as usual. The following notation will be new:

D, D', D'', X, Y, J:	arbitrary sets;
$a, \ldots, h$:	members of these sets;
ϕ, ψ, χ:	functions;
$\sqsubseteq$, $\sqsubseteq'$, $\sqsubseteq''$:	partial orderings (see 16.2) on D, D', D'' respectively;
$\sqsupseteq$, $\sqsupseteq'$, $\sqsupseteq''$:	the reverse orderings ($a \sqsupseteq b$ iff $b \sqsubseteq a$, etc.);
$\bot$, $\bot'$, $\bot''$:	the least members of D, D', D'' respectively ($\bot$ is called '*bottom*');
$(D \to D')$:	the set of all functions from D to D', i.e. functions with domain $= D$ and range $\subseteq D'$;
$[D \to D']$:	the set of all functions from D to D' that are continuous (to be defined in 16.10);
$\phi(X)$:	$\{\phi(d) : d \in X\}$, where X is a given set;
$\bigsqcup X$:	the least upper bound (supremum) of X (see 16.3);
$\bigsqcup_{n \geq p} \cdots$:	$\bigsqcup\{\cdots : n \geq p\}$;
$\bigsqcup X = \bigsqcup Y$:	$\bigsqcup X$ exists iff $\bigsqcup Y$ exists, and $\bigsqcup X = \bigsqcup Y$ if they both exist.

An informal λ-notation '$\lambda\!\!\lambda$' will be used when defining some functions. For example, suppose two sets D and D' are given, with $a_1, \ldots, a_n \in D$, and suppose ϕ is a function from D^{n+1} to D'. Then there is a function ψ from D to D' such that

$$\psi(d) \;=\; \phi(a_1, \ldots, a_n, d) \qquad \text{for all } d \in D.$$

This ψ will be called

$$\lambda\!\!\lambda d \in D.\, \phi(a_1, \ldots, a_n, d).$$

Other examples of the $\lambda\!\!\lambda$-notation are:

$$\lambda\!\!\lambda d \in D.\, \phi(\chi(d)) \quad \text{for} \quad \phi \circ \chi,$$

$$\lambda\!\!\lambda d \in D.\, b \qquad\qquad \text{for} \quad \psi \text{ such that } (\forall d \in D)(\psi(d) = b).$$

The notation has the following properties:

$$(\lambda\!\!\lambda d \in D.\phi(d))(b) \;=\; \phi(b),$$
$$\lambda\!\!\lambda d \in D.\phi(d) \;=\; \phi.$$

But note that this notation is not a new formal language. It will only be used to denote functions that are easy to define without it (though their definitions without it might be tedious). The '=' in the above two equations is not a formal λ-conversion, but is identity in set-theory as usual. It means that both sides of the above equations denote the same function in set-theory, i.e. the same set of ordered pairs.

Definition 16.2 (Partially ordered sets) A *partially ordered set* is a pair $\langle D, \sqsubseteq \rangle$ where D is a set and $\sqsubseteq$ is a binary relation on D, which is

(a) transitive, i.e. $a \sqsubseteq b$ and $b \sqsubseteq c \implies a \sqsubseteq c$,
(b) anti-symmetric, i.e. $a \sqsubseteq b$ and $b \sqsubseteq a \implies a = b$,
(c) reflexive, i.e. $a \sqsubseteq a$.

The *least member of* D (if D has one) is called $\perp$, or *bottom*; we have

$$(\forall d \in D) \quad \perp \sqsubseteq d.$$

Definition 16.3 (Least upper bounds) Let $\langle D, \sqsubseteq \rangle$ be a partially ordered set and let $X \subseteq D$. An *upper bound* (*u.b.*) of X is any $b \in D$ such that

(a) $(\forall a \in X) \quad a \sqsubseteq b$.

The *least upper bound* (or *l.u.b.* or *supremum*) of X is called $\bigsqcup X$; it is an upper bound b of X such that

(b) $(\forall c \in D) \Big((c \text{ is an u.b. of } X) \implies b \sqsubseteq c \Big)$.

Note that in general a set X need not have an upper bound; and if it has one, it need not have a least one. Thus $\bigsqcup X$ might not exist. Also, if it does exist, it might not be in X.

Exercise 16.4 * For every partially ordered set $\langle D, \sqsubseteq \rangle$, prove the following.

(a) A subset X of D cannot have two distinct least upper bounds (i.e. $\bigsqcup X$ is unique if it exists). Hence, if $b \in D$, to prove $b = \bigsqcup X$ it is enough to prove that b satisfies 16.3(a) and (b).

(b) D has a bottom (called $\perp$) iff the empty set $\emptyset$ has a l.u.b.; and

$$\perp \;=\; \bigsqcup \emptyset.$$

(c) If X, $Y \subseteq D$ and every member of X is $\sqsubseteq$ a member of Y and vice versa, then

$$\bigsqcup X = \bigsqcup Y.$$

(By Notation 16.1, this equation means that the left side exists iff the right exists, and when they both exist they are equal. Similarly for the equation in (d) below.)

(d) Let J be a set and $\{X_j : j \in J\}$ be a family of subsets of D, each X_j having a l.u.b. $\bigsqcup X_j$. If Y is the union of this family, then

$$\bigsqcup Y = \bigsqcup\{\bigsqcup X_j : j \in J\}.$$

Definition 16.5 (Directed sets) Let $\langle D, \sqsubseteq\rangle$ be a partially ordered set. A subset $X \subseteq D$ is said to be *directed* iff $X \neq \emptyset$ and every pair of members of X has an upper bound in X, i.e.

$$(\forall a, b \in X)\,(\exists c \in X)\,\big(a \sqsubseteq c \text{ and } b \sqsubseteq c\big).$$

The most important examples of directed sets are finite or infinite increasing sequences:

$$a_1 \sqsubseteq a_2 \sqsubseteq a_3 \sqsubseteq \ldots$$

An example which is not a sequence is the set of all partitions of an interval $[a, b]$; it is used in defining the Riemann integral in mathematical analysis. In mathematics in general, directed sets are used as index-sets in the theory of convergence on nets, see [Kel55, Chapter 2].

Definition 16.6 (Complete partial orders, c.p.o.s) A *c.p.o.* is a partially ordered set $\langle D, \sqsubseteq\rangle$ such that

(a) D has a least member (called $\perp$);
(b) every directed subset $X \subseteq D$ has a l.u.b. (called $\bigsqcup X$).

Notation Instead of 'the c.p.o. $\langle D, \sqsubseteq\rangle$', we shall write 'the c.p.o. D', and similarly for D', D'', etc. We shall always assume that $\sqsubseteq$ is the ordering on D, and $\sqsubseteq'$ on D' and $\sqsubseteq''$ on D''. For example, the first line of Definition 16.10 below means 'let $\langle D, \sqsubseteq\rangle$ and $\langle D', \sqsubseteq'\rangle$ be c.p.o.s'.

Remark 16.7 The above definitions might seem to be diverging from what we would expect the essential components of a λ-model to be, so let us look at the motivation for introducing partial orderings.

Scott originally built D_∞ as a model for a theory of computable higher-type functions (functions of functions). Standard accounts of computable functions from $\mathbb{N}$ to $\mathbb{N}$ emphasise partial functions, i.e. functions for which $\phi(n)$ need not have a value for all $n \in \mathbb{N}$, and at first sight it might seem natural to extend this approach to higher levels. But in Scott's theory all the functions were total. Instead of $\mathbb{N}$, he worked with

$$\mathbb{N}^+ \;=\; \mathbb{N} \cup \{\perp\} \qquad (\perp \notin \mathbb{N}),$$

where $\perp$ was an arbitrary object introduced to represent 'undefinedness' or 'garbage'.

In this approach, every partial function ϕ of natural numbers determines a total function $\phi^+ \in (\mathbb{N}^+ \to \mathbb{N}^+)$, defined thus:

$$\text{(a)} \quad \begin{cases} \phi^+(n) \;=\; \begin{Bmatrix} \phi(n) & \text{if } \phi(n) \text{ is defined} \\ \perp & \text{otherwise} \end{Bmatrix} \; (\forall n \in \mathbb{N}) \\ \phi^+(\perp) \;=\; \perp. \end{cases}$$

Introducing $\perp$ has several advantages. One is to allow us to distinguish between two kinds of constant-function. For each $p \in \mathbb{N}$, we can define

$$\text{(b)} \quad \psi_p : \qquad (\forall n \in \mathbb{N}) \quad \psi_p(n) = p, \qquad \psi_p(\perp) = \perp;$$

$$\text{(c)} \quad \psi_p' : \qquad (\forall n \in \mathbb{N}) \quad \psi_p'(n) = p, \qquad \psi_p'(\perp) = p.$$

Now $\psi_p = (\phi_p)^+$, where ϕ_p is the constant-function $\phi_p(n) = p$ for all $n \in \mathbb{N}$. In contrast, ψ_p' does not have the form ϕ^+ for any function ϕ, and theories of partial functions often omit it. Nevertheless it is programmable in practice, and Scott's theory therefore includes it.

A disadvantage of introducing $\perp$ is that, if we are not careful, we might find ourselves treating it as an output-value with the same status as a natural number. To prevent this, Scott defined the following partial order on $\mathbb{N}^+$; it corresponds to the intuition that an output $\phi(n) = \perp$ carries less information than an output $\phi(n) = m \in \mathbb{N}$.

Definition 16.8 (The set $\mathbb{N}^+$) Choose any object $\perp \notin \mathbb{N}$, and define $\mathbb{N}^+ = \mathbb{N} \cup \{\perp\}$. For all $a, b \in \mathbb{N}^+$, define

$$a \sqsubseteq b \quad\iff\quad (a = \perp \text{ and } b \in \mathbb{N}) \;\text{ or }\; \mathrm{a} = \mathrm{b}.$$

(see Figure 16:1.) The pair $\langle \mathbb{N}^+, \sqsubseteq \rangle$ will be called just $\mathbb{N}^+$.

Lemma 16.9 $\mathbb{N}^+$ *is a c.p.o.*

Proof It is easy to check that $\sqsubseteq$ is a partial order. The only directed subsets of $\mathbb{N}^+$ are (i) one-member sets, and (ii) pairs $\{\perp, n\}$ with $n \in \mathbb{N}$. Both these have obvious l.u.b.s. $\square$

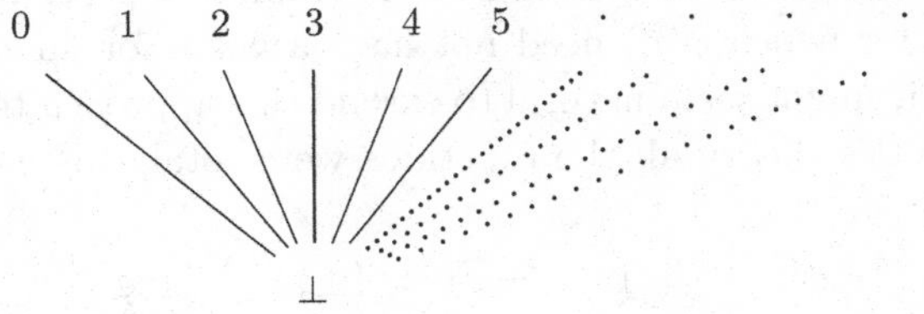

Fig. 16:1

The construction of D_∞ will begin with the c.p.o. $\mathbb{N}^+$. It will involve some properties of functions of arbitrary c.p.o.s, to be described in the next section.

16B Continuous functions

Definition 16.10 (Continuity) Let D and D' be c.p.o.s, and ϕ be a function from D to D'. We say ϕ is *monotonic* iff

$$\text{(a)} \qquad a \sqsubseteq b \quad \Longrightarrow \quad \phi(a) \sqsubseteq' \phi(b).$$

We say ϕ is *continuous* iff, for all directed $X \subseteq D$,

$$\text{(b)} \qquad \phi(\bigsqcup X) \;=\; \bigsqcup(\phi(X)).$$

In (b), $\phi(X) \;=\; \{\phi(a) : a \in X\}$, and the equation means that $\bigsqcup(\phi(X))$ exists and coincides with $\phi(\bigsqcup X)$. ($\bigsqcup X$ exists because X is directed and D is a c.p.o.)

Exercise 16.11 * Prove that every continuous function from D to D' is monotonic.

Exercise 16.12 * Prove that there are only two kinds of continuous functions from $\mathbb{N}^+$ to $\mathbb{N}^+$: those of form ϕ^+ for ϕ a partial function from $\mathbb{N}$ to $\mathbb{N}$, and those of form ψ_p' in 16.7(c).

Hint: prove that, for all functions $\chi \in (\mathbb{N}^+ \to \mathbb{N}^+)$,

$$\begin{aligned} \chi \text{ continuous} \quad &\Longleftrightarrow \quad \chi \text{ monotonic} \\ &\Longleftrightarrow \quad \chi(\bot) = \bot \;\text{ or }\; (\exists p \in \mathbb{N})(\forall \mathrm{a} \in \mathbb{N}^+)(\chi(\mathrm{a}) = \mathrm{p}). \end{aligned}$$

Exercise 16.13* Let D and D' be c.p.o.s and $\phi : D \to D'$ be monotonic. Prove that if $X \subseteq D$ is directed then so is $\phi(X)$. Hence, since D' is a c.p.o., $\phi(X)$ has a l.u.b., $\bigsqcup(\phi(X))$.

Remark 16.14 Exercise 16.13 will be used below in proofs that certain functions are continuous.

To prove a function ϕ continuous, one must prove that if X is directed then $\bigsqcup(\phi(X))$ exists and $\phi(\bigsqcup X) = \bigsqcup(\phi(X))$.

In each of the continuity proofs below, it will be fairly obvious that the function is monotonic. So by Exercise 16.13 we shall know immediately that $\bigsqcup(\phi(X))$ exists, and the proof will reduce to a fairly straightforward calculation with l.u.b.s to show that $\phi(\bigsqcup X) = \bigsqcup(\phi(X))$. We shall not have to worry in this calculation whether the l.u.b.s involved exist.

Remark 16.15 The word 'continuous' comes from the study of topology, and Scott's theory of computability was actually formulated in topological language, [Sco72]. Every c.p.o. has a topology called the *Scott topology*, whose continuous functions are exactly those in Definition 16.10; see [Bar84, Definition 1.2.3].

Definition 16.16 (The function-set $[D \to D']$) For c.p.o.s D and D', define $[D \to D']$ to be the set of all continuous functions from D to D'. For $\phi, \psi \in [D \to D']$, define

$$\phi \sqsubseteq \psi \iff (\forall d \in D)\,\big(\phi(d) \sqsubseteq' \psi(d)\big).$$

Remark 16.17 Informally, if we think of $a \sqsubseteq' b$ as meaning that a carries less or the same information as b, then $\phi \sqsubseteq \psi$ says that each output-value $\phi(d)$ carries less or the same information as $\psi(d)$.

It is easy to check that the relation $\sqsubseteq$ defined above is a partial order. Further, for all $\phi_1, \phi_2 \in [D \to D']$,

$$\text{(a)} \qquad \phi_1 \sqsubseteq \phi_2,\ d_1 \sqsubseteq d_2 \implies \phi_1(d_1) \sqsubseteq' \phi_2(d_2).$$

Also $[D \to D']$ has a least member, namely the function $\bot$ defined by

$$(\forall d \in D) \quad \bot(d) = \bot'.$$

In the special case $D = D'$, $[D \to D]$ contains the identity function I_D, whose definition is

$$(\forall d \in D) \quad I_D(d) = d.$$

Lemma 16.18 *Let D and D' be c.p.o.s Then $[D \to D']$ is a c.p.o. Furthermore, for every directed set $Y \subseteq [D \to D']$ we have*

$$(\forall d \in D) \qquad (\bigsqcup Y)(d) \;=\; \bigsqcup\{\,\phi(d) : \phi \in Y\}.$$

Proof Let $Y \subseteq [D \to D']$ be directed. For each $d \in D$, define

$$Y_d \;=\; \{\phi(d) : \phi \in Y\}. \tag{1}$$

Then Y_d is directed. (Proof: if $a, b \in Y_d$, then $a = \phi(d)$ and $b = \psi(d)$ for some $\phi, \psi \in Y$, and since Y is directed it contains $\chi \sqsupseteq \phi, \psi$; then $\chi(d) \sqsupseteq a, b$.) Also $Y_d \subseteq D'$ and D' is a c.p.o. Hence $\bigsqcup Y_d$ exists. Thus the right-hand side of the equation in the lemma is meaningful.

Define a function ψ from D to D' thus:

$$(\forall d \in D) \qquad \psi(d) \;=\; \bigsqcup Y_d. \tag{2}$$

The lemma claims that $\psi = \bigsqcup Y$. Before proving this claim, we first prove ψ continuous. Let $X \subseteq D$ be directed; then

$$\begin{aligned}
\psi(\bigsqcup X) &= \bigsqcup \left(Y_{(\bigsqcup X)}\right) && \text{by (2)}\\
&= \bigsqcup \{\phi(\bigsqcup X) : \phi \in Y\} && \text{by (1)}\\
&= \bigsqcup \{\bigsqcup(\phi(X)) : \phi \in Y\} && \text{by continuity of } \phi\\
&= \bigsqcup \{\phi(a) : a \in X \text{ and } \phi \in Y\} && \text{by 16.4(d)}\\
&= \bigsqcup \{\bigsqcup Y_a : a \in X\} && \text{by 16.4(d)}\\
&= \bigsqcup \{\psi(a) : a \in X\} && \text{by (2).}
\end{aligned}$$

(It is easy to check that all the sets above are directed and are $\subseteq D$ or D'; since D and D' are c.p.o.s, all the l.u.b.s mentioned above do exist.) Thus ψ is continuous. Hence $\psi \in [D \to D']$.

Now ψ is an u.b. of Y. Because, for all $\phi \in Y$ and $d \in D$, we have $\phi(d) \sqsubseteq \bigsqcup Y_d$ by (1), $= \psi(d)$ by (2).

Finally, $\psi \sqsubseteq$ every other u.b. χ of Y. Because, for all $d \in D$, $\chi(d)$ must be an u.b. of Y_d and hence $\sqsupseteq$ its least u.b., which is $\psi(d)$. □

Lemma 16.19 (Composition) *The composition of continuous functions is continuous. That is, if D, D', D'' are c.p.o.s and $\psi \in [D \to D']$ and $\phi \in [D' \to D'']$, and $\phi \circ \psi$ is defined by*

$$(\forall d \in D) \qquad (\phi \circ \psi)(d) \;=\; \phi(\psi(d)),$$

then

$$\phi \circ \psi \;\in\; [D \to D''].$$

Proof Straightforward. □

Definition 16.20 (Isomorphism) Let D and D' be c.p.o.s. We say *D is isomorphic to D'*, or $D \cong D'$, iff there exist $\phi \in [D \to D']$ and $\psi \in [D' \to D]$ such that

$$\psi \circ \phi = I_D, \qquad \phi \circ \psi = I_{D'}.$$

(It is easy to see that any such ϕ and ψ must be one-to-one and onto. They are also continuous, and hence are monotonic, i.e. they preserve order.)

Definition 16.21 (Projections) Let D and D' be c.p.o.s. A *projection from D' to D* is a pair $\langle\phi, \psi\rangle$ of functions with $\phi \in [D \to D']$ and $\psi \in [D' \to D]$, such that

$$\psi \circ \phi = I_D, \qquad \phi \circ \psi \sqsubseteq I_{D'}.$$

We say D' is *projected onto D by $\langle\phi, \psi\rangle$*. (See Figure 16:2.)

A projection $\langle\phi, \psi\rangle$ is a retraction in the sense of Notation 15.1, but with the extra properties that ϕ and ψ are continuous and

$$\phi \circ \psi \sqsubseteq I_{D'}.$$

It is easy to show that $\langle\phi, \psi\rangle$ makes D isomorphic to the set $\phi(D) \subseteq D'$. Also $\langle\phi, \psi\rangle$ makes the bottom members of D and D' correspond:

$$\phi(\bot) = \bot', \qquad \psi(\bot') = \bot.$$

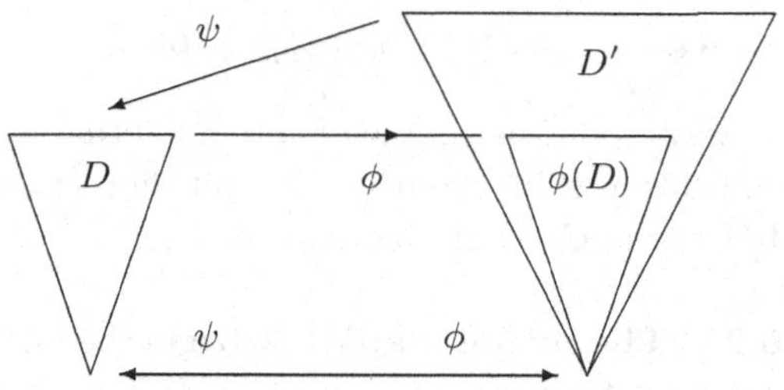

Fig. 16:2

16C The construction of D_∞

We shall build D_∞ as the 'limit' of a sequence $D_0, D_1, D_2, \ldots$ of c.p.o.s, each of which is the continuous-function set of the one before it. Their precise definition is as follows.

Definition 16.22 (The sequence D_0, D_1, D_2, ...) Define $D_0 = \mathbb{N}^+$ (see Definition 16.8), and

$$D_{n+1} = [D_n \to D_n].$$

The $\sqsubseteq$-relation on D_n will be called just '$\sqsubseteq$'; it is defined in Definition 16.16. The least member of D_n will be called $\perp_n$.

By Lemmas 16.9 and 16.18, every D_n is a c.p.o.

Discussion 16.23 To build a λ-model $\langle D_\infty, \bullet, [\![\ ]\!]\rangle$ in a standard set-theory such as ZF, we cannot take D_∞ to be a set of functions and $\bullet$ to be function-application, because in set-theory no function can be applied to itself.

Scott avoided this problem by a device which, in principle, is very simple. He took the members of D_∞ to be not just functions, but infinite sequences of functions:

$$\phi = \langle \phi_0, \phi_1, \phi_2, \ldots \rangle$$

with $\phi_n \in D_n$. Application was defined by

$$\phi \bullet \psi = \langle \phi_1(\psi_0),\ \phi_2(\psi_1),\ \phi_3(\psi_2),\ \ldots \rangle.$$

With this definition, self-application becomes immediately possible:

$$\phi \bullet \phi = \langle \phi_1(\phi_0),\ \phi_2(\phi_1),\ \phi_3(\phi_2),\ \ldots \rangle.$$

It will be a long way from this simple idea to an actual λ-model, and the definition of application will become somewhat more complicated before it gets there, but the above is its motivation.

Definition 16.24 (The initial maps) To begin the limit-construction, we embed D_0 into D_1 by a map ϕ_0 and define a reverse map ψ_0:

(a) for all $d \in D_0$, define $\phi_0(d) = \lambda\!\!\lambda a \in D_0 . d$;

(b) for all $g \in D_1$, define $\psi_0(g) = g(\perp_0)$.

That is, for $d \in D_0$, $\phi_0(d)$ is the constant-function with value d. Constant-functions are obviously continuous, so $\phi_0(d) \in D_1$; hence $\phi_0 \in (D_0 \to D_1)$. Conversely, for $g \in D_1$ we have $g(\bot_0) \in D_0$, so $\psi_0 \in (D_1 \to D_0)$. Also $\psi_0(g)$ is the least value of g, since each $g \in D_1$ is continuous and hence monotonic.

Lemma 16.25 *The pair $\langle \phi_0, \psi_0 \rangle$ is a projection from D_1 to D_0; i.e.*

(a) $\phi_0 \in [D_0 \to D_1]$ *and* $\psi_0 \in [D_1 \to D_0]$;

(b) $\psi_0 \circ \phi_0 \;=\; I_{D_0}$; *i.e.* $\psi_0(\phi_0(d)) = d$ *for all* $d \in D_0$;

(c) $\phi_0 \circ \psi_0 \;\sqsubseteq\; I_{D_1}$; *i.e.* $\phi_0(\psi_0(g)) \sqsubseteq g$ *for all* $g \in D_1$.

Proof (a) Just before the Lemma we have seen that $\phi_0 \in (D_0 \to D_1)$ and $\psi_0 \in (D_1 \to D_0)$. To prove (a) we must show further that ϕ_0 and ψ_0 are continuous. This is left as an exercise.$\star$

(b) $\psi_0(\phi_0(d)) \;=\; \phi_0(d)(\bot_0), \;=\; d$ by the definition of $\phi_0(d)$.

(c) Let $g \in D_1$. Then g is continuous and therefore monotonic, so $g(\bot_0) \sqsubseteq g(d)$ for all $d \in D_0$. Then

$$\begin{aligned} \phi_0(\psi_0(g)) &= \lambda\!\!\lambda d \in D_0 \,.\, g(\bot_0) \\ &\sqsubseteq \lambda\!\!\lambda d \in D_0 \,.\, g(d) \qquad \text{by definition of } \sqsubseteq \text{ in } D_1 \\ &= g. \end{aligned}$$

□

Discussion 16.26 We shall make the above initial projection induce a projection $\langle \phi_n, \psi_n \rangle$ from D_{n+1} to D_n for each $n \geq 1$, in a very natural way. Then, in category-theory language, D_∞ will be the inverse limit of this sequence of projections in the category of c.p.o.s and continuous functions (Figure 16:3).

For each n, we shall have $D_n \prec [D_n \to D_n]$, where '$\prec$' denotes projection, and in the limit we shall obtain

$$D_\infty \;\cong\; [D_\infty \to D_\infty].$$

Definition 16.27 (Maps between D_n and D_{n+1}) For every $n \geq 0$ we define a pair of mappings ϕ_n, ψ_n. If $n = 0$, define ϕ_0, ψ_0 as in 16.24. If $n \geq 1$ and ϕ_{n-1}, ψ_{n-1} have already been defined, define ϕ_n, ψ_n thus:

(a) $\phi_n(f) \;=\; \phi_{n-1} \circ f \circ \psi_{n-1} \qquad (\forall f \in D_n)$,

(b) $\psi_n(g) \;=\; \psi_{n-1} \circ g \circ \phi_{n-1} \qquad (\forall g \in D_{n+1})$.

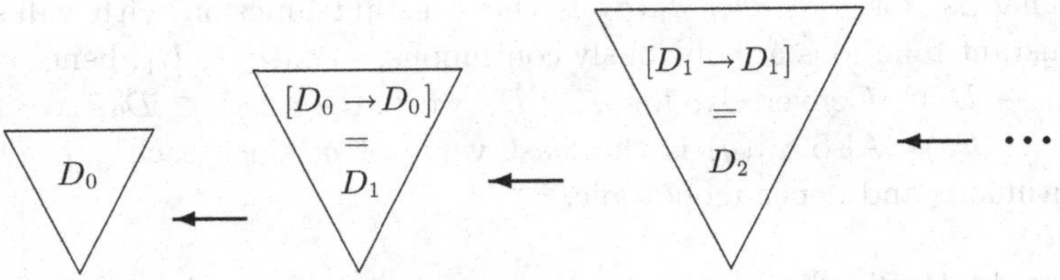

Fig. 16:3

That is

(a′) $\phi_n(f)(b) = \phi_{n-1}(f(\psi_{n-1}(b)))$ $(\forall f \in D_n, \ \forall b \in D_n)$,

(b′) $\psi_n(g)(a) = \psi_{n-1}(g(\phi_{n-1}(a)))$ $(\forall g \in D_{n+1}, \ \forall a \in D_{n-1})$.

Very roughly speaking, $\phi_n(f)$ is a function which acts on members of D_n by applying f to the 'corresponding' members of D_{n-1}, and $\psi_n(g)$ acts on members of D_{n-1} by applying g to the 'corresponding' members of D_n.

Lemma 16.28 *The pair $\langle \phi_n, \psi_n \rangle$ is a projection from D_{n+1} to D_n; i.e.*

(a) $\phi_n \in [D_n \to D_{n+1}], \quad \psi_n \in [D_{n+1} \to D_n]$;

(b) $\psi_n \circ \phi_n = I_{D_n}$;

(c) $\phi_n \circ \psi_n \sqsubseteq I_{D_{n+1}}$.

Proof We use induction on n. The basis ($n = 0$) is 16.25.

For the induction-step, let $n \geq 1$, and assume (a)–(c) for $n - 1$. To prove (a) for n, two things must be verified:

(a_1) $\phi_n \in (D_n \to D_{n+1}), \quad \psi_n \in (D_{n+1} \to D_n)$;

(a_2) ϕ_n and ψ_n are continuous.

To prove (a_1) for ϕ_n, the main step is to prove $\phi_n(f)$ continuous for all $f \in D_n$. But this follows from 16.19 and the definition of ϕ_n and part (a_2) of the induction-hypothesis for ϕ_{n-1} and ψ_{n-1}. Similarly for ψ_n.

We next prove (a_2) for ϕ_n. (The proof for ψ_n is similar.) Let $X \subseteq D_n$ be directed. It is not hard to see that ϕ_n is monotonic, so the set $\phi_n(X)$ is directed and hence $\bigsqcup(\phi_n(X))$ exists. Both $\bigsqcup(\phi_n(X))$ and $\phi_n(\bigsqcup X)$ are functions, so to prove them equal we only need prove

$$(\forall b \in D_n) \qquad \phi_n(\bigsqcup X)(b) = \left(\bigsqcup(\phi_n(X))\right)(b). \tag{3}$$

But

$$\begin{aligned}
\phi_n(\bigsqcup X)(b) &= \phi_{n-1}((\bigsqcup X)(\psi_{n-1}(b))) && \text{by 16.27(a}'\text{)}\\
&= \phi_{n-1}(\bigsqcup\{\, f(\psi_{n-1}(b)) : f \in X\}) && \text{by 16.18}\\
&= \bigsqcup\{\phi_{n-1}(f(\psi_{n-1}(b))) : f \in X\} && \text{by contin. } \phi_{n-1}\\
&= \bigsqcup\{\phi_n(f)(b) : f \in X\} && \text{by 16.27(a}'\text{)}\\
&= (\bigsqcup(\phi_n(X)))(b) && \text{by 16.18.}
\end{aligned}$$

Next we prove (b) for n. We must prove that $\psi_n(\phi_n(f)) = f$ for all $f \in D_n$; i.e. that $\psi_n(\phi_n(f))(a) = f(a)$ for all $a \in D_{n-1}$. But

$$\begin{aligned}
\psi_n(\phi_n(f))(a) &= \psi_{n-1}(\phi_n(f)(\phi_{n-1}(a))) && \text{by 16.27(b}'\text{)}\\
&= \psi_{n-1}(\phi_{n-1}(f(\psi_{n-1}(\phi_{n-1}(a))))) && \text{by 16.27(a}'\text{)}\\
&= f(a) && \text{by induc. hyp.}
\end{aligned}$$

The proof of (c) for n is similar. This ends the induction step. □

Lemma 16.29 *The maps ϕ_n and ψ_n preserve application, in the following sense: for all $a \in D_{n+1}$ and $b \in D_n$,*

(a) $\psi_{n-1}(a(b)) \sqsupseteq \psi_n(a)(\psi_{n-1}(b))$ *if $n \geq 1$;*

(b) $\phi_n(a(b)) = \phi_{n+1}(a)(\phi_n(b))$ *if $n \geq 0$.*

Proof We prove (a). (The proof of (b) is similar.) By 16.27(b′),

$$\begin{aligned}
\psi_n(a)(\psi_{n-1}(b)) &= \psi_{n-1}(a(\phi_{n-1}(\psi_{n-1}(b))))\\
&\sqsubseteq \psi_{n-1}(a(b)) && \text{by 16.28(c) for } n-1.
\end{aligned}$$

□

Exercise 16.30 * If $n \geq 2$, D_n contains the following analogue of **K**:

$$k_n = \lambda\!\!\lambda a \in D_{n-1}\,.\, \lambda\!\!\lambda b \in D_{n-2}\,.\, \psi_{n-2}(a)\,.$$

Prove that

(a) $k_n \in D_n$ for all $n \geq 2$;

(b) $\psi_1(k_2) = I_{D_0}$ and $\psi_0(\psi_1(k_2)) = \bot_0$;

(c) $\psi_n(k_{n+1}) = k_n$ for all $n \geq 2$.

(Hint: a proof of (a) must contain proofs that (a_1) for all $a \in D_{n-1}$, $k_n(a)$ is continuous, and (a_2) k_n is continuous.)

Note 16.31 If $n \geq 3$, D_n contains the following analogue of **S**:

$$s_n \;=\; \lambda\!\!\lambda a \in D_{n-1} \,.\, \lambda\!\!\lambda b \in D_{n-2} \,.\, \lambda\!\!\lambda c \in D_{n-3} \,.\, a(\phi_{n-3}(c))(b(c))\,.$$

It is tedious, but not hard, to prove that

(a) $s_n \in D_n$ for all $n \geq 3$;

(b) $\psi_2(s_3) = \lambda\!\!\lambda a \in D_1 \,.\, \lambda\!\!\lambda b \in D_0 \,.\, a(\bot_0)$, $\quad \psi_1(\psi_2(s_3)) = I_{D_0}$;

(c) $\psi_n(s_{n+1}) = s_n$ for all $n \geq 3$.

Definition 16.32 For every pair $m, n \geq 0$, a map $\phi_{m,n}$ is defined from D_m to D_n thus:

$$\phi_{m,n} \;=\; \begin{cases} \phi_{n-1} \circ \phi_{n-2} \circ \ldots \circ \phi_{m+1} \circ \phi_m & \text{if } m < n, \\ I_{D_m} & \text{if } m = n, \\ \psi_n \circ \psi_{n+1} \circ \ldots \circ \psi_{m-2} \circ \psi_{m-1} & \text{if } m > n. \end{cases}$$

Lemma 16.33

(a) $\phi_{m,n} \in [D_m \to D_n]$;

(b) $m \leq n \implies \phi_{n,m} \circ \phi_{m,n} = I_{D_m}$;

(c) $m > n \implies \phi_{n,m} \circ \phi_{m,n} \sqsubseteq I_{D_m}$;

(d) $\phi_{k,n} \circ \phi_{m,k} = \phi_{m,n}$ *if k is between m and n.*

Proof By 16.19 and 16.28. □

Definition 16.34 (Construction of D_∞) We define D_∞ to be the set of all infinite sequences

$$d \;=\; \langle d_0,\, d_1,\, d_2,\, \ldots \rangle$$

such that (for all $n \geq 0$) $d_n \in D_n$ and $\psi_n(d_{n+1}) = d_n$. A relation $\sqsubseteq$ on D_∞ is defined by setting

$$d \sqsubseteq d' \iff (\forall n \geq 0)(d_n \sqsubseteq d'_n).$$

Notation 16.35 In the rest of this chapter, 'a_n', 'b_n', '$(a \bullet b)_n$', etc. will denote the n-th member of a sequence a or b or $a \bullet b$, etc. in D_∞. Also, for $X \subseteq D_\infty$, X_n is defined by

$$X_n \;=\; \{a_n : a \in X\}.$$

16D Basic properties of D_∞

Lemma 16.36 *D_∞ is a c.p.o. Its least member is*

$$\bot \;=\; \langle \bot_0,\ \bot_1,\ \bot_2,\ \ldots \rangle,$$

where $\bot_n$ is the least member of D_n. And for all directed $X \subseteq D_\infty$,

$$\bigsqcup X \;=\; \langle \bigsqcup X_0, \bigsqcup X_1, \bigsqcup X_2, \ldots \rangle.$$

Proof Let $X \subseteq D_\infty$ be directed. Then each X_n is directed, so $\bigsqcup X_n$ exists in D_n. Further, the sequence $\langle \bigsqcup X_0, \bigsqcup X_1, \bigsqcup X_2, \ldots \rangle$ is in D_∞, because

$$\begin{aligned} \psi_n(\textstyle\bigsqcup X_{n+1}) &= \textstyle\bigsqcup(\psi_n(X_{n+1})) && \text{by continuity of } \psi_n \\ &= \textstyle\bigsqcup\{\psi_n(a_{n+1}) : a \in X\} && \text{by definition of } X_{n+1} \\ &= \textstyle\bigsqcup X_n && \text{since } \psi_n(a_{n+1}) = a_n. \end{aligned}$$

Finally, we must prove that $\langle \bigsqcup X_0, \bigsqcup X_1, \bigsqcup X_2, \ldots \rangle$ satisfies the two conditions in Definition 16.3 for being the least upper bound of X. But this is straightforward. □

Definition 16.37 (Embedding D_n into D_∞) Mappings $\phi_{\infty,n}$ from D_∞ to D_n and $\phi_{n,\infty}$ from D_n to D_∞ are defined thus:

$$\begin{aligned} (\forall d \in D_\infty) \quad \phi_{\infty,n}(d) &= d_n; \\ (\forall a \in D_n) \quad \phi_{n,\infty}(a) &= \langle \phi_{n,0}(a),\ \phi_{n,1}(a),\ \phi_{n,2}(a),\ \ldots \rangle. \end{aligned}$$

By the way, the n-th term in the sequence for $\phi_{n,\infty}(a)$ is just a, since $\phi_{n,n} = I_{D_n}$.

Lemma 16.38 *$\langle \phi_{n,\infty}, \phi_{\infty,n} \rangle$ is a projection from D_∞ to D_n; i.e.*

(a) $\phi_{n,\infty} \in [D_n \to D_\infty]$,
$\phi_{\infty,n} \in [D_\infty \to D_n]$;

(b) $\phi_{\infty,n} \circ \phi_{n,\infty} \;=\; I_{D_n}$;

(c) $\phi_{n,\infty} \circ \phi_{\infty,n} \;\sqsubseteq\; I_{D_\infty}$.

Also, if $m \leq n$ and $d \in D_m$, then

(d) $\phi_{n,\infty}(\phi_{m,n}(d)) \;=\; \phi_{m,\infty}(d)$.

Proof Straightforward. □

Lemma 16.39 *For all $a \in D_\infty$ and all $n, r \geq 0$:*

$$\begin{array}{ll} (a) & \phi_{n+r,n}(a_{n+r}) = a_n; \\ (b) & \phi_{n,\infty}(a_n) \sqsubseteq \phi_{n+1,\infty}(a_{n+1}); \\ (c) & a = \bigsqcup_{n\geq 0} \phi_{n,\infty}(a_n) = \bigsqcup_{n\geq r} \phi_{n,\infty}(a_n). \end{array}$$

Proof (a) By the definitions of D_∞ and $\phi_{n+r,n}$.

$$\begin{array}{rcll} \text{(b)} \quad \phi_{n,\infty}(a_n) & = & \phi_{n,\infty}(\psi_n(a_{n+1})) & \text{since } a \in D_\infty \\ & = & \phi_{n+1,\infty}(\phi_n(\psi_n(a_{n+1}))) & \text{by 16.38(d)} \\ & \sqsubseteq & \phi_{n+1,\infty}(a_{n+1}) & \text{by 16.28(c).} \end{array}$$

(c) Let $X = \{\phi_{n,\infty}(a_n) : n \geq 0\}$. By (b), X is an increasing sequence. Hence X is directed, so $\bigsqcup X$ exists. Also, since X is increasing, for all $r \geq 0$ we have

$$\bigsqcup X = \bigsqcup_{n\geq r} \phi_{n,\infty}(a_n). \tag{4}$$

To prove $\bigsqcup X = a$, we must prove that $(\bigsqcup X)_p = a_p$ for all $p \geq 0$. But

$$\begin{array}{rcll} \left(\bigsqcup X\right)_p & = & \left(\bigsqcup_{n\geq p} \phi_{n,\infty}(a_n)\right)_p & \text{by (4) above} \\ & = & \bigsqcup_{n\geq p} (\phi_{n,\infty}(a_n))_p & \text{by 16.36} \\ & = & \bigsqcup_{n\geq p} \phi_{n,p}(a_n) & \text{by def. of } \phi_{n,\infty} \\ & = & \bigsqcup\{a_p\} & \text{by (a)} \\ & = & a_p. & \end{array}$$

□

Remark 16.40 By Lemma 16.28, $\phi_{n,\infty}$ embeds D_n isomorphically into D_∞; i.e. the range of $\phi_{n,\infty}$ is an isomorphic copy of D_n inside D_∞. (See 16.20, 16.21 and Figure 16:2.) So it is possible to think of each d in D_n as being the same as $\phi_{n,\infty}(d)$ in D_∞, and speak of d as if it was a member of D_∞. With this convention, Lemma 16.39(b) would imply that, for each $a \in D_\infty$,

$$a_0 \sqsubseteq a_1 \sqsubseteq a_2 \sqsubseteq \ldots,$$

and 16.39(c) would say that

$$a = \bigsqcup\{a_0, a_1, a_2, \ldots\}.$$

Thus $a_0, a_1, a_2, \ldots$ could be thought of as a sequence of better and better 'approximations' to a. Also 16.38(d) implies that, modulo isomorphism,

$$D_0 \subseteq D_1 \subseteq D_2 \subseteq \ldots D_\infty.$$

Identifying members of D_n with members of D_∞ may perhaps confuse a less mathematically experienced reader a little, so it will not be done in this book; but it is standard practice in most accounts of D_∞ and similar models of λ.

Definition 16.41 (Application in D_∞) For $a, b \in D_\infty$, the set $\{\phi_{n,\infty}(a_{n+1}(b_n)) : n \geq 0\}$ will be shown in Lemma 16.42 below to be an increasing sequence; hence it has a l.u.b. Define

$$a \bullet b \;=\; \bigsqcup_{n\geq 0} \phi_{n,\infty}(a_{n+1}(b_n)).$$

Viewed in the light of Remark 16.40 above, $a \bullet b$ is the l.u.b. of an increasing sequence of approximations, $a_{n+1}(b_n)$. This is the modification of the simple definition of application in Discussion 16.23, that is needed to make D_∞ into a λ-model.

Lemma 16.42 *For all $a, b \in D_\infty$,*

$$\phi_{n,\infty}(a_{n+1}(b_n)) \;\sqsubseteq\; \phi_{n+1,\infty}(a_{n+2}(b_{n+1})).$$

Proof First,

$$\begin{aligned} \phi_n(a_{n+1}(b_n)) &= \phi_n\big(\psi_{n+1}(a_{n+2})(\psi_n(b_{n+1}))\big) && \text{since } a, b \in D_\infty \\ &\sqsubseteq \phi_n\big(\psi_n(a_{n+2}(b_{n+1}))\big) && \text{by 16.29(a)} \\ &\sqsubseteq a_{n+2}(b_{n+1}) && \text{by 16.28(c).} \end{aligned}$$

Next, apply $\phi_{n+1,\infty}$ to both sides and use 16.38(d). □

Corollary 16.42.1 *For all $a, b \in D_\infty$ and all $r \geq 0$:*

(a) $a \bullet b \;=\; \bigsqcup_{n\geq r} \phi_{n,\infty}(a_{n+1}(b_n))$;

(b) $(a \bullet b)_r \;=\; \bigsqcup_{n\geq r} \phi_{n,r}(a_{n+1}(b_n))$;

(c) $(a \bullet b)_r \;\sqsupseteq\; a_{r+1}(b_r)$.

Proof (a) By 16.41 and 16.42.
(b) By (a) and 16.36 and the definition of $\phi_{n,\infty}$.
(c) By (b) and 16.42. □

Definition 16.43 (Interpreting combinations of variables) Recall that *Vars* is the set of all variables in λ and CL. A *combination of variables* is a λ- or CL-term built from variables by application only (i.e. containing no λs or combinators). Let ρ be any mapping from *Vars* to D_∞. Then ρ generates an interpretation in D_∞ of every combination of variables, thus:

(a) $[\![x]\!]_\rho \;=\; \rho(x)$;

(b) $[\![PQ]\!]_\rho \;=\; [\![P]\!]_\rho \bullet [\![Q]\!]_\rho$.

Definition 16.44 Let $n \geq 0$. Then every mapping ρ from *Vars* to D_∞ generates, for every combination M of variables, not only the interpretation in D_∞ defined above, but also an interpretation $[\![M]\!]^n_\rho$ in D_n defined as follows:

(a) $[\![x]\!]^n_\rho \;=\; (\rho(x))_n$;

(b) $[\![PQ]\!]^n_\rho \;=\; [\![P]\!]^{n+1}_\rho([\![Q]\!]^n_\rho)$.

Example 16.45 Let $\rho(x) = a$, $\rho(y) = b$, and $\rho(z) = c$. Then

(a) $[\![xz(yz)]\!]^n_\rho \;=\; a_{n+2}(c_{n+1})(b_{n+1}(c_n))$;

(b) $[\![xx]\!]^n_\rho \;=\; a_{n+1}(a_n)$.

Remark 16.46 The interpretation $[\![M]\!]^n_\rho$ can be thought of as an 'approximation' to $[\![M]\!]_\rho$. In fact Lemma 16.48(a) below will show that as n increases, $[\![M]\!]^n_\rho$ approximates closer and closer to $[\![M]\!]_\rho$, in the sense that

$$[\![M]\!]_\rho \;=\; \bigsqcup_{n\geq 0} \phi_{n,\infty}([\![M]\!]^n_\rho).$$

This idea of approximation can, with some work, be extended from combinations of variables to λ-terms in general. Although it is a semantic concept, it gave rise in the 1970s to a new technique on the syntactical side, which involved assigning natural-number labels to parts of λ-terms, and this led to a sort of type-theory. Properties of this 'labelled λ-calculus' led to deep results about the behaviour of terms in pure untyped λ-calculus; see [Bar84, Chapter 14].

The following two lemmas will be needed in proving that D_∞ is a λ-model.

Lemma 16.47 *For all combinations M of variables, all $\rho : Vars \to D_\infty$, and all $n, r \geq 0$:*

(a) $\psi_n([\![M]\!]_\rho^{n+1}) \sqsupseteq [\![M]\!]_\rho^n$;

(b) $\phi_{n+r,n}([\![M]\!]_\rho^{n+r}) \sqsupseteq [\![M]\!]_\rho^n$;

(c) $\phi_{n+r,\infty}([\![M]\!]_\rho^{n+r}) \sqsupseteq \phi_{n,\infty}([\![M]\!]_\rho^n)$.

Proof

(a) By induction on M. The induction step uses 16.29(a).

(b) By (a) iterated.

(c) The key is the case $r = 1$. For this case,

$$\begin{aligned} \phi_{n+1,\infty}([\![M]\!]_\rho^{n+1}) &\sqsupseteq \phi_{n+1,\infty}(\phi_n(\psi_n([\![M]\!]_\rho^{n+1}))) && \text{by 16.28(c)} \\ &\sqsupseteq \phi_{n+1,\infty}(\phi_n([\![M]\!]_\rho^n)) && \text{by (a) above} \\ &= \phi_{n,\infty}([\![M]\!]_\rho^n) && \text{by 16.38(d).} \end{aligned}$$

□

Lemma 16.48 *For all combinations M of variables, all $\rho : Vars \to D_\infty$, and all $n, r \geq 0$:*

(a) $[\![M]\!]_\rho = \bigsqcup_{n \geq r} \phi_{n,\infty}([\![M]\!]_\rho^n)$;

(b) $([\![M]\!]_\rho)_r = \bigsqcup_{n \geq r} \phi_{n,r}([\![M]\!]_\rho^n)$.

Proof

(a) By (b) and 16.47(c) and the definition of $\phi_{n,\infty}$.

(b) By induction on M, as follows.

Basis ($M \equiv x$): Let $\rho(x) = d \in D_\infty$. Then $\phi_{n,r}(d_n) = d_r$ when $n \geq r$, by 16.39(a), so

$$\bigsqcup_{n \geq r} \phi_{n,r}([\![x]\!]_\rho^n) = \bigsqcup_{n \geq r} \phi_{n,r}(d_n) = \bigsqcup_{n \geq r} d_r = d_r.$$

Induction-step ($M \equiv PQ$): First,

$$\begin{aligned} ([\![PQ]\!]_\rho)_r &= \bigsqcup_{n \geq r} \phi_{n,r}\Big(([\![P]\!]_\rho)_{n+1}(([\![Q]\!]_\rho)_n)\Big) && \text{by 16.42.1(b)} \\ &= \bigsqcup_{n \geq r} \phi_{n,r}\Big(\Big(\bigsqcup_{p \geq n+1} \phi_{p,n+1}([\![P]\!]_\rho^p)\Big)\Big(\bigsqcup_{q \geq n} \phi_{q,n}([\![Q]\!]_\rho^q)\Big)\Big) \\ & && \text{by induction hypothesis} \end{aligned}$$

$$= \bigsqcup_{n\geq r} \bigsqcup_{p\geq n+1} \bigsqcup_{q\geq n} a_{n,p,q} \qquad \text{by continuity,}$$

where

$$a_{n,p,q} \;=\; \phi_{n,r}\Big(\phi_{p,n+1}([\![P]\!]^p_\rho)(\phi_{q,n}([\![Q]\!]^q_\rho))\Big). \tag{5}$$

Now by 16.47(b) applied to P and Q,

$$a_{n,p,q} \;\sqsupseteq\; \phi_{n,r}([\![P]\!]^{n+1}_\rho([\![Q]\!]^n_\rho)) \;=\; \phi_{n,r}([\![PQ]\!]^n_\rho).$$

This gives us half of (b), namely

$$\big([\![PQ]\!]_\rho\big)_r \;\sqsupseteq\; \bigsqcup_{n\geq r} \phi_{n,r}([\![PQ]\!]^n_\rho). \tag{6}$$

To complete (b) we must prove that the left side of (6) $\sqsubseteq$ the right side. For this, it is enough to prove that for each triple n, p, q in (5) there is an $m \geq r$ such that

$$a_{n,p,q} \;\sqsubseteq\; \phi_{m,r}([\![PQ]\!]^m_\rho). \tag{7}$$

Choose $m = \max\{p-1, q\}$. Then $m+1 \geq p \geq n+1$ and $m \geq r$, and

$$\begin{aligned}\phi_{p,n+1}([\![P]\!]^p_\rho) \;&\sqsubseteq\; (\phi_{p,n+1} \circ \phi_{m+1,p})([\![P]\!]^{m+1}_\rho) \qquad \text{by 16.47(b)}\\ &=\; (\psi_{n+1} \circ \ldots \circ \psi_m)([\![P]\!]^{m+1}_\rho).\end{aligned}$$

Similarly

$$\begin{aligned}\phi_{q,n}([\![Q]\!]^q_\rho) \;&\sqsubseteq\; (\phi_{q,n} \circ \phi_{m,q})([\![Q]\!]^m_\rho)\\ &=\; (\psi_n \circ \ldots \circ \psi_{m-1})([\![Q]\!]^m_\rho).\end{aligned}$$

Hence

$$\begin{aligned}a_{n,p,q} &\sqsubseteq \phi_{n,r}\Big((\psi_{n+1} \circ \ldots \circ \psi_m)([\![P]\!]^{m+1}_\rho)((\psi_n \circ \ldots \circ \psi_{m-1})([\![Q]\!]^m_\rho))\Big)\\ &\sqsubseteq (\phi_{n,r} \circ \psi_n \circ \ldots \circ \psi_{m-1})([\![P]\!]^{m+1}_\rho([\![Q]\!]^m_\rho))\\ &\qquad\qquad \text{by 16.29(a) iterated}\\ &= \phi_{m,r}([\![PQ]\!]^m_\rho). \qquad \text{which proves (7).}\end{aligned}$$

□

Example 16.49 Let $M \equiv xz(yz)$, and $\rho(x) = a$, $\rho(y) = b$, $\rho(z) = c$. Then Lemma 16.48(a) implies that

$$a \bullet c \bullet (b \bullet c) \;=\; \bigsqcup_{n\geq 0} \phi_{n,\infty}\Big(a_{n+2}(c_{n+1})(b_{n+1}(c_n))\Big).$$

16E D_∞ is a λ-model

To prove that D_∞ is a λ-model, it is quickest to first show that it is an extensional combinatory algebra and then use Theorem 15.30.

Definition 16.50 Using the k_n from Exercise 16.30, define

$$k = \langle \bot_0,\ I_{D_0},\ k_2,\ k_3,\ k_4,\ \ldots \rangle.$$

Lemma 16.51 *The above k is a member of D_∞. And, for all $a, b \in D_\infty$,*

$$k \bullet a \bullet b = a.$$

Proof First, k satisfies the conditions in 16.34 for membership of D_∞, by 16.30. Next, we apply 16.48(b) to $M \equiv uxy$ and $\rho(u) = k$, $\rho(x) = a$, $\rho(y) = b$. This gives

$$\begin{aligned}
(k \bullet a \bullet b)_r &= \bigsqcup_{n \geq r} \phi_{n,r}(k_{n+2}(a_{n+1})(b_n)) && \text{by 16.48(b)}\\
&= \bigsqcup_{n \geq r} \phi_{n,r}(\psi_n(a_{n+1})) && \text{by 16.30}\\
&= \bigsqcup \{a_r\} && \text{by 16.39(a)}\\
&= a_r && \text{since } \{a_r\} \text{ is a singleton.}
\end{aligned}$$

□

Definition 16.52 Using the s_n from Note 16.31, define

$$s = \langle \bot_0,\ I_{D_0},\ \psi_2(s_3),\ s_3,\ s_4,\ \ldots \rangle.$$

Lemma 16.53 *The above s is a member of D_∞. And, for all $a, b, c \in D_\infty$,*

$$s \bullet a \bullet b \bullet c = a \bullet c \bullet (b \bullet c).$$

Proof First, $s \in D_\infty$ by 16.31. Next, we apply 16.48(b) to $M \equiv uxyz$ and $\rho(u) = s$, $\rho(x) = a$, $\rho(y) = b$, $\rho(z) = c$. This gives

$$(s \bullet a \bullet b \bullet c)_r = \bigsqcup_{n \geq r} \phi_{n,r}\Big(s_{n+3}(a_{n+2})(b_{n+1})(c_n)\Big) \quad \text{by 16.48(b)}$$

$$= \bigsqcup_{n\geq r} \phi_{n,r}\Big(a_{n+2}(\phi_n(c_n))(b_{n+1}(c_n))\Big) \quad \text{by 16.31.}$$

Now $\phi_n(c_n) = \phi_n(\psi_n(c_{n+1})), \sqsubseteq c_{n+1}$ by 16.28(c), so

$$\begin{aligned}(s \bullet a \bullet b \bullet c)_r &\sqsubseteq \bigsqcup_{n\geq r} \phi_{n,r}\Big(a_{n+2}(c_{n+1})(b_{n+1}(c_n))\Big)\\ &= (a \bullet c \bullet (b \bullet c))_r \qquad \text{by 16.49.}\end{aligned}$$

To complete the lemma, we must prove $(s\bullet a\bullet b\bullet c)_r \sqsupseteq (a\bullet c\bullet(b\bullet c))_r$. By above, but taking the l.u.b. for $n \geq r+1$ not $n \geq r$ (which is permitted because the sequence involved is increasing), we have

$$(s \bullet a \bullet b \bullet c)_r = \bigsqcup_{n\geq r+1} \phi_{n,r}\Big(a_{n+2}(\phi_n(c_n))(b_{n+1}(c_n))\Big)$$

$$= \bigsqcup_{n\geq r+1} \phi_{n-1,r}\Big(\psi_{n-1}(a_{n+2}(\phi_n(c_n))(b_{n+1}(c_n)))\Big) \quad \text{by def. of } \phi_{n,r}$$

$$\sqsupseteq \bigsqcup_{n\geq r+1} \phi_{n-1,r}\Big(\psi_{n+1}(a_{n+2})(\psi_n(\phi_n(c_n)))(\psi_n(b_{n+1})(\psi_{n-1}(c_n)))\Big)$$

by 16.29

$$= \bigsqcup_{n\geq r+1} \phi_{n-1,r}\Big(a_{n+1}(c_n)(b_n(c_{n-1}))\Big) \quad \text{by 16.28(b) and def. of } D_\infty$$

$$= (a \bullet c \bullet (b \bullet c))_r$$

by 16.49 and since $\bigsqcup_{n\geq r+1}(\ldots(n-1)\ldots) = \bigsqcup_{n\geq r}(\ldots(n)\ldots)$.

□

Theorem 16.54 *The structure $\langle D_\infty, \bullet\rangle$ is extensional; i.e. if $a \bullet c = b \bullet c$ for all c, then $a = b$.*

Proof To prove $a = b$, it is enough to prove $a_{r+1} = b_{r+1}$ for all $r \geq 0$. (This will imply that $a_0 = b_0$ too, because $a_0 = \psi_0(a_1) = \psi_0(b_1) = b_0$.) Now a_{r+1} and b_{r+1} are functions, so to prove them equal it is enough to prove

$$(\forall d \in D_r) \quad a_{r+1}(d) = b_{r+1}(d). \tag{8}$$

Let $d \in D_r$; define $c = \phi_{r,\infty}(d)$, so $c_n = \phi_{r,n}(d)$ for $n \geq 0$. Then

$$(a \bullet c)_r = \bigsqcup_{n\geq r} \phi_{n,r}(a_{n+1}(\phi_{r,n}(d))) \qquad \text{by 16.42.1(b)}$$

$$= \bigsqcup_{n\geq r} (\psi_r \circ \ldots \circ \psi_{n-2} \circ \psi_{n-1} \circ a_{n+1} \circ \phi_{n-1} \circ \phi_{n-2} \circ \ldots \circ \phi_r)(d)$$

$$= \bigsqcup_{n\geq r} (\psi_r \circ \ldots \circ \psi_{n-2} \circ (\psi_n(a_{n+1})) \circ \phi_{n-2} \circ \ldots \circ \phi_r)(d)$$

by def. of ψ_n

$$= \bigsqcup_{n\geq r} (\psi_r \circ \ldots \circ \psi_{n-2} \circ a_n \circ \phi_{n-2} \circ \ldots \circ \phi_r)(d) \qquad \text{since } a \in D_\infty$$

$$= \bigsqcup_{n\geq r} a_{r+1}(d) \qquad \text{by repeating the above}$$

$$= a_{r+1}(d).$$

Similarly $(b \bullet c)_r = b_{r+1}(d)$. So if $a \bullet c = b \bullet c$ for all c, then $a_{r+1}(d) = b_{r+1}(d)$ for all $d \in D_r$. This is (8). □

Theorem 16.55 *D_∞ is an extensional λ-model.*

Proof By 16.51, 16.53, 16.54 and 15.30. □

Now that D_∞ has been proved to be a λ-model, a few interesting properties will be stated without proof.

Lemma 16.56 *Application in D_∞ is continuous in both variables; i.e.*

(a) $a \bullet (\bigsqcup X) = \bigsqcup\{a \bullet b : b \in X\}$,

(b) $(\bigsqcup X) \bullet b = \bigsqcup\{a \bullet b : a \in X\}$.

Proof Straightforward. [Bar84, Lemma 1.2.12 and Proposition 18.2.11 (18.3.11 in 1st edn.)]. □

Theorem 16.57

(a) A function from D_∞ to D_∞ is continuous iff it is representable in D_∞.

(b) $[D_\infty \to D_\infty]$ is a c.p.o. and is isomorphic to D_∞.

Proof By [Bar84, Theorems 18.2.15 and 18.2.16, or 18.3.15 and 18.3.16 in 1st edn.]. □

Theorem 16.58 *For every c.p.o. D: every $\phi \in [D \to D]$ has a fixed-point (i.e. a member p of D such that $\phi(p) = p$), and the least fixed point of ϕ is*

$$p_\phi = \bigsqcup_{n\geq 0} \phi^n(\bot).$$

Proof Straightforward. □

Theorem 16.59 *For D_∞, the operation of finding the least fixed-point is 'representable' in D_∞; in fact if Y is any fixed-point combinator, i.e. any combinator such that $Yx =_\beta x(Yx)$, then, for all $\phi \in [D_\infty \to D_\infty]$ and all $f \in D_\infty$ representing ϕ,*

$$[\![Y]\!] \bullet f \;=\; p_\phi.$$

Proof By [Bar84, Section 19.3]. □

Remark 16.60 It is worth noting that, although the relation '$D_\infty \models M = N$' is a semantic one, it can also be characterized in terms of pure syntax. The syntactical structures needed to do this are called 'Böhm trees' [Bar84, Chapter 10]; they are well beyond the scope of this book, but here is the characterization theorem anyway.

Theorem 16.61 *If M and N are λ-terms, $D_\infty \models M = N$ iff the Böhm trees of M and N have the same 'infinite η-normal form'.*

Proof By [Bar84, Corollary 19.2.10 (or 19.2.13 in 1st edn.)], based on the original proofs in [Hyl76] and [Wad76, Wad78]. □

Remark 16.62 The D_∞-construction in this chapter differs slightly from Scott's original one, which used complete lattices not c.p.o.s. A complete lattice is a c.p.o. in which every subset has a l.u.b. (not just every directed subset), so Scott avoided all problems of proving that l.u.b.s exist. But c.p.o.s became important in later work on other λ-models, so they have been introduced and used as the main tool here. (The c.p.o. approach was first advocated by Gordon Plotkin.)

In fact the only difference between using c.p.o.s and using lattices is in the starting-set D_0. That set was taken to be $\mathbb{N}^+$ here, but any other c.p.o. or complete lattice would have done just as well, and the rest of the construction would not have been affected. Furthermore, the proof of Theorem 16.61, which characterizes the set of equations $M = N$ satisfied by D_∞, turns out to be independent of D_0, so that set of equations is independent of D_0.

16F Some other models

Since D_∞ was made in 1969, many other ways of building λ-models have been found. A few will be described briefly after the next definition.

Definition 16.63 Two λ-models $\mathbb{D}_1$, $\mathbb{D}_2$ are called *equationally equivalent* iff they satisfy the same set of equations $M = N$ (M, N λ-terms).

16.64 The model D_A (Engeler) For any non-empty set A, define $G(A)$ to be the smallest set such that

(i) $A \subseteq G(A)$,

(ii) if $\alpha \subseteq G(A)$ is finite and $m \in G(A)$, then $(\alpha \rightarrow m) \in G(A)$, where '$(\alpha \rightarrow m)$' denotes any ordered-pair construction (such that $(\alpha \rightarrow m) \notin A$).

Define $D_A = \mathcal{P}(G(A))$, the set of all subsets of $G(A)$. Then, for all $a, b \in D_A$, define

$$a \bullet b = \{ m \in G(A) : (\exists \text{ finite } \beta \subseteq b) \ (\beta \rightarrow m) \in a \},$$

$$\Lambda(a) = \{ (\beta \rightarrow m) : \beta \text{ finite } \subseteq G(A) \text{ and } m \in a \bullet \beta \}.$$

Then $\langle D_A, \bullet, \Lambda \rangle$ is a λ-model, by [Lon83, Theorem 2.3]. The terms **K**, **S** and $\lambda xy.xy$ are interpreted in D_A thus:

$$k = \{ (\alpha \rightarrow (\beta \rightarrow m)) : \alpha, \beta \text{ finite } \subseteq G(A) \text{ and } m \in \alpha \},$$

$$s = \{ (\alpha \rightarrow (\beta \rightarrow (\gamma \rightarrow m))) : \alpha, \beta, \gamma \text{ finite } \subseteq G(A) \text{ and } m \in \alpha \bullet \gamma \bullet (\beta \bullet \gamma) \},$$

$$e = \{ (\alpha \rightarrow (\beta \rightarrow m)) : \alpha, \beta \text{ finite } \subseteq G(A) \text{ and } m \in \alpha \bullet \beta \}.$$

This D_A is the shortest known model-construction, apart from term-models. It is due to Erwin Engeler [Eng81], though a very similar idea had occurred earlier to Gordon Plotkin, see [Plo93, Part I Section 2, written in 1972]. A similar idea had also been invented by Robert Meyer to build a model of the theory CLw of weak reduction (not equality), [MBP91, Section 5, 'Fool's Model', dating from about 1973].

Sample properties of D_A:

(a) For no set A is D_A extensional, [Eng81, Section 2].

(b) D_A is equationally equivalent to the Böhm tree model mentioned in 16.67 below, [Lon83, Proposition 2.8].

(c) The above definition of Λ is not the only possible one that makes $\langle D_A, \bullet, \Lambda\rangle$ a λ-model; there exist others which make the resulting model satisfy different sets of equations, [Lon83, Theorem 4.1].

(d) Every applicative structure $\langle B, \bullet\rangle$ can be isomorphically embedded into $\langle D_B, \bullet\rangle$, [Eng81, Section 1].

16.65 The model $\mathcal{P}\omega$ (Plotkin, Scott) This model will look at first sight like a special case of D_A, with some trivial differences. But these differences will not be as trivial as they seem.

Let $\mathcal{P}\omega$ be the set of all subsets of $\mathbb{N}$. Let $\subseteq$ be set-inclusion as usual. For all $i, j \in \mathbb{N}$, let $\lceil i, j \rceil$ be the number corresponding to the pair $\langle i, j\rangle$ in some given recursive one-to-one coding of ordered pairs in $\mathbb{N}$, for example the coding shown at the end of Note 10.4. Let $\alpha_0, \alpha_1, \alpha_2, \ldots$ be some given recursive enumeration of all the finite sets of natural numbers. For each α_i and each $m \in \mathbb{N}$, the notation '$(\alpha_i \to m)$' will be used for $\lceil i, m \rceil$.

Define, for $a, b \in \mathcal{P}\omega$,

$$a \bullet b = \{ m \in \mathbb{N} : (\exists \alpha_i \subseteq b)\big((\alpha_i \to m) \in a\big)\},$$

$$\Lambda(a) = \{ (\alpha_i \to m) : m \in a \bullet \alpha_i \}.$$

The construction-details can be found in [Bar84, Section 18.1 (18.2 in 1st edn.)]. Proofs of basic properties, including that $\langle \mathcal{P}\omega, \bullet, \Lambda\rangle$ is a λ-model, are in [Bar84, Sections 19.1 and 19.3] and [Sco76].

Sample properties:

(a) $\mathcal{P}\omega$ is not extensional [Sco76, Theorem 1.2(iii)].

(b) $\mathcal{P}\omega$ is equationally equivalent to the Böhm tree model mentioned in 16.67 below [Bar84, Corollary 19.1.19(ii)].

(c) $\mathcal{P}\omega$ is a complete lattice. Also $[\mathcal{P}\omega \to \mathcal{P}\omega] = (\mathcal{P}\omega \to \mathcal{P}\omega)_{rep}$ [Bar84, Corollary 18.2.8 (18.1.8 in 1st edn.)].

(d) Each of the combinatory algebras $\langle \mathcal{P}\omega, \bullet\rangle$ and $\langle D_A, \bullet\rangle$ can be isomorphically embedded into the other (if A is countable), but they are not isomorphic [Lon83, Propositions 4.7, 4.10].

Other properties of $\mathcal{P}\omega$ can be found in [San79], [BL84, Section 2], [LM84], and [Koy84]. This model was chosen by Stoy to be the basis of his textbook on denotational semantics, [Sto77].

Warning: $P\omega$ is really a set of models, not just a single model. In fact, different codings $\lceil i, m \rceil$ and enumerations $\alpha_0, \alpha_1, \alpha_2, \ldots$ give different versions of $P\omega$, which all have the above properties, but may differ interestingly in some other ways; see [BB79] or [Bar84, Exercise 19.4.7]. Models built by the $P\omega$ method are called *graph models.*[1]

16.66 Filter models (Coppo, Dezani and collaborators) Types are usually introduced into λ-calculus to restrict the set of terms which can be formed, so models of typed λ are in principle simpler to build than models of untyped λ. But there is an alternative type-system, that of *intersection types*, from which a wide variety of models can be constructed, called *filter models.* And these are models of untyped λ, although derived from a type-system. The first explicit description of a filter model was in [BCD83]. But also D_∞ can be viewed as a filter model, see [ADH04, Theorem 6]. For some introductions to intersection types, see the reading list at the end of Chapter 12 of the present book; some constructions and studies of filter models can be found in [CDHL84], [CDZ87] and [ABD06].

16.67 Some other models

Term models: for each formal theory whose axioms and rules include those of $\lambda\beta$, the corresponding term model, defined as in 15.16, is a λ-model.

Barendregt's Böhm-tree model $\mathcal{B}$ has trees of syntactical expressions as its members. (Not all these trees are finite.) Its construction and basic properties are described in [Bar84, Section 18.3 (18.4 in 1st edn.)]. One of these properties is

$$\mathcal{B} \models M = N \iff M \text{ has the same Böhm tree as } N.$$

Plotkin's model $\mathcal{T}^\omega$ was described in [Plo78]. Its properties are similar to $\mathcal{P}\omega$, but it is not a lattice. In [BL80] it is proved to be equationally equivalent to the Böhm tree model, and hence to $\mathcal{P}\omega$ and D_A.

Sanchis' hypergraph structure is a development of the $\mathcal{P}\omega$ construction, see [San79]. It is an interesting example of a combinatory algebra which is not a λ-model; the latter fact was proved in [Koy84, Chapter 4].

J. Zashev has described two general procedures for generating combinatory algebras; see [Zas01, pp. 1733–1734, and comments in Section 5]. He points out that some of these algebras are λ-models, one being

[1] By (b) above, all graph models are equationally equivalent. But this does not imply that they are isomorphic or even have the same cardinality; there are many differences between mathematical structures that cannot be expressed in the language of $\lambda\beta$.

closely related to $P\omega$, and refers to work of D. Skordev dating back to 1976.

Remark 16.68 (Other approaches to model-building) Roughly speaking, in building a λ-model the main problem has been to create a structure $\langle D, \bullet \rangle$ such that the members of D behave like functions, and yet $a \bullet b$ is defined for all $a, b \in D$. However, there are also some other approaches to the semantics of λ and CL.

(1) One could change the set-theory in which models are defined and built. The usual Zermelo–Fraenkel set theory has an *axiom of foundation* which prevents self-memberships $a \in a$ and infinite descending $\in$-chains $\{a_{n+1} \in a_n : n \geq 1\}$ from existing. In a *non-well-founded set theory* this axiom is altered, such chains can exist, and one can build λ-models $\langle D, \bullet \rangle$ whose members are genuine functions and whose $\bullet$ is genuine function-application. This was first proposed and done by von Rimscha, [Rim80]. Some comments on non-well-founded models are in [Plo93, pp. 375–377], and a readable general account of non-well-founded set theories is the short book [Acz88].

(2) One could abandon the requirement that $a \bullet b$ be defined for all a and b. This results in structures that may be called *partial models.* Two examples are:

(a) *Uniformly reflexive structures* (*u.r.s.s*). These are models of a certain axiomatized abstract theory of partial recursive functions. The simplest u.r.s. is the set $\mathbb{N}$ with $a \bullet b$ defined as $\{a\}(b)$, where $\{a\}$ is the partial recursive function whose Gödel number is a. If $\{a\}(b)$ has no output-value, then $a \bullet b$ is not defined, so the model is not 'total'. The u.r.s. concept first appeared in [Str68] and [Wag69], and was also studied in [Fri71, Bye82a, Bye82b] and the references in them.

(b) *Models of typed λ-calculi.* As mentioned at the end of Chapter 15, this concept of model first appeared in [Hen50, pp. 83–84]. In it, $a \bullet b$ is only defined when the types of a and b are suitably related, otherwise the concept is like that of model of untyped λ.

(3) One could build a model of a theory of reduction instead of equality. Examples are the 'Fool's Model' in [MBP91, Section 5] for CLw, and the similar model in [Plo94, Section 4] for $\lambda\beta$.

(4) Another alternative approach originated in the field of algebraic logic: *lambda abstraction algebras* are related to λ-calculus like boolean algebras are related to propositional logic, and cylindric and polyadic

algebras to predicate logic (roughly speaking). They are described in [PS95] and [PS98]; also [Sal00] contains a useful short survey (besides some original results).

Further reading

Chapters 5 and 18–20 of [Bar84] give a more advanced treatment of λ-models than the present book. Chapter 5 covers the various definitions of the model concept; Chapter 18 describes the constructions of $\mathcal{P}\omega$, D_∞ and the Böhm-tree model; Chapter 19 gives some of their key structural properties, and Chapter 20 looks at a few general properties of models.

For D_∞, the relevant passages of [Bar84] are Sections 1.2, 5.4, 18.2, 19.2–3 and parts of Chapter 20. Analyses of the structure of D_∞ are included in [Hyl76] and [Wad76, Wad78]. Also [Sco76] is partly about D_∞. Of Scott's original accounts of D_∞, the earliest were only handwritten and copies are hard to find, but those published include [Sco70b], [Sco72], [Sco73], [Sco80a], [Sco82a] and [Sco82b].

For $P\omega$, the relevant passages of [Bar84] are Sections 18.1, 19.1, 19.3, and parts of Chapter 20. For discussion and motivation besides technical results, [Sco76] is still of interest.

Plotkin's original 1972 proposal for a model like D_A was eventually published in [Plo93, Part I]. A later discussion of D_A and $P\omega$ and similar models is in [Plo93, Part II].

For more recent work on graph models two very useful sources are the survey papers [Ber00] and [Ber05], and the substantial bibliographies they contain.

Part of the motivation for building λ-models lay in *denotational semantics*, the approach to the semantics of programming languages which was first proposed in the 1960s by Christopher Strachey in Oxford. The invention of D_∞ and $P\omega$ turned this subject into a major branch of computer science. The handbook article [Mos90] is a suitable introduction, and other introductions are in the textbooks [Gun92] and [Win01], as well as the older book [Sto77] by one of the subject's pioneers.

In the field of mathematics, the ideas involved in D_∞ also gave rise to a new subject, *domain theory*. Introductions to this subject can be found in [Gun92], [Rey98] and [Win01], and more technical accounts can be found in, for example, [AJ94] and [GHK+03].

Appendix A1
Bound variables and α-conversion

In Chapter 1 the technicalities of bound variables, substitution and α-conversion were merely outlined. This is the best approach at the beginning. Indeed, most accounts of λ omit details of these, and simply assume that clashes between bound and free variables can always be avoided without problems; see, for example, the 'variable convention' in [Bar84, Section 2.1.13]. The purpose of this appendix is to show how that assumption can be justified.

Before starting, it is worth mentioning two points. First, there is a notation for λ-calculus that avoids bound variables completely. It was invented by N. G. de Bruijn, see [Bru72], and in it each bound variable-occurrence is replaced by a number showing its 'distance' from its binding λ, in a certain sense. De Bruijn's notation has been found useful when coding λ-terms for machine manipulation; examples are in [Alt93, Hue94, KR95]. But, as remarked in [Pol93, pp. 314–315], it does not lead to a particularly simple definition of substitution, and most human workers still find the classical notation easier to read.

For such workers, the details of α-conversion would not be avoided by de Bruijn's notation, but would simply be moved from the stage of manipulating terms to that of translating between the two notations.

The second point to note is shown by the following two examples: if we simply deleted $\equiv_\alpha$ from the rules of λ-calculus, we would lose the confluence of both $\triangleright_{\beta\eta}$ and $\triangleright_\beta$. Thus there is no way to entirely avoid dealing with $\equiv_\alpha$ in the standard λ-notation.

Example A1.1 Let $P \equiv \lambda x.((\lambda y.y)x)$. Then P is an η-redex and contains a β-redex $(\lambda y.y)x$, and

$$P \triangleright_{1\eta} \lambda y.y, \qquad P \triangleright_{1\beta} \lambda x.x,$$

and without $\equiv_\alpha$ these cannot be reduced to the same term.

Example A1.2 Let $P \equiv (\lambda x.(\lambda y.yx))Q$, where $Q \equiv (\lambda u.v)y$. Then Q is a β-redex and $Q \triangleright_{1\beta} v$, so

$$\begin{array}{rll} P & \triangleright_{1\beta} & (\lambda x.(\lambda y.yx))v \\ & \triangleright_{1\beta} & [v/x](\lambda y.yx) \\ & \equiv & \lambda y.yv. \end{array}$$

Also P is a β-redex, and

$$\begin{array}{rlll} P & \triangleright_{1\beta} & [Q/x](\lambda y.yx) & \\ & \equiv & \lambda z.[Q/x][z/y](yx) & \text{by Chapter 1's 1.12(g),} \\ & \equiv & \lambda z.zQ & \text{where } z \notin FV(Q(yx)) \text{ so } z \not\equiv y, \\ & \triangleright_{1\beta} & \lambda z.zv. & \end{array}$$

Without $\equiv_\alpha$, we cannot reduce $\lambda y.yv$ and $\lambda z.zv$ to the same term, so $\equiv_\alpha$ cannot be avoided if we want confluence. (Also changes of bound variables cannot be avoided if we want the definition of substitution to be as general as possible.)

Exercise A1.3 By the way, the term P in the above example is not a λI-term; show that in the λI-calculus the following (typable) term P' could serve instead. Let u, v, x, y (in that order) be the first four variables of the language of λ-calculus, and define

$$P' \equiv (\lambda x.S)v, \quad \text{where} \quad S \equiv (\lambda yv.uvy)x.$$

(Show, using Chapter 1's 1.12(g) carefully, that P' β-reduces without α-steps to both $\lambda y.uyv$ and $\lambda x.uxv$.)

Hence a rigorous treatment of λ-calculus in the usual notation must include α-conversion. To do this rigorously, the commonest approach is to say that λ-calculus is not really about λ-terms, but about *equivalence-classes of λ-terms under the relation of congruence* ($\equiv_\alpha$). The individual terms are then viewed as representatives of their classes, and a proof must be given that they may be replaced by other representatives whenever necessary.

The goal of the present appendix is to justify this '*congruence-class*' approach. The main lemmas will be stated here, but their proofs will merely be sketched, as they are straightforward and boring. (Full details have been worked out in several unpublished theses, for example [Sch65, Part II, Chapter 3] and [Hin64, Chapter 4]; and other careful treatments of $\equiv_\alpha$, with discussions, are in [Pol93] and [VB03].)

The first move will be to define a simpler basic α-conversion step, and prove that it generates the same relation $\equiv_\alpha$ as the original one.

Definition A1.4 (α_0-contraction, reduction, etc.) We say that P *α_0-contracts to* Q, or $P \triangleright_{1\alpha_0} Q$, iff P can be changed to Q by replacing an occurrence of a term $\lambda x.M$ by $\lambda y.[y/x]M$, where $y \notin FV(xM)$ and neither x nor y is bound in M.

We say P *α_0-reduces to* Q, or $P \triangleright_{\alpha_0} Q$, iff P can be changed to Q by a finite (perhaps empty) series of such contractions, and P *α_0-converts to* Q, or $P \equiv_{\alpha_0} Q$, iff P can be changed to Q by a finite (perhaps empty) series of α_0-contractions and reversed α_0-contractions.

Lemma A1.5 *If $y \notin FV(xM)$ and x, y are not bound in M, then:*

(a) $[y/x]M$ is obtained by simply changing x to y throughout M;

(b) $x \notin FV([y/x]M)$, $x \not\equiv y$, and x, y are not bound in $[y/x]M$;

(c) $[x/y][y/x]M \equiv M$;

(d) $\lambda y.[y/x]M \triangleright_{1\alpha_0} \lambda x.M$, so the relation $\triangleright_{1\alpha_0}$ is symmetric;

(e) $P \equiv_{\alpha_0} Q \iff P \triangleright_{\alpha_0} Q$;

(f) $P \equiv_{\alpha_0} Q \implies FV(P) = FV(Q)$;

(g) for all $P, x_1, \ldots, x_n$, there exists P' such that $P \triangleright_{\alpha_0} P'$ and none of $x_1, \ldots, x_n$ is bound in P'.

Proof For (a): the conditions on x and y imply that the definition of $[y/x]M$ does not use Chapter 1's 1.12(g), (d). For (b): use (a) and the conditions on x and y. For (c): use (a) with x, y reversed (which holds by (b)), combined with (a). For (d): we have $\lambda y.[y/x]M \triangleright_{1\alpha_0} \lambda x.[x/y][y/x]M$ by (b), and $[x/y][y/x]M \equiv M$ by (c). For (e): use (d). For (f) and (g): use (a). □

Definition A1.6 (α-contraction) We say P *α-contracts to* Q, or $P \triangleright_{1\alpha} Q$, iff P can be changed to Q by replacing an occurrence of a term $\lambda x.M$ by $\lambda y.[y/x]M$, where $y \notin FV(M)$.

The relation $\equiv_\alpha$ was defined by a finite series of α-contractions, in Chapter 1's Definition 1.17.

In that definition of $\equiv_\alpha$, reversed contractions were not mentioned, so the symmetry of $\equiv_\alpha$ was not immediately obvious, and had to be stated as a separate lemma, Chapter 1's Lemma 1.19. The proof of that lemma was omitted. The first application of α_0 will be to fill in that gap by proving the equivalence of $\equiv_\alpha$ and $\equiv_{\alpha_0}$; see Lemma A1.8 below.

Lemma A1.7 *For all M, x and $y \notin FV(xM)$, there exists M' such that y is neither free nor bound in M' and x is not bound in M', and*

$$M \triangleright_{\alpha_0} M', \qquad [y/x]M \triangleright_{\alpha_0} [y/x]M'.$$

Proof By induction on M (i.e. on the length of M), with cases as in the definition of $[y/x]M$. □

Lemma A1.8 *Every α-contraction can be done by a series of α_0-contractions. Hence by A1.5(e) the relations $\equiv_\alpha$, $\equiv_{\alpha_0}$, $\triangleright_{\alpha_0}$ are the same.*

Proof If $y \notin FV(xM)$, then, for the M' in A1.7, we get $\lambda x.M \triangleright_{\alpha_0} \lambda x.M'$, which $\triangleright_{1\alpha_0}$ $\lambda y.[y/x]M'$, which $\triangleright_{\alpha_0}$ $\lambda y.[y/x]M$ by A1.7, A1.5(e). □

Exercise A1.9* Lemma A1.8 implies that an α-contraction can always be reversed by a series of further α-contractions. Show that it cannot always be reversed by a single α-contraction (contrary to a claim in [CF58, bottom of p. 91]).

Now, which of the lemmas in Chapter 1's Section 1B need to be proved in this appendix? The first two, 1.15 and 1.16, do not mention or depend on $\equiv_\alpha$. The next, 1.19, has just been proved above. Lemma 1.20 rests on a proof in [CF58, p. 95, Section 3E Theorem 2(c)]; that proof is adequate without the present appendix, although the use of α_0 instead of α might simplify it a little. Finally, Lemma 1.21, which says substitution is 'well-behaved' with respect to $\equiv_\alpha$, comes from the following lemma.

Lemma A1.10

(a) $M \equiv_\alpha M' \implies [N/x]M \equiv_\alpha [N/x]M'$;

(b) $N \equiv_\alpha N' \implies [N/x]M \equiv_\alpha [N'/x]M$.

Proof For (a): use [CF58, Theorem 2(a) p. 95, proof on pp. 96–103].

For (b): by Lemma A1.5(g), change M to a term M' whose bound variables do not occur in NN'. Then Chapter 1's 1.12(g) is not used in $[N/x]M'$ or $[N'/x]M'$, so it is easy to prove $[N/x]M' \equiv_\alpha [N'/x]M'$. Then use (a). □

The next four lemmas are needed in the proof of the Church-Rosser theorem, see Appendix A2. They connect β-redexes, $\equiv_\alpha$ and substitution.

Notation A1.11 The notation $\Gamma(R)$ will be used in the next lemmas for the contractum of an arbitrary redex R. So, for a β-redex $R \equiv (\lambda x.M)N$ we shall say $\Gamma(R) \equiv [N/x]M$, and for an η-redex $R \equiv \lambda x.Mx$ we shall say $\Gamma(R) \equiv M$.

Lemma A1.12 *If R is a β-redex and no variable free in xN is bound in R, then $[N/x]R$ is a β-redex and*

$$\Gamma([N/x]R) \;\equiv_\alpha\; [N/x](\Gamma(R)).$$

Proof Let $R \equiv (\lambda v.U)V$. Then $\Gamma(R) \equiv [V/v]U$. By assumption, $v \notin FV(xN)$, so, by Chapter 1's 1.12,

$$[N/x]R \;\equiv\; (\lambda v.[N/x]U)\,[N/x]V.$$

Hence

$$\begin{aligned}\Gamma([N/x]R) \;&\equiv\; [\,([N/x]V)/v\,]\,[N/x]\,U\\ &\equiv_\alpha\; [N/x]\,[V/v]\,U \qquad\qquad \text{by Chapter 1's 1.16(c), 1.20.}\end{aligned}$$

□

Lemma A1.13 *If $R \equiv_\alpha R'$ and R is a β-redex, then so is R' and*

$$\Gamma(R) \;\equiv_\alpha\; \Gamma(R').$$

Proof By A1.8 we can assume R goes to R' by one replacement $\lambda x.M \triangleright_{1\alpha_0} \lambda y.[y/x]M$. Let $R \equiv (\lambda v.U)V$. If $\lambda x.M$ is in U or V, use A1.10. If $\lambda x.M \equiv \lambda v.U$, the result comes from Chapter 1's 1.16(a) and 1.20. □

Lemma A1.14 *Let $P \equiv_\alpha P'$. Let P contain occurrences $R_1, \dots, R_n$ of some β-redexes. Then P' contains β-redex-occurrences $R'_1, \dots, R'_n$, such that, for all $i, j \le n$,*

(a) R'_i, R'_j are related (one inside the other, or non-overlapping, or identical) exactly as R_i, R_j are related;

(b) if contracting R_i changes P to P_i, then contracting R'_i changes P' to a term $P'_i \equiv_\alpha P_i$.

Proof Let $P \triangleright_{1\alpha_0} P'$ by replacing $\lambda x.M$ by $\lambda y.[y/x]M$. For those R_i containing $\lambda x.M$, use A1.13. For those in M, use A1.12 with $N \equiv y$. □

Corollary A1.14.1 (Postponement of α-conversions) *If $P \triangleright_\beta Q$ by k β-contractions with possibly some α-conversions between, then there exista a term Q' such that $P \triangleright_\beta Q'$ by k β-steps with no α-steps between, and $Q' \equiv_\alpha Q$.*

Proof By A1.14(b), case $i = 1$, used at most k times. □

By the way, Lemma A1.14 does not claim that $R_i' \equiv_\alpha R_i$. For example, let

$$P \equiv \lambda x.(\lambda u.ux)v, \quad P' \equiv \lambda y.(\lambda u.uy)v, \quad R_1 \equiv (\lambda u.ux)v.$$

Then $R_1' \equiv (\lambda u.uy)v, \not\equiv_\alpha R_1$.

Lemma A1.15 *If $P \triangleright_\beta P'$ and $Q \triangleright_\beta Q'$, then $[P/x]Q \triangleright_\beta [P'/x]Q'$.*

Proof It is enough to prove the result when $P \triangleright_{1\beta} P'$ or $P \equiv_\alpha P'$, and $Q \triangleright_{1\beta} Q'$ or $Q \equiv_\alpha Q'$. We show here only the least easy case.

If $P \triangleright_{1\beta} P'$ and $Q \triangleright_{1\beta} Q'$, first α-convert Q to a term $Q^\star$ in which no variable free in xP is bound. Then Chapter 1's 1.12(g) is not used in $[P/x]Q^\star$, and, by Chapter 1's 1.30, the same holds for $[P'/x]Q^\star$. Hence $[P/x]Q^\star \triangleright_\beta [P'/x]Q^\star$ by simply reducing the substituted occurrences of P, so, by A1.10,

$$[P/x]Q \equiv_\alpha [P/x]Q^\star \triangleright_\beta [P'/x]Q^\star.$$

But by A1.14.1 with $n = 1$, $Q^\star \triangleright_\beta Q'$ by one β-step followed by α-steps, so A1.12 and A1.10 give

$$[P'/x]Q^\star \triangleright_\beta [P'/x]Q'.$$

The other three cases, in which $P \equiv_\alpha P'$ or $Q \equiv_\alpha Q'$, are easier. □

Analogues of A1.12–A1.15 also hold for $\triangleright_\eta$, with easier proofs.

Appendix A2
Confluence proofs

Definition A2.1 (See Figure A2:1 below.) A binary relation $\triangleright$ between λ-terms or CL-terms is said to be *confluent* iff, for all terms P, M, N,

$$P \triangleright M \text{ and } P \triangleright N \implies (\exists \text{ term } T)\ M \triangleright T \text{ and } N \triangleright T. \qquad (1)$$

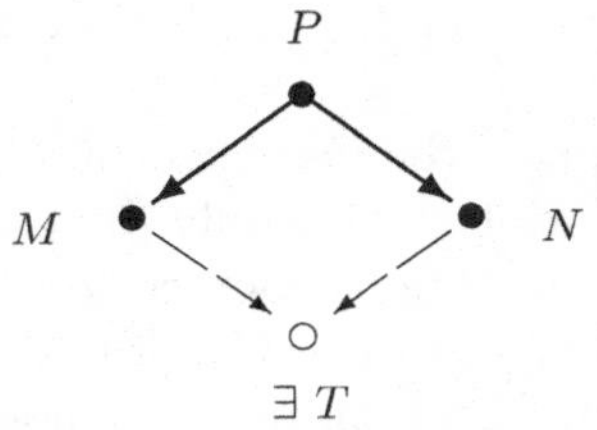

Fig. A2:1

A2A Confluence of β-reduction

This section will present a proof of Theorem 1.32 in Chapter 1, which stated that $\triangleright_\beta$ in λ-calculus is confluent. The first confluence-proof for $\triangleright_\beta$ was made by Alonzo Church and his student Barkley Rosser in 1935 [CR36, Section 1], but was not particularly simple. A much simpler proof was made in 1971 by Per Martin-Löf using a method originated by William Tait in 1965. The proof below will be based on this method and will try to show the principles behind it that make it work. (Other accounts of the Tait–Martin-Löf method can be found in [Bar84, Theorem 3.2.8] or [Tak95, Section 1].)

The next section will give outline proofs of confluence for $\triangleright_w$ in CL and several other reducibility relations, by variants of the same method.

Notation A2.2 Recall from Chapter 3's Definition 3.15 that a *β-reduction* in λ is a series (perhaps empty or infinite) of β- and α-contractions, and its *length* is the number of its β-contractions (perhaps 0 or ∞).

By Appendix A1's Lemma A1.8, we can assume all α-contractions in a reduction are α_0-contractions.

In the present appendix, *redex* always means a particular occurrence of a redex in a given term. For example, 'Let R, S be redexes in P' means 'Let R, S be occurrences of redexes in P'. For *occurrence*, see the note after Chapter 1's Definition 1.7.

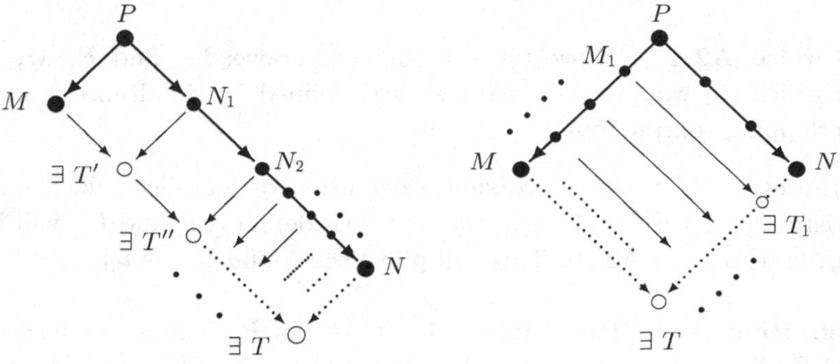

Fig. A2:2

Discussion A2.3 (Strategy for proving confluence) We might hope to prove $\triangleright_\beta$ confluent by proving the one-step relation $\triangleright_{1\beta}$ confluent, i.e.

$$P \triangleright_{1\beta} M,\ P \triangleright_{1\beta} N \implies (\exists\, T)\ M \triangleright_{1\beta} T,\ N \triangleright_{1\beta} T. \tag{2}$$

If (2) held, we could deduce (1) by the method sketched in Figure A2:2: we could first prove (1) in the special case that $P \triangleright_{1\beta} M$, by induction on the length of the reduction from P to N as shown in the left-hand diagram in Figure A2:2; and we could then deduce the general case by induction on the length of the reduction from P to M as in the right-hand part of Figure A2:2.

Unfortunately (2) is not always true. For example, let

$$P \equiv (\lambda y.uyy)(\mathsf{I}z) \qquad (\text{where } \mathsf{I} \equiv (\lambda x.x));$$

then $P \triangleright_{1\beta} u(\mathsf{I}z)(\mathsf{I}z)$ and $P \triangleright_{1\beta} (\lambda y.uyy)z$, and $(\lambda y.uyy)z \triangleright_{1\beta} uzz$, but $u(\mathsf{I}z)(\mathsf{I}z)$ cannot be reduced to uzz in just one step.

But $u(\mathsf{I}z)(\mathsf{I}z)$ can be reduced to uzz by two non-overlapping steps 'in parallel'. So our second hope might be to define a concept of 'parallel

β-reduction' $\triangleright_{1\text{par}}$, and prove

$$P \triangleright_{1\text{par}} M,\ P \triangleright_{1\text{par}} N \implies (\exists\, T)\ M \triangleright_{1\text{par}} T,\ N \triangleright_{1\text{par}} T. \qquad (3)$$

If 'parallel' was defined in such a way that every single contraction was a special case of a parallel reduction, then the confluence of $\triangleright_\beta$ would follow from (3) by the method of Figure A2.2.

Unfortunately the obvious definition, that a parallel reduction consists of simultaneous non-overlapping contractions, does not satisfy (3).

Exercise A2.4 * Prove the last sentence above; i.e. find P, M, N for which (3) would fail if 'parallel' was defined by simultaneous non-overlapping contractions.

However, there is a more subtle definition of 'parallel' which does satisfy (3); it will be given in the next two definitions, and (3) will be proved in Lemma A2.10. This will prove the confluence of $\triangleright_\beta$.

Definition A2.5 (Residuals) Let a λ-term P contain β-redexes R and S. When R is contracted, let P change to P'. The *residuals* of S with respect to R are redexes in P', defined as follows (from [CR36, pp. 473–475]).

Case 1: R, S are non-overlapping parts of P. Then contracting R leaves S unchanged. We call the unchanged S in P' the *residual* of S.

Case 2: $R \equiv S$. Then contracting R is the same as contracting S. We say S has *no residual* in P'.

Case 3: R is a proper part of S, i.e. R is a part of S and $R \not\equiv S$. Then S has form $(\lambda x.M)N$ and R is in M or in N. Contracting R changes M to a term M', or N to N'. This changes S to $(\lambda x.M')N$ or $(\lambda x.M)N'$ in P'; we call this the *residual* of S.

Case 4:[1] S is a proper part of R. Then R has form $(\lambda x.M)N$ and S is in M or in N.

Subcase 4a: S is in M. When $[N/x]M$ is formed from M, then S is changed to a redex S' with one of the forms

$$[N/x]S, \qquad [N/x][z_1/y_1]\dots[z_n/y_n]S, \qquad S,$$

depending on how many times Chapter 1's clause 1.12(g) is used in

[1] Case 4 is not needed in the confluence proof. It is included here only because it is often used in other studies of reductions.

making $[N/x]M$, and on whether S is in the scope of a λx in M. We call this S' the *residual* of S.

Subcase 4b: S is in N. When $[N/x]M$ is made, there is an occurrence of S in each substituted N. We call these the *residuals* of S. (If there are $k \geq 0$ free occurrences of x in M, then S will have k residuals.)

Definition A2.6 (Parallel reductions) Let $R_1, \ldots, R_n$ $(n \geq 0)$ be redexes in a λ-term P. An R_i is called *minimal* in $\{R_1, \ldots, R_n\}$ iff none of $R_1, \ldots, R_n$ is a proper part of R_i. A *parallel reduction* of $\{R_1, \ldots, R_n\}$ in P is a reduction obtained by first contracting a minimal R_i, then a minimal residual of $R_1, \ldots, R_n$, and continuing to contract minimal residuals until no residuals are left, and finally perhaps doing some α-conversions. Iff a parallel reduction changes P to a term Q, we say

$$P \triangleright_{1\text{par}} Q.$$

Note A2.7 Every non-empty set of redexes in a λ-term has a minimal member (and possibly more than one). Hence every set of redexes in a λ-term has at least one parallel reduction. The following are easy to prove.

(a) A parallel reduction of an n-member set has length exactly n. (Since the contracted redexes are minimal, only Cases 1–3 of Definition A2.5 apply in determining residuals, so each redex has at most one residual; hence there are $n - 1$ residuals after the first step, $n - 2$ after the second, etc.)

(b) A parallel reduction of a one-member set of redexes consists of a single contraction (perhaps followed by some α-steps). Conversely, every one-step reduction is a parallel reduction of a one-member set.

(c) A parallel reduction of the empty set is just a (perhaps empty) series of α-conversions. Conversely, every α-conversion is a parallel reduction of the empty set.

(d) An example of a non-parallel reduction is the following; the redex contracted at the second step is not a residual of any redex in P.

$$\begin{aligned} P \;\equiv\; (\lambda x.xy)(\lambda z.z) \;&\triangleright_{1\beta}\; (\lambda z.z)y \\ &\triangleright_{1\beta}\; y \qquad \equiv\; Q. \end{aligned}$$

(e) The relation $\triangleright_{1\text{par}}$ is not transitive. For example, in (d) the two contractions count as two parallel reductions by (b), but there is not a single parallel reduction from P to Q.

(f) If $M \triangleright_{1\text{par}} M'$ and $N \triangleright_{1\text{par}} N'$, then $MN \triangleright_{1\text{par}} M'N'$.

(g) If $M \triangleright_{1\text{par}} M'$, then $\lambda x.M \triangleright_{1\text{par}} \lambda x.M'$.

Lemma A2.8 (Preservation of parallel reductions by $\equiv_\alpha$) *For λ-terms and β-reduction:*

$$P \triangleright_{1\text{par}} Q \;\; \textit{and} \;\; P \equiv_\alpha P' \quad \Longrightarrow \quad P' \triangleright_{1\text{par}} Q.$$

Proof By induction on the length of the reduction from P to Q, using Lemma A1.14 in the induction step. (See also A1.14.1.) □

Lemma A2.9 (Preservation of parallel reductions by substitution) *For λ-terms and β-reduction:*

$$M \triangleright_{1\text{par}} M' \;\; \textit{and} \;\; N \triangleright_{1\text{par}} N' \quad \Longrightarrow \quad [N/x]M \triangleright_{1\text{par}} [N'/x]M'.$$

Proof By Lemma A2.8 above, and Appendix A1's Lemma A1.5(g), we may assume that no variable bound in M is free in xNM, and that the given reductions of M and N have no α-steps.

We proceed by induction on M. Let $M \triangleright_{1\text{par}} M'$ by a parallel reduction of redexes $R_1, \ldots, R_n$ in M.

Case 1: $M \equiv x$. Then n must be 0, so $M' \equiv M \equiv x$. Hence

$$[N/x]M \;\equiv\; N \;\triangleright_{1\text{par}}\; N' \;\equiv\; [N'/x]M'.$$

Case 2: $x \notin FV(M)$. Then $x \notin FV(M')$ by Chapter 1's Lemma 1.30, so

$$[N/x]M \;\equiv\; M \;\triangleright_{1\text{par}}\; M' \;\equiv\; [N'/x]M'.$$

Case 3: $M \equiv \lambda y.M_1$ and $y \not\equiv x$ and $x \in FV(M_1)$. Then each β-redex in M is in M_1. We have assumed the given reduction of M has no α-steps, so M' must have form $\lambda y.M_1'$ where $M_1 \triangleright_{1\text{par}} M_1'$. Hence

$$\begin{array}{rcll} [N/x]M & \equiv & [N/x](\lambda y.M_1) & \\ & \equiv & \lambda y.[N/x]M_1 & \text{by Ch. 1's 1.12(f) since } y \notin FV(N), \\ & \triangleright_{1\text{par}} & \lambda y.[N'/x]M_1' & \text{by induction hypothesis,} \\ & \equiv & [N'/x]M' & \text{by Ch. 1's 1.12(e), (f)} \\ & & & \quad \text{since } y \notin FV(N') \text{ by Ch. 1's 1.30.} \end{array}$$

Case 4: $M \equiv M_1 M_2$ and each R_i is in M_1 or in M_2. Then M' has form $M_1' M_2'$ where $M_j \triangleright_{1\text{par}} M_j'$ for $j = 1, 2$. Hence

$$\begin{array}{lll} [N/x]M & \equiv & ([N/x]M_1)([N/x]M_2) \\ & \triangleright_{1\text{par}} & ([N'/x]M_1')([N'/x]M_2') \text{ by ind. hyp. and A2.7(f),} \\ & \equiv & [N'/x]M'. \end{array}$$

Case 5: $M \equiv (\lambda y.L)Q$ and one R_i, say R_1, is M itself and the others are in L or Q. Then R_1 contains $R_2, \ldots, R_n$, so, by the definition of 'parallel reduction', its residual must be contracted last in the given parallel reduction of M. Hence this reduction has form

$$\begin{array}{llll} M \equiv (\lambda y.L)Q & \triangleright_{1\text{par}} & (\lambda y.L')Q' & (L \triangleright_{1\text{par}} L',\ Q \triangleright_{1\text{par}} Q') \\ & \triangleright_{1\beta} & [Q'/y]L' & \\ & \equiv & M'. & \end{array}$$

By the induction hypothesis there exist parallel reductions of $[N/x]L$ and $[N/x]Q$; each one may have some α-steps at the end, say

$$\begin{array}{llll} [N/x]L & \triangleright_{1\text{par}} & L^\star & \equiv_\alpha [N'/x]L', \\ [N/x]Q & \triangleright_{1\text{par}} & Q^\star & \equiv_\alpha [N'/x]Q', \end{array}$$

where the reductions to $L^\star$ and $Q^\star$ have no α-steps. Hence

$$\begin{array}{lll} [N/x]M \equiv & (\lambda y.[N/x]L)([N/x]Q) & \text{by Ch. 1's 1.12(c), (f)} \\ & & \text{since } y \notin FV(xN), \\ \triangleright_{1\text{par}} & (\lambda y.L^\star)Q^\star & \text{without } \alpha\text{-steps,} \\ \triangleright_{1\beta} & [Q^\star/y]L^\star & \\ \equiv_\alpha & [([N'/x]Q')/y][N'/x]L' & \text{by above and Ch. 1's 1.21,} \\ \equiv_\alpha & [N'/x][Q'/y]L' & \text{by Ch. 1's 1.16(c), 1.20, since} \\ & & y \notin FV(xNM) \supseteq FV(xN'Q'), \\ \equiv & [N'/x]M'. & \end{array}$$

The above reduction is a parallel reduction, as required. □

Lemma A2.10 (Confluence of parallel reductions) *For λ-terms and β-reduction:*

$$P \triangleright_{1\text{par}} A,\quad P \triangleright_{1\text{par}} B \quad \Longrightarrow \quad (\exists\, T)\ A \triangleright_{1\text{par}} T,\ \ B \triangleright_{1\text{par}} T.$$

Proof By Lemma A2.8 above, we may assume that the two given reductions of P have no α-steps. We shall use induction on P.

Case 1: $P \equiv x$. Then $A \equiv B \equiv P$. Choose $T \equiv P$.

Case 2: $P \equiv \lambda x.P_1$. Then all β-redexes in P are in P_1, and we have assumed the given reductions have no α-steps, so

$$A \equiv \lambda x.A_1, \qquad B \equiv \lambda x.B_1,$$

where $P_1 \triangleright_{1\mathrm{par}} A_1$ and $P_1 \triangleright_{1\mathrm{par}} B_1$. By the induction-hypothesis there exists T_1 such that

$$A_1 \triangleright_{1\mathrm{par}} T_1, \qquad B_1 \triangleright_{1\mathrm{par}} T_1.$$

Choose $T \equiv \lambda x.T_1$.

Case 3: $P \equiv P_1 P_2$ and all the redexes involved in the parallel reductions are in P_1, P_2. Then the induction-hypothesis gives us T_1 and T_2; choose $T \equiv T_1 T_2$.

Case 4: $P \equiv (\lambda x.M)N$ and just one of the given parallel reductions involves contracting P's residual; say it is $P \triangleright_{1\mathrm{par}} A$. Then that reduction has form

$$\begin{array}{rcll} P & \equiv & (\lambda x.M)N & \\ & \triangleright_{1\mathrm{par}} & (\lambda x.M')N' & (M \triangleright_{1\mathrm{par}} M',\ N \triangleright_{1\mathrm{par}} N') \\ & \triangleright_{1\beta} & [N'/x]M' & \\ & \equiv & A. & \end{array}$$

And the other given parallel reduction has form

$$\begin{array}{rcll} P & \equiv & (\lambda x.M)N & \\ & \triangleright_{1\mathrm{par}} & (\lambda x.M'')N'' & (M \triangleright_{1\mathrm{par}} M'',\ N \triangleright_{1\mathrm{par}} N'') \\ & \equiv & B. & \end{array}$$

The induction-hypothesis applied to M, N gives us M^+, N^+ such that

$$M' \triangleright_{1\mathrm{par}} M^+, \qquad M'' \triangleright_{1\mathrm{par}} M^+;$$

$$N' \triangleright_{1\mathrm{par}} N^+, \qquad N'' \triangleright_{1\mathrm{par}} N^+.$$

Choose $T \equiv [N^+/x]M^+$. Then there is a parallel reduction from A to T, thus:

$$\begin{array}{rcll} A & \equiv & [N'/x]M' & \\ & \triangleright_{1\mathrm{par}} & [N^+/x]M^+ & \text{by Lemma A2.9.} \end{array}$$

To construct a parallel reduction from B to T, first split the parallel reductions of M'' and N'' into β-part and α-part, thus:

$$M'' \triangleright_{1\mathrm{par}} M^\star \equiv_\alpha M^+, \qquad N'' \triangleright_{1\mathrm{par}} N^\star \equiv_\alpha N^+,$$

where the reductions to $M^\star$ and $N^\star$ have no α-steps. Then

$$\begin{array}{lll} B & \equiv & (\lambda x.M'')N'' \\ & \rhd_{1\mathrm{par}} & (\lambda x.M^\star)N^\star \quad \text{without } \alpha\text{-steps} \\ & \rhd_{1\beta} & [N^\star/x]M^\star \\ & \equiv_\alpha & [N^+/x]M^+ \quad \text{by Chapter 1's 1.21.} \end{array}$$

Case 5: $P \equiv (\lambda x.M)N$ and both the given parallel reductions involve contracting P's residual. Then these reductions have form

$$\begin{array}{lll} P & \equiv & (\lambda x.M)N \\ & \rhd_{1\mathrm{par}} & (\lambda x.M')N' \\ & \rhd_{1\beta} & [N'/x]M' \\ & \equiv & A, \end{array} \qquad \begin{array}{lll} P & \equiv & (\lambda x.M)N \\ & \rhd_{1\mathrm{par}} & (\lambda x.M'')N'' \\ & \rhd_{1\beta} & [N''/x]M'' \\ & \equiv & B. \end{array}$$

Apply the induction-hypothesis to M and N as in Case 4, and choose $T \equiv [N^+/x]M^+$. Then Lemma A2.9 gives the result, similarly to Case 4. □

Theorem A2.11 (= 1.32, Church-Rosser theorem for $\rhd_\beta$) *For λ-terms, the relation $\rhd_\beta$ is confluent; i.e.*

$$P \rhd_\beta M,\ P \rhd_\beta N \implies (\exists T)\ M \rhd_\beta T,\ N \rhd_\beta T.$$

Proof By A2.7(c) and (b), each α- or β-step is a special case of a parallel reduction, so P reduces to M by a finite series of parallel reductions. Similarly for N. Then the method sketched in Discussion A2.3 and Figure A2:2 gives the result. □

A2B Confluence of other reductions

Theorem A2.12 (= 7.13, Church-Rosser theorem for $\rhd_{\beta\eta}$) *For λ-terms, the relation $\rhd_{\beta\eta}$ introduced in Definitions 7.7 and 7.8 is confluent; i.e.*

$$P \rhd_{\beta\eta} M,\ P \rhd_{\beta\eta} N \implies (\exists\, T)\ M \rhd_{\beta\eta} T,\ N \rhd_{\beta\eta} T.$$

Proof First, extend Definition A2.5 (*Residuals*) to cover η-redexes. Cases 1 and 2 of that definition do not change. Case 4 is not needed here. (If desired, its details are in [CF58, Section 4B2].) Case 3 changes as follows.

Case 3η: R is a proper part of S. There are four possible subcases:

3a: $S \equiv (\lambda x.M)N$ and R is in M or N. Contracting R changes S to a term $(\lambda x.M')N$ or $(\lambda x.M)N'$; we call this the *residual* of S.

3b: $S \equiv (\lambda x.M)N$ and $R \equiv \lambda x.M$. R must be an η-redex and $M \equiv Lx$ for some L with $x \notin FV(L)$. Contracting R changes S to LN; we say S has *no residual.*

3c: $S \equiv \lambda x.Mx$ and R is in M. Contracting R changes S to $\lambda x.M'x$, for some M'. And $x \notin FV(M) \implies x \notin FV(M')$ by Chapter 7's Lemma 7.12(a). We call $\lambda x.M'x$ the *residual* of S.

3d: $S \equiv \lambda x.Mx$ and R is a β-redex $\equiv Mx$. Then $M \equiv (\lambda y.L)$ for some L, and contracting R changes S to $\lambda x.[x/y]L$; we say S has *no residual.*

(In subcases 3b and 3d, it can easily be seen that contracting R produces the same result as contracting S, modulo $\equiv_\alpha$.)

Next, define *parallel reductions* exactly as in A2.6.

Then Lemmas A2.8, A2.9 and A2.10 can be extended to $\beta\eta$ by adding extra cases to their proofs. (*Exercise:* Do this.)

The confluence of $\triangleright_{\beta\eta}$ then follows, as in the proof of A2.11. □

By the way, a different confluence proof for $\triangleright_{\beta\eta}$ is in [Bar84, Section 3.3].

We now turn from λ to CL.

Theorem A2.13 (= 2.15, Church-Rosser theorem for $\triangleright_w$ in CL) *For CL-terms, the relation $\triangleright_w$ is confluent; i.e.*

$$P \triangleright_w M,\ P \triangleright_w N \quad \Longrightarrow \quad (\exists\, T)\ M \triangleright_w T,\ N \triangleright_w T.$$

Proof First, adjust Definition A2.5 (*Residuals*) to suit weak redexes in CL. Cases 1 and 2 do not change. Cases 3 and 4 will both turn out to be irrelevant to the proof, and can be omitted.[2]

[2] Case 3 is that R is a proper part of S. Then $S \equiv \mathbf{I}X$ or $\mathbf{K}XY$ or $\mathbf{S}XYZ$, and R is in X, Y or Z. Contracting R changes S to a term S' with one of the forms $\mathbf{I}X'$, $\mathbf{K}X'Y$, $\mathbf{K}XY'$, $\mathbf{S}X'YZ$, $\mathbf{S}XY'Z$, $\mathbf{S}XYZ'$, for some X', Y' or Z'; we can call this S' the *residual* of S.
Case 4 is that $R \equiv \mathbf{I}X$ or $\mathbf{K}XY$ or $\mathbf{S}XYZ$, and S is in X, Y or Z. Contracting R produces X or X or $XZ(YZ)$ with obvious corresponding occurrences of S. These may be called the *residuals* of S. (If S is in Y in $\mathbf{K}XY$ then S has no residual; if S is in Z in $\mathbf{S}XYZ$ then S has two residuals; otherwise S has just one.)

Next, define a *parallel reduction* in a term P to be a simultaneous contraction of a set of non-overlapping redexes in P. (This definition was too simple to serve in a confluence proof in λ, but it will work in CL, where there are no bound variables.)

Finally, prove Lemma A2.10 by induction on P. The proof is straightforward. (*Exercise:* write it out.) □

(The confluence of $\triangleright_w$ was proved first in [Ros35, p. 144 Theorem T12], also in [CHS72, Section 11B2, Theorem 3].)

Remark A2.14 (Reduction with Z)
In Chapter 4's Discussion 4.25 and Definition 4.26, three new atoms $\widehat{0}$, $\widehat{\sigma}$ and Z were added to pure λ and CL, and reducibility relations $\triangleright_{\beta\mathsf{Z}}$ (in λ) and $\triangleright_{w\mathsf{Z}}$ (in CL) were defined by adding to the definitions of $\triangleright_\beta$ and $\triangleright_w$ the following contractions (one for each $n \geq 0$):

$$\mathsf{Z}\,\widehat{n} \;\triangleright_1\; \overline{n}_{\mathrm{Ch}},$$

where $\widehat{n} \equiv \widehat{\sigma}^n\,\widehat{0}$ and $\overline{n}_{\mathrm{Ch}}$ is the Church numeral for n. The terms $\mathsf{Z}\,\widehat{0}$, $\mathsf{Z}\,\widehat{1}$, $\mathsf{Z}\,\widehat{2}$, etc. are called Z-*redexes*.

Theorem A2.15 (Church-Rosser theorem for reduction with Z)
The relations $\triangleright_{\beta\mathsf{Z}}$ in λ and $\triangleright_{w\mathsf{Z}}$ in CL are confluent.

Proof (for $\triangleright_{\beta\mathsf{Z}}$ in λ) First, a Z-redex $\mathsf{Z}\,\widehat{n}$ cannot contain any other Z- or β-redex.

Extend Definition A2.5 (*Residuals*) to cover Z-redexes. Cases 1 and 2 do not change, and Case 4 is not needed in the confluence proof.

> **Case 3_Z:** R is a proper part of S. Then S cannot be a Z-redex, so $S \equiv (\lambda x.M)N$ and R is in M or N. Contracting R changes S to a term $(\lambda x.M')N$ or $(\lambda x.M)N'$; we call this term the *residual* of S.

Next, define *parallel reductions* exactly as in A2.6. Then Lemmas A2.8, A2.9 and A2.10 can be extended to Z-redexes by adding some easy extra cases to their proofs. The confluence of $\triangleright_{\beta\mathsf{Z}}$ then follows.

The proof for $\triangleright_{w\mathsf{Z}}$ in CL is simpler; just as in the proof of Theorem A2.13, parallel reductions are simultaneous contractions of sets of non-overlapping redexes. □

Remark A2.16 (Typed terms) The confluence proofs in this appendix are valid also for typed terms. To prove this, all we need to check is that if P is a typed term, and a redex R in P is contracted, then the result is a typed term with the same type as P. With care, this property can be seen to hold for all the typed systems in Chapter 10.

Note A2.17 (Parallel reductions) Parallel reductions as defined in A2.6 originated in Curry and Feys' 1958 book [CF58, Section 4C2], and they were used in an abstract confluence-proof in [Hin69, p. 547] under the name '*minimal complete developments*'. They were given a particularly simple inductive definition by Tait and Martin-Löf, as mentioned at the start of this appendix, and were used by Takahashi in [Tak95] to prove, very neatly, not only confluence but most of the main general theorems about β- and $\beta\eta$-reductions in λ-calculus. The name 'parallel reductions' is due to Takahashi.

Incidentally, although this fact was not needed for the confluence proofs above, it is fairly easy to prove that, if P contains β-redexes $R_1, \ldots, R_n$, then all parallel reductions of $\{R_1, \ldots, R_n\}$ produce the same term Q (modulo $\equiv_\alpha$). Indeed, this is true of all complete developments of $\{R_1, \ldots, R_n\}$ (i.e. reductions whose steps are residuals of $\{R_1, \ldots, R_n\}$ and in which all residuals are contracted), although the proof is not so easy [CF58, pp. 113–130].

Deep results on the structure of reductions are described in [Bar84, Chapters 3, 11–14]. A summary of a machine-readable formalization of these and later results is in Huet's [Hue94].

Further reading Studies of confluence in more abstract settings can be found in the sources mentioned in Remark 3.25.

Appendix A3
Strong normalization proofs

As we have seen in Chapter 10, the main property of typed systems not possessed by untyped systems is that all reductions are finite, and hence every typed term has a normal form. In this appendix we shall prove this theorem for the simply typed systems in Chapter 10, and for an extended system from which the consistency of first-order arithmetic can be deduced.

The proofs will be variations on a method due to W. Tait, [Tai67]. (See also [TS00, Sections 6.8, 6.12.2] or [SU06, Sections 5.3.2–5.3.6].) Simpler methods are known for pure λ and CL, but Tait's is the easiest to extend to more complex type-systems.

We begin with two definitions which have meaning for any reduction-concept defined by sequences of replacements. The first is a repetition of Definition 10.14. The second is the key to Tait's method.

Definition A3.1 (Normalizable terms) A typed or untyped CL- or λ-term X is called *normalizable* or *weakly normalizable* or *WN* with respect to a given reduction concept, iff it reduces to a normal form. It is called *strongly normalizable* (*SN*) iff all reductions starting at X are finite.

As noted in Chapter 10, SN implies WN. Also the concept of SN involves the distinction between finite and infinite reductions, whereas WN does not, so SN is a fundamentally more complex concept than WN.

Definition A3.2 (Computable terms) For simply typed CL- or λ-terms, the concept of *strongly computable* (*SC*) *term* is defined by induction on the number of occurrences of '$\to$' in the term's type:

(a) a term of atomic type is SC iff it is SN;

(b) a term $X^{\rho\to\sigma}$ is SC iff, for every SC term Y^{ρ}, the term $(XY)^{\sigma}$ is SC.

Weakly computable (*WC*) is defined similarly, with 'WN' instead of 'SN' in (a). (WC terms are usually called just *computable*.)

A3A Simply typed λ-calculus

In this section, *types* are the simple types of Definition 10.1, and *terms* are simply-typed λ-terms as defined in 10.5.

Theorem A3.3 (SN for $\lambda\beta^{\rightarrow}$, cf. Theorem 10.15) *In the simply typed λ-calculus, there are no infinite β-reductions.*

Proof The theorem says that all terms are SN (with respect to $\triangleright_\beta$). We shall prove that

(a) *every SC term is SN,*
(b) *every term is SC.*

The actual proof will consist of six simple notes and three lemmas, and the last lemma will be equivalent to the theorem.

Note A3.4 *Each type τ can be written in a unique way in the form $\tau_1 \to \ldots \to \tau_n \to \theta$, where θ is atomic and $n \geq 0$.*

Note A3.5 *It follows immediately from Definition A3.2(b) that if*

$$\tau \equiv \tau_1 \to \ldots \to \tau_n \to \theta$$

where θ is atomic, then a term X^τ is SC iff, for all SC terms

$$Y_1^{\tau_1}, \ldots, Y_n^{\tau_n},$$

the term $(XY_1 \ldots Y_n)^\theta$ is SC. And it follows from Definition A3.2(a) that $(XY_1 \ldots Y_n)^\theta$ is SC iff it is SN.

Note A3.6 *If X^τ is SC, then every term which differs from X^τ only by changes of bound variables is also SC. And the same holds for SN.*

Note A3.7 *By Definition A3.2(b), if $X^{\rho\to\sigma}$ is SC and Y^ρ is SC, then $(XY)^\sigma$ is SC.*

Note A3.8 *If X^τ is SN, then every subterm of X^τ is SN, because any infinite reduction of a subterm of X^τ would give rise to an infinite reduction of X^τ.*

Note A3.9 *If $[N^\rho/x^\rho]M^\tau$ is SN, then so is M^τ, because any infinite reduction of M^τ would give rise to an infinite reduction of $[N^\rho/x^\rho]M^\tau$ by substituting N^ρ into every step (cf. Lemma A1.15).*

Lemma A3.10 *Let τ be any type. Then*

(a) every term $(aX_1 \dots X_n)^\tau$, where a is an atom, $n \geq 0$, and $X_1, \dots, X_n$ are all SN, is SC;

(b) every atomic term a^τ is SC;

(c) every SC term of type τ is SN.

Proof Part (b) is merely the special case $n = 0$ of (a). We prove (a) and (c) together by induction on the number of occurrences of '$\to$' in τ.

Basis: τ is an atom. For (a): since $X_1, \dots, X_n$ are SN, $aX_1 \dots X_n$ must be SN. Hence it is SC by Definition A3.2(a).

For (c): Use Definition A3.2(a).

Induction step: $\tau \equiv \rho \to \sigma$. For (a): let Y^ρ be SC. By the induction hypothesis (c), Y^ρ is SN. Using the induction hypothesis (a), we get that $(aX_1 \dots X_n Y)^\sigma$ is SC. Hence, so is $(aX_1 \dots X_n)^\tau$ by Definition A3.2(b).

For (c): let X^τ be SC, and let x^ρ not occur (free or bound) in X^τ. By the induction hypothesis (a) with $n = 0$, x^ρ is SC. Hence, by Note A3.7, $(Xx)^\sigma$ is SC. By the induction hypothesis (c), $(Xx)^\sigma$ is also SN. But then by Note A3.8, X^τ is SN as well. □

Lemma A3.11 *If $[N^\rho/x^\rho]M^\sigma$ is SC, then so is $(\lambda x^\rho . M^\sigma)N^\rho$, provided that N^ρ is SC if x^ρ is not free in M^σ.*

(This lemma says that if the contractum of a typed β-redex R is SC, and all terms (if any) that are cancelled when R is contracted are SC, then R is SC.)

Proof Let $\sigma \equiv \sigma_1 \to \dots \to \sigma_n \to \theta$, where θ is atomic, and let

$$M_1^{\sigma_1}, \ \dots, \ M_n^{\sigma_n}$$

be SC terms. Since $[N^\rho/x^\rho]M^\sigma$ is SC, it follows by Note A3.5 that

$$(([N/x]M)M_1 \dots M_n)^\theta \tag{1}$$

is SN. The lemma will follow by Note A3.5 if we can prove that

$$((\lambda x . M)NM_1 \dots M_n)^\theta \tag{2}$$

is SN. Now since (1) is SN, so are all its subterms; these include

$$[N/x]M, \ M_1, \ \dots, \ M_n.$$

Hence M is SN by Note A3.9. Also, by hypothesis and by part (c) of the preceding lemma, N is SN if it does not occur in $[N/x]M$. Therefore, an infinite reduction of (2) cannot consist entirely of contractions in M, N, M_1, ..., M_n. Hence, such a reduction must have the form

$$\begin{array}{lll} (\lambda x.M)NM_1\ldots M_n & \rhd_\beta & (\lambda x.M')N'M'_1\ldots M'_n \\ & \rhd_{1\beta} & ([N'/x]M')M'_1\ldots M'_n \\ & \rhd_\beta & \ldots \end{array}$$

where $M \rhd_\beta M'$, $N \rhd_\beta N'$, etc. From the reductions $M \rhd_\beta M'$ and $N \rhd_\beta N'$ we get $[N/x]M \rhd_\beta [N'/x]M'$ by Lemma A1.15; hence, we can construct an infinite reduction of (1) thus:

$$\begin{array}{lll} ([N/x]M)M_1\ldots M_n & \rhd_{1\beta} & ([N'/x]M')M'_1\ldots M'_n \\ & \rhd_\beta & \ldots \end{array}$$

This contradicts the fact that (1) is SN. Hence, (2) must be SN. □

Lemma A3.12 *For every typed term M^τ:*

(a) M^τ is SC;

(b) For all $x_1^{\rho_1},\ldots,x_n^{\rho_n}$ $(n \geq 1)$, and all SC terms $N_1^{\rho_1}$, ..., $N_n^{\rho_n}$ such that (for $i = 2,\ldots,n$) none of $x_1,\ldots,x_{i-1}$ occurs free in N_i, the term $M^\star \equiv [N_1/x_1]\ldots[N_n/x_n]M$ is SC.

(Part (a) is all that is needed to prove the SN theorem, but the extra strength of (b) is needed to make the proof of the lemma work. In fact (a) is a special case of (b), namely $N_i \equiv x_i$ for $i = 1,\ldots,n$, since every x_i is SC by Lemma A3.10(b).)

Proof We prove (b) by induction on the length of M. (Note that, by our usual convention, $x_1,\ldots,x_n$ are distinct.)

Case 1. $M \equiv x_i$ and $\tau \equiv \rho_i$. Then $M^\star \equiv N_i$. (If $i = 1$, this is trivial; if $i \geq 2$ then $M^\star \equiv [N_1/x_1]\ldots[N_{i-1}/x_{i-1}]N_i$, which is N_i by the assumption in (b).) But N_i is SC by assumption, so $M^\star$ is SC.

Case 2. M is an atom distinct from $x_1, x_2,\ldots,x_n$. Then $M^\star \equiv M$, which is SC by Lemma A3.10(b).

Case 3. $M \equiv M_1M_2$. Then $M^\star \equiv M_1^\star M_2^\star$. By the induction hypothesis, $M_1^\star$ and $M_2^\star$ are SC, and so $M^\star$ is SC by Note A3.7.

Case 4. $M^\tau \equiv (\lambda x^\rho.M_1^\sigma)$, where $\tau \equiv \rho \to \sigma$. By Note A3.6, we can assume that x does not occur free in any of $N_1,\ldots,N_n$, x_1, ..., x_n. Then $M^\star \equiv \lambda x.M_1^\star$ by Definition 1.12(f).

To show that $M^\star$ is SC, we must prove that for all SC terms N^ρ, the term $M^\star N$ is SC. But

$$\begin{aligned} M^\star N &\equiv (\lambda x.M_1^\star)N \\ &\triangleright_{1\beta} [N/x]M_1^\star \\ &\equiv [N/x][N_1/x_1]\dots[N_n/x_n]M_1, \end{aligned}$$

which is SC by the induction hypothesis applied to M_1 and the sequence $N, N_1, \dots N_n$. Then $M^\star N$ is SC by Lemma A3.11. □

This completes the proof of Theorem A3.3. □

By making a minor change, we can extend this proof to $\lambda\beta\eta^{\rightarrow}$, as follows.

Theorem A3.13 (SN for $\boldsymbol{\lambda\beta\eta^{\rightarrow}}$, cf. Remark 10.17) *In the simply typed λ-calculus, there are no infinite βη-reductions.*

Proof The same as Theorem A3.3 except that in Lemma A3.11, near the end of the proof, we need to allow for the possibility that an infinite reduction of $(\lambda x.M)NM_1\dots M_n$ has the form

$$\begin{aligned} (\lambda x.M)NM_1\dots M_n &\triangleright_{\beta\eta} (\lambda x.M')N'M_1'\dots M_n' \\ &\equiv (\lambda x.Px)N'M_1'\dots M_n' \\ &\triangleright_{1\eta} PN'M_1'\dots M_n' \\ &\triangleright_{\beta\eta} \dots, \end{aligned}$$

where $M \triangleright M'$, etc. and $x \notin \mathrm{FV}(P)$. But in this case we can construct an infinite reduction of $([N/x]M)M_1\dots M_n$ as follows:

$$\begin{aligned} ([N/x]M)M_1\dots M_n &\triangleright_{\beta\eta} ([N'/x]M')M_1'\dots M_n' \\ &\equiv PN'M_1'\dots M_n' \\ &\triangleright_{\beta\eta} \dots, \end{aligned}$$

and this contradicts the fact that (1) in the proof of A3.11 is SN. □

A3B Simply typed CL

In this section, *types* are the simple types of Definition 10.1, and *terms* are simply-typed CL-terms as defined in 10.19.

Theorem A3.14 (SN for $\boldsymbol{CLw^{\rightarrow}}$, cf. Theorem 10.26) *In simply typed CL, there are no infinite weak reductions.*

Proof Modify the proof of Theorem A3.3 as follows.

In Lemma A3.10(a) and (b), insert an assumption that a is a non-redex atom (i.e. is not an $\mathbf{S}_{\gamma,\delta,\epsilon}$, $\mathbf{K}_{\gamma,\delta}$ or $\mathbf{I}_\gamma$ for any types γ, δ, ϵ). The proof of Lemma A3.10 is unchanged.

Delete Lemma A3.11, which is not needed for CL-terms.

In Lemma A3.12, delete (b), which is not needed now. In that lemma's proof, Case 4 is not needed. But Case 2 must be augmented by a proof that the atomic combinators are SC. This comes from the following lemma.

Lemma A3.15 *The atomic combinators $\mathbf{S}_{\rho,\sigma,\tau}$, $\mathbf{K}_{\sigma,\tau}$, $\mathbf{I}_\tau$ are SC, for all types ρ, σ, τ.*

Proof (a) $\mathbf{S}_{\rho,\sigma,\tau}$ has type $(\rho \to \sigma \to \tau) \to (\rho \to \sigma) \to \rho \to \tau$. Let

$$\tau \equiv \tau_1 \to \ldots \to \tau_n \to \theta,$$

where θ is atomic and $n \geq 0$, and let $X^{\rho\to\sigma\to\tau}$, $Y^{\rho\to\sigma}$, Z^ρ, $U_1^{\tau_1}$, ..., $U_n^{\tau_n}$ be any SC terms. The term

$$\mathbf{S}XYZU_1 \ldots U_n \tag{3}$$

has type θ, an atom, so, by Note A3.5, to prove $\mathbf{S}$ is SC it is enough to prove (3) is SN.

If an infinite reduction of (3) existed, it could not proceed entirely inside X, Y, Z, U_1, ..., U_n, because these SC terms are SN by Lemma A3.10(c). Therefore it would have form

$$\begin{aligned} \mathbf{S}XYZU_1 \ldots U_n \;&\triangleright_w\; \mathbf{S}X'Y'Z'U_1' \ldots U_n' \\ &\triangleright_{1w}\; X'Z'(Y'Z')U_1' \ldots U_n' \\ &\triangleright_w\; \ldots, \end{aligned}$$

where $X \triangleright_w X'$, $Y \triangleright_w Y'$, etc. Hence we could make an infinite reduction starting at $XZ(YZ)U_1 \ldots U_n$.

But X, Y, Z are SC, so $XZ(YZ)$ is SC by Note A3.7. Hence the term $XZ(YZ)U_1 \ldots U_n$ is SN, by Note A3.5, and an infinite reduction starting at this term is impossible. Therefore (3) is SN and so $\mathbf{S}$ is SC.

(b) $\mathbf{K}_{\sigma,\tau}$ has type $\sigma \to \tau \to \sigma$. Let $\sigma \equiv \sigma_1 \to \ldots \to \sigma_n \to \theta$, where θ is atomic and $n \geq 0$, and let X^σ, Y^τ, $U_1^{\sigma_1}$, ..., $U_n^{\sigma_n}$ be any SC terms. To prove $\mathbf{K}$ is SC, it is enough to prove the following term is SN:

$$\mathbf{K}XYU_1 \ldots U_n. \tag{4}$$

An infinite reduction of (4) would have form

$$\begin{aligned} \mathbf{K}XYU_1 \dots U_n \;&\triangleright_w\; \mathbf{K}X'Y'U_1' \dots U_n' \\ &\triangleright_{1w}\; X'U_1' \dots U_n' \\ &\triangleright_w\; \dots, \end{aligned}$$

where $X \triangleright_w X'$, etc. This would give rise to an infinite reduction starting at $XU_1 \dots U_n$. But this is impossible, because X is SC which implies $XU_1 \dots U_n$ is SN by Note A3.5. Therefore (4) is SN and so $\mathbf{K}$ is SC.

(c) The proof that $\mathbf{I}_\tau$ is SC is like those for $\mathbf{S}$ and $\mathbf{K}$. □

Using the preceding lemma, we can prove that every typed CL-term M^τ is SC by induction on the length of M, as in the proof of Lemma A3.12, Cases 1–3. This completes the proof of Theorem A3.14. □

A3C Arithmetical system

To show the versatility of Tait's method, we shall here apply it to an extension of simply typed CL which has played an important rôle in proofs of consistency.

The *arithmetical extension of CL* was discussed in 4.25 and defined in 4.26. It was proved confluent in Theorem A2.15. Types were assigned to its terms by the rules of $\mathrm{TA}_{\mathrm{C}}^{\rightarrow}$ shown in Definition 11.5, augmented by the basis $\mathcal{B}_{\mathbf{Z}}$ shown in Example 11.40.

Now, the formal first-order theory of natural numbers is usually called *Peano Arithmetic* (*PA*). A definition is in [SU06, Section 9.2], for example. Kurt Gödel's famous second incompleteness theorem implies that, if PA is consistent, every proof of its consistency must contain a 'non-arithmetical' step; i.e., very roughly speaking, a step that is too complex to be translated into a valid proof in PA when the formulas and syntax of PA are coded as numbers.

The theory of PA is outside the scope of this book. But it is worth noting here that one way of proving PA consistent (discovered by Gödel himself) is to translate it into a typed version CL$\mathbf{Z}^{\rightarrow}$ of the arithmetical extension of CL, and deduce its consistency from the confluence and WN theorems for CL$\mathbf{Z}^{\rightarrow}$. The deduction of consistency can be done by 'arithmetical' means, and so can the confluence proof. Hence the proof of WN for CL$\mathbf{Z}^{\rightarrow}$ must contain a non-arithmetical step.

In the present section we shall briefly define CL$\mathbf{Z}^{\rightarrow}$ and prove WN for it, in fact SN.

More details can be found in other books. For example, there are outlines of Gödel's consistency proof for PA or HA (the intuitionistic analogue of PA, whose consistency problem is equivalent) in [Sho01,

Chapter 8] and [HS86, Chapter 18]; there are descriptions of his interpretation of arithmetic in CL in [TD88, Volume 1 Chapter 3 Section 3, Volume 2 Chapter 9] and [SU06, Chapters 9, 10], with normalization proofs in [TD88, Volume 2 Chapter 9 Section 2], [SU06, Section 10.3] and [GLT89, Chapter 7]. There is a comprehensive treatment of Gödel's proof in [Tro73]: Sections 1.1.1–1.3.10 define and discuss HA, Sections 2.2.1–2.2.35 define a system like $CL\mathbf{Z}^{\rightarrow}$ and prove SN for it, and Sections 3.5.1–3.5.4 describe Gödel's translation of HA into that system. Gödel's consistency-proof was first published in [Göd58]; but Gödel gave no details of λ or CL or WN-proofs, just a few hints.

Definition A3.16 *Types* are defined as in 10.1, with only one atomic type, $\mathbf{N}$ (for the set of all natural numbers).

Recall the notation $\mathbf{N}_\tau \equiv (\tau \to \tau) \to \tau \to \tau$ for every type τ.

Definition A3.17 The *terms* of $CL\mathbf{Z}^{\rightarrow}$ are typed CL-terms as defined in 10.19, with, besides the combinators, just the following typed atomic constants:

(a) $\widehat{0}^{\mathbf{N}}$ to denote zero; $\widehat{\sigma}^{(\mathbf{N}\to\mathbf{N})}$ for the successor function;
(b) atoms $\mathbf{Z}^{(\mathbf{N}\to\mathbf{N}_\tau)}$ called *iterators*, one for each type τ.

Note A3.18 The types of the iterators are the same as those assigned to $\mathbf{Z}$ in the basis $\mathcal{B}_{\mathbf{Z}}$ in 11.40. We shall call $\mathbf{Z}^{(\mathbf{N}\to\mathbf{N}_\tau)}$ just '$\mathbf{Z}_\tau$' for short. Type-superscripts will be omitted unless needed for emphasis.

For $m = 0, 1, 2, \ldots$ we shall write $\widehat{m} \equiv \widehat{\sigma}^{\,m}\,\widehat{0}$ and call $\widehat{m}$ a '*numeral*'. Clearly $\widehat{m}$ has type $\mathbf{N}$.

Abstraction [ ] is defined as usual by 2.18, or equivalently 10.24.

Other notation conventions are the same as in Chapter 10.

Exercise A3.19 (Typed Church numerals) For every τ, find suitable typed versions of $\mathbf{S}$, $\mathbf{B}$, $\mathbf{K}$, $\mathbf{I}$ such that $(\mathbf{SB})^m(\mathbf{KI})$ has type $\mathbf{N}_\tau$ for all $m \geq 0$. (Hint: see 11.8(e)–(g).) We shall call this version of $(\mathbf{SB})^m(\mathbf{KI})$ the *Church numeral* $\overline{m}_\tau$. It is easy to see that, for all $X^{\tau\to\tau}$ and Y^τ,

$$\overline{m}_\tau XY \;\triangleright_w\; X^m Y.$$

Definition A3.20 (Typed *w*Z-reduction) *Reduction* $\triangleright_{w\mathbf{Z}}$ is weak reduction as defined in 2.9, with extra contractions

$$\mathbf{Z}_\tau\widehat{m} \;\triangleright_{w\mathbf{Z}}\; \overline{m}_\tau$$

(for all $m \geq 0$ and all types τ), cf. Definition 4.26. A $\mathbf{Z}$-*redex* is any term $\mathbf{Z}_\tau \widehat{m}$, and its *contractum* is $\overline{m}_\tau$. (Both $\mathbf{Z}_\tau \widehat{m}$ and $\overline{m}_\tau$ have type $\mathbf{N}_\tau$.)

Equality $=_{w\mathbf{Z}}$ is defined by contractions and reversed contractions as usual. A $w\mathbf{Z}$-*normal form* is a term containing no $w\mathbf{Z}$-redexes.

Reduction $\triangleright_{w\mathbf{Z}}$ is confluent (cf. Theorem A2.15), so each term reduces to at most one $w\mathbf{Z}$-normal form.

Exercise A3.21 This exercise shows some of the scope of CL$\mathbf{Z}^{\rightarrow}$; however, it is not needed in the SN proof.

(a) **(Predecessor)** Let $\rho \equiv (\mathbf{N} \to \mathbf{N}) \to \mathbf{N}$, and let

$$\widehat{\pi} \;\equiv\; [x^{\mathbf{N}}]\,.\,\mathbf{Z}_\rho\, x\,\big([u^\rho, v^{\mathbf{N}\to\mathbf{N}}]\,.\,v\,(u\,\widehat{\sigma})\big)\,\big(\mathbf{K}_{\mathbf{N},\mathbf{N}\to\mathbf{N}}\widehat{0}\big)\,\mathbf{I}_{\mathbf{N}} \qquad (5)$$

(cf. $\overline{\pi}_{\text{Bund-Urb}}$ in 4.13). Show that $\widehat{\pi}$ has type $\mathbf{N} \to \mathbf{N}$, and that

$$\widehat{\pi}\,\widehat{0} \triangleright_{w\mathbf{Z}} \widehat{0}, \qquad \widehat{\pi}\,(\widehat{\sigma}\,\widehat{k}) \triangleright_{w\mathbf{Z}} \widehat{k} \quad (\forall k \geq 0).$$

(b) **(Recursion combinators)** For every type τ, a CL$\mathbf{Z}^{\rightarrow}$-term $\mathbf{R}_\tau$ can be built, with type

$$\tau \to (\mathbf{N} \to \tau \to \tau) \to \mathbf{N} \to \tau, \qquad (6)$$

and such that, for all X^τ, $Y^{\mathbf{N}\to\tau\to\tau}$ and all $k \geq 0$,

$$\left.\begin{aligned} \mathbf{R}_\tau X\,Y\,\widehat{0} \quad &=_{w\mathbf{Z}} \quad X, \\ \mathbf{R}_\tau X\,Y\,(\widehat{\sigma}\widehat{k}) \quad &=_{w\mathbf{Z}} \quad Y\,\widehat{k}\,(\mathbf{R}_\tau X Y \widehat{k}\,). \end{aligned}\right\} \qquad (7)$$

Show, using (6), that both sides of the equations in (7) are genuine typed terms and have the same type, namely τ.
Show that the following $\mathbf{R}_\tau$ satisfies (6) and (7). (It is from [CHS72, p.283] and is due mainly to Kleene.)[1]

$$\mathbf{R}_\tau \;\equiv\; [x^\tau, y^{(\mathbf{N}\to\tau\to\tau)}, u^{\mathbf{N}}]\,.\,\mathbf{Z}_{(\mathbf{N}\to\tau)}\, u\,(M_\tau y)(\mathbf{K}_{\tau,\mathbf{N}}\, x)\, u\,, \qquad (8)$$

where

$$M_\tau \;\equiv\; [y^{(\mathbf{N}\to\tau\to\tau)}, v^{(\mathbf{N}\to\tau)}, w^{\mathbf{N}}]\,.\,\mathbf{S}_{\mathbf{N},\tau,\tau}\; y\, v\,(\widehat{\pi} w). \qquad (9)$$

(c) **(Pairing)** For every type τ, construct a CL$\mathbf{Z}^{\rightarrow}$-term $\mathbf{D}^\star_\tau$ with type $\tau \to \tau \to \mathbf{N} \to \tau$, such that, for all X^τ and Y^τ,

$$\mathbf{D}^\star_\tau\, X\,Y\widehat{0} \;=_{w\mathbf{Z}}\; X, \qquad \mathbf{D}^\star_\tau\, X\,Y\widehat{k+1} \;=_{w\mathbf{Z}}\; Y.$$

(Hint: insert types into $[x, y].\mathbf{R}x(\mathbf{K}(\mathbf{K}y))$.)

[1] The $\mathbf{R}$ in 4.25 (32) like $\mathbf{R}_{\text{Bernays}}$ is not used here, because an attempt to insert $\mathbf{Z}_\tau$ and types into that $\mathbf{R}$ would only give $\mathbf{R}_{\mathbf{N}}$, not $\mathbf{R}_\tau$ for all τ: see [CHS72, Theorem 13D1, p. 280].

Theorem A3.22 (SN for CL$\mathbf{Z}^{\rightarrow}$) *No term of* CL$\mathbf{Z}^{\rightarrow}$ *can be the start of an infinite* $w\mathbf{Z}$*-reduction.*

Proof We modify the proof of Theorem A3.3 as follows. In Lemma A3.10, insert an assumption that a is neither a combinator nor a $\mathbf{Z}_\tau$ (although a is allowed to be $\widehat{0}$ or $\widehat{\sigma}$); the proof of that lemma is unchanged. Delete A3.11 and A3.12(b) which are now redundant, and delete Case 4 from A3.12's proof.

To complete the proof, it only remains to show that all atoms $\mathbf{Z}_\tau$ are SC; the following lemma does this. (Its part (b) is needed in the proof of (a).)

Lemma A3.23 *Let τ be any type. Then*

(a) $\mathbf{Z}_\tau$ *is SC;*
(b) for all $m \geq 0$, the Church numeral $\overline{m}_\tau$ is SC.

Proof Let $\tau \equiv \tau_1 \rightarrow \ldots \rightarrow \tau_n \rightarrow \mathbf{N}$, with $n \geq 0$. Recall that the types of $\mathbf{Z}_\tau$ and $\overline{m}_\tau$ are, respectively,

$$\mathbf{N} \rightarrow (\tau \rightarrow \tau) \rightarrow \tau \rightarrow \tau, \qquad (\tau \rightarrow \tau) \rightarrow \tau \rightarrow \tau.$$

In what follows, $V^{\mathbf{N}}$, $X^{\tau\rightarrow\tau}$, Y^τ, $U_1^{\tau_1}$, ..., $U_n^{\tau_n}$ will be any SC terms of the types shown.

Proof that (b) $\Longrightarrow$ (a). To prove that $\mathbf{Z}_\tau$ is SC, it is enough to prove that the following term is SN:

$$\mathbf{Z}_\tau VXYU_1 \ldots U_n. \tag{10}$$

But V, X, Y, U_1, ..., U_n are SN by Lemma A3.10(c), so an infinite reduction of (10) would have form

$$\begin{aligned} \mathbf{Z}_\tau VXYU_1 \ldots U_n \ &\rhd_{w\mathbf{Z}}\ \mathbf{Z}_\tau \widehat{m} X'Y'U_1' \ldots U_n' \\ &\rhd_{\mathbf{Z}}\ \overline{m}_\tau X'Y'U_1' \ldots U_n' \\ &\rhd_w\ \ldots, \end{aligned}$$

where $V \rhd_{w\mathbf{Z}} \widehat{m}$ for some $m \geq 0$, and $X \rhd_{w\mathbf{Z}} X'$, etc. Hence we could make an infinite reduction of $\overline{m}_\tau XYU_1 \ldots U_n$, contrary to (b).

Proof of (b). To prove that $\overline{m}_\tau$ is SC, it is enough, by Note A3.5, to prove the following term is SN (for all SC terms X, Y, U_1, ..., U_n):

$$\overline{m}_\tau XYU_1 \ldots U_n. \tag{11}$$

We shall do this by induction on m.

Basis ($m = 0$ *and* $\overline{m} \equiv \mathbf{KI}$). Since X, Y, U_1, ..., U_n are SN by Lemma A3.10(c), an infinite reduction of (11) must have form

$$\begin{array}{llll} \mathbf{KI}XYU_1\ldots U_n & \rhd_{w\mathbf{Z}} & \mathbf{I}Y'U_1'\ldots U_n' & (Y \rhd_w Y', \text{etc.}) \\ & \rhd_{w\mathbf{Z}} & Y''U_1''\ldots U_n'' & (Y' \rhd_w Y'', \text{etc.}) \\ & \rhd_{w\mathbf{Z}} & \ldots & \end{array}$$

This would give rise to an infinite reduction of $YU_1\ldots U_n$, contrary to the assumption that Y is SC.

Induction step (m to $m+1$). Assume (11) is SN for all SC terms X, Y, U_1, ..., U_n. Now $\overline{m+1} \equiv \mathbf{SB}\overline{m}$, and hence an infinite reduction of the term $\overline{m+1}XYU_1\ldots U_n$ must have form

$$\begin{array}{llll} \mathbf{SB}\overline{m}XYU_1\ldots U_n & \rhd_{w\mathbf{Z}} & \mathbf{SB}\overline{m}X'Y'U_1'\ldots U_n' & (X \rhd X', \text{etc.}) \\ & \rhd_{1w} & \mathbf{B}X'(\overline{m}X')Y'U_1'\ldots U_n' & \\ & \rhd_{w\mathbf{Z}} & \mathbf{B}X'WY'U_1'\ldots U_n' & (\overline{m}X' \rhd \text{some } W) \\ & \rhd_{w\mathbf{Z}} & \mathbf{B}X''W''Y''U_1''\ldots U_n'' & (X' \rhd X'', \text{etc.}) \\ & \equiv & \mathbf{S}(\mathbf{KS})\mathbf{K}X''W''Y''U_1''\ldots U_n'' & \\ & \rhd_w & X''(W''Y'')U_1''\ldots U_n'' & \\ & \rhd_{w\mathbf{Z}} & \ldots & \end{array}$$

From this we could make the following infinite reduction:

$$X(\overline{m}XY)U_1\ldots U_n \;\rhd\; X''(W''Y'')U_1''\ldots U_n'' \;\rhd\; \ldots \tag{12}$$

Now $\overline{m}XY$ is SC. To prove this, it is enough, by Note A3.5, to show that $\overline{m}XYU_1\ldots U_n$ is SN (for all SC terms U_1, ..., U_n); and the latter holds by the induction hypothesis.

But X is assumed to be SC, so $X(\overline{m}XY)$ is SC by Definition A3.2(b). Hence $X(\overline{m}XY)U_1\ldots U_n$ is SN by Note A3.5. Thus (12) is impossible. Therefore the analogue of (11) for $\overline{m+1}$ is SN. □

This completes the proof of Theorem A3.22. □

Remark A3.24 (Arithmetizability) The discussion at the start of the present section noted that any proof of SN or WN for $\mathrm{CL}\mathbf{Z}^{\rightarrow}$ must contain at least one 'non-arithmetical' step. In fact, it can be shown that there is such a step right at the start: the definitions of SC and WC for $\mathrm{CL}\mathbf{Z}^{\rightarrow}$ are not expressible in PA (see [Tro73, Section 2.3.11]).

Also the definition of SN is not arithmetical, since 'infinite reduction' is not a first-order arithmetical concept. (For pure λ or CL, the concept 'X is SN' can be made arithmetical by re-wording it as 'there exists n

(depending on X) such that all reductions of X have less than n steps'. But for $CL\mathbf{Z}^{\rightarrow}$ this does not work.)

Remark A3.25 (Recursion combinators) Instead of adding $\mathbf{Z}_\tau$, one can add *typed recursion combinators* $\mathbf{R}_\tau$ to CL, each having type $\tau \rightarrow (\mathbf{N} \rightarrow \tau \rightarrow \tau) \rightarrow \mathbf{N} \rightarrow \tau$ and reduction-axioms

$$\left.\begin{array}{lll} \mathbf{R}_\tau XY\widehat{0} & \triangleright_{w\mathbf{R}} & X, \\ \mathbf{R}_\tau XY(\widehat{\sigma k}) & \triangleright_{w\mathbf{R}} & Y\widehat{k}(\mathbf{R}_\tau XY\widehat{k}). \end{array}\right\} \qquad (13)$$

The system $CL\mathbf{R}^{\rightarrow}$ so defined is equivalent to $CL\mathbf{Z}^{\rightarrow}$, in the sense that in $CL\mathbf{Z}^{\rightarrow}$ one can build terms $\mathbf{R}_\tau$ satisfying (13) with '=' instead of '$\triangleright$' (see Exercise A3.21(b)), and in $CL\mathbf{R}^{\rightarrow}$ one can build terms $\mathbf{Z}_\tau$ such that $\mathbf{Z}_\tau \widehat{m} \triangleright_{w\mathbf{R}} \overline{m}$. (Try $\mathbf{R}_\tau(\mathbf{KI})(\mathbf{K}(\mathbf{SB}))$ with suitable types.)

SN holds for $CL\mathbf{R}^{\rightarrow}$. The previous **Z**-proof can fairly easily be modified; alternatively, proofs can be found in several sources, for example [San67], [HS86, Appendix 2, Theorem A2.6] and [TD88, Chapter 9, Section 2]. The first of these uses a different method from Tait's, invented independently. The other two use Tait's method. In the third, WN and SN are proved separately (Sections 2.10, 2.16).

The advantage of using $\mathbf{R}_\tau$ instead of $\mathbf{Z}_\tau$ is that defining recursion is simpler and more direct. The price to pay is technical: a **Z**-redex cannot contain other redexes, but an **R**-redex can, and this makes the proof of confluence for $\triangleright_{w\mathbf{R}}$ is slightly more complicated than for $\triangleright_{w\mathbf{Z}}$, cf. Theorem A2.15.

Remark A3.26 (λ-calculus version) Instead of CL, we could begin with λ-calculus and add $\mathbf{Z}_\tau$ (or $\mathbf{R}_\tau$). Then we could prove SN for $\beta\mathbf{Z}$- or $\beta\mathbf{R}$-reduction by a proof very like the one given here for CL.

Proofs of SN for $\triangleright_{\beta\mathbf{R}}$ can be found, for example, in [Ste72, Chapter 4, Section 8], [Tro73, Chapter II Theorem 2.2.31], [GLT89, Chapter 7] and [SU06, Section 10.3].

Appendix A4
Care of your pet combinator

This Appendix was contributed by Carol Hindley to [HS86]. We believe its plain common-sense advice is still very valid despite changing fashions in care, and therefore reprint it here.

Combinators make ideal pets.

Housing They should be kept in a suitable axiom-scheme, preferably shaded by Böhm trees. They like plenty of scope for their contractions, and a proved extensionality is ideal for this.

Diet To keep them in strong normal form a diet of mixed free variables should be given twice a day. Bound variables are best avoided as they can lead to contradictions. The exotic **R** combinator needs a few Church numerals added to its diet to keep it healthy and active.

House-training If they are kept well supplied with parentheses, changed daily (from the left), there should be no problems.

Exercise They can be safely let out to contract and reduce if kept on a long corollary attached to a fixed point theorem, but do watch that they don't get themselves into a logical paradox while playing around it.

Discipline Combinators are generally well behaved but a few rules of inference should be enforced to keep their formal theories equivalent.

Health For those feeling less than weakly equal a check up at a nearby lemma is usually all that is required. In more serious cases a theorem (Church–Rosser is a good general one) should be called in. Rarely a trivial proof followed by a short remark may be needed to get them back on their feet.

Travel If you need to travel any distance greater than the length of M with your combinators try to get a comfortable Cartesian Closed Category. They will feel secure in this and travel quite happily.

Choosing your combinator Your combinators should be obtained from a reputable combinatory logic monograph. Make sure that you are given the full syntactic identity of each combinator. A final word: *do* consider obtaining a recursive function; despite appearances, they can make charming pets!

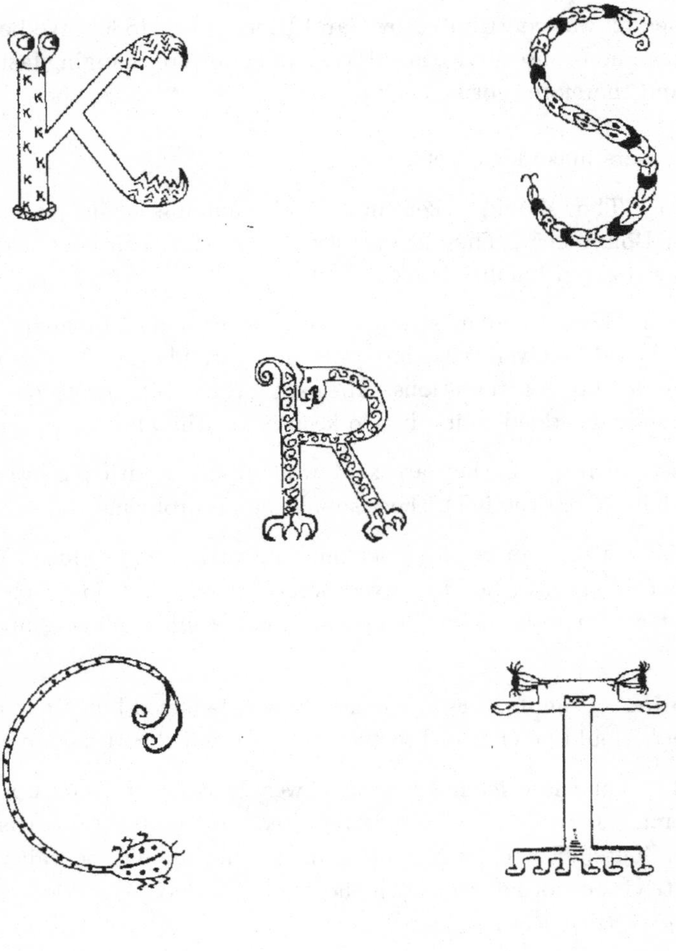

Appendix A5
Answers to starred exercises

1.4 (To help the reader, outer parentheses are shown larger; but actually all parentheses should be the same size.)

(a) $\Big(((xy)z)(yx)\Big)$, (d) $\Big(\Big((\lambda u\,.\,((vu)u)\,)\,z\Big)\,y\Big)$,

(b) $\Big(\lambda x\,.\,((ux)y)\Big)$, (e) $\Big(((ux)(yz))\,(\lambda v.(vy))\Big)$,

(c) $\Big(\lambda u.(u\,(\lambda x.y))\Big)$, (f) $\Big(\Big(\Big(\Big(\lambda x.(\lambda y.(\lambda z.((xz)(yz))))\Big)\,u\Big)\,v\Big)\,w\Big)$.

1.8 (a) $\lambda xy.xy \;\equiv\; (\lambda x.(\lambda y.(\underline{xy})))$.

(b) $x(uv)(\lambda u.v(uv))uv \;\equiv\; ((((x(\underline{uv}))(\lambda u.(v(\underline{uv})))) \,u)\,v)$.

(c) No. In fact $\lambda u.uv \;\equiv\; (\lambda u.(uv))$,
and $\lambda u.u \;\equiv\; (\lambda u.u)$, which does not occur in $(\lambda u.(uv))$.

1.14 (a) $\lambda y.\,uv(\lambda w.\,vw(uv))$; (c) $y\,(\lambda z.(\lambda y.vy)z)$, where $z \not\equiv v, y, x$;
(b) $\lambda y.\,(\lambda y.xy)(\lambda x.x)$; (d) $\lambda x.zy$.

1.28 Here are suitable reductions. (In each term, an underline shows the redex to be contracted in the next step.) In (c) and (f) there are other possible reductions. (But they give the same nf's, modulo $\equiv_\alpha$.)

(a) $\underline{(\lambda x.xy)(\lambda u.vuu)} \;\rhd_{1\beta}\; [(\lambda u.vuu)/x]\,(xy) \;\equiv\; \underline{(\lambda u.vuu)\,y}$
$\rhd_{1\beta}\; [y/u]\,(vuu) \;\equiv\; vyy.$

(b) First, $(\lambda xy.yx)uv$ is really $\big((\lambda x.(\lambda y\,.\,yx)\,u\big)\,v$. Then

$\Big(\underline{(\lambda x.(\lambda y.yx))\,u}\Big)\,v \;\rhd_{1\beta}\; \Big([u/x]\,(\lambda y.yx)\Big)\,v \;\equiv\; \underline{(\lambda y.yu)\,v}$
$\rhd_{1\beta}\; [v/y]\,(yu) \;\equiv\; vu.$

(c) $\underline{(\lambda x.\,x(x(yz))x)(\lambda u.uv)} \;\rhd_{1\beta}\; [(\lambda u.uv)/x]\,(x(x(yz))x)$
$\equiv\; (\lambda u.uv)\,\big(\,\underline{(\lambda u.uv)\,(yz)}\,\big)\,(\lambda u.uv)$
$\rhd_{1\beta}\; (\lambda u.uv)\,\big([(yz)/u](uv)\big)\,(\lambda u.uv)$
$\equiv\; \underline{(\lambda u.uv)\,((yz)v)}\,(\lambda u.uv)$
$\rhd_{1\beta}\; \big(\,[((yz)v)/u]\,(uv)\,\big)\,(\lambda u.uv)$
$\equiv\; ((yz)v)v\,(\lambda u.uv)$ which is a nf ($\equiv yzvv(\lambda u.uv)$).

(d) $\underline{(\lambda x.xxy)(\lambda y.yz)} \rhd_{1\beta} [(\lambda y.yz)/x](xxy) \equiv \underline{(\lambda y.yz)(\lambda y.yz)}\, y$
$\rhd_{1\beta} [(\lambda y.yz)/y](yz)\, y \equiv \underline{(\lambda y.yz)\, z}\, y$
$\rhd_{1\beta} ([z/y](yz))\, y \equiv zzy.$

(e) $(\lambda xy.xyy)(\lambda u.uyx) \equiv \underline{(\lambda x.(\lambda y.xyy))(\lambda u.uyx)}$
$\rhd_{1\beta}$ $[(\lambda u.uyx)/x](\lambda y.xyy)$
$\equiv$ $[(\lambda u.uyx)/x](\lambda z.xzz)$ by def. of substitution, 1.12(g),
$\equiv$ $\lambda z\,.\,\underline{(\lambda u.uyx)zz}$
$\rhd_{1\beta}$ $\lambda z\,.\,([z/u](uyx))z \equiv \lambda z.zyxz$ which is a nf.

To avoid having to change y to z while substituting, it is usually better to change bound variables at the start of the reduction, thus (β-reductions are allowed to contain α-steps):

$$(\lambda xy.xyy)(\lambda u.uyx) \equiv_\alpha (\lambda vw.vww)(\lambda u.uyx) \rhd_\beta \lambda w.wyxw.$$

(f) First, $(\lambda xy.yx)u \equiv (\lambda x.(\lambda y.yx))u \rhd_{1\beta} [u/x](\lambda y.yx) \equiv \lambda y.yu$. Also $(\lambda xy.yx)v \rhd_{1\beta} \lambda y.yv$. Hence
$(\lambda xyz.xz(yz))((\lambda xy.yx)u)((\lambda xy.yx)v)\, w$
$\rhd_\beta$ $(\lambda xyz.xz(yz))(\lambda y.yu)(\lambda y.yv)\, w$
$\rhd_\beta$ $(\lambda y.yu)\, w\, ((\lambda y.yv)w)$ by three contractions
$\rhd_\beta$ $wu(wv)$ by two contractions.

1.35 (a) If M contained a redex $(\lambda u.V)W$, then $[N/x]M$ would contain a redex obtained by substitution from $(\lambda u.V)W$.

(b) Let $\Omega \equiv (\lambda x.xx)(\lambda x.xx)$, which has no β-nf. Then $x\Omega$ has no β-nf. Choose $M \equiv x\Omega$. Choose $N \equiv \lambda y.z$. Then $[N/x]M \equiv (\lambda y.z)\Omega$ which reduces to z, which is a nf.

1.36 (Due to B. Intrigila) Let $\Omega \equiv (\lambda x.xx)(\lambda x.xx)$. Choose P to be $\lambda y.\, y(\lambda uvw.w)\Omega$, and Q to be $\lambda z.z\Omega$. Then $PQ \rhd_\beta \lambda w.w$.

1.38 To avoid confusion, it is safer to change some bound variables first:

$$(\lambda xyz.xzy)(\lambda xy.x) \equiv_\alpha (\lambda xyz.xzy)(\lambda uv.u)$$
$$\rhd_{1\beta} \lambda yz.(\lambda uv.u)zy \quad \rhd_\beta \lambda yz.z;$$

$$(\lambda xy.x)(\lambda x.x) \equiv_\alpha (\lambda xy.x)(\lambda w.w) \rhd_{1\beta} \lambda y.(\lambda w.w)$$
$$\equiv \lambda yw.w \qquad \equiv_\alpha \lambda yz.z.$$

1.42 (a) For all M, N: $M =_\beta (\lambda xy.x)MN$ since $(\lambda xy.x)MN \rhd_\beta M$,
$= (\lambda xy.y)MN$ by proposed new axiom,
$=_\beta N$.

(b) Let $\mathsf{K} \equiv \lambda xy.x$. Then $(\mathsf{K}X)Y =_\beta X$. Hence, for all M, N:

$$(\lambda xy.yx)(\mathbf{K}M)(\mathbf{K}N) =_\beta (\mathbf{K}N)(\mathbf{K}M) =_\beta N,$$
$$(\lambda x.x)(\mathbf{K}M)(\mathbf{K}N) =_\beta (\mathbf{K}M)(\mathbf{K}N) =_\beta M.$$

Also $(\lambda xy.yx)(\mathbf{K}M)(\mathbf{K}N) = (\lambda x.x)(\mathbf{K}M)(\mathbf{K}N)$ would follow from the proposed new axiom. These equations together imply $M = N$.

2.8 (a) Simultaneous substitution is defined in CL thus:

$$[U_1/x_1,\ldots,U_n/x_n]x_i \equiv U_i \quad \text{for } 1 \le i \le n;$$
$$[U_1/x_1,\ldots,U_n/x_n]a \equiv a \quad \text{if } a \text{ is an atom} \notin \{x_1,\ldots,x_n\},$$
$$[U_1/x_1,\ldots,U_n/x_n](XY) \equiv \big([U_1/x_1,\ldots,U_n/x_n]X\ [U_1/x_1,\ldots,U_n/x_n]Y\big).$$

(b) The given identity is true if (for $1 \le i \le n$) U_i contains none of x_1, $\ldots$, x_n. It is also true under the weaker condition that (for $2 \le i \le n$) U_i contains none of x_1, $\ldots$, x_{i-1}.

2.13 $\underline{\mathbf{SIK}x} \rhd_{1w} \underline{\mathbf{I}x}(\mathbf{K}x) \rhd_{1w} x(\mathbf{K}x)$. This is a nf.

$\underline{\mathbf{SSK}x\,y} \rhd_{1w} \underline{\mathbf{S}x(\mathbf{K}x)\,y} \rhd_{1w} xy(\underline{\mathbf{K}xy}) \rhd_{1w} xyx.$

$\underline{\mathbf{S}(\mathbf{SK})xy} \rhd_{1w} \underline{\mathbf{SK}y(xy)} \rhd_{1w} \underline{\mathbf{K}(xy)(y(xy))} \rhd_{1w} xy.$

$\underline{\mathbf{S}(\mathbf{KS})\mathbf{S}\,x}\,y\,z \rhd_{1w} \underline{\mathbf{KS}x}(\mathbf{S}x)yz \rhd_{1w} \underline{\mathbf{S}(\mathbf{S}x)yz}$

$\rhd_{1w} \underline{\mathbf{S}xz(yz)} \rhd_{1w} x(yz)(z(yz)).$

$\underline{\mathbf{SBBI}}\,x\,y \rhd_{1w} \big(\mathbf{BI}(\mathbf{BI})x\big)\,y \rhd_w \underline{\mathbf{I}(\mathbf{BI}x)}\,y$ by Example 2.11,

$\rhd_{1w} \mathbf{BI}xy \rhd_w \underline{\mathbf{I}(xy)} \rhd_{1w} xy.$

2.17 One answer is: $\mathbf{B}' \equiv \mathbf{S}(\mathbf{K}(\mathbf{SB}))\mathbf{K}$, where $\mathbf{B} \equiv \mathbf{S}(\mathbf{KS})\mathbf{K}$; and $\mathbf{W} \equiv \mathbf{SS}(\mathbf{KI})$. There are other possible answers.

2.22 $[x].u(vx) \equiv \mathbf{S}([x].u)([x].vx)$ by 2.18(f), $\equiv \mathbf{S}(\mathbf{K}u)v$ by 2.18(a),(c).
$[x].x(\mathbf{S}y) \equiv \mathbf{S}([x].x)([x].\mathbf{S}y)$ by 2.18(f), $\equiv \mathbf{SI}(\mathbf{K}(\mathbf{S}y))$ by 2.18(b),(a).
$[x].uxxv \equiv \mathbf{S}([x].uxx)([x].v)$ by 2.18(f); then use 2.18(f),(a) to get
$\equiv \mathbf{S}(\mathbf{S}([x].ux)([x].x))(\mathbf{K}v)$, $\equiv \mathbf{S}(\mathbf{S}u\mathbf{I})(\mathbf{K}v)$ by 2.18(c),(b).

2.26 $[x,y,z].xzy \equiv \mathbf{S}(\mathbf{S}(\mathbf{KS})(\mathbf{S}(\mathbf{KK})\mathbf{S}))(\mathbf{KK})$. This $\not\equiv$ the $\mathbf{C}$ in 2.12, but has some similarities with it. For $[x,y,z].y(xz)$ and $[x,y].xyy$ we get exactly the terms $\mathbf{B}'$ and $\mathbf{W}$ shown in the answer to 2.17.

2.30 $\mathbf{BWBI}x \rhd_w \mathbf{W}(\mathbf{BI})x \rhd_w \mathbf{BI}xx \rhd_w \mathbf{I}(xx) \rhd_{1w} xx;$
also $\mathbf{SII}x \rhd_{1w} \mathbf{I}x(\mathbf{I}x) \rhd_{1w} x(\mathbf{I}x) \rhd_{1w} xx.$

2.34 (a) The pairing-combinator $\mathbf{D}$ most often used in the literature comes from [Chu41, p. 30]: $\mathbf{D} \equiv [x,y,z].zxy$, with its two projections $\mathbf{D}_i \equiv [u].u([x_1,x_2].x_i)$ for $i = 1, 2$. Another is given in Note 4.14.

(b) If A exists, then $\mathbf{S} =_w A\mathbf{K} =_w A(\mathbf{KKK}) =_w \mathbf{K}$, contrary to 2.32.3.

(c) If X is a nf, it is obviously minimal. If X is not a nf, then it contains a weak redex. But a weak redex never contracts to itself. (This is obvious for $\mathbf{I}U \triangleright_w U$ and $\mathbf{K}UV \triangleright_w U$; for $\mathbf{S}UVW \triangleright_w UW(VW)$, if $(\mathbf{S}UV)W \equiv (UW)(VW)$ then $W \equiv VW$, which is impossible.) Hence, if X is not a nf, X must be non-minimal.

If $\mathbf{W}XY \triangleright_w XYY$ was a contraction, we could have $\mathbf{WWW} \triangleright_w \mathbf{WWW}$.

3.5 (a) Let $\mathbf{Y} \equiv \mathbf{Y}_{\text{Curry-Ros}} \equiv \lambda x.(\lambda y.x(yy))(\lambda y.x(yy))$. Then

$$\begin{array}{rlll} \mathbf{Y}X & =_{\beta,w} & VV & \text{where } V \equiv \lambda z.X(zz) \text{ where } z \notin FV(X) \\ & \equiv & (\lambda z.X(zz))V & \text{since } V \equiv \lambda z.X(zz), \\ & =_{\beta,w} & X(VV) & \\ & =_{\beta,w} & X(\mathbf{Y}X) & \text{by the first line reversed.} \end{array}$$

(b) The exercise requires terms $X_1, \ldots, X_k$ such that, for $1 \le i \le k$,

$$X_i y_1 \ldots y_n \ =_{\beta,w}\ [X_1/x_1, \ldots, X_k/x_k]\, Z_i. \tag{1}$$

To get them, we can combine the k given equations into one, solve the combined equation by applying Corollary 3.3.1, and then split the solution into k parts. But to make this method work, the details need care.[1]

First, make a k-tuple combinator and k projection-combinators, by analogy with Exercise 2.34: let $\mathbf{D}^{(k)} \equiv \lambda x_1 \ldots x_k z\,.\, z x_1 \ldots x_k$ and $\mathbf{D}_i^{(k)} \equiv \lambda u.\, u(\lambda x_1 \ldots x_k . x_i)$ $(1 \le i \le k)$. These satisfy

$$\mathbf{D}_i^{(k)}\big(\mathbf{D}^{(k)} x_1 \ldots x_k\big) \ \triangleright_{\beta,w}\ x_i. \tag{2}$$

Choose a variable $x \notin FV(x_1 \ldots x_k y_1 \ldots y_n Z_1 \ldots Z_k)$; define, for $1 \le i \le k$,

$$E_i \ \equiv\ \lambda y_1 \ldots y_n . \mathbf{D}_i^{(k)}(x y_1 \ldots y_n), \quad Z_i^\star \ \equiv\ [E_1/x_1, \ldots, E_k/x_k]\, Z_i. \tag{3}$$

By Corollary 3.3.1, solve the equation $x y_1 \ldots y_n = \mathbf{D}^{(k)} Z_1^\star \ldots Z_k^\star$. This gives a term X, not containing any of $y_1, \ldots, y_n$, such that

$$X y_1 \ldots y_n \ =_{\beta,w}\ \mathbf{D}^{(k)}([X/x]Z_1^\star) \ldots ([X/x]Z_k^\star). \tag{4}$$

Define, for $1 \le i \le k$,

$$X_i \ \equiv\ [X/x]E_i \ \equiv\ \lambda y_1 \ldots y_n . \mathbf{D}_i^{(k)}(X y_1 \ldots y_n). \tag{5}$$

Then, for $1 \le i \le k$,

$$[X/x]Z_i^\star \ \equiv\ [X_1/x_1, \ldots, X_k/x_k]\, Z_i. \tag{6}$$

[1] More care than they received in [HS86]! Its answer was incorrect, as several readers pointed out.

Finally, for $1 \le i \le k$,

$$\begin{aligned} X_i y_1 \dots y_n &=_{\beta,w} \mathbf{D}_i^{(k)}(Xy_1 \dots y_n) && \text{by (5)},\\ &=_{\beta,w} \mathbf{D}_i^{(k)}(\mathbf{D}^{(k)}([X/x]Z_1^\star)\dots([X/x]Z_k^\star)) && \text{by (4)},\\ &=_{\beta,w} [X/x]Z_i^\star && \text{by (2)},\\ &\equiv [X_1/x_1,\dots,X_k/x_k]\,Z_i && \text{by (6)}. \end{aligned}$$

3.12 (a) (i) Choose $n = 2$ and $L_1 \equiv \lambda xy.y$, $L_2 \equiv \lambda xy.x$.

(ii) Choose $n = 5$, $L_1 \equiv \lambda xy.yx$, $L_2 \equiv L_3 \equiv L_4 \equiv \lambda x.x$, $L_5 \equiv \lambda xy.x$. (These answers are by John D. Stone. They have the property that each L_i is either a *permutator* (such as $\lambda xy.yx$ or $\lambda xyz.yxz$) or a *selector* (such as $\lambda xy.x$ or $\lambda x.x$ or $\lambda xyz.y$). It is known that suitable $L_1,\dots,L_n$ for Böhm's theorem can always be found with this property. But the choice of $n, L_1,\dots,L_n$ is not unique; e.g. for (ii) above, we could choose $n = 4$ and $L_1 \equiv \lambda x.x$, $L_2 \equiv \lambda u.u(\lambda xy.y)$, $L_3 \equiv \lambda xyz.y$, $L_4 \equiv \lambda xy.y$.)

(b) First, if a closed term Y is a strong nf, then Yx weakly reduces to a strong nf Z (proof by induction on Definition 3.8). By Lemma 3.10, Z is also a weak nf. Hence so is xZ. Therefore by Corollary 2.32.3, $Z \neq_w xZ$. But the equation $Yx =_w x(Yx)$ would imply $Z =_w xZ$.

(c) In CL, $\mathbf{Y}_{\text{Curry-Ros}} \equiv \mathbf{S}WW$, where $W \equiv \mathbf{S}(\mathbf{S}(\mathbf{KS})\mathbf{K})(\mathbf{K}(\mathbf{SII}))$. It seems abstraction often produces weak nfs. To change 'often' to 'always', look at Definition 2.18: omit clause (c) and restrict clause (a) to the case that M is an atom. By Remark 2.23, the resulting term (which we call here '$[x]^{fab}.M$') has the property that $([x]^{fab}.M)X \triangleright_w [X/x]M$. By induction on M, one can prove that $[x]^{fab}.M$ is always a weak nf, even when M is not one; e.g. $[x]^{fab}.(\mathbf{IK}) \equiv \mathbf{S}(\mathbf{KI})(\mathbf{KK})$. Finally, choose

$$X' \equiv [y_1,\dots,y_n]^{fab}.Z.$$

4.10 First, we prove $m \dot- (k+1) = \pi(m \dot- k)$. (*Case* 1: if $k < m$ then $k+1 \le m$, so $m \dot- k = m - k$ and $m \dot- (k+1) = m - (k+1) = \pi(m-k) = \pi(m \dot- k)$. *Case* 2: if $k \ge m$ then $k+1 > m$, so $m \dot- (k+1) = 0 = m \dot- k = \pi(m \dot- k)$ since $\pi(0) = 0$.)

Hence $m \dot- (k+1) = \pi(\Pi_2^3(k, m \dot- k, m))$. Also $m \dot- 0 = m = \Pi_1^1(m)$. Now Π_1^1, Π_2^3 are primitive recursive by 4.8(III), and so is π by 4.9. Hence $\dot-$ is primitive recursive by 4.8(V) with

$$n = 1, \qquad \psi = \Pi_1^1, \qquad \chi = \Pi_2^3.$$

4.16 (a) The definition of ϕ can be written thus: $\phi(0) = 2$, $\phi(k+1) = 3 + \phi(k) = \sigma(\sigma(\sigma(\phi(k))))$. To represent ϕ, choose:

$$\overline{\phi} \equiv \mathbf{R}\,(\overline{\sigma}(\overline{\sigma}\overline{0}))\,Y, \quad \text{where} \quad Y \equiv \lambda xy.\,\overline{\sigma}(\overline{\sigma}(\overline{\sigma}y)).$$

Then $\overline{\phi}(\overline{0}) \equiv \mathbf{R}\overline{2}Y\overline{0} =_{\beta,w} \overline{2}$ by (6) in the proof of Theorem 4.11. Also

$$\overline{\phi}\,(\overline{k+1}) \equiv \mathbf{R}\,\overline{2}\,Y\,\overline{k+1} =_{\beta,w} Y\,\overline{k}\,(\mathbf{R}\,\overline{2}\,Y\,\overline{k}) \quad \text{by (6)}$$
$$=_{\beta,w} Y\,\overline{k}\,(\overline{\phi}\,\overline{k})$$
$$=_{\beta,w} \overline{\sigma}\,(\overline{\sigma}\,(\overline{\sigma}\,(\overline{\phi}\,\overline{k}))).$$

(b) First: $Add(m,0) = m$, $Add(m,k+1) = Add(m,k)+1$;
$Mult(m,0) = 0$, $Mult(m,k+1) = Add(Mult(m,k),m)$;
$Exp(m,0) = 1$, $Exp(m,k+1) = Mult(Exp(m,k),m)$.

Suitable representatives using $\mathbf{R}$:

$$\overline{Add} \equiv \lambda uv\,.\,\mathbf{R}\,u\,Y\,v, \quad \text{where } Y \equiv \lambda xy\,.\,\overline{\sigma}\,y;$$
$$\overline{Mult} \equiv \lambda uv\,.\,\mathbf{R}\,\overline{0}\,Y\,v, \quad \text{where } Y \equiv \lambda xy\,.\,\overline{Add}\,u\,y;$$
$$\overline{Exp} \equiv \lambda uv.\,\mathbf{R}\,\overline{1}\,Y\,v, \quad \text{where } Y \equiv \lambda xy.\,\overline{Mult}\,u\,y.$$

(c) For $\dot{-}$: $m \dot{-} (k+1) = \pi(m \dot{-} k)$ by the answer to 4.10. Also $m \dot{-} 0 = m$. Representative: $\lambda x\,.\,\mathbf{R}x(\lambda u.\overline{\pi}\,)$.

(d) Short representatives, by Rosser [Chu41, pp. 10, 30]: $\overline{Add}_{\text{Rosser}} \equiv \lambda uvxy.ux(vxy)$, $\overline{Mult}_{\text{Rosser}} \equiv \lambda uvx.u(vx)$, $\overline{Exp}_{\text{Rosser}} \equiv \lambda uv.vu$.

4.27 (From [CHS72, Section 13A3, Theorem 2]) Suppose π could be represented by a term P. Then $P\widehat{0} =_{\beta,w} \widehat{0}$, $P\widehat{k+1} =_{\beta,w} \widehat{k}$. Since $\widehat{0}$ and $\widehat{\sigma}$ are atoms, we could substitute any terms for them and the conversions '$=_{\beta,w}$' would stay correct. Substitute $\mathbf{K}$ for $\widehat{0}$ and $\mathbf{KS}$ for $\widehat{\sigma}$. This makes $\widehat{k+1} =_{\beta,w} \mathbf{S}$ for all $k \geq 0$. Hence, after the substitution, we would get

$$\mathbf{S} =_{\beta,w} \widehat{1} =_{\beta,w} P\widehat{2} =_{\beta,w} P\mathbf{S} =_{\beta,w} P\widehat{1} =_{\beta,w} \widehat{0} \equiv \mathbf{K}.$$

5.8 Let $\mathcal{A}$ be the set of all closed λI-terms and $\mathcal{B}$ be the set of all non-closed λI-terms.

5.9 (a) [Bar84, Theorem 20.2.5] Let the range of F have $n \geq 2$ members, say $M_1, \ldots, M_n$ (modulo $=_{\beta,w}$). Define $\mathcal{A}_i$ to be the set $\{X : FX =_{\beta,w} M_i\}$. Then $\mathcal{A}_1, \ldots, \mathcal{A}_n$ are non-empty and closed under conversion.

As mentioned in 5.7, the theory of $=_{\beta,w}$ can be written out as formal axioms and rules. Hence the set $\{\langle X,Y\rangle : FX =_{\beta,w} Y\}$ is recursively enumerable ('r.e.'), and $\{X : FX =_{\beta,w} M_i\}$ is r.e. too. Let $\mathcal{B} = \mathcal{A}_2 \cup \ldots \cup \mathcal{A}_n$. Then $\mathcal{B}$ is r.e. Since its complement is $\mathcal{A}_1$ which is also r.e., both $\mathcal{B}$ and $\mathcal{A}_1$ must be recursive, contrary to Theorem 5.6.

(b) Let T, N be as in the proof of 5.6. Choose $y \notin FV(F)$ and define, by analogy with (10) in Chapter 5,

$$X_F \equiv H'\ulcorner H'\urcorner, \quad \text{where } H' \equiv \lambda y.F(Ty(Ny)).$$

7.6 To derive (ξ) in $\lambda\beta_{-\xi+\zeta}$, we deduce $\lambda x.M = \lambda x.M'$ from an equation $M = M'$ thus. Rule (β) gives $(\lambda x.M)x = [x/x]M \equiv M$. We assume $M = M'$. And (β) with rule (σ) give $M' = (\lambda x.M')x$. From these, rule (τ) gives $(\lambda x.M)x = (\lambda x.M')x$. Then ($\zeta$) gives $\lambda x.M = \lambda x.M'$.

8.3 For (ζ): let $X \equiv \mathsf{S}(\mathsf{K}u)\mathsf{I}$ and $Y \equiv u$. Then $Xx =_w ux \equiv Yx$ but $X \neq_w Y$. For (ξ): let $X \equiv \mathsf{S}(\mathsf{K}u)\mathsf{I}x$, $Y \equiv ux$. Then $X =_w Y$ but $[x].X \equiv \mathsf{S}(\mathsf{K}u)\mathsf{I}$ and $[x].Y \equiv u$, so $[x].X \neq_w [x].Y$.

9.19 (a) (From [CF58, Section 6F, Theorem 3].) If $U \succ X$ and $U \succ Y$, then $X =_{Cext} Y$ by 8.17(d), so $X_\lambda =_{\lambda ext} Y_\lambda$ by 9.17(c). Hence, by 7.16.1, there exists T such that $X_\lambda \triangleright_{\beta\eta} T$ and $Y_\lambda \triangleright_{\beta\eta} T$. Then, by 9.18(1), $X_{\lambda H_\eta} \succ T_{H_\eta}$ and $Y_{\lambda H_\eta} \succ T_{H_\eta}$. That is, by 9.17(a), $X \succ T_{H_\eta}$ and $Y \succ T_{H_\eta}$.

(b) (From [CF58, Section 6F, p. 221].) Choose $X \equiv \mathsf{SK}$, $Y \equiv \mathsf{KI}$. By 8.16(a), $X \succ Y$. But $X_\lambda \equiv (\lambda xyz.xz(yz))(\lambda uv.u)$, which $\beta\eta$-reduces in three steps to three terms, none of which is $\equiv_\alpha \mathsf{K}_\lambda \mathsf{I}_\lambda$.

(c) By induction on Definition 3.8, X in strong nf implies $X \equiv M_{H_\eta}$ for some M in β-nf. By 7.14, this M has a $\beta\eta$-nf. Also η-contractions in M do not change M_{H_η}, since

$$(\lambda x.Px)_{H_\eta} \;\equiv\; [x]^\eta.(P_{H_\eta}x) \;\equiv\; P_{H_\eta} \quad \text{if } x \notin \mathrm{FV}(P).$$

Finally, by induction on the clauses of Lemma 1.33, M in β-nf implies M_{H_η} in strong nf.

9.28 Let $X_\lambda =_\beta \lambda x.M$. Then by the Church-Rosser theorem, 1.41, $X_\lambda \triangleright_\beta T$ and $\lambda x.M \triangleright_\beta T$ for some T. From the latter, T must have form $\lambda x.Q$ with $M \triangleright_\beta Q$.

Since $X_\lambda \triangleright_\beta T \equiv \lambda x.Q$, the standardization theorem [Bar84, Theorem 11.4.7] gives a standard reduction from X_λ to $\lambda x.Q$. In a standard reduction, no 'internal' contraction can precede a 'head' contraction, i.e. a contraction of a redex whose leftmost λ is the leftmost symbol of the whole term (except for parentheses). And internal contractions cannot change a non-abstraction-term into an abstraction-term. Hence the standard reduction from X_λ to $\lambda x.Q$ must first change X_λ to an abstraction-term $\lambda x.P$ by head-contractions, then change P to Q.

Now apply the mapping H_β. Head-contractions can be seen to translate into CL as weak reductions. Hence

$$(X_\lambda)_{H_\beta} \;\triangleright_w\; (\lambda x.P)_{H_\beta} \;\equiv\; [x]^\beta.(P_{H_\beta}).$$

But, by 9.27, $(X_\lambda)_{H_\beta} \equiv X$ and $[x]^\beta.(P_{H_\beta})$ is fnl.

9.30 (b) $\mathsf{SK} =_{C\beta} \mathsf{KI}$, because $(\mathsf{SK})_\lambda \equiv_\alpha (\lambda xyz.xz(yz))(\lambda uv.u) \rhd_\beta \lambda yz.z$ and $(\mathsf{KI})_\lambda \equiv_\alpha (\lambda uv.u)(\lambda x.x) \rhd_\lambda \lambda vx.x \equiv_\alpha \lambda yz.z$. Also $\mathsf{SK} \neq_w \mathsf{KI}$ by 2.32.3, because SK, KI are distinct weak nfs.

(c) $\mathsf{S}(\mathsf{KI})yz \rhd_w \mathsf{KI}z(yz) \rhd_w \mathsf{I}(yz) \rhd_w yz$, and $\mathsf{I}yz \rhd_w yz$, so

$$\mathsf{S}(\mathsf{KI})yz =_w \mathsf{I}yz;$$

hence, by rule (ζ) twice, $\mathsf{S}(\mathsf{KI}) =_{C ext} \mathsf{I}$. Also $\mathsf{S}(\mathsf{KI}) \neq_{C\beta} \mathsf{I}$, because $(\mathsf{S}(\mathsf{KI}))_\lambda \rhd_\beta \lambda xy.xy$ and $\lambda xy.xy \not\rhd_\beta \lambda x.x$.

11.8 (a)

$$\dfrac{\overset{(\to\mathsf{K})}{\mathsf{K} : (\sigma\to\sigma)\to\tau\to\sigma\to\sigma} \qquad \overset{(\to\mathsf{I})}{\mathsf{I} : \sigma\to\sigma}}{\mathsf{KI} : \tau\to\sigma\to\sigma\,.}\,(\to\mathrm{e})$$

(b) Let $\mu \equiv \sigma\to\tau$, $\nu \equiv \rho\to\sigma$, and $\pi \equiv \rho\to\tau$:

$$\dfrac{\overset{(\to\mathsf{S})}{\mathsf{S} : (\mu\to\nu\to\pi)\to(\mu\to\nu)\to\mu\to\pi} \qquad \overset{\text{By Example 11.7}}{\mathsf{B} : \mu\to\nu\to\pi}}{\mathsf{SB} : (\mu\to\nu) \to \mu\to\pi\,.}\,(\to\mathrm{e})$$

(c) Let $\mu \equiv \sigma\to\sigma\to\tau$, $\nu \equiv \sigma\to\sigma$, and $\pi \equiv \sigma\to\tau$:

$$\dfrac{\dfrac{\overset{(\to\mathsf{S})}{\mathsf{S} : (\mu\to\nu\to\pi)\to(\mu\to\nu)\to\mu\to\pi} \qquad \overset{(\to\mathsf{S})}{\mathsf{S} : \mu\to\nu\to\pi}}{\mathsf{SS} : (\mu\to\nu)\to\mu\to\pi}\,(\to\mathrm{e}) \qquad \overset{\text{By (a)}}{\mathsf{KI} : \mu\to\nu}}{\mathsf{SS}(\mathsf{KI}) : \mu\to\pi\,.}\,(\to\mathrm{e})$$

(d)

$$\dfrac{\overset{(\to\mathsf{K})}{\mathsf{K} : (\sigma\to\tau\to\sigma)\to\rho\to\sigma\to\tau\to\sigma} \qquad \overset{(\to\mathsf{K})}{\mathsf{K} : \sigma\to\tau\to\sigma}}{\mathsf{KK} : \rho\to\sigma\to\tau\to\sigma\,.}\,(\to\mathrm{e})$$

(e) Apply (a), taking the special case that the σ in (a) is the same as the present type τ, and the τ in (a) is $\tau\to\tau$ for the present τ.

(f) Apply (b), taking the special case $\rho \equiv \tau \equiv \sigma$.

(g) Apply rule $(\to\mathrm{e})$ repeatedly to (e) and (f).

11.9 (a) Here is a deduction of $\mathbf{S}UVW:\tau$ whose only non-axiom assumptions are $U:\rho\to\sigma\to\tau$, $V:\rho\to\sigma$, $W:\rho$:

$$\dfrac{\dfrac{\dfrac{\overset{(\to\mathbf{S})}{\mathbf{S}:(\rho\to\sigma\to\tau)\to(\rho\to\sigma)\to\rho\to\tau} \qquad U:\rho\to\sigma\to\tau}{\mathbf{S}U:(\rho\to\sigma)\to\rho\to\tau} \qquad V:\rho\to\sigma}{\mathbf{S}UV:\rho\to\tau} \qquad W:\rho}{\mathbf{S}UVW:\tau\,.}$$

(b)

$$\dfrac{\dfrac{U:\rho\to\sigma\to\tau \qquad W:\rho}{UW:\sigma\to\tau} \qquad \dfrac{V:\rho\to\sigma \qquad W:\rho}{VW:\sigma}}{UW(VW):\tau\,.}$$

(c) and (d)

$$\dfrac{\dfrac{\overset{(\to\mathbf{K})}{\mathbf{K}:\rho\to\sigma\to\rho} \qquad U:\rho}{\mathbf{K}U:\sigma\to\rho} \qquad V:\sigma}{\mathbf{K}UV:\rho\,,} \qquad\qquad \dfrac{\overset{(\to\mathbf{I})}{\mathbf{I}:\rho\to\rho} \qquad U:\rho}{\mathbf{I}U:\rho\,.}$$

(e)

$$\dfrac{x:\rho\to\sigma \qquad x:\rho}{xx:\sigma\,.}$$

11.15 (a) First, $x:\rho\to\sigma\to\tau,\ y:\sigma,\ z:\rho \vdash_{\mathrm{TA}_{\mathrm{C}}^{\to}} xzy:\tau$ thus:

$$\dfrac{\dfrac{x:\rho\to\sigma\to\tau \qquad z:\rho}{xz:\sigma\to\tau} \qquad y:\sigma}{xzy:\tau\,.}$$

Hence by Corollary 11.14.1,

$$\vdash_{\mathrm{TA}_{\mathrm{C}}^{\to}} \quad \big([x,y,z].xzy\big):(\rho\to\sigma\to\tau)\to\sigma\to\rho\to\tau\,.$$

(b) First, $x:\tau,\ y:\tau,\ z:\mathbf{N}_\tau \vdash_{\mathrm{TA}_{\mathrm{C}}^{\to}} z(\mathbf{K}y)x:\tau$ thus:

$$\dfrac{\dfrac{z:(\tau\to\tau)\to\tau\to\tau \qquad \dfrac{\overset{(\to\mathbf{K})}{\mathbf{K}:\tau\to\tau\to\tau} \qquad y:\tau}{\mathbf{K}y:\tau\to\tau}}{z(\mathbf{K}y):\tau\to\tau} \qquad x:\tau}{z(\mathbf{K}y)x:\tau\,.}$$

Hence by Corollary 11.14.1,

$$\vdash_{\mathrm{TA}_C^{\to}} \quad ([x,y,z].\,z(\mathbf{K}y)x) : \tau \to \tau \to \mathbf{N}_\tau \to \tau\,.$$

(c) Given any τ, let $\xi \equiv \mathbf{N}_\tau \equiv (\tau\to\tau)\to\tau\to\tau$. By 11.8(e) and (g) applied to ξ instead of τ, we get $\vdash \overline{0} : \mathbf{N}_\xi$ and $\vdash \overline{1} : \mathbf{N}_\xi$. Also, by 11.8(f), $\vdash \overline{\sigma} : \mathbf{N}_\tau \to \mathbf{N}_\tau$. Hence, using 11.15(b), from two assumptions $y : \mathbf{N}_\tau \to \mathbf{N}_\tau \to \mathbf{N}_\tau$ and $v : \mathbf{N}_\xi \to \mathbf{N}_\tau$ we can deduce

$$\mathbf{D}\,(\overline{\sigma}(v\overline{0}))\,(y(v\overline{0})(v\overline{1})) : \mathbf{N}_{\mathbf{N}_\tau} \to \mathbf{N}_\tau\,.$$

Note that $\mathbf{N}_{\mathbf{N}_\tau} \equiv \mathbf{N}_\xi$. Then Corollary 11.14.1 gives

$$\vdash_{\mathrm{TA}_C^{\to}} \quad Q : (\mathbf{N}_\tau \to \mathbf{N}_\tau \to \mathbf{N}_\tau) \to (\mathbf{N}_\xi \to \mathbf{N}_\tau) \to \mathbf{N}_\xi \to \mathbf{N}_\tau\,.$$

We must make a deduction that will give

$$x : \mathbf{N}_\tau,\; y : \mathbf{N}_\tau \to \mathbf{N}_\tau \to \mathbf{N}_\tau,\; u : \mathbf{N}_{\tau^\star} \quad \vdash_{\mathrm{TA}_C^{\to}} \quad u(Qy)(\mathbf{D}\overline{0}x)\overline{1} : \mathbf{N}_\tau\,.$$

Note that $\tau^\star \equiv \mathbf{N}_{\mathbf{N}_\tau} \to \mathbf{N}_\tau \equiv \mathbf{N}_\xi \to \mathbf{N}_\tau$; hence

$$\mathbf{N}_{\tau^\star} \equiv ((\mathbf{N}_\xi \to \mathbf{N}_\tau) \to \mathbf{N}_\xi \to \mathbf{N}_\tau) \to (\mathbf{N}_\xi \to \mathbf{N}_\tau) \to \mathbf{N}_\xi \to \mathbf{N}_\tau\,.$$

Note also that $\vdash \overline{0} : \mathbf{N}_\tau$, by 11.8(e). Using these facts, the required deduction is not hard to construct.

12.9 (a)

$$\dfrac{\dfrac{\overset{1}{[y:\sigma]}}{\lambda y.y : \sigma\to\sigma}\,(\to\mathrm{i}-1)}{\lambda xy.y : \tau\to\sigma\to\sigma\,.}\,(\to\mathrm{i}-\mathrm{v})$$

(b)

$$\dfrac{\dfrac{\dfrac{\dfrac{\overset{1}{[x:\sigma\to\tau]} \qquad \dfrac{\dfrac{\overset{2}{[u:(\sigma\to\tau)\to\rho\to\sigma]} \quad \overset{1}{[x:\sigma\to\tau]}}{ux : \rho\to\sigma}\,(\to\mathrm{e}) \quad \overset{3}{[y:\rho]}}{uxy : \sigma}\,(\to\mathrm{e})}{x(uxy) : \tau}\,(\to\mathrm{e})}{\lambda y.x(uxy) : \rho\to\tau}\,(\to\mathrm{i}-3)}{\lambda xy.x(uxy) : (\sigma\to\tau)\to\rho\to\tau}\,(\to\mathrm{i}-1)}{\lambda uxy.x(uxy) : ((\sigma\to\tau)\to\rho\to\sigma)\to(\sigma\to\tau)\to\rho\to\tau\,.}\,(\to\mathrm{i}-2)$$

(c)

$$\dfrac{\dfrac{\dfrac{\dfrac{\overset{1}{[x:\sigma\to\sigma\to\tau]}\quad\overset{2}{[y:\sigma]}}{xy:\sigma\to\tau}\,(\to\mathrm{e})\qquad\overset{2}{[y:\sigma]}}{xyy:\tau}\,(\to\mathrm{e})}{\lambda y.xyy:\sigma\to\tau}\,(\to\mathrm{i}-2)}{\lambda xy.xyy:(\sigma\to\sigma\to\tau)\to\sigma\to\tau\,.}\,(\to\mathrm{i}-1)$$

(d)

$$\dfrac{\dfrac{\dfrac{\overset{1}{y:\sigma}}{\lambda z.y:\tau\to\sigma}\,(\to\mathrm{i}-\mathrm{v})}{\lambda yz.y:\sigma\to\tau\to\sigma}\,(\to\mathrm{i}-1)}{\lambda xyz.y:\rho\to\sigma\to\tau\to\sigma\,.}\,(\to\mathrm{i}-\mathrm{v})$$

(e) In (a), let the σ in (a) be the present τ, and let the τ in (a) be the present $\tau\to\tau$.

(f) In (b), take the special case $\rho\equiv\sigma\equiv\tau$.

(g) Note that $x^0y\equiv y$ and $x^ny\equiv x(x^{n-1}y)$ for $n\geq 1$. Build, for every $n\geq 0$, a deduction $\mathcal{D}_n$ of $x^ny:\tau$ from assumptions $x:\tau\to\tau$ and $y:\tau$, thus: $\mathcal{D}_0$ is the one-step deduction $y:\tau$, and if $\mathcal{D}_{n-1}$ has already been built, build $\mathcal{D}_n$ thus:

$$\dfrac{x:\tau\to\tau\qquad\begin{matrix}\mathcal{D}_{n-1}\\ x^{n-1}y:\tau\end{matrix}}{x(x^{n-1}y):\tau\,.}\,(\to\mathrm{e})$$

Then apply $(\to\mathrm{i})$ twice, thus:

$$\dfrac{\dfrac{\begin{matrix}\mathcal{D}_n\\ x^ny:\tau\end{matrix}}{\lambda y.x^ny:\tau\to\tau}\,(\to\mathrm{i},\ \text{discharging } y:\tau \text{ in } \mathcal{D}_n)}{\lambda xy.x^ny:(\tau\to\tau)\to\tau\to\tau\,.}\,(\to\mathrm{i},\ \text{discharging } x:\tau\to\tau \text{ in } \mathcal{D}_n)$$

12.15 Since $\mathbf{B}\equiv\lambda xyz.x(yz)$, any $\mathrm{TA}_\lambda^{\to}$-deduction of a type for $\mathbf{B}$ must begin with a deduction for $x(yz)$ using rule $(\to\mathrm{e})$; this must have form

$$\dfrac{x:\sigma\to\tau\qquad\dfrac{y:\rho\to\sigma\qquad z:\rho}{yz:\sigma}\,(\to e)}{x(yz):\tau\,,}\,(\to e)$$

where ρ, σ, τ can be any types. The next steps in the deduction must come from three applications of ($\to$i); hence the result.

12.16 Since $\mathbf{Y}_{\text{Curry-Ros}} \equiv \lambda x.(\lambda y.x(yy))(\lambda y.x(yy))$, any $\text{TA}_\lambda^{\to}$-deduction of a type for $\mathbf{Y}_{\text{Curry-Ros}}$ must contain a deduction for $\lambda y.x(yy)$. This must begin with steps of form

$$\dfrac{x:\sigma\to\tau \qquad \dfrac{y:\rho\to\sigma \qquad y:\rho}{yy:\sigma}\,(\to e)}{x(yy):\tau\,.}\,(\to e)$$

Then ($\to$i) must be applied. But the condition in ($\to$i) prevents this, because the two assumptions for y have different types (see Remark 12.8).

12.31 (a) In Theorem 12.30, take H to be H_η. Then $(X_\lambda)_H \equiv X$ by 9.11, so 12.30(a) and 12.30(b) together give the result.

(b) Let $M \equiv \lambda xy.xy$. Then $(a\to b)\to a\to b$ is a p.t. of M. Hence a shorter type such as $c\to c$ cannot be assigned to M. But $c\to c$ is a p.t. of $\mathbf{I}$, and $M_{H_\eta} \equiv [x].([y].xy) \equiv [x].x \equiv \mathbf{I}$.

(c) For H_w and H_β, M_H is typable iff M is typable, and both have the same p.t. In fact, for all environments Γ, $\Gamma \vdash_{\text{TA}_C^{\to}} M_H:\tau$ iff $\Gamma \vdash_{\text{TA}_\lambda^{\to}} M:\tau$.

Proof-outline: By 12.30(b), it is enough to prove that

$$\Gamma \vdash_{\text{TA}_C^{\to}} M_H:\tau \quad\Longrightarrow\quad \Gamma \vdash_{\text{TA}_\lambda^{\to}} M:\tau. \tag{7}$$

We prove (7) by induction on $lgh(M)$. The difficult case is $M \equiv \lambda x.P$, with $M_H \equiv [x].(P_H)$. By 9.23 for H_w and 9.27 for H_β, $[x].(P_H)$ is functional. It is easy to see this implies τ is not an atom, so $\tau \equiv \rho\to\sigma$.

We may assume x is not a subject in Γ. Then by rule ($\to$e),

$$\Gamma,\ x:\rho \vdash_{\text{TA}_C^{\to}} (([x].P_H)x):\sigma.$$

But $([x].P_H)x \rhd_w P_H$ by 2.21, so by 11.19, $\Gamma,\ x:\rho \vdash_{\text{TA}_C^{\to}} P_H:\sigma$. Hence by the induction hypothesis,

$$\Gamma,\ x:\rho \vdash_{\text{TA}_\lambda^{\to}} P:\sigma,$$

and the conclusion of (7) follows by rule ($\to$i).

14.10 A combinatory algebra has ≥ 2 members. But, if $i = k$ or $k = s$ or $s = i$, we shall prove $d = i$ for all $d \in D$.

First, if $i = k$ then, for all $c, d \in D$, $c \bullet d = (i \bullet c) \bullet d = (k \bullet c) \bullet d = c$. In particular, taking $c = i$ we get $i \bullet d = i$ and hence $d = i \bullet d = i$.

Second, if $k = s$ then, for all $b, c, d \in D$, $b \bullet d = (k \bullet b \bullet c) \bullet d = (s \bullet b \bullet c) \bullet d = b \bullet d \bullet (c \bullet d)$. Taking $b = k \bullet i$ and $c = i$, this gives $i = k \bullet i \bullet d = b \bullet d = b \bullet d \bullet (c \bullet d) = k \bullet i \bullet d \bullet (i \bullet d) = i \bullet (i \bullet d) = d$.

Third, if $s = i$ then, for all $b, c, d \in D$, $b \bullet d \bullet (c \bullet d) = s \bullet b \bullet c \bullet d = i \bullet b \bullet c \bullet d = b \bullet c \bullet d$. Taking $b = k$ and $c = i$ gives $d = i$.

15.9 Assume 15.3(a)–(c) and 15.8(a) or (b). Clearly 15.8(a) implies 15.3(f).

For 15.3(d), use induction on M. In the case $M \equiv \lambda x.P$ the goal is to prove $[\![\lambda x.P]\!]_\rho = [\![\lambda x.P]\!]_\sigma$. This comes from 15.8(b), since, for all $d \in D$,

$$\begin{aligned}[\![\lambda x.P]\!]_\rho \bullet d &= [\![P]\!]_{[d/x]\rho} \text{ by 15.3(c)}, = [\![P]\!]_{[d/x]\sigma} \text{ by induc. hyp.},\\ &= [\![\lambda x.P]\!]_\sigma \bullet d \text{ by 15.3(c)}.\end{aligned}$$

For 15.3(e): by Lemma A1.8 in Appendix A1, it can be assumed that $y \notin \mathrm{FV}(xM)$ and neither x nor y is bound in M. By 15.8(b) it is enough to prove $[\![\lambda x.M]\!]_\rho \bullet d = [\![\lambda y.[y/x]M]\!]_\rho \bullet d$ for all ρ and all $d \in D$. By 15.3(c), this is equivalent to

$$[\![M]\!]_{[d/x]\rho} = [\![[y/x]M]\!]_{[d/y]\rho} \quad \text{(for all } \rho \text{ and all } d \in D). \qquad (8)$$

We prove (8) by induction on M. In the case $M \equiv \lambda v.P$, we have $[y/x]M \equiv \lambda v.[y/x]P$ by the assumed restrictions on x, y. By 15.8(a) it is enough to prove $[\![\lambda v.P]\!]_{[d/x]\rho} \bullet e = [\![\lambda v.[y/x]P]\!]_{[d/y]\rho} \bullet e$ for all $e \in D$. By 15.3(c), this is equivalent to

$$[\![P]\!]_{[e/v][d/x]\rho} = [\![[y/x]P]\!]_{[e/v][d/y]\rho}. \qquad (9)$$

But $[e/v][d/x]\rho = [d/x][e/v]\rho$ since $x \not\equiv v$, and similarly $[e/v][d/y]\rho = [d/y][e/v]\rho$. And $[\![P]\!]_{[d/x][e/v]\rho} = [\![[y/x]P]\!]_{[d/y][e/v]\rho}$ by the induction hypothesis applied to P and $[e/v]\rho$. Hence (9) holds, and (8) follows. (Note: we cannot use Lemma 15.10(a) to prove (8), because the proof of 15.10(a) uses (e), which we are trying to prove here.)

15.15 If $\langle D, \bullet, [\![\ ]\!]\rangle$ is a λ-model, then, for all ρ, M, $x \notin \mathrm{FV}(M)$, $d \in D$:

$$\begin{aligned}[\![\lambda x.Mx]\!]_\rho \bullet d &= [\![(\lambda x.Mx)x]\!]_{[d/x]\rho} && \text{by 15.3(b)},\\ &= [\![Mx]\!]_{[d/x]\rho} && \text{by 15.10(b)},\\ &= [\![M]\!]_\rho \bullet d && \text{by 15.3(b)}.\end{aligned}$$

Hence, if $\langle D, \bullet, [\![\ ]\!]\rangle$ is extensional, then $[\![\lambda x.Mx]\!]_\rho = [\![M]\!]_\rho$.

For the converse, let $a \bullet d = b \bullet d$ for all $d \in D$. Take any distinct x, u, v and let $\rho(u) = a$ and $\rho(v) = b$. Then $[\![ux]\!]_{[d/x]\rho} = a \bullet d$ by 15.3(b), $= b \bullet d$ by assumption, $= [\![vx]\!]_{[d/x]\rho}$. So, by 15.3(f), $[\![\lambda x.ux]\!]_\rho = [\![\lambda x.vx]\!]_\rho$. Hence, if $\langle D, \bullet, [\![\ ]\!]\rangle$ satisfies (η), then $[\![u]\!]_\rho = [\![v]\!]_\rho$, that is $a = b$.

16.4 (a) If b_1 and b_2 are l.u.b.s of X, then by 16.3(b) applied to both we have $b_1 \sqsubseteq b_2$ and $b_2 \sqsubseteq b_1$. Hence $b_1 = b_2$ by anti-symmetry, 16.2(b).

(b) Every $d \in D$ is an u.b. of $\emptyset$, because $(\forall a \in D)(a \in \emptyset \Rightarrow a \sqsubseteq d)$ holds vacuously. Hence $\bot$ (iff it exists) is the least u.b. of $\emptyset$.

(c) Every u.b. b of Y is an u.b. of X, because if $a \in X$ then $a \sqsubseteq$ some $d \in Y$ and hence $a \sqsubseteq b$. Similarly, every u.b. of X is an u.b. of Y. Hence X and Y have the same set (call it B) of u.b.s. But $\bigsqcup X$ exists iff B has a least member, and similarly for $\bigsqcup Y$. Hence result.

(d) Let $Y = \bigcup\{X_j : j \in J\}$ and $Z = \{\bigsqcup X_j : j \in J\}$. First, every u.b. b of Y is an u.b. of Z. Because, for every j, $X_j \subseteq Y$ so b is an u.b. of X_j and hence $b \sqsupseteq \bigsqcup X_j$.

Conversely, every u.b. b of Z is an u.b. of Y. Because, if $a \in Y$ then $a \in X_j$ for some j, so $a \sqsubseteq \bigsqcup X_j$ which is in Z and hence is $\sqsubseteq b$.

Thus Y and Z have the same set of u.b.s; hence result.

16.11 Let $\phi : D \to D'$ be continuous and $a \sqsubseteq b$ in D. Then $\{a, b\}$ is directed and $\bigsqcup\{a, b\} = b$. By 16.10(b), $\phi(b) = \bigsqcup\{\phi(a), \phi(b)\}$. Hence $\phi(a) \sqsubseteq \phi(b)$.

16.12 In $\mathbb{N}^+$, $a \sqsubseteq b \iff a = b$ or ($a = \bot$ and $b \in \mathbb{N}$). So the only directed subsets of $\mathbb{N}^+$ are singletons $\{\bot\}$ or $\{n\}$ or pairs $\{\bot, n\}$ ($n \in \mathbb{N}$). Hence χ is continuous iff $\chi(\bot) \sqsubseteq \chi(n)$ for all $n \in \mathbb{N}$.

Thus χ is continuous $\iff$ χ is monotonic. Also χ is continuous $\iff$ either $\chi(\bot) = \bot$ or $\chi(a)$ has the same value for all $a \in \mathbb{N}^+$.

In the latter case, if this value is $p \in \mathbb{N}$ then $\chi = \psi_p'$. If $\chi(\bot) = \bot$, then $\chi = \phi^+$, where $\phi(n) = \chi(n)$ if $\chi(n) \in \mathbb{N}$ and $\phi(n)$ has no value if $\chi(n) = \bot$.

16.13 If $a, b \in \phi(X)$, then $a = \phi(e)$ and $b = \phi(f)$ for some $e, f \in X$. Since X is directed, we have $e, f \sqsubseteq g$ for some $g \in X$. Let $c = \phi(g)$. Then $c \in \phi(X)$ and $a, b \sqsubseteq c$ since ϕ is monotonic.

16.25 (a) To prove ϕ_0 continuous, we must prove $\phi_0(\bigsqcup X) = \bigsqcup(\phi_0(X))$ for all directed $X \subseteq D_0$. Now $D_0 = \mathbb{N}^+$, see 16.8. If X is a singleton, then so is $\phi_0(X)$ and the result is trivial. If not, then $X = \{\bot_0, n\}$ for some $n \in \mathbb{N}$, so $\bigsqcup X = n$, and $\phi_0(\bigsqcup X) = \lambda\!\!\lambda a \in D_0 . n$. Also $\phi_0(X) = \{\lambda\!\!\lambda a \in D_0 . \bot_0, \lambda\!\!\lambda a \in D_0 . n\}$, so $\bigsqcup \phi_0(X) = \lambda\!\!\lambda a \in D_0 . n$.

To prove ψ_0 continuous, we must prove $\psi_0(\bigsqcup Y) = \bigsqcup(\psi_0(Y))$ for all directed $Y \subseteq D_1$. That is, prove $(\bigsqcup Y)(\bot_0) = \bigsqcup\{g(\bot_0) : g \in Y\}$. But this equation is true by 16.18.

16.30 (a) $D_n = [D_{n-1} \to D_{n-1}]$ and $D_{n-1} = [D_{n-2} \to D_{n-2}]$. For all $a \in D_{n-1}$, $k_n(a) = \lambda\!\!\lambda b \in D_{n-2} . \psi_{n-2}(a)$, which is a constant-function and therefore continuous. Also $\psi_{n-2}(a) \in D_{n-2}$, therefore $k_n(a) \in [D_{n-2} \to D_{n-2}]$, i.e. $k_n(a) \in D_{n-1}$. Hence $k_n \in (D_{n-1} \to D_{n-1})$.

To prove $k_n \in [D_{n-1} \to D_{n-1}]$, we must prove k_n continuous. Let $X \subseteq D_{n-1}$ be directed. It is easy to prove k_n monotonic, so by 16.13, $\bigsqcup(k_n(X))$ exists $\in D_{n-1}$. To prove $k_n(\bigsqcup X) = \bigsqcup(k_n(X))$: since they are both functions we must prove that $k_n(\bigsqcup X)(b) = (\bigsqcup(k_n(X)))(b)$ for all $b \in D_{n-2}$. But

$$\begin{array}{rcll} k_n(\bigsqcup X)(b) & = & \psi_{n-2}(\bigsqcup X) & \text{by definition of } k_n \\ & = & \bigsqcup(\psi_{n-2}(X)) & \text{by continuity of } \psi_{n-2} \\ & = & \bigsqcup\{\psi_{n-2}(a) : a \in X\} & \text{by definition of } \psi_{n-2}(X) \\ & = & \bigsqcup\{k_n(a)(b) : a \in X\} & \text{by definition of } k_n \\ & = & (\bigsqcup\{k_n(a) : a \in X\})(b) & \text{by 16.18} \\ & = & (\bigsqcup k_n(X))(b) & \text{by definition of } k_n(X). \end{array}$$

(b) To prove $\psi_1(k_2) = I_{D_0}$, prove $(\forall a \in D_0)(\psi_1(k_2)(a) = a)$, thus:

$$\begin{array}{rcll} \psi_1(k_2)(a) & = & \psi_0(k_2(\phi_0(a))) & \text{by 16.27(b}')\\ & = & k_2(\phi_0(a))(\perp_0) & \text{by 16.24(b)} \\ & = & \psi_0(\phi_0(a)) & \text{by definition of } k_2 \\ & = & a & \text{by 16.25(b).} \end{array}$$

Also $\psi_0(\psi_1(k_2)) = \perp_0$; because, by above, $\psi_0(\psi_1(k_2)) = \psi_0(I_{D_0})$, $= I_{D_0}(\perp_0)$ by 16.24(b).

(c) To prove that $\psi_n(k_{n+1}) = k_n$, let $a \in D_{n-1}$ and $b \in D_{n-2}$. Then

$$\begin{array}{rll} \psi_n(k_{n+1})(a)(b) & = \psi_{n-1}(k_{n+1}(\phi_{n-1}(a)))\,(b) & \text{by 16.27(b}')\\ & = \psi_{n-1}(\lambda\!\!\lambda c \in D_{n-1}\,.\,\psi_{n-1}(\phi_{n-1}(a)))\,(b) & \text{by def. of } k_{n+1} \\ & = \psi_{n-1}(\lambda\!\!\lambda c \in D_{n-1}\,.\,a)\,(b) & \text{by 16.28(b)} \\ & = \psi_{n-2}((\lambda\!\!\lambda c \in D_{n-1}\,.\,a)(\phi_{n-2}(b))) & \text{by 16.27(b}') \text{ for } \psi_{n-1} \\ & = \psi_{n-2}(a) & \\ & = k_n(a)(b) & \text{by definition of } k_n. \end{array}$$

A1.9 We have $\lambda xy.yx \equiv \lambda x.(\lambda y.yx) \triangleright_{1\alpha} \lambda y.[y/x](\lambda y.yx) \equiv \lambda yz.zy$, where z is chosen by Chapter 1's Definition 1.12(g). For this single α-contraction we need two steps to reverse it.

A2.4 Choose $P \equiv (\lambda x.R_1)R_2$, where $R_1 \equiv (\lambda y.xyz)w$, $R_2 \equiv (\lambda u.u)v$. Choose $M \equiv [R_2/x]R_1 \equiv (\lambda y.R_2yz)w$. Then $P \triangleright_{1\text{par}} M$ by contracting P itself. Choose $N \equiv (\lambda x.xwz)v$. Then $P \triangleright_{1\text{par}} N$ by contracting R_1, R_2 simultaneously. The only terms to which N can be reduced are N and vwz. Neither of these can be obtained from M by non-overlapping simultaneous contractions.

References

[ABD06] F. Alessi, F. Barbanera and M. Dezani. Intersection types and lambda models. *Theoretical Computer Science*, 355:108–126, 2006.

[Acz88] P. Aczel. *Non-Well-Founded Sets.* CSLI (Centre for the Study of Language and Information), Ventura Hall, Stanford University, Stanford, CA 94305-4115, USA, 1988.

[ADH04] F. Alessi, M. Dezani and F. Honsell. Inverse limit models as filter models. In D. Kesner, F. van Raamsdonk and J. Wells, editors, *HOR'04, Proceedings of Workshop on Higher Order Rewriting, 2004*, pages 3–25, Aachen, Germany, 2004. Technische Hochschule Aachen. AIB2004-03, ISSN 0935-3232.

[AJ94] S. Abramsky and A. Jung. Domain theory. In S. Abramsky, D. Gabbay and T. Maibaum, editors, *Handbook of Logic in Computer Science*, volume 3, pages 1–168. Clarendon Press, Oxford, England, 1994. Also available online.

[AL91] A. Asperti and G. Longo. *Categories, Types and Structures. An Introduction to Category Theory for the Working Computer Scientist.* M.I.T. Press, Cambridge, Mass., USA, 1991.

[Alt93] T. Altenkirch. A formalization of the strong normalization proof for System F in LEGO. In M. Bezem and J. F. Groote, editors, *Typed Lambda Calculi and Applications*, volume 664 of *Lecture Notes in Computer Science*, pages 13–28. Springer-Verlag, Berlin, 1993.

[And65] P. B. Andrews. *A Transfinite Type Theory with Type Variables.* North-Holland Co., Amsterdam, 1965.

[And02] P. B. Andrews. *An Introduction to Mathematical Logic and Type Theory: to Truth Through Proof.* Kluwer, Dordrecht, Netherlands, 2002. 2nd edn. (1st was 1986, Academic Press, USA).

[Bac78] J. Backus. Can programming be liberated from the von Neumann style? *Communications of the ACM*, 21(8):613–641, 1978.

[Bar73] H. P. Barendregt. Combinatory logic and the axiom of choice. *Indagationes Mathematicae* 35: 203–221, 1973. Journal also appears as *Proc. Nederl. Akad. van Wetenschappen.*

[Bar74] H. P. Barendregt. Pairing without conventional restraints. *Zeitschrift für Mathematische Logik und Grundlagen der Mathematik*, 20:289–306, 1974. Journal now called *Mathematical Logic Quarterly.*

[Bar84] H. P. Barendregt. *The Lambda Calculus, its Syntax and Semantics.* North-Holland Co., Amsterdam, 1984. 2nd (revised) edn., reprinted 1997 (1st edn. was 1981).

[Bar92] H. P. Barendregt. Lambda calculi with types. In S. Abramsky, D. Gabbay and T. Maibaum, editors, *Handbook of Logic in Computer Science, Volume 2, Background: Computational Structures*, pages 117–309. Clarendon Press, Oxford, England, 1992.

[BB79] J. Baeten and B. Boerboom. Ω can be anything it shouldn't be. *Indagationes Mathematicae*, 41:111–120, 1979. Journal also appears as *Proc. Nederl. Akad. van Wetenschappen.*

[BCD83] H. P. Barendregt, M. Coppo and M. Dezani. A filter lambda model and the completeness of type assignment. *Journal of Symbolic Logic*, 48:931–940, 1983.

[BDPR79] C. Böhm, M. Dezani, P. Peretti, and S. Ronchi. A discrimination algorithm inside $\lambda\beta$-calculus. *Theoretical Computer Science*, 8:271–291, 1979.

[BDS] H. P. Barendregt, W. Dekkers, and R. Statman. *Typed Lambda Calculus, Volume 1.* In preparation.

[Ber93] S. Berardi. Encoding of data types in pure construction calculus: a semantic justification. In H. Huet and G. Plotkin, editors, *Logical Environments*, pages 30–60. Cambridge University Press, 1993.

[Ber00] C. Berline. From computation to foundations via functions and application: the λ-calculus and its webbed models. *Theoretical Computer Science*, 249:81–161, 2000.

[Ber05] C. Berline. Graph models of λ-calculus at work, and variations. At website, 2005. Web address hal.ccsd.cnrs.fr/ccsd-00004473/en/.

[Bet99] I. Bethke. Annotated Bibliography of Lambda Calculi, Combinatory Logics and Type Theory. At website, 1999. File type '.ps'. Web address www.science.uva.nl/~inge/Bib/.

[BG66] C. Böhm and W. Gross. Introduction to the CUCH. In E. Caianiello, editor, *Automata Theory*, pages 35–65. Academic Press, New York, 1966.

[BHS89] M. W. Bunder, J. R. Hindley and J. P. Seldin. On adding (ξ) to weak equality in combinatory logic. *Journal of Symbolic Logic*, 54:590–607, 1989.

[BK80] H. P. Barendregt and K. Koymans. Comparing some classes of lambda-calculus models. In Hindley and Seldin [HS80], pages 287–301.

[BL80] H. P. Barendregt and G. Longo. Equality of λ-terms in the model T^{ω}. In Hindley and Seldin [HS80], pages 303–337.

[BL84] K. Bruce and G. Longo. A note on combinatory algebras and their expansions. *Theoretical Computer Science*, 31:31–40, 1984.

[BN98] F. Baader and T. Nipkow. *Term Rewriting and All That.* Cambridge University Press, England, 1998.

[Böh68] C. Böhm. Alcune proprietà delle forme β-η-normali nel λ-K-calcolo. Pubblicazione no. 696, Istituto per le Applicazioni del Calcolo, C.N.R., Roma, 1968.

[Bru70] N. G. de Bruijn. The mathematical language AUTOMATH. In M. Laudet, D. Lacombe, L. Nolin and M. Schützenberger, editors, *Symposium on Automatic Demonstration, IRIA Versailles 1968*, volume 125 of *Lecture Notes in Mathematics*, pages 29–61. Springer-Verlag, Berlin, 1970.

[Bru72] N. G. de Bruijn. Lambda calculus notation with nameless dummies, a tool for automatic formula manipulation. *Indagationes Mathematicae*, 34:381–392, 1972.

[Bun02] M. W. Bunder. Combinators, proofs and implicational logics. In D. M. Gabbay and F. Guenthner, editors, *Handbook of Philosophical Logic*, volume 6, pages 229–286. Springer (Kluwer), Berlin, 2002.

[Bye82a] R. Byerly. An invariance notion in recursion theory. *Journal of Symbolic Logic*, 47:48–66, 1982.

[Bye82b] R. Byerly. Recursion theory and the lambda calculus. *Journal of Symbolic Logic*, 47:67–83, 1982.

[Car86] L. Cardelli. A polymorphic λ-calculus with Type : Type. Technical report, Systems Research Center of Digital Equipment Corporation, Palo Alto, California, May 1986.

[CC90] F. Cardone and M. Coppo. Two extensions of Curry's type inference system. In P. Odifreddi, editor, *Logic and Computer Science*, volume 31 of *APIC Studies in Data Processing*, pages 19–76. Academic Press, USA, 1990.

[CC91] F. Cardone and M. Coppo. Type inference with recursive types: syntax and semantics. *Information and Computation*, 92(1):48–80, 1991.

[CD78] M. Coppo and M. Dezani. A new type assignment for λ-terms. *Archiv für Mathematische Logik*, 19:139–156, 1978. Journal now called *Archive for Mathematical Logic.*

[CDHL84] M. Coppo, M. Dezani, F. Honsell and G. Longo. Extended type structures and filter lambda models. In G. Lolli, G. Longo and A. Marcja, editors, *Logic Colloquium '82*, pages 241–262. North-Holland Co., Amsterdam, 1984.

[CDS79] M. Coppo, M. Dezani and P. Sallé. Functional characterization of some semantic equalities inside λ-calculus. In H. Maurer, editor, *Automata, Languages and Programming, Sixth Colloquium*, volume 71 of *Lecture Notes in Computer Science*, pages 133–146. Springer-Verlag, Berlin, 1979.

[CDV81] M. Coppo, M. Dezani, and B. Venneri. Functional characters of solvable terms. *Zeitschrift für Mathematische Logik*, 27:45–58, 1981. Journal now called *Mathematical Logic Quarterly.*

[CDZ87] M. Coppo, M. Dezani, and M. Zacchi. Type theories, normal forms and D_∞-lambda models. *Information and Computation*, 72:85–116, 1987.

[CF58] H. B. Curry and R. Feys. *Combinatory Logic, Volume I.* North-Holland Co., Amsterdam, 1958. 1st. edn. (3rd edn. 1974).

[CH88] T. Coquand and G. Huet. The calculus of constructions. *Information and Computation*, 76:95–120, 1988.

[ÇH98] N. Çağman and J. R. Hindley. Combinatory weak reduction in lambda calculus. *Theoretical Computer Science*, 198:239–247, 1998.

[CHS72] H. B. Curry, J. R. Hindley and J. P. Seldin. *Combinatory Logic, Volume II.* North-Holland Co., Amsterdam, 1972.

[Chu36a] A. Church. A note on the Entscheidungsproblem. *Journal of Symbolic Logic*, 1:40–41, 1936. See also correction in pp. 101–102.

[Chu36b] A. Church. An unsolvable problem of elementary number theory. *American Journal of Mathematics*, 58:345–363, 1936.

[Chu40] A. Church. A formulation of the simple theory of types. *Journal of Symbolic Logic*, 5:56–68, 1940.

[Chu41] A. Church. *The Calculi of Lambda Conversion.* Princeton University Press, Princeton, New Jersey, USA, 1941.

[Coh87] D. E. Cohen. *Computability and Logic.* Ellis-Horwood, England, 1987.

[CR36] A. Church and J. B. Rosser. Some properties of conversion. *Transactions of the American Mathematical Society*, 39:472–482, 1936.

[Cro94] R. Crole. *Categories for Types.* Cambridge University Press, England, 1994.

[Cur30] H. B. Curry. Grundlagen der kombinatorischen Logik. *American Journal of Mathematics*, 52:509–536, 789–834, 1930.

[Cur34] H. B. Curry. Functionality in combinatory logic. *Proceedings of the National Academy of Sciences of the USA*, 20:584–590, 1934.

[Cur69] H. B. Curry. Modified basic functionality in combinatory logic. *Dialectica*, 23:83–92, 1969.

[Daa94] D. T. van Daalen. The language theory of Automath, Chapter 1 Sections 1–5. In Nederpelt *et al.* [NGdV94], pages 163–200. From author's thesis, University of Eindhoven 1980.

[Dal97] D. van Dalen. *Logic and Structure.* Springer-Verlag, Berlin, 1997. 3rd edn.

[Ded87] Richard Dedekind. *Was sind und was sollen die Zahlen?* Friedrich Vieweg & Sohn, Braunschweig, 1887. (10th edn. 1965).

[End00] H. B. Enderton. *A Mathematical Introduction to Logic.* Harcourt/ Academic Press, New York, 2000. 2nd edn.

[Eng81] E. Engeler. Algebras and combinators. *Algebra Universalis*, 13:389–392, 1981.

[Fia05] J. L. Fiadero. *Categories for Software Engineering.* Springer-Verlag, Berlin, 2005.

[Fit58] F. B. Fitch. Representation of sequential circuits in combinatory logic. *Philosophy of Science*, 25:263–279, 1958.

[Fre93] G. Frege. *Grundgesetze der Arithmetik.* Verlag Hermann Pohle, Jena, 1893. Two vols. Reprinted 1962 as one vol. by Georg Olms, Hildesheim, Germany, and 1966 as No. 32 in series *Olms Paperbacks*.

[Fri71] H Friedman. Axiomatic recursive function theory. In R. Gandy and C. E. M. Yates, editors, *Logic Colloquium '69*, pages 113–137. North-Holland Co., Amsterdam, 1971.

[Geu93] H. Geuvers. *Logic and Type Systems.* Ph.D. thesis, Catholic University of Nijmegen, 1993.

[Geu01] H. Geuvers. Induction is not derivable in second order dependent type theory. In S. Abramsky, editor, *Proceedings of Typed Lambda Calculus and Applications (TLCA 2001), Krakow, Poland, May 2001*, volume 2044 of *Lecture Notes in Computer Science*, pages 166–181. Springer, 2001.

[GHK+03] G. Gierz, K. Hofmann, K. Keimel, J. Lawson, M. Mislove and D. Scott. Continuous lattices and domains. In *Encyclopedia of Mathematics and its Applications*, volume 93. Cambridge University Press, England, 2003.

[Gir71] J.-Y. Girard. Une extension de l'interprétation de Gödel à l'analyse, et son application à l'élimination des coupures dans l'analyse et la théorie des types. In J. E. Fenstad, editor, *Proceedings of the Second Scandinavian Logic Symposium*, pages 63–92. North-Holland Co., Amsterdam, 1971.

[Gir72] J.-Y. Girard. *Interprétation fonctionnelle et élimination des coupures de l'arithmétique d'ordre supérieur.* Ph.D. thesis, University of Paris VII, France, 1972.

[GLT89] J.-Y. Girard, Y. Lafont, and P. Taylor. *Proofs and Types.* Cambridge University Press, England, 1989.

[Göd58] K. Gödel. Über eine bisher noch nicht benützte Erweiterung des finiten Standpunktes. *Dialectica,* 12:280–287, 1958. English translation: *On a hitherto unexploited extension of the finitary standpoint,* in *Journal of Philosophical Logic* 9 (1980) pp. 133–142. Two other English translations with notes: pp. 217–251, 271–280 of *Kurt Gödel Collected Works, Vol. II, Publications 1938–1974,* edited by S. Feferman *et al.*, Oxford University Press 1990.

[Gra05] C. Grabmeyer. *Relating Proof Systems for Recursive Types.* Ph.D. thesis, Free University, Amsterdam, 2005.

[Gun92] C. Gunter. *Semantics of Programming Languages.* M.I.T. Press, Cambridge, Massachusetts, USA, 1992.

[Han04] C. Hankin. *An Introduction to Lambda Calculi for Computer Scientists.* King's College Publications, London, England, 2004. Revised edn. of *Lambda Calculi,* Clarendon Press, Oxford, 1994.

[Hen50] L. Henkin. Completeness in the theory of types. *Journal of Symbolic Logic,* 15:81–91, 1950.

[HHP87] R. Harper, F. Honsell and G. Plotkin. A framework for defining logics. In *Proceedings Second Symposium of Logic in Computer Science (Ithaca, NY),* pages 194–204. IEEE, 1987.

[Hin64] J. R. Hindley. *The Church-Rosser Theorem and a Result in Combinatory Logic.* Ph.D. thesis, University of Newcastle upon Tyne, England, 1964.

[Hin67] J. R. Hindley. Axioms for strong reduction in combinatory logic. *Journal of Symbolic Logic,* 32:224–236, 1967.

[Hin69] J. R. Hindley. The principal type-scheme of an object in combinatory logic. *Transactions of the American Mathematical Society,* 146:29–60, 1969.

[Hin77] J. R. Hindley. Combinatory reductions and lambda reductions compared. *Zeitschrift für Mathematische Logik,* 23:169–180, 1977. Journal now called *Mathematical Logic Quarterly.*

[Hin78] J. R. Hindley. Reductions of residuals are finite. *Transactions of the American Mathematical Society,* 240:345–361, 1978.

[Hin79] J. R. Hindley. The discrimination theorem holds for combinatory weak reduction. *Theoretical Computer Science,* 8:393–394, 1979.

[Hin92] J. R. Hindley. Types with intersection, an introduction. *Formal Aspects of Computing,* 4:470–486, 1992.

[Hin97] J. R. Hindley. *Basic Simple Type Theory.* Cambridge University Press, England, 1997.

[HL70] J. R. Hindley and B. Lercher. A short proof of Curry's normal form theorem. *Proceedings of the American Mathematical Society,* 24:808–810, 1970.

[HL80] J. R. Hindley and G. Longo. Lambda-calculus models and extensionality. *Zeitschrift für Mathematische Logik,* 26:289–310, 1980. Journal now called *Mathematical Logic Quarterly.*

[HLS72] J. R. Hindley, B. Lercher and J. P. Seldin. *Introduction to Combinatory Logic.* Cambridge University Press, England, 1972. Also Italian (revised) edn: *Introduzione alla Logica Combinatoria,* Boringhieri, Torino, 1975.

[How80] W. A. Howard. The formulæ-as-types notion of construction. In Hindley and Seldin [HS80], pages 479–490. Manuscript circulated 1969.

[HS80] J. R. Hindley and J. P. Seldin, editors. *To H. B. Curry, Essays on Combinatory Logic, Lambda Calculus and Formalism.* Academic Press, London, 1980.

[HS86] J. R. Hindley and J. P. Seldin. *Introduction to Combinators and λ-calculus.* Cambridge University Press, England, 1986.

[Hue93] G. Huet. An analysis of Böhm's theorem. *Theoretical Computer Science*, 121:154–167, 1993.

[Hue94] G. Huet. Residual theory in λ-calculus: a formal development. *Journal of Functional Programming*, 4:371–394, 1994.

[Hyl76] J. M. E. Hyland. A syntactic characterization of the equality in some models for the lambda calculus. *Journal of the London Mathematical Society, Series 2*, 12:361–370, 1976.

[Jac99] B. Jacobs. *Categorical Logic and Type Theory.* North-Holland Co., Amsterdam, 1999.

[Kel55] J. L. Kelley. *General Topology.* Van Nostrand, New York, 1955.

[Kle36] S. C. Kleene. λ-definability and recursiveness. *Duke Mathematical Journal*, 2:340–353, 1936.

[Kle52] S. C. Kleene. *Introduction to Metamathematics.* Van Nostrand, New York, 1952.

[KLN04] F. Kamareddine, T. Laan and R. Nederpelt. *A modern Perspective on Type Theory: from its Origins until Today.* Kluwer, Dordrecht, Boston and London, 2004.

[Klo80] J. W. Klop. *Combinatory Reduction Systems.* Ph.D. thesis, University of Utrecht, 1980. Published by Mathematisch Centrum, 413 Kruislaan, Amsterdam.

[Klo92] J. W. Klop. Term rewriting systems. In S. Abramsky, D. Gabbay, and T. Maibaum, editors, *Handbook of Logic in Computer Science, Volume 2: Background, Computational Structures*, pages 1–116. Oxford University Press, England, 1992.

[Koy82] C. P. J. Koymans. Models of the lambda calculus. *Information and Control*, 52:306–332, 1982. (Journal now called *Information and Computation*).

[Koy84] C. P. J. Koymans. *Models of the Lambda Calculus.* Ph.D. thesis, University of Utrecht, The Netherlands, 1984.

[KR95] F. Kamareddine and A. Rios. A λ-calculus à la de Bruijn with explicit substitutions. In M. Hermenegildo and S. D. Swierstra, editors, *Programming Languages, Implementations, Logics and Programs, 7th International Symposium*, volume 982 of *Lecture Notes in Computer Science*, pages 45–62. Springer-Verlag, Berlin, 1995.

[Kri93] J.-L. Krivine. *Lambda-Calculus, Types and Models.* Ellis-Horwood, U.S.A. and Prentice-Hall, U.K., 1993. English translation of *Lambda-calcul, Types et Modèles*, Masson, Paris 1990.

[KvOvR93] J. W. Klop, V. van Oostrom, and F. van Raamsdonk. Combinatory reduction systems: introduction and survey. *Theoretical Computer Science*, 121(1–2):279–308, 1993.

[Lam80] J. Lambek. From λ-calculus to cartesian closed categories. In Hindley and Seldin [HS80], pages 375–402.

[Lan65] P. J. Landin. A correspondence between ALGOL 60 and Church's lambda notation. *Communications of the ACM*, 8:89–101, 158–165, 1965.

[Lan66] P. J. Landin. The next 700 programming languages. *Communications of the ACM*, 9(3):157–166, 1966.

[Läu65] H. Läuchli. Intuitionistic propositional calculus and definably non-empty terms. *Journal of Symbolic Logic*, 30:263, 1965. Abstract only.

[Läu70] H. Läuchli. An abstract notion of realizability for which intuitionistic predicate calculus is complete. In A. Kino, J. Myhill and R. Vesley, editors, *Intuitionism and Proof Theory*, pages 227–234. North-Holland Co., Amsterdam, 1970. Proceedings of conference at Buffalo, N.Y. 1968.

[Ler63] B. Lercher. *Strong Reduction and Recursion in Combinatory Logic.* Ph.D. thesis, Mathematics Department, Pennsylvania State University, USA, 1963.

[Ler67a] B. Lercher. The decidability of Hindley's axioms for strong reduction. *Journal of Symbolic Logic*, 32:237–239, 1967.

[Ler67b] B. Lercher. Strong reduction and normal form in combinatory logic. *Journal of Symbolic Logic*, 32:213–223, 1967.

[Ler76] B. Lercher. Lambda-calculus terms that reduce to themselves. *Notre Dame Journal of Formal Logic*, 17:291–292, 1976.

[LM84] G. Longo and S. Martini. Computability in higher types and the universal domain $P\omega$. In M. Fontet and K. Mehlhorn, editors, *STACS 84, Symposium of Theoretical Aspects of Computer Science*, volume 166 of *Lecture Notes in Computer Science*, pages 186–197. Springer-Verlag, Berlin, 1984.

[LM91] G. Longo and E. Moggi. Constructive natural deduction and its ω-set interpretation. *Mathematical Structures in Computer Science*, 1(2):215–254, 1991.

[Lon83] G. Longo. Set-theoretical models of λ-calculi: theories, expansions, isomorphisms. *Annals of Mathematical Logic*, 24:153–188, 1983. Journal now called *Annals of Pure and Applied Logic.*

[LS86] J. Lambek and P. J. Scott. *Introduction to Higher Order Categorical Logic.* Cambridge University Press, England, 1986.

[Luo90] Z. Luo. *An extended calculus of constructions.* Ph.D. thesis, Univerisity of Edinburgh, 1990.

[Mac71] S. MacLane. *Categories for the Working Mathematician.* Springer-Verlag, Berlin, 1971.

[MBP91] R. K. Meyer, M. W. Bunder and L. Powers. Implementing the "fool's model" of combinatory logic. *Journal of Automated Reasoning*, 7:597–630, 1991.

[McC60] J. McCarthy. Recursive functions of symbolic expressions and their computation by machine. *Communications of the ACM*, 3:184–195, 1960.

[Men97] E. Mendelson. *Introduction to Mathematical Logic.* Chapman and Hall, New York, 1997. 4th edn.

[Mey82] A. R. Meyer. What is a model of the lambda calculus? *Information and Control*, 52:87–122, 1982. Journal now called *Information and Computation.*

[Mez89] M. Mezghiche. On pseudo-Cβ-normal form in combinatory logic. *Theoretical Computer Science*, 66:323–331, 1989.

[Mic88] G. Michaelson. *An Introduction to Functional Programming through Lambda Calculus.* Addison-Wesley, England and USA, 1988.

[Mil78] R. Milner. A theory of type polymorphism in programming. *Journal of Computer and System Sciences*, 17:348–375, 1978.

[Mit96] J. C. Mitchell. *Foundations for programming Languages.* M.I.T. Press, Cambridge, Massachusetts, USA, 1996.

[ML75] P. Martin-Löf. An intuitionistic theory of types: predicative part. In H. E. Rose and J. C. Shepherdson, editors, *Logic Colloquium '73*, pages 73–118, North-Holland Co., Amsterdam, 1975.

[Mos90] P. Mosses. Denotational semantics. In J. van Leeuwen, editor, *Handbook of Theoretical Computer Science, Volume B: Formal Methods and Semantics*, pages 575–631. Elsevier, Amsterdam and M.I.T. Press, Cambridge, Massachusetts, USA, 1990.

[NG94] R. P. Nederpelt and J. H. Geuvers. Twenty-Five Years of Automath Research. In Nederpelt *et al.* [NGdV94], pages 3–54.

[NGdV94] R. P. Nederpelt, J. H. Geuvers and R. C. de Vrijer, editors. *Selected Papers on Automath.* Elsevier, Amsterdam, 1994.

[Pie91] B. C. Pierce. *Basic Category Theory for Computer Scientists.* M.I.T. Press, Cambridge, Massachusetts, USA, 1991.

[Pie02] B. C. Pierce. *Types and Programming Languages.* M.I.T. Press, Cambridge, Massachusetts, USA, 2002.

[Plo74] G. D. Plotkin. The λ-calculus is ω-incomplete. *Journal of Symbolic Logic*, 39:313–317, 1974.

[Plo78] G. D. Plotkin. T^{ω} as a universal domain. *Journal of Computer and System Sciences*, 17:209–236, 1978.

[Plo93] G. D. Plotkin. Set-theoretical and other elementary models of the λ-calculus. *Theoretical Computer Science*, 121:351–409, 1993. (Updated version of a paper informally circulated in 1972).

[Plo94] G. D. Plotkin. A semantics for static type-inference. *Information and Computation*, 109:256–299, 1994.

[Pol93] R. Pollack. Closure under alpha-conversion. In H. Barendregt and T. Nipkow, editors, *Types for Proofs and Programs*, volume 806 of *Lecture Notes in Computer Science*, pages 313–332. Springer-Verlag, Berlin, 1993.

[Pot80] G. Pottinger. A type assignment for the strongly normalizable λ-terms. In Hindley and Seldin [HS80], pages 561–579.

[Pra65] D. Prawitz. *Natural Deduction.* Almqvist and Wiksell, Stockholm, 1965. Reissued in 2006, with new preface and errata-list, by Dover Inc., Mineola, N.Y., USA.

[PS95] D. Pigozzi and A. Salibra. Lambda abstraction algebras: representation theorems. *Theoretical Computer Science*, 140:5–52, 1995.

[PS98] D. Pigozzi and A. Salibra. Lambda abstraction algebras: coordinatizing models of lambda calculus. *Fundamenta Informaticae*, 33:149–200, 1998.

[Rau06] W. Rautenberg. *A Concise Introduction to Mathematical Logic.* Springer-Verlag, Berlin, 2006.

[RC90] S. Reeves and M. Clarke. *Logic for Computer Science.* Addison-Wesley Co., U.S.A., 1990.

[RdL92] G. R. Renardel de Lavalette. Strictness analysis via abstract interpretation for recursively defined types. *Information and Computation*, 99(2):154–177, 1992.

[Rév88] G. Révész. *Lambda-calculus, Combinators and Functional Programming.* Cambridge University Press, England, 1988.

[Rey74] J. C. Reynolds. Towards a theory of type structure. In B. Robinet, editor, *Programming Symposium*, volume 19 of *Lecture Notes in Computer Science*, pages 408–425. Springer-Verlag, Berlin, 1974.

[Rey98] J. C. Reynolds. *Theories of Programming Languages.* Cambridge University Press, England, 1998.

[Rez82] A. Rezus. *A Bibliography of Lambda-Calculi, Combinatory Logics and Related Topics.* Mathematisch Centrum, 413 Kruislaan, Amsterdam, 1982. ISBN 90-6196234-X.

[Rim80] M. von Rimscha. Mengentheoretische Modelle des λK-Kalküls. *Archiv für Mathematische Logik*, 20:65–74, 1980. Journal now called *Archive for Mathematical Logic.*

[Ros35] J. B. Rosser. A mathematical logic without variables, Part 1. *Annals of Mathematics, Series 2*, 36:127–150, 1935. Also Part 2: *Duke Mathematical Journal* 1 (1935), pp. 328–355.

[Ros50] P. Rosenbloom. *The Elements of Mathematical Logic.* Dover Inc., New York, 1950.

[Ros55] J. B. Rosser. *Deux Esquisses de Logique.* Gauthier-Villars, Paris, and Nauwelaerts, Louvain, 1955.

[Ros73] B. K. Rosen. Tree manipulating systems and Church-Rosser theorems. *Journal of the Association for Computing Machinery*, 20:160–187, 1973.

[Sal78] P. Sallé. Une extension de la théorie des types en λ-calcul. In G. Ausiello and C. Böhm, editors, *Automata, Languages and Programming, Fifth Colloquium*, volume 62 of *Lecture Notes in Computer Science*, pages 398–410. Springer-Verlag, Berlin, 1978.

[Sal00] A. Salibra. On the algebraic models of lambda calculus. *Theoretical Computer Science*, 249:197–240, 2000.

[San67] L. E. Sanchis. Functionals defined by recursion. *Notre Dame Journal of Formal Logic*, 8:161–174, 1967.

[San79] L. E. Sanchis. Reducibilities in two models for combinatory logic. *Journal of Symbolic Logic*, 44:221–234, 1979.

[Sch24] M. Schönfinkel. Über die Bausteine der mathematischen Logik. *Mathematische Annalen*, 92:305–316, 1924. English translation: *On the building blocks of mathematical logic*, in *From Frege to Gödel*, edited by J. van Heijenoort, Harvard University Press, USA 1967, pp. 355–366.

[Sch65] D. E. Schroer. *The Church-Rosser Theorem.* Ph.D. thesis, Cornell University, 1965. Informally circulated 1963.

[Sch76] H. Schwichtenberg. Definierbare Funktionen im λ-Kalkül mit Typen. *Archiv für Mathematische Logik*, 17:113–114, 1976.

[Sco70a] D. S. Scott. Constructive validity. In M. Laudet, D. Lacombe, L. Nolin and M. Schützenberger, editors, *Symposium on Automatic Demonstration*, volume 125 of *Lecture Notes in Mathematics*, pages 237–275. Springer-Verlag, Berlin, 1970. (Proceedings of a conference in Versailles 1968).

[Sco70b] D. S. Scott. Outline of a mathematical theory of computation. In *Proceedings of the Fourth Annual Princeton Conference on Information Sciences and Systems*, pages 169–176. Department of Electrical Engineering, Princeton University, 1970.

[Sco72] D. S. Scott. Continuous lattices. In F. W. Lawvere, editor, *Toposes, Algebraic Geometry and Logic*, volume 274 of *Lecture Notes in Mathematics*, pages 97–136, Berlin, 1972. Springer-Verlag. (Informally circulated in 1970).

[Sco73] D. S. Scott. Models for various type-free calculi. In P. Suppes and others, editors, *Logic, Methodology and Philosophy of Science IV*, pages 157–187. North-Holland Co., Amsterdam, 1973. (Proceedings of a conference in 1971).

[Sco76] D. S. Scott. Data types as lattices. *SIAM Journal on Computing*, 5:522–587, 1976.

[Sco80a] D. S. Scott. Lambda calculus: some models, some philosophy. In J. Barwise *et al.*, editors, *The Kleene Symposium*, pages 223–265. North-Holland Co., Amsterdam, 1980.

[Sco80b] D. S. Scott. Relating theories of the λ-calculus. In Hindley and Seldin [HS80], pages 403–450.

[Sco82a] D. S. Scott. Domains for denotational semantics. In M. Nielsen and E. Schmidt, editors, *Automata, Languages and Programming, Ninth International Colloquium*, volume 140 of *Lecture Notes in Computer Science*, pages 577–613. Springer-Verlag, Berlin, 1982.

[Sco82b] D. S. Scott. Lectures on a mathematical theory of computation. In M. Broy and G. Schmidt, editors, *Theoretical Foundations of Programming Methodology*. D. Reidel Co., Dordrecht, The Netherlands, 1982.

[Sco93] D. S. Scott. A type-theoretical alternative to ISWIM, CUCH, OWHY. *Theoretical Computer Science*, 121:411–440, 1993. (Informally circulated in 1969).

[Sel77] J. P. Seldin. A sequent calculus for type assignment. *Journal of Symbolic Logic*, 42:11–28, 1977.

[Sel79] J. P. Seldin. Progress report on generalized functionality. *Annals of Mathematical Logic*, 17:29–59, 1979. Condensed from manuscript *Theory of Generalized Functionality*, informally circulated in 1975. Journal now called *Annals of Pure and Applied Logic*.

[Sel97] J. P. Seldin. On the proof theory of Coquand's calculus of constructions. *Annals of Pure and Applied Logic*, 83:23–101, 1997.

[Sel00a] J. P. Seldin. A Gentzen-style sequent calculus of constructions with expansion rules. *Theoretical Computer Science*, 243:199–215, 2000.

[Sel00b] J. P. Seldin. On lists and other abstract data types in the calculus of constructions. *Mathematical Structures in Computer Science*, 10:261–276, 2000.

[Sho01] J. R. Shoenfield. *Mathematical Logic*. A. K. Peters, USA, 2001. (1st edn. by Addison-Wesley 1967).

[Sim00] H. Simmons. *Derivation and Computation*. Cambridge University Press, England, 2000.

[Smu85] R. M. Smullyan. *To Mock a Mocking-Bird*. Alfred Knopf Inc., U.S.A., 1985. Also Oxford University Press, England, 1990.

[Ste72] S. Stenlund. *Combinators, λ-terms and Proof Theory*. D. Reidel Co., Dordrecht, The Netherlands, 1972.

[Sto77] J. Stoy. *Denotational Semantics: The Scott–Strachey Approach to Programming Language Theory*. M.I.T. Press, Cambridge, Massachusetts, USA, 1977.

[Sto88] A. Stoughton. Substitution revisited. *Theoretical Computer Science*, 59(3):317–325, 1988.

[Str68] H. R. Strong. Algebraically generalized recursive function theory. *I.B.M. Journal of Research and Development*, 12:465–475, 1968.

[SU06] M. H. Sorensen and P. Urzyczyn. *Lectures on the Curry–Howard Isomorphism*. Elsevier, Amsterdam, 2006.

[Tai67] W. W. Tait. Intensional interpretations of functionals of finite type. *Journal of Symbolic Logic*, 32:198–212, 1967.

[Tak91] Masako Takahashi. *Theory of Computation, Computability and Lambda Calculus.* Kindai Kagaku Sha, Tokyo, 1991. In Japanese.

[Tak95] Masako Takahashi. Parallel reductions in λ-calculus. *Information and Computation*, 118:120–127, 1995. Earlier version: *J. Symbolic Computation* 7 (1989), 113–123.

[TD88] A. S. Troelstra and D. van Dalen. *Constructivism in Mathematics, an Introduction.* North-Holland Co., Amsterdam, 1988. (Vols. 1 and 2).

[Tro73] A. S. Troelstra, editor. *Metamathematical Investigations of Intuitionistic Arithmetic and Analysis*, volume 344 of *Lecture Notes in Mathematics.* Springer-Verlag, Berlin, 1973. (Also 2nd edn. 1993, publ. as Preprint no. X-93-05 by Institute for Logic, Language and Computation, University of Amsterdam. Plantage Muidergracht 24, 1018TV Amsterdam).

[TS00] A. S. Troelstra and H. Schwichtenberg. *Basic Proof Theory.* Cambridge University Press, England, 2000.

[Tur76] D. A. Turner. *SASL Language Manual.* University of St. Andrews, Scotland, 1976.

[VB03] R. Vestergaard and J. Brotherton. A formalised first-order confluence proof for the λ-calculus using one-sorted variable names. *Information and Computation*, 183:212–244, 2003.

[vBJ93] L. S. van Benthem Jutting. Typing in Pure Type Systems. *Information and Computation*, 105:30–41, 1993.

[Wad76] C. P. Wadsworth. The relation between computational and denotational properties for Scott's D_∞ models of the lambda-calculus. *SIAM Journal of Computing*, 5:488–521, 1976.

[Wad78] C. P. Wadsworth. Approximate reduction and lambda-calculus models. *SIAM Journal of Computing*, 7:337–356, 1978.

[Wag69] E. Wagner. Uniformly reflexive structures. *Transactions of the American Mathematical Society*, 144:1–41, 1969.

[Win01] G. Winskel. *The Formal Semantics of Programming Languages, an Introduction.* M.I.T. Press, USA, 2001. (1st edn. 1993).

[Wol03] V. E. Wolfengagen. *Combinatory Logic in Programming.* JurInfoR Ltd., Moscow, Russia, 2003. 2nd edn., in English.

[Wol04] V. E. Wolfengagen. *Methods and Means for Computation with Objects.* JurInfoR Ltd., Moscow, Russia, 2004. In Russian.

[Zas01] J. Zashev. On the recursion theorem in iterative operative spaces. *Journal of Symbolic Logic*, 66:1727–1748, 2001.

List of symbols

Index

Printed in the United States
By Bookmasters